THE ART OF THE MOTORCYCLE

THE ART OF THE MOTORCYCLE

GUGGENHEIM MUSEUM

Contents

Catalogue Index

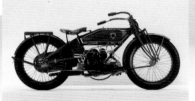

4. FN Four • 498 cc •
1908 • Belgium, p. 108

5. Pierce Four • 43 ci •
1910 • United States, p. 110

6. Flying Merkel Model V • 54 ci •
1911 • United States, p. 112

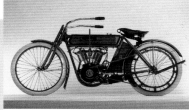

7. Harley-Davidson Model 7D • 49 ci •
1911 • United States, p. 116

8. Cyclone • 61 ci •
1914 • United States, p. 118

14. Monet & Goyon Moto Légère •
117 cc • 1922 • France, p. 142

15. Neracar • 14 ci •
1922 • United States, p. 144

16. BMW R32 • 494 cc •
1923 • Germany, p. 148

17. Harley-Davidson 8-Valve Board Track Racer •
61 ci • 1923 • United States, p. 152

18. Moto Guzzi C4V • 498 cc •
1924 • Italy, p. 154

24. MGC N3BR • 245 cc •
1932 • France, p. 174

25. Dollar V4 • 748 cc •
1933 • France, p. 178

26. Gnôme et Rhône M1 • 306 cc •
1934 • France, p. 182

27. BMW World Land-Speed Record • 493 cc •
1937 • Germany, p. 186

28. Triumph Speed Twin • 498 cc •
1938 • United Kingdom, p. 190

34. Sunbeam S7 • 487 cc •
1947 • United Kingdom, p. 212

35. Indian Chief • 1,206 cc •
1948 • United States, p. 216

36. Solex Vélosolex • 45 cc •
1948 • France, p. 218

37. Imme R100 • 99 cc •
1949 • West Germany, p. 222

38. Jackson-Rotrax JAP Speedway • 490 cc •
1949 • United Kingdom, p. 226

44. Harley-Davidson KR • 750 cc •
1957 • United States, p. 246

45. Harley-Davidson Sportster XL • 883 cc •
1957 • United States, p. 248

46. Triumph Twenty-One • 350 cc •
1958 • United Kingdom, p. 252

47. BSA Gold Star Clubmans • 499 cc •
1960 • United Kingdom, p. 260

48. Honda CB92 Benly Super Sport • 125 cc •
1960 • Japan, p. 264

49. NSU Supermax • 247 cc •
1961 • West Germany, p. 266

50. Ducati Elite • 204 cc •
1962 • Italy, p. 268

51. Honda CR110 • 50 cc •
1962 • Japan, p. 270

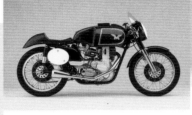

52. Matchless G50 • 496 cc •
1962 • United Kingdom, p. 272

53. Norton Manx • 498 cc •
1962 • United Kingdom, p. 276

59. Kreidler Florett • 49 cc •
1965 • West Germany, p. 288

60. Triumph T120 Bonneville • 650 cc •
1967 • United Kingdom, p. 292

61. Harley-Davidson Easy Rider Chopper • 1,200 cc •
1969 (1993 replica) • United States, p. 294

62. BSA Rocket 3 • 740 cc •
1969 • United Kingdom, p. 302

63. Kawasaki Mach III • 498 cc •
1969 • Japan, p. 304

69. MV Agusta 750S • 743 cc •
1973 • Italy, p. 320

70. Triumph X75 Hurricane • 750 cc •
1973 • United Kingdom, p. 324

71. Ducati 750SS • 748 cc •
1974 • Italy, p. 326

72. Laverda SFC • 744 cc •
1974 • Italy, p. 328

73. Honda GL1000 Gold Wing • 999 cc •
1975 • Japan, p. 332

79. Benelli Sei • 906 cc •
1984 • Italy, p. 352

80. Kawasaki GPZ900R Ninja • 908 cc •
1984 • Japan, p. 356

81. BMW K100RS • 987 cc •
1985 • West Germany, p. 358

82. BMW R80 G/S Paris-Dakar • 980 cc •
1985 • West Germany, p. 360

83. Buell RS1200 • 1,203 cc •
1989 • United States, p. 362

89. Aprilia Moto 6.5 • 649 cc •
1995 • Italy, p. 380

90. Honda EXP-2 • 402 cc •
1995 • Japan, p. 384

91. Beta Techno • 272 cc •
1997 • Italy, p. 386

92. BMW R1200 C • 1,170 cc •
1997 • Germany, p. 388

93. Morbidelli V8 • 847 cc •
1997 • Italy, p. 390

54. Parilla GS • 247 cc •
1962 • Italy, p. 278

55. Vespa GS • 146 cc •
1962 • Italy, p. 280

56. Honda C100 Super Cub • 49 cc •
1963 • Japan, p. 282

57. Velocette Venom • 499 cc •
1963 • United Kingdom, p. 284

58. Bultaco Sherpa T • 244 cc •
1965 • Spain, p. 286

64. Norton Commando 750 Fastback •
745 cc • 1969 • United Kingdom, p. 308

65. Derbi 50 Grand Prix • 49 cc •
1970 • Spain, p. 310

66. Honda CB750 Four • 736 cc •
1970 • Japan, p. 312

67. Harley-Davidson Super Glide "Night Train" •
1,200 cc • 1971 • United States, p. 314

68. Harley-Davidson XR750 • 750 cc •
1972 • United States, p. 318

74. BMW R90S • 898 cc •
1976 • West Germany, p. 336

75. Harley-Davidson XLCR • 1,000 cc •
1977 • United States, p. 338

76. Moto Guzzi Le Mans 1 • 844 cc •
1978 • Italy, p. 340

77. Suzuki Katana • 997 cc •
1982 • Japan, p. 346

78. Honda VF750F "Interceptor" • 748 cc •
1983 • Japan, p. 350

84. Yamaha Vmax • 1,198 cc •
1989 • Japan, p. 366

85. Ducati M900 "Monster" • 904 cc •
1993 • Italy, p. 372

86. Yamaha GTS1000 • 1,003 cc •
1993 • Japan, p. 374

87. Britten V1000 • 985 cc •
1994 • New Zealand, p. 376

88. Ducati 916 • 916 cc •
1994 • Italy, p. 378

94. Italjet Formula 50 LC • 49 cc •
1998 • Italy, p. 392

95. MV Agusta F4 • 750 cc •
1998 • Italy, p. 394

THE ART OF THE MOTORCYCLE

Solomon R. Guggenheim Museum, New York
June 26–September 20, 1998

The Field Museum of Natural History, Chicago
November 7, 1998–March 21, 1999

Guggenheim Museum Bilbao
fall 1999

This exhibition is made possible by BMW.

The Frank O. Gehry installation is made possible by Banana Republic.

Transportation assistance is provided by Lufthansa German Airlines.

Sponsor's Statement

More than eight years ago, Thomas Krens approached BMW with his idea for a museum exhibit featuring the motorcycle as a cultural phenomenon. For Mr. Krens, looking at the motorcycle in this way seemed perfectly natural. For BMW, which has been creating motorcycles of character since 1923, it was every bit as natural to view the motorcycle as a phenomenon that influences, and is influenced by, culture—in other words, not merely as two wheels and an engine; not just as a motor vehicle or industrial product; and much more than a halfway point between bicycle and automobile.

The world's first motorcycle was assembled before the turn of the century, a year before the first automobile. At the time, the motorcycle was little more than a melding of bicycle and internal-combustion-engined cycle; yet it was a development whose relevance to transportation, society, and prosperity would begin to become apparent some two decades later. BMW's own history began in 1916 with aircraft engines; in 1923, the first BMW motorcycle, the R32, made its debut at the Paris Auto Salon.

In the motorcycle, one sees an all-encompassing reflection of the very nature of mobility. At the turn of the century, mobility was a necessity: it meant work, bread, survival. Today, mobility of course remains a necessity; but in the world's advanced societies it is also much more: an expression of freedom, of being where we want to be when we want to be there. Over the century of the motorcycle's existence, it has ridden the high and low points of history, reflecting society and the diverse directions it has taken. The motorized two-wheeler, originally a vehicle of necessity, has evolved into a means of expressing individuality and a symbol of active, optimistic lifestyles.

As the motorcycle's role in society has evolved, so has its design; so, equally, has its value to society. From the artistic viewpoint it is three-dimensional: a composition of many elements of form, design, and aesthetics, always reflecting the time in which it is conceived and produced. Without exaggeration, it is possible to say that the motorcycle is one of the icons of our century, representing significant achievements in both technology and culture. The Guggenheim has recognized its particular meaning for the 20th century and shares with BMW the belief that the motorcycle, as an object of cultural value, richly deserves this recognition.

For both the Guggenheim and BMW, it is a *raison d'être* to continually challenge the ordinary; to merge the boundaries between technology and art; and to illuminate the synergies between engineering and culture. Both institutions feel an obligation to observe, act upon, and lead societal trends, as well as to support the development of new concepts, both technological and cultural. Both perceive technology and cultural values as equal elements in today's world. Both institutions think not in merely national, but rather in global dimensions; both are prepared to pursue the new, the innovative, the unconventional.

On the occasion of the 75th anniversary of BMW motorcycles, BMW is proud and honored to sponsor an exhibition that we think will help illuminate the far-reaching interaction between technology and culture. For the outstanding exhibit and catalogue *The Art of the Motorcycle*, we are profoundly indebted to the Solomon R. Guggenheim Foundation.

—*Bernd Pischetsrieder, Chairman of the Board, BMW AG*

Project Team

Curator
Thomas Krens

Curatorial
Charles Falco, Curatorial Adviser
Ultan Guilfoyle, Curatorial Adviser
Matthew Drutt, Associate Curator for Research
Sarah Botts, Executive Assistant to the Director
Vanessa Rocco, Project Curatorial Assistant

Film and Video Program
John Hanhardt, Senior Curator of Film and Media Arts
Maria-Christina Villaseñor, Assistant Curator of Film and Media Arts
Art Simon, Guest Curator

Technical and Historical Advisory Board
Thomas Krens, Chairman
Richard Gaul, Cochairman
George Barber
Beverly St. Clair Baird
Otis Chandler
Nobby Clark
Matthew Drutt
David Edwards
Bud Ekins
Don Emde
Charles Falco
Ultan Guilfoyle
Stefan Knittel
Harry Lindsay
Yves Macaire
Sammy Miller
Peter Noever
Bernard Salvat
John Surtees
Philip Tooth
Joachim Vogt
Ed Youngblood

Photography
David Heald, Chief Photographer and Director
    of Photographic Services
Ellen Labenksi, Assistant Photographer
Kimberly Bush, Photography and Permissions Associate
Werner Diesenroth
Gabriele Diesenroth-Sirius
Josef Holzl
Christoph Kuhn
Florian Rappmannsberger

Exhibition Design
Frank O. Gehry and Associates

Exhibition Graphics
Arnell Group
Let There Be Neon, Inc., New York

Art Services and Preparation
Karen Meyerhoff, Director of Exhibition and Collection
    Management and Design
Guillermo Ovalle, Assistant Registrar
Eleanor Nagy, Associate Conservator for Sculpture
Nobby Clark, Technical Consultant
Scott Wixon, Manager of Art Services and Preparations
Peter Read, Manager of Exhibition Fabrication and Design
Richard Gombar, Construction Manager
James Cullinane, Senior Exhibition Technician
Barry Hylton, Art Services and Preparations Project Leader
Stephen Engelman, Fabrication Specialist
Derek DeLuco, Art Handler
Jack Davidson
Jen Doyle
Craig Drennen
Megan Dyre
Matt Schwede
Jocelyn Groom, Exhibition Design Coordinator
Ana Linnemann, Graphic Designer

Catalogue, Design
Richard Pandiscio
Peter Stemmler, Senior Designer

Catalogue, Editorial and Production
Anthony Calnek, Director of Publications
Elizabeth Levy, Managing Editor/Manager of Foreign Editions
Elizabeth Franzen, Manager of Editorial Services
Esther Yun, Assistant Production Manager
Carol Fitzgerald, Associate Editor
Domenick Ammirati, Editorial Assistant
Melissa Secondino, Production Assistant
Stephanie Fleischmann
Lisa Cohen
Deborah Drier
Olga Han
Anita Leclerc
Phil Patton
Emily Russell
Diana Stoll
Thad Ziolkowski

Interns
Reginal Harper
Ari Hiroshige
L. Frances Hui
Christiane Ibach
Sylvia Omedes
Beatrice Trussardi

Lenders to the Exhibition

American Honda Motor Company, Inc., Torrance, Calif.
The Barber Vintage Motorsports Museum, Birmingham, Ala.
Glenn M. Bator
BMW AG, Munich
Dominique Buisson
Ron Bussey
King Juan Carlos of Spain, courtesy of Cagiva Motor SpA, Varese
The Otis Chandler Vintage Museum of Transportation and Wildlife,
    Oxnard, Calif.
Ron Commo
Alain Cortot
Derbi-Nacional Motor S.A., Barcelona
Deutsches Zweirad-Museum, Neckarsulm, Germany
Deutsches Museum, Munich
Ducati Motor SpA, Bologna
David Edwards
William Eggers
Elf-Antar France, Paris
Laurence L. Forstall
Mick Frew
Peter Gagan
Michel Gagnaire
The Gilbert family
Gérard Gruschwitz
Henry Ford Museum & Greenfield Village, Dearborn, Mich.
John Hoover, courtesy of Kawasaki Motor Corp., USA, Irvine, Calif.
Mr. and Mrs. Dennis E. Huamán
James M. Hunter
Italjet, USA, Huntington, New York
Matthew Janquitto, Vintage Imports
Dale Keesecker
Chris Le Sauvage
D. J. Light
Harry Lindsay
Jean Malleret
Reed Martin
Mark Mederski, courtesy of The Motorcycle Heritage Museum, Westerville, Ohio
Franck Meneret
The Sammy Miller Museum, Bashley Manor, England
John Mishanec
Moto Guzzi SpA, Mandello del Lario, Italy
Musée de l'Ile-de-France, Sceaux
Musée des Arts et Métiers (CNAM), Paris
Karl-Heinz Mutschler
National Air and Space Museum, Smithsonian Institution, Washington, D.C.
W. Eric Oddy
David Percival
Alain Petitjean
Primm Racing Collection/Vintage Iron, Fresno, Calif.
Private collection, Verona, Italy
Maxine and Kurt Ritthaler
SCM Group, Rimini
Jack Silverman, Silverman Museum Racing, Aspen, Colo.
Daniel K. Statnekov
Doug Strange
Andrew Sturgeon
Peter Swider
Jerry Tamanini
Mr. and Mrs. Alexander B. Wattles
Guy Webster
Yamaha Motor Corporation, USA, Cypress, Calif.

Thomas Krens

Preface

The motorcycle is a perfect metaphor for the 20th century. . . . Invented at the beginning of the industrial age, its evolution tracks the main currents of modernity. The object and its history represent the themes of technology, engineering, innovation, design, mobility, speed, rebellion, desire, freedom, love, sex, and death. . . . For much of society, the motorcycle remains a forbidden indulgence, an object of fascination, fantasy, and danger. Park the latest Ducati, Harley, Honda, or BMW on a street corner in any city or town in the world, and a crowd will gather. . . . It is hard to imagine the motorcycle twenty years from now. Like the modern age it reflects, the motorcycle would seem to have an uncertain future. They cannot be built any bigger or faster without leaving the road, and space-age design certainly must have its own limitations. . . . As a practical machine whose history has been one of relentless improvements and design evolution, the motorcycle as a form class at the end of the 20th century embodies its own end-game paradox. Logic and physics suggest it has reached the end of its evolutionary potential, but somehow we know that cannot be completely true. As such, however, it is a quintessential symbol of the insecurity and optimism of our time.

—*T. Krens, notes from Guggenheim Museum curatorial meeting, Oct. 1993*

The principal message of Walter Benjamin's prescient essay "The Work of Art in the Age of Mechanical Reproduction" (1936) is an explicit warning about technology's threat to the original work of art. Benjamin suggested that increasingly sophisticated means for reproducing imagery could lead to an attenuation of purportedly "authentic" cultural experience through the proliferation of second-generation images, which do not have the "aura" of the original. Furthermore, the capacity of new mediums like photography and film to extend the reach of culture to a far wider audience tends to erode the traditional aesthetic ideals and refined artistic purpose that has defined the history of art over the course of the last century. While Benjamin's immediate objective was to use this fundamental insight to leverage a Marxist analysis of culture and aesthetics for a political argument against Fascism, it is his observation about the gradual evolution of aesthetic values that has a particular relevance for the rationalization of an exhibition of motorcycles in an art museum. Benjamin's conclusion that "the transformation of the (cultural) superstructure . . . takes place far more slowly than that of the substructure" is an obvious but essential insight to the mechanics of cultural change. He notes that as our uses for culture multiply through the exploitation of the expressive potential of new mediums, new attitudes emerge that "brush aside a number of outmoded concepts, such as creativity and genius, eternal value and mystery," to posit a significantly broader framework for cultural exploration and experience.

It seems obvious that an exhibition like *The Art of the Motorcycle* at the Guggenheim challenges the *conventional* notion of the art museum by exploiting the significantly broader framework. If the institution's original mission is interpreted as a mandate to present paintings and drawings, then motorcycles have no place on the Guggenheim's ramp. But the contemporary museum is no longer simply a sanctuary for sacred objects. The gradual changes in the substructure have been taking place for years. Like all other social institutions, the art museum has continued to evolve, responding to new directions in artistic creativity and to pressures and demands from a better informed, better educated, and more demanding audience. Special exhibitions in general are more complex, more informative, and more carefully designed and presented than ever before. The containers have become works of art in and of themselves. None of these developments are particularly new—major museums have had departments devoted to design for a good many years. Frank Lloyd Wright, among others, established the notion of architecture as art, and exhibitions have become increasingly imaginative and sophisticated since *The Treasures of Tuthankhamen* in 1977. What is new is the widespread feeling that the environment has changed, that the traditional models for cultural mediation are no longer adequate, and that new, infinitely complex cultural forms and institutions are in the process of formation.

Perhaps Benjamin would have been troubled by the replacement of the auratic work of art with mechanically produced objects such as motorcycles, but that distinction is irrelevant in today's discourse. The accumulation of changes in the substructure has produced a new world of cultural activity and diversity that he would scarcely recognize. The transformation of the superstructure has been profound. Although new paradigms still need to be defined, a wider vision of art and culture in society has nevertheless created new responsibilities and opportunities for art museums and cultural institutions. The new museum has a complex mission. It must, on the one hand, continue to fulfill its historical role of stewardship: the collection, preservation, and presentation of important works of art and cultural developments. At the same time, it must address a broad range of new implicit responsibilities. It must recognize, for example, the significance and validity of new generations of creative artists whose work, ideas, and visual language have been shaped by MTV, rap music, the Internet, and contemporary critical theory as well as traditional art history. It must also respond to evolving demands on its capacity for cultural mediation and education from an increasingly sophisticated audience.

Within this complex situation, the art museum has the opportunity to play a leadership role, both as interlocutor and participant. Necessarily, this role must reflect the subtleties and complexities of a late century culture with shifting boundaries and an unprecedented level of interconnectivity. In this new territory, *The Art of the Motorcycle,* as an exhibition project, is of particular significance for the Guggenheim. Its content, context, rationale, and structure offer a multifaceted opportunity for information and interpretation. The centerpiece of the project is the precise and comprehensive survey of the history of motorcycle design expressed through 111 machines—from an 1868 Michaux-Perreaux (fig. i), a 19th-century big-wheeled bicycle with a steam engine attached under the seat, to a 1998 MV Agusta (cat. no. 95), a sleek, Italian-designed sportbike capable of a speed of 170 miles per hour. The history of the motorcycle describes the history and evolution of the modern age. In the Guggenheim Museum, Frank Gehry's extraordinary installation design for the exhibition is an integral part of the experience. Recognizing the implicit potential of Frank Lloyd Wright's rotunda to express fantasies of movement and speed, Gehry has fashioned a space that is as artistically evocative and technologically savvy as the machines on display. By cladding the interior of the Guggenheim rotunda in highly reflective stainless steel, Gehry both transforms and emphasizes the essence of Wright's structure, and suggests the sensuousness and industrial elegance of motorcycle design. Art, architecture, and industrial design mirror each other in constantly shifting ways. Equally integral to the exhibition is this carefully crafted catalogue. The images reproduced here—particularly those views of the motorcycles photographed in black and white against a minimal white background—attempt to neutralize the surrounding environment and present the machines in a standardized format. The detailed entries and documentation accompanying each motorcycle in the catalogue and the exhibition have been contributed by a group of renowned motorcycle historians to support the integrity and scope of the checklist. A range of superb essays as well as nine personal and critical commentaries situate motorcycles in a broader historical context and cultural milieu, from individual experiences to analyses of the iconic value of the motorcycle. The last element of the project is a film program, which evaluates the real and mythic place that motorcycles occupy in 20th-century media. The cultural experience of *The Art of the Motorcycle* then, is the sum of its parts: the historical evolution represented by the machines themselves; the notions of thematic transformation and reflection in the installation; the documentation and contextualization of the objects in the catalogue and the impressions of the contributing authors; and, the representation of motorcycles in media and in discussion.

The Art of the Motorcycle then is organized as a cultural event. The distinctions separating content from context are blurred; the exhibition becomes a contemporary creative experience that in its various richness of choices mirrors our own environment. *The Art of the Motorcycle* is an obvious challenge to the conventional mission of the museum to present those objects of high material culture that are authentic, unique, and grounded in tradition and history. But is it, as critic Hilton Kramer recently told *The Wall Street Journal* (22 May 1998), staking out his position in advance of the event, "a bald-faced ploy to bring in money and whatever attendance might come rolling in on motorcycles," or is there a deeper impulse at work here, something softer, more evolutionary, that reflects the subtle shifting of the uses, functions, and purposes—and perhaps the expanding frame—of cultural institutions. As a contemporary institution engaging scholarship, seriousness of purpose, traditional methodology, and considered interpretation, the Guggenheim continues in its original mission. Designed as an event, and with a certain level of authority—the luxury of sheer numbers of motorcycles affording a detailed and subtle presentation—*The Art of the Motorcycle* signals the beginning of the transformation of the cultural superstructure.

A precise collection of circumstances has shaped this exhibition. For the past five years, the Solomon R. Guggenheim Foundation has been expanding internationally and now has museums or exhibition spaces in four countries. With the Gehry-designed

Guggenheim Museum in Bilbao, Spain, which opened in fall 1997, the Foundation has built one of the greatest buildings of the century. It has expanded its collection in innovative ways, and its programming has ranged from major retrospectives devoted to established 20th-century artists such as Robert Rauschenberg, to concise and focused exhibitions on important periods in the careers of historical figures such as Max Beckmann and Robert Delaunay, to broad cultural overviews such as *The Great Utopia*, an exhibition devoted to the avant-garde in Russia, and *China: 5,000 Years*, which brought together ancient treasures with modern art in a single narrative. The Guggenheim Foundation has made a commitment to exploring new art, new artists, and new mediums. It has, perhaps, in the words of Michael Kimmelman, "extend(ed) the reach of the art museum today in ways that other museums don't imagine." (*The New York Times*, 19 April 1998)

From a practical perspective, an art museum's special-exhibition programming should fit into a strategic plan. Any given exhibition project should not only be considered for its short-term impact as such, but how it influences the long-term profile of the institution by contributing to the definition of the issues, ideas, and concepts that determine the institution's cultural "voice." The Guggenheim, as an institution, has defined its mission to explore 20th-century and contemporary culture in all of its richness and presence. This includes painting and sculpture, architecture and design, photography and new media; the arts of Asia, Africa, and South America, as well as those of Europe and America, and classical, historical, and other non-20th century manifestations that offer some insight or perspective on current cultural preoccupations.

The Art of the Motorcycle is part of that trajectory of exhibition programming at the Guggenheim that will broaden the museum's cultural reach and engender its more active participation in the interpretation of contemporary art and culture. The genesis of *The Art of the Motorcycle* dates from 1991; the project results from the convergence of several ideas. That the Guggenheim is expanding its international presence and thematic frame has already been established: art, architecture, design, and new media are intended to be the four main elements of its portfolio. The impact of the Museum's expanding base and increased competency in the conceptualization and organization of exhibitions means that it can occasionally take on projects outside its specific in-house expertise and develop them into clear and powerful cultural commentaries. More specifically, however, Norman Rosenthal, Exhibitions Secretary at the Royal Academy of Arts in London, inadvertently provided the conceptual framework for this exhibition when he invited the Guggenheim to collaborate on an exhibition of 20th-century painting and sculpture, the overarching ambition of which—like other end-of-the-century summary and celebration efforts—was to capture the spirit, essence, and complexity of the 20th century in the visual arts. Ultimately, the exhibition proved impossible to realize in New York. Not only was the topic and its range vast and resistant to comprehensive summary, but from a practical perspective it immediately became clear that denial of important loans would become an insurmountable problem. Major institutions with seminal works were reluctant to part with them at such a portentous time precisely because of the importance of those works to the definition of institutional achievement. In other words, it was impossible to make an exhibition of the 20th century and include the most precious and rarest works of the 20th century. That the themes of the century could be revealed through primary and secondary if not seminal works simply had less appeal for the Guggenheim, and it ultimately withdrew from the project. The notion of staging an exhibition that captured the spirit, development, and imagination of the 20th century prevailed however. General research into motorcycles was initiated.

One hundred and thirty years ago neither the bicycle nor the engine existed in the forms we are familiar with. In 1868 Louis Perreaux installed and patented a steam engine in the first commercially successful pedal bicycle; by 1894, the Hildebrand brothers and Alois Wolfmüller had patented a water-cooled, two-cylinder gasoline engine in a bicycle type frame, the first commercially produced motorcycle with an internal-combustion engine. More than a product of the industrial revolution, the motorcycle quickly took on broader significance. Embodying the more abstract themes of speed, rebellion, progress, freedom, sex, and danger, the motorcycle has been immortalized as a cultural icon that has transformed with the times. The limits imposed by the possible form and function of the motorcycle, and the breadth of variation that have been expressed within these limitations, provide a vehicle for examining the motorcycle as a possible metaphor for the 20th century.

The approach to constructing a definitive survey of motorcycles was serious and rigorous. A curatorial team with a deep sense for the material and a broad information network was identified, and the methodology for selecting and presenting the motorcycles was adopted and implemented. The criteria for selecting machines to be included in *The Art of the Motorcycle* are fairly straightforward. Except for the seven pre-production motorcycles that open the exhibition, the selection not only spans the century of motorcycle production that evolved from the first patented combination of steam engine and bicycle frame in 1868, but also the technological progress and the cultural, sociological, and economic factors that define and characterize the 20th century. In addition to these, marketing, the expectations and desires of consumers, and the ebb and flow of national economies are all manifested in the components and form of the motorcycle. The sheer number of types of motorcycles—production, studio-built one-offs, customized, sidecar additions, and the many categories of motorcycle racing—is vast. To extract a narrative from the array of functions and dictates that motorcycles represent, the choices have been refined to a group of singularly 20th-century defining elements: technological innovation, design excellence and aesthetics, and social function. All of the motorcycles in the exhibition are a product of more than one of these criteria.

The pursuit of speed can be seen as a primary factor in the advancement of singularly 20th-century technologies, from the measure of light, sound, and atomic particles to the development of military weapons and the nature of warfare, to the transformation of our concept of distance. The earliest machines in this exhibition are the outcome of a period of tremendous experimentation and technological innovation that was underway in every industrialized country in the world. By the first years of the 20th century, after a decade of intense experimentation and competition, essentially all the features of the machines on the market today were in place in practically all motorcycles in production. Competition and speed provided the impetus for development of motorcycles in these early years; the American phenomenon of board-track racing (where the riders rode their stripped-down and incredibly fast machines around a steeply banked wooden course) attracted large audiences, and often fatalities for both riders and spectators. The Indian Board Track Racer (cat. no. 10), which debuted in 1911, garnered valuable publicity for the company by winning numerous championships and setting new track records.

As the century continued, the division between race-ready and road motorcycles narrowed, and increasingly race technology has been adapted as a performance and marketing essential that customers are ready to pay for. But while Grand Prix racing attracts huge audiences via television and pays huge dividends as a marketing device, 1990s motorcycle technology still reflects the individualist, experimental, hand-built nature of early motorcycle development, as embodied by the radical and successful Britten V-1000 (cat. no. 87), built by designer John Britten in 1994. The 20th century's mania for harnessing technology to conquer new territory finds its pure form in the motorcycle; since the early days of board-track racing, and Glenn Curtiss's spectacular record-breaking accomplishment in 1907 on his experimental Curtiss V-8 (cat. no. 3), myriad competition categories have developed to accommodate new areas of special-interest motorcycle technology and audiences, such as those for trials and enduro racing.

The story of 20th-century industrial design is manifested in the many approaches to the arrangement of the motorcycle's functioning elements catalogued in this exhibition. BMW's R32, 1923 (cat. no. 16), as just one example, is a model of Bauhaus-caliber design, with its emphasis on practicality, efficiency, and sleek forms capable of being mass-produced through the use of inexpensive, industrial materials. Motorcycle design runs the gamut from styling—the projection of technical sophistication or a look which functions to project something about the identity of the rider—to machines whose technical components find a harmonious union with their function in the distribution of their parts. Beautiful design at the hands of a technician is manifested in the Imme, 1949 (cat. no. 37), designed by Norbert Riedl, whose ingenious reorganization of the machine's frame broke with fifty years of tradition to create one of the most innovative motorcycles of the postwar era. The Suzuki Katana (cat. no. 77) was an example of successful design styling to create the most radical-looking production sportbike of the early 1980s. Design that creates a mythos about the motorcycle and its rider found its origins in the great mid-century American motorcycle marques Harley-Davidson and Indian, and at the hands of GI's returning from the war who customized their bikes for performance on the Californian dry lakes. These "Bob-Jobs" evolved into "Choppers" known for their performance and appearance, and the Easy Rider Chopper (cat. no. 61) in the exhibition is one of the enduring icons of the Californian 1960s.

With the Super Cub (cat. no. 56), Honda targeted the new rider and proposed the antithesis of Marlon Brando in his *Wild One* incarnation. From technical innovations like its automatic clutch and the use of plastic for its leg shields and front fenders, to its cheerful red-and-white styling, the Super Cub was designed to appeal to a non-motorcycle market. Motorcycle production has been buffeted by changing economies and demographics, but in turn it has also impacted the function of daily life. Early attempts at marketing motorbikes for women, like the Megola, 1922 (cat. no. 13), or the Monet & Goyon Moto Légère, 1922 (cat. no. 14), nicknamed "priest's bike" (a frocked clergyman could have operated this machine without entangling his clothes) and the Vélosolex (cat. no. 36), find their apotheosis in the Super Cub and Piaggio's Vespa (cat. no. 55). In both Depression-era and postwar Europe, manufacturers sought to broaden their markets and sustain cheap mass production. More recently motorcycle riding has become almost exclusively a leisure activity. Radical changes in the work/leisure landscape and the evolution of industries and events for recreation have contributed to the appetite for sport and luxury bikes.

The Art of the Motorcycle has resulted from the support and efforts of a great many individuals and institutions, who are acknowledged elsewhere in this catalogue. I am especially indebted to Bernd Pischetsrieder, Chairman and CEO of BMW and his team, whose support and enthusiasm from the inception of this project have been inspiring. I would also like to thank Lufthansa German Airlines and Frederick W. Reid, a Guggenheim Trustee and President and COO of Lufthansa for their generous support of this project.

Essays

Charles M. Falco

Issues in the Evolution of the Motorcycle

The motorcycle, at its core, is both an object of commerce and a fetish. As such, it embodies the dreams and desires of its owners and enthusiasts. These expectations, in turn, have been shaped and abetted by the breathtaking technological progress of this century. This, together with a novel combination of cultural, sociological, and gender-related factors, has determined when, and why, certain technologies appeared in the designs of specific motorcycles. Because these elements overlap, a strictly chronological approach cannot capture this evolution in all its richness. Moreover, in a field of design dominated by technology, a year-by-year chronology risks implying a linear sequence of development. As we'll see, this would be far from the truth.

Conceptually, the 1868 Michaux-Perreaux and the 1998 MV Agusta F-4 are both little more than bicycles with engines, but that the motorcycle has changed in the 130 years between these two machines is obvious. Indeed, 130 years ago, neither the bicycle nor the engine existed in the forms in which we now know them. The origins of motorcycle technology date back to the steam engines of Thomas Savery and Thomas Newcomen in the 17th century. Toward the end of the 19th century, however, the pace of experimentation and development picked up dramatically. A compact engine may be the most obvious component needed for making a motorcycle, but the invention of pneumatic tires (Dunlop, 1888; Michelin, 1895), the roller chain (Renold, 1880), and an appropriate frame geometry (Starley, 1886) were all equally necessary.[1] And thanks to the extraordinarily rapid technological changes taking place, these elements were coming together simultaneously. Within a very short time, all that was lacking was a practical, self-contained motorcycle engine. Until about 1890, just what type of motor that would be was an open question.

Late in the 19th century, the steam engine emerged as a power source for propelling personal vehicles. A hundred years earlier, James Watt had perfected the Newcomen steam engine for industrial uses. Large steam-powered carriages were already in public use in England as early as the 1820s. Eventually, on December 26, 1868, Louis Guillaume Perreaux patented a design for a steam engine to be installed on the first commercially successful pedal bicycle, built by Pierre and Ernest Michaux in France. The solid iron frame of the Michaux bicycle, which was manufactured at a rate of several hundred per year, made

24

it a natural choice for the 61-kg Perreaux engine. All that was needed was to remove the cranks and pedals from the front wheel, substitute an arched backbone to make room for the steam engine, and add pulleys for transmitting the power to the rear wheel. This final modification was described in a June 14, 1871, addition to Perreaux's patent, and the resulting 87-kg motorcycle was fabricated later that year. Similar efforts to develop steam-powered motorcycles were under way in other countries, as well. In the United States, Sylvester Roper's machine, built circa 1869, was another early example.

Fortunately for those who cringe at the thought of sitting with a steam boiler between their legs, all but a few motorcycles produced today are powered by four-cycle internal-combustion engines. The four-stroke cycle—the induction of a fresh fuel and air mixture into the cylinder, its compression by the piston, the ignition and subsequent expansion of the hot gasses to work against the piston, and finally, the expulsion of the spent mixture into the atmosphere—was first proposed by Alphonse Beau de Rochas in 1862 and made into a working engine by Nikolaus Otto in 1876. Nine years later, Gottlieb Daimler built a lightweight version of one of these engines, installed it in a wooden chassis, and created the first "motor-cycle" powered by internal combustion. But this crude vehicle had four wheels and bore only a superficial resemblance to an actual motorcycle, and Daimler soon abandoned his *Reitwagen mit Petroleum Motor* to focus on producing a practical automobile. It took nine more years for the first commercial production of motorcycles to begin.

In 1894, five years after abandoning their own steam-engine project, Henry and Wilhelm Hildebrand joined with Alois Wolfmüller of Munich to patent a water-cooled, two-cylinder, four-cycle gasoline engine in a bicycle-type frame. Made under license in France, approximately one thousand of the machines were eventually produced. Unfortunately, their design, which linked the connecting rods of the massive 1,489-cc engine directly to the rear wheel, was fundamentally flawed. Unable to keep pace with rapid developments in the nascent motorcycle industry, the company went out of business in 1897. In many ways, however, the founding of this company was every bit as significant as Daimler's experimental vehicle of a decade earlier. The number of machines produced indicates the demand that already existed for two-wheeled transport.

Fig. 1. Michaux-Perreaux Steam Velocipede, 1868, France. Musée de l'Ile-de-France, Sceaux.

Fig. 2. Hildebrand & Wolfmüller, 1,489 cc, 1894, Germany. Deutches Zweirad-Museum, Neckarsulm, Germany.

Another representative early production model was the 1901 Indian, whose engine was derived from that of the De Dion Bouton automobile. By copying it, George Hendee and Oscar Hedstrom were able to enter production relatively easily. Their company was a success; along with Harley-Davidson, it was one of only two U.S. manufacturers to survive into the 1930s. It's clear at a glance that the Indian's engine was adapted as an afterthought to fit into a standard bicycle frame. By contrast, it's evident that the frame of the FN was specifically designed to house an engine. The engine itself was particularly remarkable: Paul Kelecom's complex shaft-drive, four-cylinder machine appeared at a time when most manufacturers were producing much cruder one-cylinder, belt-driven machines. The intrinsic strengths of the FN design kept it in production for more than twenty years.

By 1903, the engine had found its final resting place in the space beneath the tank, and the spray carburetor and magneto had been developed to replace the unreliable surface carburetor and the hazardous open flame of hot-tube ignition. Everything was essentially

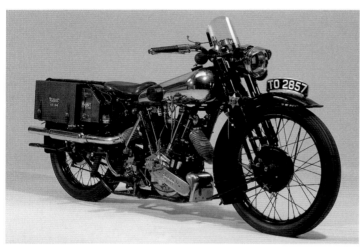

Fig. 3. Indian Single, 16 ci, 1901, United States.
The Otis Chandler Vintage Museum of Transportation
and Wildlife, Oxnard, Calif.

Fig. 4. Brough Superior SS100 Alpine Grand Sport,
988 cc, 1926, United Kingdom. Collection of Jack Silverman,
Silverman Museum Racing, Aspen, Colo.

in place, and the changes since then have mostly been gradual refinements. But those refinements improved performance many times over. The 1901 Indian weighed some one hundred pounds and produced less than 2 hp from its 16-ci (260-cc) engine. By the 1920s, developments in engine technology originating in the aircraft industry of World War I had boosted the output of a typical 300-cc engine to more than 15 hp. Harnessing this additional power without twisting or distorting the frame required an increase in overall weight to approximately three hundred pounds. The 1994 Ducati 916 weighs only 50 percent more than these machines, yet its engine produces nearly ten times the power. This was made possible by the development of materials technology, which allowed engineers to design structures of tremendous strength without a corresponding increase in weight. A simple example is the substitution of aluminum for steel. Although the reduced weight of aluminum provides significant performance advantages over low-carbon structural steels, a typical aluminum alloy costs roughly five times as much per kilogram as steel. However, the aluminum frame of the 1925 Molteni shows that motorcycle designers were already exploiting the advantages of high-performance materials.

The Racer's Edge

Other than the choice of color, every aspect of the 1915 Indian 8-Valve Board Track Racer was designed solely to get it around the track faster than its competitors. Its high-performance engine, developed by Oscar Hedstrom several years earlier with four valves for each cylinder, established a number of official world speed and distance records. Other racing machines, such as the 1953 AJS E-95 or the 1957 Harley-Davidson KR, were similarly specialized. The Harley was a very successful dirt-track racer of the 1950s and 1960s. One should not conclude, however, that such racing machines represented motorcycle design in its purest form, for each was designed to compete within a set of rules that typically specified minimum overall weight and other mechanical aspects, in addition to engine size. Nonetheless, the impact of racing on the evolution of motorcycles cannot be understated.

In 1926, George Brough guaranteed that the Brough Superior SS100 Alpine Grand Sport could reach a top speed of 100 mph, although few of England's roads of the time could sustain such a speed. Produced at a rate of fewer than one a day for a period of twenty years, Brough Superiors were virtually handcrafted. Over an 11-year period, T. E. Lawrence, one of the marque's most famous riders, averaged 27,000 miles a year on a series of six SS100 (and one SS80) models before he was killed on one in a low-speed crash when he swerved to avoid a bicyclist. Historically, cyclists have been willing to pay a premium for performance that few could effectively use. Motorcycles such as the Brough Superior spent most of their lives at speeds easily achievable on machines a third of the size. Such has continued to be the case. The 1954 Vincent Black Shadow Series C was designed to exacting standards of materials, craftsmanship, and performance. The adjustable foot controls, the use of stainless steel, and the dual side-stands that also pivoted to elevate the front of the machine for changing tires set it apart from its contemporaries. At the time it was introduced, its top speed of 120 mph made it the fastest production vehicle available.

Design trends beyond those of motorcycling have also influenced styles, although the results often emerged in diluted form. An Art Deco influence is visible in several of the machines from the 1920s and '30s. At other times, cultural forces from within motorcycling itself have played major roles.[2] The single-cylinder 1962 Matchless G50, with its lightweight magnesium castings and overhead camshaft, was designed and produced in very limited numbers for the purpose of winning races. The handlebars and the seat were positioned to achieve minimum wind resistance and therefore maximum speed—although this configuration was not necessarily the most comfortable for the rider. With an engine of only one cylinder, the G50 gained reliability and maneuverability over machines with multi-cylinder engines, at the cost of somewhat reduced maximum horsepower. As such, it was an example of one approach to the Grand Prix racing of the time. The enthusiasts who built British "Café Racers" of the 1950s and '60s wanted their motorcycles to have the appearance of Grand Prix racers, so they took their styling cues from such machines. This prompted manufacturers to design production machines such as the 1963 Velocette Venom. With its large fuel tank, alloy rims, twin-leading-shoe front brake, lowered handlebars, and racing-style seat, the Venom emulates the style of the G50 in a machine intended for everyday use.

The minor cosmetic modifications made to stock machines that first surfaced in postwar America (for example, see the 1940 Indian Sport Scout "Bob-Job") were the first stirrings of the impulse that eventually led to highly stylized "Choppers," epitomized by the motorcycles crafted for *Easy Rider* (1969). The clean, extended front ends of those bikes can be seen in the 1973 Triumph X75 Hurricane. Although it was made in England, this machine was styled in central Illinois by Craig Vetter, working as an independent designer. Vetter's "American" design can be contrasted directly with the "English" design of the BSA Rocket 3, since Vetter began his work with a standard 1969 Rocket 3. In general, however, mainstream motorcycles have been less strongly affected by fashion trends than have other items of industrial design. The 1973 Triumph X75, which, in retrospect, was not such a radical departure from the conventional designs of the time, was viewed with considerable skepticism when it first appeared. Fewer than 1,200 of the machines were sold, compared to 27,000 of the Triumph Trident, a more traditional design. (The 1967 T120 Bonneville is a similarly traditional Triumph.)

Contrary to the clichéd perception that motorcyclists are individualists who choose to ride as a way of demonstrating their unique identity, they are, in fact, quite conservative. Manufacturers are keenly aware that cyclists have been reluctant to accept revolutionary designs, even ones with performance advantages. Although BMW's 1985 water-cooled, four-cylinder K100RS was a radical departure from its sixty-year tradition of air-cooled transverse "boxer" twins, the engine was mounted transversely in the frame and styled to look like the older engine. Again, ten years later, when BMW introduced its innovative Telelever front suspension on machines such as the R1100RS, it was styled to resemble the conventional front ends that motorcyclists were used to seeing. Now, as well as in the past, motorcycle designs that push too far beyond contemporary designs risk failure in the marketplace.

The 1993 Ducati M900 "Monster" was a significant departure from design norms. By the late 1980s, most large-displacement street motorcycles were created either as "cruisers" or as "sportbikes." The cruiser category was represented by machines such as

Fig. 5. Vincent Black Shadow Series C, 998 cc, 1954, United Kingdom. The Otis Chandler Vintage Museum of Transportation and Wildlife, Oxnard, Calif.

Fig. 6. Matchless G50, 496 cc, 1962, United Kingdom. The Barber Vintage Motorsports Museum, Birmingham, Ala.

the 1971 Harley-Davidson Super Glide "Night Train," on which the rider sat upright while traveling at moderate speeds along fairly straight roads. The modern sportbike evolved out of machines such as the 1985 Suzuki GSXR, which resembled the high-speed racers built for maneuverability on twisting roads. They were designed with a full fairing and placed the rider in a crouched position to reduce wind resistance. In contrast to cruisers, several national and international racing series exist for modified sportbikes, which has affected sales of their production counterparts. As a consequence, considerable developmental effort has been devoted to these machines, and their performance levels have escalated considerably. However, the Ducati M900 dispensed with the fairing that had hidden most engines for the previous decade, put the rider in a more upright position, and thereby established a new trend, one that combined some aspects of the "naked" styling of cruisers with the high performance and maneuverability of sportbikes.

Because fairings are easy to damage but expensive to replace, because motorcycles can function without them, and perhaps because of the sameness of fully faired machines, young riders of the 1990s have taken to turning damaged sportbikes into stripped-down "streetfighters." A damaged sportbike that's only a few years old can be purchased for a third of the price of a new machine, yet it provides its owner with an engine that produces only a few horsepower less than the latest model. Removing extraneous parts boosts the power-to-weight ratio and allows the owner to exercise his or her creativity, as well. No doubt these streetfighters will influence styles of the coming years.

The Lady Riders

Examining the open-loop frame of the 1922 Monet & Goyon Moto Légère, one might conclude that it was designed for a woman. Actually, this machine was developed to provide transportation for the many parish priests in France, allowing them to ride while wearing their cassocks. With few exceptions, motorcycle designers have been male, and most designs were developed specifically to appeal to men. Even today, women account for less than 10 percent of all motorcycle riders in the U.S., and the percentage was surely lower at the turn of the century. That is not to say that women haven't been involved in motorcycles from the earliest times. As early as 1897, both Coventry and Humber marketed motorcycles in England made specifically for women. They were manufactured using the open-frame style of women's bicycles of the time. In that same year, Mrs. F. H. de Veulle rode a Coventry Motette woman's motor bicycle the hundred miles from Coventry to London, where she received a diamond ring from the company's owner for her accomplishment. To appreciate what was involved in this ride, understand that in 1897 there were no paved roads in England, other than those that were covered with irregular cobblestones. Moreover, the ignition system on Mrs. de Veulle's motorcycle consisted of an open-flame burner on one end of a platinum tube inserted into the cylinder, and the carburetor was simply a pan of fuel whose vapors were sucked into the engine. Even the most minor accident often resulted in a conflagration.[3]

The Vespa and the Honda C100 Super Cub were styled to appeal to women without simultaneously alienating men. Both sold in very large numbers, influencing other manufacturers to copy the designs. Despite the popularity of such models, however, women still constitute a fairly small minority of motorcyclists. This fact has had significant consequences for the designs of the machines. Although the styling of certain industrial objects—pens, razors, even automobiles—might be aimed at men, their functionality is largely gender-neutral. Such is not the case for the motorcycle.

For one thing, there's the sheer physicality of the machines. The unique single-sided front suspension of the 1993 Yamaha GTS1000 was developed by James Parker to bypass some of the limitations of the conventional telescopic fork suspension, which came into widespread use shortly after World War II. With any suspension system, the farther it can telescope, the better a motorcycle can react to irregularities in the pavement. The 31-inch height of the GTS1000's seat was a compromise the designer made between suspension and physiology. The most common configuration for modern street motorcycles puts the seat 30 to 32 inches above the ground, which allows the average male rider to touch the ground with both feet when stopped. Fewer than 3 percent of women are as tall as the average man, and they generally lack the upper-body strength to support a 450-pound machine.

Fig. 8. Monet & Goyon Moto Légère, 117 cc, 1922, France. Collection of Michel Gagnaire.

What's in a Motor?

Most of the motorcycles highlighted here were powered by four-cycle engines. The two-cycle form of the internal-combustion engine was patented in 1892, and the remarkable water-cooled engine in the 1929 Scott Squirrel Sprint Special was the result of the determined efforts of Alfred A. Scott, beginning as early as 1900. In the Scott engine, induction and expansion processes overlapped during one cycle, with compression and exhaust overlapping during the other. As a result, it produced twice the number of power impulses as a four-cycle engine during every revolution. With its combination of light weight and high power output, the Scott Squirrel won the 1912 and 1913 Isle of Man Senior TT, one of the most prestigious motorcycle races of the time. With the engine low in the frame and its purple fuel tank stowed below the seat, the basic Scott design lasted for a half-century.

Subsequent improvements to the two-cycle engine, such as the elegant Schnuerle loop-scavenging system, were first deployed in Germany in such machines as the DKW RT125. This was one of the most advanced designs of the time, and DKW's influence was seen later in the BSA Bantam and Harley-Davidson Hummer, both of which were copied from DKW drawings that were taken as war reparations. During the 1960s, the power output of these engines increased considerably, due largely—but not exclusively—to the work of Suzuki, along with Kawasaki and Yamaha. The Kawasaki Mach III was a direct result of those efforts. Although it had an engine of only 498 cc, this motorcycle was able to accelerate more rapidly than practically any other vehicle on the road. In one decade, the two-cycle engine had evolved from a device suitable largely for inexpensive transport to the engine of choice for many racing teams and high-performance enthusiasts.

Alas, the engine was to run afoul of the U.S. Environmental Protection Agency. Although it was not explicitly banned, it was nearly impossible for a two-cycle engine to meet exhaust-emissions standards. An exception was the Yamaha RD400 of the mid '80s, which demonstrated that with sufficient effort, it was possible for a two-cycle engine to comply with the then-current regulations. But the lengths to which Yamaha had to go to obtain EPA certification made this labor a less than practical engineering solution. Certainly, one cannot ignore the environmental costs of air pollution, yet the fact remains that the two-cycle engine has far fewer working parts than a four-cycle engine, which means a lower production cost and hence a lower purchase price. Consequently, engineers continue trying to overcome the emissions problem. Honda's experimental EXP-2 engine has a valve in the exhaust port that controls the pressure in the cylinder during a critical period of the cycle. The result is an engine that has significantly reduced emissions as well as increased fuel economy.

Fig. 9. Yamaha GTS1000, 1,003 cc, 1993, Japan. Courtesy of Yamaha Motor Corporation, USA, Cypress, Calif.

Fig. 10. Scott Squirrel Sprint Special, 620 cc, 1929, United Kingdom. The Barber Vintage Motorsports Museum, Birmingham, Ala.

Words such as sidevalve, four-valve, overhead-cam, or Desmo all refer to specific aspects of the head of the engine. Even dual-carburetor, which seems to describes a different component entirely, refers to the performance of the head. A head performs three essential functions: It delivers air and fuel to the inside of the engine, dissipates the heat generated by combustion, and expels the hot gasses. The head is the single most important part of an engine and has received the attention of generations of engineers, resulting in many designs that are beautiful in their own right; for example, consider the heads on the engines of the 1914 Cyclone, 1953 AJS, 1962 Matchless G50, 1974 Ducati 750SS, and 1973 MV Agusta 750S.

A motorcycle engine generates power by ingesting as much air and fuel as possible (15 times as much air as fuel), igniting it, then venting the spent mixture with minimal restriction. Unfortunately, the laws of thermodynamics dictate that much of the energy released by the burning fuel is lost in the form of heat rather than delivered as power to the rear wheel. The more power extracted from an engine, the more wasted heat is generated. Very little can be done about this wasted power other than removing it as efficiently as possible to avoid damaging the engine. Until about twenty years ago, most motorcycle engines relied on air cooling, necessitating cooling fins to transfer efficiently the heat from the engine to the air. The low-power engines of the early years of the century generated relatively small amounts of heat, so materials of low thermal conductivity such as cast iron could be used, and cooling fins could be fairly small. However, as engine power increased, aluminum replaced cast iron, and deeper cooling fins became essential. The heads on the 1924 Moto Guzzi C4V and the 1962 Norton Manx illustrate the improvement in casting techniques during this period.

The Cycling Century

Taking one's hand off the accelerator, it's fascinating to follow the gradual transformation of motorcycle shape and style as a whole, from the 1915 Iver Johnson through the 1938 Triumph Speed Twin and 1970 Honda CB750 Four to the 1993 Ducati M900. All of these are outstanding examples of machines designed to provide a level of performance well beyond what's needed for basic transportation. The quality of the materials and the machine work used in the Iver Johnson were significantly higher than that of most of its contemporaries. Edward Turner's twin-cylinder engine for the Speed Twin, introduced at a time when single-cylinder machines dominated the English market, proved to be one of the most long-lived designs in motorcycling history. It was used for the next fifty years in Triumph's entire range of vertical twins (and triples), including the Bonneville, and was copied by numerous other manufacturers. Honda's CB750 was the world's first truly mass-produced four-cylinder machine. Honda was far from the first with this engine configuration—witness the 1908 FN Four and 1910 Pierce Four—but thanks to Honda's excellent design, high quality, and the economies of mass production, the CB750 brought such features as overhead-camshaft multi-cylinder engines and disc brakes to the general motorcycling public. And the Ducati M900, cited earlier, by boldly stripping away the ubiquitous fairing, created a new and extraordinary hybrid machine.

These transformations serve to illustrate the overall evolution of motorcycle design, but there have been many interesting, and sometimes important, digressions and discontinuities, as well. Consider the 1922 Megola, the 1922 Neracar, the 1925 Böhmerland, and the 1930 Majestic. Although the Megola's design was quite unorthodox, nearly two thousand were produced over four years. The touring version of the machine shielded the rider with sheet metal for partial protection from the elements and adopted a comfortable feet-forward riding position and rear springing, which was unusual for machines of this period. The Megola's five-cylinder, four-cycle engine was coupled to the front wheel via a 6 to 1 gear ratio, providing 15 firing impulses for each revolution of the wheel. This design resulted in an exceptionally smooth operation. However, overcoming the inertia of the rapidly spinning 30 kg made turning sharply more difficult than is the case with a more conventional machine.

The Neracar represented another approach to protecting riders from the elements. Unlike the Megola, the Neracar was designed as an inexpensive machine. It was first produced with a two-cycle engine and primitive friction drive, although later versions had a four-cycle engine with a gearbox, as well as rear springing. In spite of its utilitarianism, the Neracar's low center of gravity and hub-center steering were quite innovative, and the styling of the bodywork was very pleasing. A decade later, designer Georges Roy revisited some of these ideas when he produced his remarkable Majestic. Roy went one step further, fully enclosing the Majestic's engine to protect the rider from grease and oil, making the machine attractive to a broader spectrum of riders.

Like the Megola, the Böhmerland deserves special mention as one of the most unusual motorcycles ever produced in quantity. Albin Liebisch designed his long-wheelbase machines to carry three people and produced them in various forms from 1923 until 1939. These machines were remarkable not only for their length and their construction from large-diameter tubing but also for Liebisch's use of bright and contrasting colors at a time when muted tones were the standard.

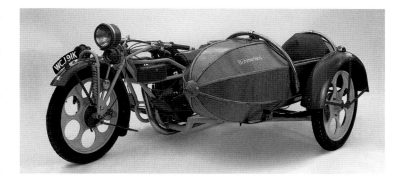

Truly, two-wheeled motorization has undergone a vast and amazing evolution since the day L. G. Perreaux installed his steam engine in a Michaux bicycle some one hundred thirty years ago. What began as a mongrel contraption fabricated out of a bicycle that was never intended to be motorized, and an engine that was never meant to propel it, evolved into a fleet of finely pedigreed machines. The cruiser and the chopper, the scooter and the sportbike, the magnificent eccentrics and the evolutionary dead ends—all of them embodied the dream of rolling freely down the open road. What good fortune it was that such a unique interaction of society, culture, and gender, and design innovation and technological progress, gave rise to an individualized, even intimate, means of conveyance that has stirred hearts for generations.

Fig. 11. Honda CB750 Four, 736 cc, 1970, Japan.
Collection of David Edwards.

Fig. 12. Böhmerland, 598 cc, 1925, Czechoslovakia.
Collection of D. J. Light.

Notes

1. C. F. Caunter, *Motorcycles: A Technical History*, 3rd ed. (London: Her Majesty's Stationary Office, 1982).

2. Maz Harris, *Bikers: Birth of a Modern Day Outlaw* (London: Faber & Faber, 1985).

3. "Ixion"/B. H. Davies, *Motor Cycle Reminiscences* (London: Iliffe & Sons, ca. 1920).

Mark C. Taylor and José Márquez

Cycles of Paradox

Most people live completely absorbed in worldly joys and sorrows; they are the benchwarmers who do not take part in the dance. The knights of infinity are the ballet dancers and have elevation. They make the upward movement and come down again, and this, too, is not an unhappy diversion and is not unlovely to see. But every time they come down, they are unable to assume the posture immediately, they waver for a moment, and this wavering shows that they are aliens. It is more or less conspicuous according to their skill, but even the most skillful of these knights cannot hide this wavering. One does not need to see them in the air; one needs only to see them the instant they touch and have touched the earth— and then one recognizes them. But to be able to come down in such a way that instantaneously one seems to stand and to walk, to change the leap into life into walking, absolutely to express the sublime in the pedestrian—that only the knight can do, and this is the one and only marvel.

—Søren Kierkegaard, *Fear and Trembling*, 1843

Riding fast on a motorcycle is a tremendously exhilarating and challenging game. This game has rules and barriers. There's something to win, something to lose, and a purpose for each individual who plays the game. It demands your attention. The consequences of a major mistake can be severe—severe enough to make the game worth playing well.

—Keith Code, *A Twist of the Wrist*, 1983

The Road, the Writer

The motorcyclist encounters the road as a writer encounters the page. There is no proper approach, no correct path, no true line. The page is never blank but is always littered with tracks and debris left by those who have gone before. Lines cross and crisscross to create intersections without warning signs. The road twists and turns, banks and slopes, becomes straight and narrows down, develops a new surface, throws up gravel, sand, oil, water. To ride is to write and to write is to read and rewrite a text that has already been written.

Neither writing nor riding is possible without a certain violence. As the writer inscribes paper with ink and words, so the motorcyclist cuts a line through sheer space using angles and velocity as letters and punctuation. Whether ink or rubber, the trace is never direct even when the course seems to be straight. Far from a passive medium, the road is a site of resistance that solicits the imagination of the rider. The body of the road forces the body of the rider/bike to negotiate a high-speed balancing act. A right curve in the road leads the rider to drift to the left before carving out a long, deliberate line to the right. Though the road is the pretext, the rider's lines can never be written in advance. Where rubber meets the road, improvisation is unavoidable. Since curves unexpectedly appear and disappear, the rider can never know what's around the next bend. The rider must become fully aware of the road by reading signs that are never completely legible. Nothing is secure—readiness is all.

The inscription of the line is the mark of style. Though the road seems fixed, no two ride it the same way. It's not the words but their inflection, their rhythm, their balance, their spacing that creates style. Slight changes have important consequences; the turn of a phrase, like the turn of the wheel, can change everything in the twinkling of an eye. Never lightweight, seemingly minor adjustments might be matters of life and death. Riding and writing are deadly serious endeavors. Mistakes, which can never be erased, are sometimes fatal. The curve, which may last only a split second, can become a death sentence.

The bike joins rider and road at the hip. No longer two but not yet one, the trail of the road is the tale of the rider. The bike is a pen, the road, the rider's unfinished autobiography.

Lane-Splitting, Margins

As the motorcycle accelerates between two lanes of heavy highway traffic, overtaking a car on the left and a truck on the right, it is virtually impossible not to cry: "Dear God, she's. . . ."

A critical situation. If nobody moves, nobody gets hurt.

The rider who splits lanes relies on nearly mystical vision to guide her along the thin painted lines on the road. Like a trapeze artist or tightrope

Fig. 1. U.S. Grand Prix, Laguna Seca, Calif., 1994.

walker, the lane-splitter never looks down but only ahead; she gazes into an ever-shrinking window of opportunity that opens and closes between fast-moving lanes of traffic. To lane-split is to know both the security of a motorcycle's superior agility and the insecurity of its dangerous invisibility. Passing speeding cars may sometimes be risky, but lane-splitting is something altogether different.

Unlike the many aspects of motorcycling that tend to be highly individual and strictly personal, lane-splitting lends a social dimension to riding. The lane-splitter is a parasite who lives off surrounding traffic. Never following the road proper, lane-splitting always occurs at the boundary, on the edge, along the margin. Neither here nor there, the (un)canny motorcyclist rides alone in the company of others.

When the motorcyclist rides between lanes, she secures for herself an unstable position that is both apart from and yet integral to the road. Riding the edge, she opens a space that is nowhere. Always venturing beyond society's regulated flows, the lane-splitter gambles by taking seemingly senseless risks. Simultaneously attractive and repulsive to car and truck drivers who play by the rules, lane-splitters both provoke fear and loathing and inspire envy and jealousy. "What was that?" asks the dazzled driver as she is buzzed by a motorcyclist passing on her right. For a split second, the motorcyclist appears to be "within" her lane. For the motorcyclist, however, roads have no lanes but only lines waiting to be traced. Coloring outside the lines is said to be a child's game. Not surprisingly, drivers sitting in their sports-utility vehicles, minivans, or station wagons often deride motorcyclists as childish and irresponsible. But lane-splitters know that the meaning of responsibility is determined by where you sit and how you ride.

What is at stake in lane-splitting is precisely the social game of traffic: a struggle for recognition and self-definition in the interplay of mixed vehicles on shared roadways. Solitary car drivers who are unwilling to fill their five-seaters with other passengers are just as reluctant to share lanes with motorcyclists. Lane-splitters scorn those who stick to the straight and narrow and insist that the only action that counts is on the margin. Each considers the other an unthinking fool. Car culture can no more tolerate lane-splitting than lane-splitters can stay on the left or on the right. Both reckless prank and practical tactic, lane-splitting lies at the heart of motorcycling's largely misunderstood methodical madness.

Helmets, Style

With the exception of rare transcendent experiences, motorcycling is not one but many—its styles are as varied as the cultures in which it makes sense. In the modern-day American West, the helmetless motorcyclist is as ubiquitous as designer jeans. Against this backdrop of simulated frontier living, the choice to ride without a helmet is often no choice at all but, rather, an unavoidable demand of fashion.

Beyond the serpentine coastal roads of California, western highways usually follow perfectly straight lines. This trajectory leads to an emphasis on controlled cruising that makes the fast-cornering motorcycle of European and Japanese racing culture both unnecessary and impractical. On the straightaway, the preferred ride is a low and heavyset galleon: a Harley or a Harley wanna-be. With foot pegs only a few inches off the ground, even if the Harley-esque rider wanted to take a tight corner at high speeds, he could not avoid scraping the road. In fact, the very presence of chrome components—especially polished chrome foot pegs—suggests that in this style of motorcycling, the bike and the road are expected to maintain a respectful distance at all times.

Having done away with fast-paced cornering, the art of motorcycling over deserted, rectilinear highways becomes a strangely laid-back leisure sport. Every rider becomes an Easy Rider. As the rider's emphasis drifts from high-performance machinery to the pantomime of a low-maintenance lifestyle, the helmet is the first piece of "baggage" to go. Since only a handful of components is needed to create a given tableau of motorcycling, it makes little sense to refer to any element—whether fashion, machinery, or safety gear—as an accessory. No element is of secondary significance because all are interrelated; every piece is, in some sense, primary. Thus, when the helmet goes, the bike is transformed, and when the bike changes, the helmet goes. In the story of motorcycling, the helmet is as telling in its absence as in its presence.

As life insurance policies go, the helmet is a good investment. Traumatized brains rarely mend as cleanly as shattered bones. Faced with such dreadful odds, the simple-minded accountant wonders why anyone would be so reckless as to ride a two-wheeled vehicle at high speeds without a helmet. The answer, it appears, is not to be found in any conscious risk analysis but in the dictates of an aesthetically designed experience that is wholly dependent on context for content. In the world of casual cruisers, crashing seems as impossible or as unlikely as suddenly encountering a series of switchback turns on a flat desert highway.

The helmet or its absence corresponds to an imaginary vector by reflecting a particular understanding of the meaning of riding as occurring in and through a particular place. The litany of practical, pseudo-practical, and blatantly impractical objections to helmets are rationalizations of decisions made for other reasons. The refusal to wear a helmet is not an act of courage but an aesthetic statement.

The aesthetics of the helmet are on display in any European-styled city where racing motorcycles reign supreme. In this setting, the use of helmets is no less contrived and creative than its conscious eschewal. But instead of riders flagrantly parading through the streets with little more than bandanas tied around their heads, one finds a dazzling array of helmets ranging from cheap to expensive, and stock to painted gear.

Fig. 2. Italian Grand Prix, Mugello, 1997.

The difference is one of posture: while the urban street racer (or, less charitably, the "café racer") may have no intention of actually scraping his foot pegs on a tight turn, his fancy helmet projects precisely the opposite image. In the final analysis, the accidental function of a helmet during a crash is insignificant when compared to its overdetermined aesthetic effect. The helmet is a matter of style rather than substance, and of aesthetics rather than utility.

Pipes, Postscript

On the street, the intense camaraderie between motorcycle riders is something of an anachronism in this age of virtual and non-virtual gated communities. Whether the occasion is a fallen bike or merely a dead battery, a rider in need of assistance can always expect help from other motorcyclists, who often initially appear in disguise. The man in the pickup truck, the woman behind the counter, the delivery boy, the well-heeled exec reveal themselves to be motorcyclists when one of their own is in distress.

The roots of this impromptu society of motorcycle riders are not occult, nor do they stem from what many have identified as antisocial or misanthropic tendencies. Even members of rival clubs share in the general society of motorcyclists in moments of need. At first glance, it might seem a marvel that any communal roots can grow in the seemingly barren soil of a motorcyclist's lonely and aloof spirit. Since motorcycling is experienced, first and foremost, as a silent and solitary encounter of rider, road, and bike, what binds riders together might initially appear to be a spiritual equivalence based on their discrete and unique experiences. But something else draws bikers together. As is often the case, community is born of opposition: the immediate and universal bond among motorcyclists is forged as if from without by the constant threat of cars and their "drivers."

For some motorcylists, an ideal world would be one in which they had their own roads. Having come of age in the crucible of mixed traffic, however, most contemplate such a fantasy with indignant scorn. The modern motorcyclist defines himself or herself in contradistinction to car drivers. The biker is what the driver is not and, of course, vice versa. The survival of the two-wheel species turns on a daily life-and-death struggle between bike and car (or truck) for control of the road. Obviously, in this day and age, the car is king. But what is not so obvious to the vast majority of travelers who do not ride motorcycles is how lethal cars are. Their very safety, security, and simplicity enable them to maim and kill all the more efficiently.

Riding a motorcycle demands total concentration; driving a car or the now-popular "light" truck, by contrast, requires little more than a single hand, leaving the other hand free to make telephone calls, send faxes, log on, apply makeup, eat a burger, drink a beer, play with the radio knob, or turn the pages of a newspaper. While the motorcyclist resists all such distractions, his fate often rests in hands that are not on the wheel. When worlds as well as bikes collide, helicopter-bound newscasters invariably report "an accident involving a motorcycle." It is as if the motorcyclist were a parasite engaged in an endless coevolutionary struggle with a host that is trying to eliminate him.

Living on the margins of mainstream automotive society, the motorcycle rider quickly realizes she is not welcome on the open road. Indeed, it is not uncommon for the rider to become the target of a car driver's bizarre sense of four-wheeled justice. The presence of the motorcyclist poses a troubling question for automotive society: Who is the outlaw? The motorcyclist makes a conscious decision not only to ride but to ride in traffic. In this casting of lots, the rider has no choice but to become all too aware of the stakes as well as the rewards of riding. For those who can forgive fellow travelers who know not what they do, the bliss of motorcycling comes precisely from knowing that the road must be reclaimed, again and again, if only by deft maneuver and guerrilla tactics. Never safe and secure, the motorcyclist seeks to affirm her presence along different lines.

Whence the kinship among motorcycle riders that generates a variety of codes, badges, banners, and rituals. There are the group rallies, which inspire thousands of motorcyclists to reclaim a special road in one fell swoop; there are the bars where sacred stories are spun and tales retold; there are esoteric magazines devoted to different tribes and their specialized fashions. These texts, fabrics, and colors distinguish motorcyclists from one another and, more importantly, differentiate riders from drivers. Among all these marks of difference, none is more pronounced and telling than the sound of the motorcycle's tail pipes.

The sound of pipes trail a bike like an exclamation mark or an ellipsis but never a period. A phrasing, which begins with rapid firing in the bike's engine, quickly issues from the tail pipes as expressive exhaust. To the tutored ear, the deafening roar of an American cruiser, the throaty gargle of an Italian sport bike, the clean zip of a Japanese street racer are each layered with associations. In addition to identifying the make and model of a bike, these signatures convey myriad meanings far exceeding the rider's need for pedestrian approval—or myopic obsession with acceleration. The pipes are to the motorcyclist's identity what the unconscious is to the Freudian subject: a largely inaccessible reservoir of feeling and meaning, which is a remainder of a collective spirit. In both cases, one must listen at least twice for the significance of the utterances. For those with ears to hear, the invisible society of motorcyclists is maintained by the sound of its tail pipes.

The contours of a sleek bike, the brilliance of polished chrome, or an armful of artful tattoos all appear and disappear in the blink of an eye or the twist of the wrist. Evanescent as images, they finally fail to inspire witnesses with any lasting promise of life after the moment. But the sound of the departed motorcycle, the postscript of its pipes, lingers, remains, and beckons.

Knee Pads, Balance

Imagine traveling alone at 60 mph, with a roaring motorcycle between your legs, the road rushing beneath you, and nothing but a light helmet on your head. As the curve approaches, you lean the bike and smoothly shift your weight as you lower your knee toward the ground. With a suddenness that is not abrupt, you find yourself "hanging out." Action/reaction . . . weight/counterweight. To "hang out" is to counter the weight of the motorcycle with the weight of the rider. The faster you are traveling as you head into the curve, the lower you must lean to "make" the turn. The aim, of course, is to cut it as close as possible without falling.

When the angle becomes precarious, the knee becomes a third wheel. Pads are an extra layer of skin waiting to be peeled when not enough becomes too much. The knee pad is not a sign of weakness but a badge of courage worn proudly by elite riders who have achieved extraordinary technical mastery. Hanging out is the dream of many that is realized by few.

The pad marks the turning point in the complex relationship of bike, rider, and road. It is, as always, a matter of balance. Force and counterforce stage a play that is as delicate as it is complicated. It is as if rider and bike were moving in three directions at once. Where the vectors meet there is a still point at which motion and rest become indistinguishable. It is a strange calculus that never quite adds up: three-in-one . . . one-in-three. An equilibrium that seems to be perfect.

Balance can be maintained—if at all—only momentarily. Like a finger running across sandpaper, the knee pad scrapes the surface of the road, informing the rider of the road's textures and confirming his angle of descent. While the rider writes by carving lines through the road, the road writes by scraping lines into the rider's skin. Pads do not merely protect but also offer supplemental writing surfaces waiting to be inscribed. For those who know how to read, the knee pad declares: "In taking turns, I've gone over the edge and I will do so again and again for as long as I can ride. My life depends on it."

It seems odd for so much to turn the knee. It is, after all, a fragile joint, which, as every athlete knows, is easily injured. And yet, we can move forward only on bended knee. For the motorcyclist, the knee is the pivot of riding. The art of motorcycling is precisely the continuous negotiation of critical angles. Improbable though it may seem, the best riders never quite fit but are always angular—they are "all elbows and knees."

Fall, Falling

To fall off a speeding motorcycle and survive is the impossible event that underwrites all motorcycling. The motorcyclist is aware of falling from day one. Falling is the inevitable catastrophe that nevertheless must be avoided, the inescapable fate that must be permanently deferred. Riders, who also happen to be good liars, sometimes insist that the thought of falling never claims their attention. This lie is not simply false but is a necessary self-deception in which truth is spoken indirectly: the rider must always think of falling but never acknowledge the thought.

Fig. 3. Austrian Grand Prix, the Oestereichring, 1996.

Paradoxically, the fall is inevitable yet avoidable. It is, as always, self-consciousness that leads to the fall. The obsession with falling paralyzes the rider moving into heavy traffic, creates a deadly hesitation heading into a turn, slows the rider down when he should be speeding up. The successful rider must negotiate twists and turns that extend far beyond the road by simultaneously thinking and not thinking of falling. When thinking is not thinking, the heaviest thought becomes frightfully light—as if there were nothing to it. What lends this nothingness its weight is, of course, the incontestable fact that we are physical, vulnerable, mortal.

Having fallen and survived, the rider faces an important decision: "Do I continue to ride?" In a sense, this question has always already been asked when confronting the fear of falling. Yet, in the world of the fallen, it takes on added significance. Those who say "No" and turn away are usually forgiven, for their brothers and sisters understand their fear and know its force all too well. Not riding is no sin for those who have fallen. There are others, however, who insist that you cannot be a real biker until you fall. For them, biking begins

rather than ends with falling. To say "Yes" to motorcycling after a fall is to confess weakness in a way that transforms it into strength. The initiated realize that some lessons can only be learned by falling:

1. When the rider senses he may go over, he must decide: Do I release the bike, or do I attempt to change its course? If nothing can be done to avert the crash, the rider must abandon his motorcycle. It is crucial that he very quickly create as much distance as possible between himself and his motorcycle. If the gap is too small, he risks being run over or crushed by his own bike. Unruly motion cannot be mastered by strategies of control.

2. At the critical moment, the rider must make himself absolutely limp. If, struggling to avoid his fate, the motorcyclist hits the ground stiff, he risks shattering his bones. If, however, he accepts the fall without resistance, the impact will ripple through his body and he may avoid serious fractures. To relax suddenly—a split second before hitting the road at 60 mph—can save the rider from suffering grave injuries.

3. Upon impact, the rider cannot move, for the ride is not yet over. Little more than a sentient corpse, the rider must slide along the road until nothing is moving. If the rider attempts to get up before coming to a complete stop, he will bounce along the ground like a toy ball about to be shred from the impact. If the rider simply lets go and allows body and bike to go their separate ways, gliding across the surface of the road, it is possible to survive virtually unscathed. In the moment of release, opposites collide: stunned, scarred, horrified, yet thrilled, joyful, ecstatic, the rider declares: "Everything seems to be in one piece!"

The use of leather in motorcycling jackets and racing suits is not, as many suspect, a bold fashion statement. There is nothing superfluous about these animal hides, which protect fallen riders from losing their own skin. While weatherproof synthetic materials have recently made inroads on the riding apparel market, leathers are still the most effective low-friction protective material. Peeling skins allow the rider to glide across the road's surface.

To survive a fall, riders must learn that the three rules of the road teach one lesson: The only way to hang on is to let go. The problem is not to avoid falling, which is impossible, but to learn to fall gracefully. Though the rider is constantly responsible, the outcome is always out of his hands. If resistance can be resisted by translating "No" into "Yes," dreadful fatality can become blissful fatalism.

For the professional racer, falling is not a question of "if" but "when." Having made a sport of crossing the line between chance and fatalism, the rider no longer refers to falling by its proper name but says: "I had to put the bike down"—as if in moments of falling he were always in control. "Dropping," "going down," "breaking in the leathers" all suggest a world in which death lies elsewhere—beyond the realm of motorcycling. Ecce Homo: the Risen Rider.

Rider, Riders

In the mid-'80s, Marvel Comics popularized the story of a group of motorcycle stunt men with an eerie ability to conjure up a supernatural motorcyclist named Ghost Rider. Disguised as an all-American group of Boy Scout types with a propensity for stumbling into difficulties, they toured the United States staging a motorcycle circus for audiences young and old. When trouble found the apparently innocent stuntmen, they would all lapse into a coma of sorts, and from their collective dream the figure of the Ghost Rider would emerge.

Dressed in a black-leather jacket with matching pants, and seated on an incredibly powerful black classic motorcycle, the Ghost Rider kills the bad guys and saves the day. Performing morally ambivalent acts of heroism on behalf of the comatose stunt riders, the Ghost Rider is a mere flaming skeleton. Death or life? Good or evil? Creative or destructive? What spirit haunts this blazing skull and bones?

A man on a Harley is giving his young son a ride through the streets of downtown. The playful child lets go of his father and raises his skinny arms to form a cross. As the motorcycle slowly roars down city streets, the father follows the boy's lead and lets go of the handlebars. With no hands steering the bike, the machine is guided by their joint balancing act.

Driving through a deserted, postindustrial neighborhood, a man in a car detects a motorcycle behind him. Noticing that the bike is a black-and-white cruiser and the motorcyclist, dressed in black pants and black leather jacket, is wearing a white helmet with dark sunglasses, the driver suspects he is being followed by a Highway Patrol officer. Fearful of committing a moving violation, he slows down just as the motorcyclist revs his engine and passes him on the left. Only then does the driver of the car realize that the rider is just masquerading as a motorcycle cop and is heading to one of the area's leather clubs. Befuddled, the driver picks up his pace and focuses on the next stoplight.

There is little traffic during the week on the tree-lined, two-lane road that passes by the country general store. When the red sports bike arrives with rider and passenger, the clerk reacts warily: "One more crotch rocket," he thinks to himself. The passenger gets off the bike and walks into the store. Removing her helmet, she asks to use the bathroom. "Round the side," the clerk answers, waiting to see if the rider will buy some gas. Sure enough, the rider walks into the store, takes off her helmet, and asks for ten dollars of unleaded.

As motorcycle clubs go, the chapter that meets by the loading docks is a tame outfit. The riders are in their forties and fifties, with enough white beards among them to mark their years clearly. Though in recent years, the presence of a growing number of Japanese cruisers has begun to put a damper on their DIY spirit, the art of motorcycle maintenance is still the main draw of the club. There is plenty of good cheer in this fraternity of African-American riders. After all, theirs is the only club in the state formed by and for the brothers who live to ride.

Around the corner from the motorcycle repair shop is a dingy, smelly bar frequented mostly by motorcyclists. The bikes outside range from grasshopper-styled dirt bikes to gargantuan touring machines. It just so happens that customers of the repair shop like to stand outside and look at the bikes parked by the bar. Their reactions range from admiration and envy to condescension and scorn. On this particular day, two young men are engaged in the usual motorcycle talk outside the repair shop, when they spy a classic Italian sports bike parked in front of the bar. Filled with interest and desire, they begin speculating about how much mechanical know-how it takes to keep such a classic bike in running order. Having just concluded that "the owner must be a master mechanic," a man in a neatly tailored two-piece suit and tie walks out of the bar. "Another lawyer," one of the men scoffs. "Probably getting on that black K bike." But, of course, the man in the suit jumps on his classic Italian sports bike, kick starts it, and takes off without ever looking back.

Dirt Bikes, Levity

For the architect, building is a matter of light. Even though they are constructed in order to shelter, structures are designed to display light. Though they seem undeniably real, no one has ever seen buildings like those pictured in magazines, journals, and catalogues. It is as if these buildings were made to be photographed. Not only is everything in place and completely clean, but light is captured at the precise moment its glow seems most perfect.

Fig. 5. Extreme biking.

Magazines are as important to biking as they are to architecture. The relation between text and image, on the one hand, and structure and event on the other, is neither simple nor one-way. Texts/images produce structures/events as much as structures/events generate texts/images. For the dirt biker, the stunt is performed for the gaze of the camera and the thrill of the audience as much as for the pleasure of the rider. The stylized dance between rider and dirt bike is carefully choreographed with an eye to the photographic image. On the glossy pages of *Dirt Bike Magazine*, motorcycles and riders are undoubtedly real, even though it is hard to believe that the extraordinary moves captured in the flick of the camera's shutter have actually occurred. As page after page of images frames riders against the background of a horizonless sky, the world of dirt biking appears to be suspended above a ground that has vanished.

Covered from helmet to boot with dust and mud, the dirt biker roams on two wheels where most four-wheel-drive vehicles dare not tread. In addition to watching for rocks, trenches, and bushes, the dirt biker must also worry about the consistency of the road. While most on-road motorcyclists dread the thought of encountering gravel or a puddle on the far side of a turn, the dirt biker is disappointed if the trail does not throw surprises his way. Weaving, dodging, crouching, and stretching, the dirt biker, perched on his high-suspension machine, defiantly navigates all the ups, downs, and in-betweens of rugged earth. When nowhere is off limits, riding becomes an endless series of stunts. Traversing a road that is not a road, the aggressive perversity of the dirt biker transforms the art of staying on top of an ever-changing situation into a matter of course. His transgressive gestures suggest the aesthetic of a trickster who is always out of bounds. The only constant in his bewildering succession of maneuvers is the shrill, tinny sound of the dirt bike's whining two-stroke engine.

Like architecture made to be photographed, dirt biking suspends the foundations of mass, weight, angle, contour, and surface. Lightweight dirt bikes are built to soar—ten, twenty, even fifty feet in the air—in arcs that confound our expectations of what motorcycles are meant to do. Carefully crouched, the rider aims the front fender at an insanely steep hill or muddy ramp, rolls the throttle, and lets go. As bike departs earth, the rider rises from his seat while clinging to the handlebars ever so lightly. The skill of the off-road rider is demonstrated less by the takeoff than the landing on dangerous tracks and trails pockmarked with hidden crevices and covered with scattered debris. Since the levity of riding can never be separated from the pull of gravity, the artful dirt biker is always making double movements of release and return. Like a ballet dancer who lands without wavering or missing a step, the motorcyclist who lands as if taking off has learned the priceless lesson of negotiating the boundaries between heaven and earth. Neither too heavy nor too light, the accomplished dirt biker covers ground that somehow is never fully there. The improbable lightness of the dirt biker is a levity that is deadly serious.

Shifting, Punctuation

Cars and motorcycles are heading in opposite directions. Equipped with automatic transmission and cruise control as well as plug-ins for computers, cellular telephones, fax machines, and televisions, automobiles are becoming an ever-more automated auto-mobile. At the end of this road lies the computer-operated automated highway, which makes drivers obsolete. For the motorcyclist, by contrast, improving technology increases the need for timely knowledge, manual dexterity, and physical agility. Shifty riders know that lines flow smoothly only when skillfully punctuated.

The motorcycle is necessarily a manual machine that requires the rider to shift with a smooth combination of hand and footwork. Hand clutch and foot lever must operate as if they were one. As when cornering or merely balancing on the straightaway, effective shifting is impossible unless the rider's mind bends into her body and her body becomes an extension of her   he complex contours of the motorcycle's engine are opaque to the eye but visible t   r's body as she accelerates, shedding one gear after another, while always asking h   \t what point does this motorcycle want to be shifted from first to second? Where   igine speed between second and third gears? Can the course from first to fifth gea   dled in a way that erases disruptive periods and creates a continuous smooth curve   ard greater and greater velocity?" Neither starting nor stopping, shifting is the interruption that makes continuity possible.

When shifting, coordination is not merely a means to an end but an end in itself. Traveling at great speed is not the same as approaching great speed; only the latter is a true test of the rider's skill. The avid motorcyclist longs for a silent harmony between person and machine created by smooth shifting. There are, of course, riders who like to cut corners with motorcycles engineered solely to achieve speed quickly and effortlessly. These "crotch rockets" require mindless concentration and daring rather than cultivated skill and know-how. For riders who seek self-knowledge, however, shifting is a form of meditation whose lesson is the inseparability of continuity and discontinuity.

Speed, Slowness

Q: "What is the human body at 100 mph?"
A: "Dead weight."

There is a special fondness for speed in our age—a virtual fetish for all things faster than fast. Motorcycles—especially the newer, high-tech models—are often thrown into the mix of death and sex drives as visible proof that the boundaries of gravity dissolve with the exponential multiplication of mass by velocity. From this point of view, electronic stock trading and cellular telephones seem to go hand-in-hand with fuel-injected, air-cooled motorcycles painted either bright yellow or bright red.

But to equate motorcycles with this sense of frictionless and effortless speed is to miss the pointlessness of the speeding bike. Motorcycles travel at neither "the speed of business" nor "the speed of life." The motorcycle actually has nothing to do with "rush hour"; nor does it belong to the frenzied universe created by Guaranteed Overnight Delivery. In contrast to purposeful speed, the motorcyclist approaches speed slowly and painfully in rushes lasting no more than a few seconds, which betray no concern for direction or arrival. To ride a motorcycle seriously is to go nowhere fast.

Speed is both necessary and superfluous to the motorcyclist. Without adequate acceleration, a two-wheeled bike simply falls over on its side and remains inert. For reasons of basic physics, speed is the lifeblood of motorcycling. Thus, there can be no motorcycling without speed. But to think of the motorcycle as creating speed is tantamount to insisting that human lungs produce the air that nourishes them. Speed, like the air pulsating through us, always originates elsewhere.

It is, of course, undeniable that motorcycles inspire a sense of speed that other vehicles do not. But what the speeding biker registers has nothing to do with increasing miles per hour or managing revolutions per minute clocked on a tachometer. A different economy is at play: the speed of the motorcycle leads to release rather than accumulation.

In a certain sense, a motorcycle exhausts speed by allowing the rider simultaneously to experience and escape it. As the mechanical rhythms of the bike and road overtake the rider's body and mind, a paradox gradually emerges: while traveling very fast, you do not seem to be moving. At a critical point, speed becomes slowness and motion is transformed into rest. This rest is, however, precarious. Physical stimuli inform you of your particular bodily predicament, but you remain at a loss for an adequate psychological response. Your violently unstable position in time and space makes you extremely vulnerable to your own mistakes and to the errors of others as well as to unforeseeable catastrophes arising from the intersection of bike and road. When everything hangs in the balance, you learn that speed can never be conquered. All you can do is to "hang on" and "ride it out." To hang on you must, as always, let go.

Locked into patterns of repetition, riders who test the limits of speed always narrow the scope of the motorcycle by reducing it to a variant of the rocket, the arrow, or the measuring stick. But motorcycles are not built for the straight and narrow. To the contrary, the best bikes are designed to navigate tricky curves. When you reach the end of the road, you finally discover that the meaning of speed turns on the act of cornering.

Cornering

"Once you go sideways you never come back."
—License-plate holder, bolted sideways
on a red Honda Hawk in San Francisco

Make no mistake about it, cornering is the essence of motorcycling. No model, no engine, no design trend, no biker fashion is as central to the experience and meaning of motorcycling as the act of cornering.

Since motorcycle tires cannot turn at high speeds, the rider must lead the bike around the curve. The faster the motorcyclist is traveling, the greater she will have to lean her body and bike into the curve and the farther she will have stretch her arms across the handlebars in the opposite direction of the turn. This strange combination of leaning into the turn and counter-steering away from it is called "cornering." Odd as the coordination of these two opposite movements might seem, it constitutes the alternating rhythm of riding.

Fig. 6. Michael Doohan, 1995 500 World Champion.

As one's body leans into the turn, rider and riding become one. Even if knees do not scrape the ground, the angle of lean allows the rider to "dip" his hands into the rush of the road. Cornering reveals the true dynamic of the motorcycle: as the bike leans into the turn, the physical laws, which give the motorcycle its magical charm, finally become visible. Apparently defying gravity, the motorcyclist lowers the bike while accelerating; the lower the lean, the greater the acceleration must be. The technical goal is to balance centripetal and centrifugal forces. The experience that results when this is achieved is sheer exhilaration.

Though the situation seems tense, the rider must always exhale when cornering. Nothing can be held in or kept back. The slightest hesitation can topple the delicate balance of forces needed to drop and lift the bike through a twisting curve. Whereas car drivers are instructed to slow down in turns, the motorcyclist has no choice but to accelerate while cornering. Increasing speed catapults the rider into places unknown.

The practical implications of cornering are often confounding. While descending along a winding, mountain road, the motorcyclist must roll the throttle before each bend and can only decelerate when the road straightens out. This inverted cycle of speed and slowness must be repeated at every turn. When entering a freeway entry ramp, the motorcyclist begins a long, gradual arc of acceleration as the turn slowly narrows. Contrary to expectation, speed stabilizes, if only briefly.

In the act of cornering, all the paradoxes of motorcycling come into play. When opposites no longer collide but are held in balance, danger is momentarily domesticated. In this instant, the motorcyclist expresses the sublime in the pedestrian. But the moment passes as quickly as it arrives and, thus, must be repeated again and again.

Those who play the game of motorcycling well not only ride to live but live to ride.

Hunter S. Thompson

Cycle World, *March 1995*

Song of the Sausage Creature

There are some things nobody needs in this world, and a bright red, hunchback, warp-speed 900 cc café racer is one of them—but I want one anyway, and on some days I actually believe I need one. That is why they are dangerous.

Everybody has fast motorcycles these days. Some people go 150 miles an hour on two-lane blacktop roads, but not often. There are too many oncoming trucks and too many radar cops and too many stupid animals in the way. You have to be a little crazy to ride these super-torque high-speed crotch rockets anywhere except a racetrack—and even there, they will scare the whimpering shit out of you. . . . There is, after all, not a pig's eye worth of difference between going head-on into a Peterbilt or sideways into the bleachers. On some days you get what you want, and on others, you get what you need.

When Cycle World called me to ask if I would road-test the new Harley Road King, I got uppity and said I'd rather have a Ducati superbike. It seemed like a chic decision at the time, and my friends on the superbike circuit got very excited. "Hot damn," they said, "We will take it to the track and blow the bastards away."

"Balls," I said. "Never mind the track. The track is for punks. We are Road People. We are Café Racers."

The Café Racer is a different breed, and we have our own situations. Pure speed in sixth gear on a 5,000-foot straightaway is one thing, but pure speed in third gear on a gravel-strewn downhill ess turn is quite another.

But we like it. A thoroughbred Café Racer will ride all night through a fog storm in freeway traffic to put himself into what somebody told him was the ugliest and tightest decreasing-radius turn since Genghis Khan invented the corkscrew.

Café Racing is mainly a matter of taste. It is an atavistic mentality, a peculiar mix of low style, high speed, pure dumbness, and overweening commitment to the Café Life and all its dangerous pleasures. . . . I am a Café Racer myself, on some days—and many nights for that matter—and it is one of my finest addictions. . . .

I am not without scars on my brain and my body, but I can live with them. I still feel a shudder in my spine every time I see a picture of a Vincent Black Shadow, or when I walk into a public restroom and hear crippled men whispering about the terrifying Kawasaki Triple

. . . I have visions of compound femur-fractures and large black men in white hospital suits holding me down on a gurney while a nurse called "Bess" sews the flaps of my scalp together with a stitching drill.

Ho, ho. Thank God for these flashbacks. The brain is such a wonderful instrument (until God sinks his teeth into it). Some people hear Tiny Tim singing when they go under, and others hear the song of the Sausage Creature.

When the Ducati turned up in my driveway, nobody knew what to do with it. I was in New York, covering a polo tournament, and people had threatened my life. My lawyer said I should give myself up and enroll in the Federal Witness Protection Program. Other people said it had something to do with the polo crowd.

The motorcycle business was the last straw. It had to be the work of my enemies, or people who wanted to hurt me. It was the vilest kind of bait, and they knew I would go for it.

Of course. You want to cripple the bastard? Send him a 130-mph café racer. And include some license plates, so he'll think it's a streetbike. He's queer for anything fast.

Which is true. I have been a connoisseur of fast motorcycles all my life. I bought a brand-new 650 BSA Lightning when it was billed as "the fastest motorcycle ever tested by Hot Rod magazine." I have ridden a 500-pound Vincent through traffic on the Ventura Freeway with burning oil on my legs and run the Kawa 750 Triple through Beverly Hills at night with a head full of acid . . . I have ridden with Sonny Barger and smoked weed in biker bars with Jack Nicholson, Grace Slick, Ron Zigler, and my infamous old friend, Ken Kesey, a legendary Café Racer.

Some people will tell you that slow is good—and it may be, on some days—but I am here to tell you that fast is better. I've always believed this, in spite of the trouble it's caused me. Being shot out of a cannon will always be better than being squeezed out of a tube. That is why God made fast motorcycles, Bubba. . . .

So when I got back from New York and found a fiery red rocket-style bike in my garage, I realized I was back in the road-testing business.

The brand-new Ducati 900 Campione del Mundo Desmodue Supersport double-barreled magnum Cafe Racer filled me with feelings of lust every time I looked at it. Others felt the same way. My garage quickly became a magnet for drooling superbike groupies. They quarreled and bitched at each other about who would be first to help me evaluate my new toy. . . . And I did, of course, need a certain spectrum of opinions, besides my own, to properly judge this motorcycle. The Woody Creek Perverse Environmental Testing Facility is a long way from Daytona or even top-fuel challenge sprints on the Pacific Coast Highway, where teams of big-bore Kawasakis and Yamahas are said to race head-on against each other in death-defying games of "chicken" at 100 miles an hour. . . .

No. Not everybody who buys a high-dollar torque-brute yearns to go out in a ball of fire on a public street in L.A. Some of us are decent people who want to stay out of the emergency room, but still blast through neo-gridlock traffic in residential districts whenever we feel like it. . . . For that we need fine Machinery.

Which we had—no doubt about that. The Ducati people in New Jersey had opted, for reasons of their own, to send me the 900SP for testing—rather than their 916 crazy-fast, state-of-the-art superbike track racer. It was far too fast, they said—and prohibitively expensive—to farm out for testing to a gang of half-mad Colorado cowboys who think they're world-class Café Racers.

The Ducati 900 is a finely engineered machine. My neighbors called it beautiful and admired its racing lines. The nasty little bugger looked like it was going 90 miles an hour when it was standing still in my garage.

Taking it on the road, though, was a genuinely terrifying experience. I had no sense of speed until I was going 90 and coming up fast on a bunch of pickup trucks going into a wet curve along the river. I went for both brakes, but only the front one worked, and I almost went end over end. I was out of control staring at the tailpipe of a U.S. Mail truck, still stabbing frantically at my rear brake pedal, which I just couldn't find . . . I am too tall for these New Age roadracers; they are not built for any rider taller than five-nine, and the rearset brake pedal was not where I thought it would be. Midsize Italian pimps who like to race from one café to another on the boulevards of Rome in a flat-line prone position might like this, but I do not.

I was hunched over the tank like a person diving into a pool that got emptied yesterday. Whacko! Bashed on the concrete bottom, flesh ripped off, a Sausage Creature with no teeth, f-cked-up for the rest of its life.

We all love Torque, and some of us have taken it straight over the high side from time to time—and there is always Pain in that. . . . But there is also Fun, the deadly element, and Fun is what you get when you screw this monster on. BOOM! Instant takeoff, no screeching or squawking around like a fool with your teeth clamping down on your tongue and your mind completely empty of everything but fear.

No. This bugger digs right in and shoots you straight down the pipe, for good or ill.

On my first takeoff, I hit second gear and went through the speed limit on a two-lane blacktop highway full of ranch traffic. By the time I went up to third, I was going 75 and the tach was barely above 4,000 rpm. . . .

And that's when it got its second wind. From 4,000 to 6,000 in third will take you from 75 to 95 mph in two seconds—and after that, Bubba, you still have fourth, fifth, and sixth. Ho, ho.

I never got to sixth gear, and I didn't get deep into fifth. This is a shameful admission for a full-bore Café Racer, but let me tell you something, old sport: This motorcycle is simply too goddam fast to ride at speed in any kind of normal road traffic unless you're ready to go straight down the centerline with your nuts on fire and a silent scream in your throat.

When aimed in the right direction at high speed, though, it has unnatural capabilities. This I unwittingly discovered as I made my approach to a sharp turn across some railroad tracks, saw that I was going way too fast and that my only chance was to veer right and screw it on totally, in a desperate attempt to leapfrog the curve by going airborne.

It was a bold and reckless move, but it was necessary. And it worked: I felt like Evel Knievel as I soared across the tracks with the rain in my eyes and my jaws clamped together in fear. I tried to spit down on the tracks as I passed them, but my mouth was too dry. . . . I landed hard on the edge of the road and lost my grip for a moment as the Ducati began fishtailing crazily into oncoming traffic. For two or three seconds I came face to face with the Sausage Creature. . . .

But somehow the brute straightened out. I passed a school bus on the right and then got the bike under control long enough to gear down and pull off into an abandoned gravel driveway where I stopped and turned off the engine. My hands had seized up like claws and the rest of my body was numb. I felt nauseous and I cried for my mama, but nobody heard, then I went into a trance for 30 or 40 seconds until I was finally able to light a cigarette and calm down enough to ride home. I was too hysterical to shift gears, so I went the whole way in first at 40 miles an hour.

Whoops! What am I saying? Tall stories, ho, ho. . . . We are motorcycle people; we walk tall and we laugh at whatever's funny. We shit on the chests of the Weird. . . .

But when we ride very fast motorcycles, we ride with immaculate sanity. We might abuse a substance here and there, but only when it's right. The final measure of any rider's skill is the inverse ratio of his preferred Traveling Speed to the number of bad scars on his body. It is that simple: If you ride fast and crash, you are a bad rider. If you go slow and crash, you are a bad rider. And if you are a bad rider, you should not ride motorcycles.

The emergence of the superbike has heightened this equation drastically. Motorcycle technology has made such a great leap forward. Take the Ducati. You want optimum cruising speed on this bugger? Try 90 mph in fifth at 5,500 rpm—and just then, you see a bull moose in the middle of the road. WHACKO. Meet the Sausage Creature.

Or maybe not: The Ducati 900 is so finely engineered and balanced and torqued that you can do 90 mph in fifth through a 35-mph zone and get away with it. The bike is not just fast—it is extremely quick and responsive, and it will do amazing things. . . . It is a little like riding the original Vincent Black Shadow, which would outrun an F-86 jet fighter on the takeoff runway, but at the end, the F-86 would go airborne and the Vincent would not, and there was no point in trying to turn it. WHAMO! The Sausage Creature strikes again.

There is a fundamental difference, however, between the old Vincents and the new breed of superbikes. If you rode the Black Shadow at top speed for any length of time, you would almost certainly die. That is why there are not many life members of the Vincent Black Shadow Society. The Vincent was like a bullet that went straight; the Ducati is like the magic bullet in Dallas that went sideways and hit JFK and the Governor of Texas at the same time. It was impossible. But so was my terrifying sideways leap across railroad tracks on the 900SP. The bike did it easily with the grace of a fleeing tomcat. The landing was so easy I remember thinking, goddamnit, if I had screwed it on a little more I could have gone a lot further.

Maybe this is the new Café Racer macho. My bike is so much faster than yours that I dare you to ride it, you lame little turd. Do you have the balls to ride this BOTTOMLESS PIT OF TORQUE?

That is the attitude of the New Age superbike freak, and I am one of them. On some days they are about the most fun you can have with your clothes on. The Vincent just killed you a lot faster than a superbike will. A fool couldn't ride the Vincent Black Shadow more than once, but a fool can ride a Ducati 900 many times, and it will always be bloodcurdling kind of fun. That is the Curse of Speed which has plagued me all my life. I am a slave to it. On my tombstone they will carve, "IT NEVER GOT FAST ENOUGH FOR ME."

Ted Polhemus

The Art of the Motorcycle: Outlaws, Animals, and Sex Machines

Although the modern motorcycle is now 100 years old, the mythology of the modern motorcyclist—the outlaw biker—has taken only half that time to resolve into vivid, larger-than-life iconographic focus.

In July 1947, the rural California town of Hollister (previously famous only for producing 70 percent of America's garlic crop) hosted a motorcycle rally. The idea was to bring together two-wheeled sportsmen from the surrounding area to compete for trophies in various events. What Hollister got instead (or in addition) was an "invasion" of filthy, dirty, punk, barbarian "animals" who, according to various press reports, got drunk and disorderly, damaged property, and terrorized the law-abiding locals. According to a contemporary report in *Life* magazine:

> On the fourth of July weekend, 4,000 members of a motorcycle club roared into Hollister, California, for a three-day convention. They quickly tired of ordinary motorcycle thrills, and turned to more exciting stunts. Racing their bikes down the main street and through traffic lights, breaking furniture and mirrors. Some rested awhile by the curb. Others hardly paused. Police arrested many for drunkenness and indecent exposure but could not restore order. Frankly, after two days, the cyclists left with a brazen explanation. "We like to show off. It's just a lot of fun." But Hollister's police chief took a different view. Wailed he, "It's just one hell of a mess."[1]

Fig. 1. Hollister Riots, July 6, 1947.

In fact, as Hunter S. Thompson noted in *Hell's Angels*, the small police force of 29 actually had things under control quite quickly; there were limited fines and arrests—at most the revelers got 90 days in jail for indecent exposure—and only 50 people were treated at the local hospital, all for minor injuries.[2] Thompson's cooler assessment wasn't published until 1966; in

Fig. 2. Still from Laslo Benedek's *The Wild One*, 1954.

the immediate aftermath of the Hollister incident, numerous sensationalized press reports appeared, including *Harper's* jazzed-up, fictionalized account by Frank Rooney, "The Cyclist's Raid."[3] It was this story that provided the initial inspiration for one of the most socioculturally influential films of all time, Laslo Benedek's *The Wild One* (1954), which starred the young Marlon Brando.[4] This cinematic version of what happened in Hollister played a dramatic part in shaping the iconography of the motorcyclist. But the seeds of a full-scale moral panic had already been sewn in 1947.

The photographs accompanying the *Life* article cut "decent," "God-fearing" America to the quick. There was the image of strangely dressed barbarians on one side of the town's main street, and a clean-cut, small-town fold on the other, with only a couple of nervous-looking cops in-between.[5] There was another of a huge brute slumped back on his bike, staring unblinkingly into the camera, a beer in each hand. This was the stuff of nightmares, and many a law-abiding American parent must have trembled at the prospect of such a barbarian horde roaring into their cozy hamlet.

It was bad enough that such satanic characters might lurk in city alleyways—such things had always been suspected—but the very mobility of these degenerate motorcyclists, their apparent eagerness to travel from their urban habitats to small towns, sent an icy chill down the spine. Having won the war overseas, America now woke up to a terrible threat from within, little realizing how many of these disturbing-looking motorcyclists were actually veterans of World War II, who (like those who would return from fighting in Vietnam in the 1960s) were finding it hard to adjust to the comparative tedium of civilian life.

49

Fig. 3. Still from Dennis Hopper's *Easy Rider*, 1969.

But if America as a whole was troubled by the reports of the Hollister incident, the respectable members of the American Motorcycle Association were devastated. Overnight the image of the motorcyclist as daring sportsman had been replaced by that of the beer-swilling, chest-baring, laid-back degenerate. Urgently and energetically, the leaders and ordinary members of the AMA bombarded the press with letters in an effort at spin control. Paul Brokaw, editor of *Motorcyclist Magazine*, wrote to *Life* to tell its readers that:

Words are difficult to express my shock. . . . We regret to acknowledge that there was a disorder in Hollister—not the act of 4,000 motorcyclists, but rather a small percentage of that number, aided by a much larger group of nonmotorcycling hellraisers and mercenary-minded bar-keepers. We in no manner defend the culprits—in fact, drastic action is under way to avoid recurrences of such antics. You have, however, in presentation of this obnoxious picture, seared a pitiful brand on the character of tens of thousands of innocent, clean-cut, respectable, law-abiding young men and women who are the true representatives of an admirable sport.[6]

The same point—the attempt to isolate the trouble to a small percentage of motorcyclists—formed the core of the AMA's spirited defense. Responding to a call from the League of California Cities to ban all motorcycle rallies, the AMA issued a press release arguing that "the disruptive cyclists were possibly one percent of the total number of motorcyclists at the time. Only one percent of motorcyclists are hoodlums and troublemakers."[7] Furthermore, the AMA announced that it would "outlaw" such "hoodlums and troublemakers" from its membership.[8]

In so doing, the organization inadvertently mythologized the very element that it sought to eradicate. The immediate, obvious effect of the AMA's press release was to bring together all those disparate motorcycle gangs who had previously been warring with each other. Thus, groups like the Gypsy Jokers, the Road Rats, Satan's Slaves, and the Booze Fighters (who would become the Hells Angels) all officially regrouped under the badge of "1-percenters," becoming a united force in opposition to both the police and the AMA.[9]

The other, arguably even more significant, effect of the AMA's action stemmed from the use of the word *outlaw*. While using it as a verb—referring to the intention to kick these bums out of the organization—the AMA couldn't avoid resurrecting the deep, reverberating connotations of this word as a noun. As Hunter S. Thompson points out in *Hell's Angels*, this subculture largely derived its vision of itself from the cinema, and here was a fertile field from which sprang visions of the outlaw as gutsy individualist, if not hero. By 1947, the Hollywood western had finely tuned the idea of the outlaw as defiant nonconformist as well as social outcast. From *The Great Train Robbery* (1903), which ends, strangely, with one of the bandits staring directly into the camera and firing his gun at the audience, to Howard Hughes' *The Outlaw* (1943), the Western outlaw was a figure that inspired not only fear and loathing, but also awe.

Indeed, that most archetypal character of the western, "the good-bad man" is inevitably at least part outlaw in a world that is itself outside the reach of the long arm of the law.[10] Affording the western outlaw an appealing, even heroic dimension, Hollywood was not only tapping into American history (Jesse James, Billy the Kid, Bonnie and Clyde, Butch

Cassidy and the Sundance Kid, Derringer) but also reaching back to European history to replant within the New World that ancient mythology of good-bad, nonconformist outlaws, such as Rob Roy, the late 17th- and early 18th-century Scottish clan leader who, deprived of his estate by the English, stole cattle and sold protection against thieves; and, of course, Robin Hood, the 12th-century English outlaw who, as every child knows, robbed the rich to give to the poor.

The *American Heritage Dictionary of the English Language* tells us that the word *outlaw* derives from the Old Norse *ütlagr*, which denoted a person who, because of criminal acts, had to give his property to the crown and could be killed without recrimination. This is obviously a dangerous position to be in and one that no sane person would actively seek out. Yet, from Robin Hood to the present day, the outlaw has taken on positive, attractive, and often desirable connotations—connotations that the AMA inadvertently gave as a PR present to those they sought to eradicate from their midst. By labeling the Booze Fighters and other groups "outlaw motorcycle gangs," the AMA provided these riders with a mythologi-

Fig. 4. Still from Francis Ford Coppola's *Rumble Fish*, 1983.

cally trenchant label which recast "troublemakers and hooligans" as modern-day, industrialized, "righteous outlaws" who, instead of mere horses, rode powerful, motorized "hogs."[11]

While the outlaw as popular hero may have a long history, the extent of his attraction has not been constant. In wartime he becomes an "in-law," fighting fire with fire on behalf of his own country.[12] But whenever the powers that be—the government, the king, tribal leaders—are held in high esteem by the general populace, he slides, irrevocably, into the role of evil, antisocial villain. Conversely, the unpopularity of the king and the aristocracy in 12th-century England is clear from the way that Robin Hood's courage and chivalry were lauded in the popular ballads that constituted both the "music charts" and the tabloids of the day.

On the face of it, therefore, the apparently sunny days of Eisenhower's prosperous postwar America would seem an unlikely setting for any return to a pro-outlaw mentality. Yet, in addition to the "1-percenter" bikers, we also at this time find the emergence of other subcultures whose nonconformist rebellion against authority courted and sometimes openly embraced an outlaw mentality. The Beats in particular, typically middle-class and college-educated, defiantly placed themselves outside the embrace of the status quo; in their enthusiasm for illegal drugs, they also placed themselves in open opposition to the law of the land.

While we tend to view these two nonconformist subcultures—the Beats and the bikers—as opposed, it was often difficult to tell them apart in the late 1940s and early '50s. The Beats, of course, loved jazz and all aspects of "hip" Black culture. Stanley Kramer and Marlon Brando both saw *The Wild One* as a "hipster" film, as the movie's constant patter of jive-talking dialogue and their comments in various interviews indicate.[13]

Perhaps it was so shocking to the culture at large to discover people who had deliberately opted for an outlaw lifestyle that they were lumped together, regardless of style of dress, mode of transport, political inclination, or any other subcultural differences.[14] Yet, in many ways, this conflation was entirely appropriate. In addition to a fondness for illegal drugs and a rejection of authority, a rootless, ever-searching mobility forged a logical link between the Beats and the bikers. Of course, from earliest times the outlaw has been defined by his (and theoretically, her) lack of land ownership and sense of geographic displacement. Like the pirate (a seagoing form of outlaw), Robin Hood, Rob Roy, Billy the Kid, et al., were without a home they could legitimately call their own. Robin Hood and his band of merry men were illegal squatters in Sherwood Forest. Of course, Beats and bikers, unlike their historical counterparts, both chose the nomadic life, rather than having it forced upon them.

Neither had much in common with that landowning, white-picket-fenced(-in) American Dream, which, especially in its suburban multiplication, spread across the country like a brushfire. What was it that drove the Beats, bikers, and other nonconformist rebels from this paradise, compelling them to become nomadic outlaws? Clearly World War II, like all wars, had torn apart the social and cultural fabric. Accelerating industrialization and urbanization, increased multicultural interfacing, and geographic mobility had all contributed to a radical departure from that cozy stereotype of Norman Rockwell's America. In a very real sense, therefore, it is fatuous to suggest, as I have above, that these outlaw rebels were choosing to eject themselves from Paradise: by this time, the American Dream had been revealed as a dream, and only the perpetually somnolent could ignore this. Arguably, too, it had never really existed, this persistent Norman Rockwell vision of small-town, WASP America. But now that so many people were living and working far away from where they were born, now that the white Anglo-Saxons were only a fictional majority, now that even chickens were produced in factories, for many this dream was, all too obviously, history.

In addition, the decade immediately after World War II saw an unprecedented level of conformity brought to bear on a nation which had previously celebrated regional and personal differences. The system of franchising which swept across America brought virtually identical Howard Johnson's, Carvels, McDonald's, and so on to cities and towns that had previously been known for their distinctive cuisines, attitudes, lifestyles, and products. At the same time, the new medium of television was imposing a remarkably uniform vision of the American Way across different regions, classes, races, and religions— a vision of Mr. and Mrs. America and their 2.5 children, wood-paneled recreation room, and paved barbecue pit that afforded remarkably little scope for personal distinctiveness. TV and the advertising that went with it turned up the heat on the melting pot until all that was left was a homogeneous, unappealing goo (instead of jambalaya, red beans and rice, Irish stew, and pasta).

Set against this ever-constricting funnel of conformity were two increasingly popular romantic visions: the freedom of the open road and the Wild West's good-bad outlaw who, quite frankly, didn't give a damn. Putting the two together may have sent shivers of fear and loathing down the spine, but more often than most cared to admit, they were accompanied by shivers of longing and desire. As Thompson puts it, the motorcycle outlaws:

> . . . are acting out the daydreams of millions . . . who don't wear any defiant insignia and who don't know how to be outlaws. The streets of every city are thronged with men who would pay all the money they could get their hands on to be transformed—even for a day—into hairy, hard-fisted brutes

who walk over cops, extort free drinks from terrified bartenders and then thunder out of town on big motorcycles after raping the banker's daughter. Even people who think the Angels should all be put to sleep find it easy to identify with them. They command a fascination, however reluctant, that borders on psychic masturbation.[15]

The gradual triumph of desire over disdain for the outlaw motorcyclist can be seen in high fashion's embrace of the black leather motorcycle jacket; in the swelling numbers that take part each year in the massive biker get-togethers in Daytona, Sturgis, and Le Mans; in the popularity of musicals like *Grease* and TV shows like *Happy Days*; in the emergence of motorcycling theme restaurants like Harley-Davidson Cafés in New York City and Las Vegas; in the extent to which tattooing has become a more accepted form of body decoration; in the sales of rough and ready biker magazines like *Easy Rider*; in the sky-rocketing prices paid for customized Harleys; and even in the fact that the Guggenheim Museum has chosen to present a major exhibition, *The Art of the Motorcycle*.[16] But we can focus on this transformation most succinctly by examining how three important films—*The Wild One*, *Easy Rider,* and *Rumble Fish*—portrayed the outlaw motorcyclist.

In 1954, *The Wild One* gave us not one but two varieties of outlaw motorcyclist. In addition to the angst-ridden existentialist Johnny (Marlon Brando) there is Lee Marvin's surly, brutish Chico, who seems to come alive only when provoking or engaging in a fight. Although it is Johnny who remains forever the enigmatic star (and, as such, monopolized our popular vision of the outlaw biker for almost two decades), Chico actually seems more true to life—the fictional precursor of those disturbing real-life characters like Tiny, Sonny, Dirty Ed, Filthy Phil, Charger Charlie the Child Molester, Magoo, Animal, and Buzzard, all of whom we encounter in Thompson's *Hell's Angels*. In this sense, it is Chico rather than Johnny who properly deserves the name *The Wild One*: unenculturated, outside all civilized conventions, he is the cinema's first portrayal of an animal on a machine.

Unequivocally sexy and stylish on the one hand, Brando's Johnny is flawed by indecision and confusion on the other hand. Brando's skillful performance shows how his character's essential attractiveness is undercut by a pathetic frailty. His weakness keeps poking through, and thereby explaining, the brittle façade of his macho toughness. Like Betty, the small-town girl who almost falls for him, we find this outlaw initially desirable, but, in the end, an unacceptable option for escape. If Johnny knows neither where he's coming from nor where he's headed, how can we contemplate going there with him? This is, of course,

Fig. 5. Still from Kenneth Anger's *Scorpio Rising*, 1963.

Fig. 6. Red River, New Mexico, 1993.

Fig. 7. Sturgis, South Dakota.

exactly how it had to be in 1954. Benedek went as far as he could, letting us admire the outlaw biker's style but refraining from making him into a hero.

Things were different, however, in 1969, when the low-budget but phenomenally successful *Easy Rider* was released. Billy (Dennis Hopper) and especially Captain America (Peter Fonda) are good-bad guys straight out of any western (and, as the breathtaking scenery never fails to remind us, this is a contemporary western). As such they are heroes—"righteous outlaws"—from start to finish. So they bring cocaine over the border and sell it to a convincingly sleazy Phil Spector. But sometimes a man's got to do what a man's got to do, not only to survive, but for the sake of the dream.

On one level, Billy and Captain America's dream is simply to get themselves and their chopper bikes to New Orleans for Mardi Gras. But we also know that their dream is nothing less than making America (and, hey, the world) a better place. It is this ideologically tinged aspiration that ultimately makes them heroes. While Chico and Johnny are just stumbling through life from meaningless fight to psychotic retribution (in Chico's case) or existential maelstrom (in Johnny's case), Captain America and Billy have a purpose. As such they are modern-day, motorized Robin Hoods operating with courage and chivalry within their outlaw domain. When Captain America concludes, "We blew it," we are not as convinced as he that their quest has been in vain. When they are killed (by the sort of "normal" American who would have been a "good," if overzealous, citizen in *The Wild One*) we mourn for them.

By the time Francis Ford Coppola made *Rumble Fish* in 1983, the public was clearly so entranced by the motorcycle outlaw that it could accept him not only as hero, but as a god, all-seeing and all-knowing, who resides above the foibles of humanity. Mickey Rourke's Motorcycle Boy is so mythic that he doesn't even need a real name. He is a presence more than he is a character, who vanishes into the horizon for long, mysterious periods, then shows up at just the right moment to save his brother in a gang fight. He is so cool that he sees the world only in black and white. Having done it all as a gang leader, he has the philosophical and ethical substance to realize that violence is only a necessary evil. In the end, he becomes a Christ figure, calculatedly sacrificing himself for the sake of his brother's redemption and (an environmentalist touch, this) a tank full of fish.

We have come far from the image of mindless brute, worthless punk, or delinquent animal to *deus super machina*.

But to this rational calculation of the motorcyclist outlaw's heroic acceptability, we must add his role as an object of pure lust. For good or for ill, at his worst as well as his best, this mythic character has always had the raw frisson of sexuality on his (or her) side—as outlaw status and the thundering power of the machine fuse into a unique and potent system of desire.[17] Transcending everyday reality and the impotence of conformity, not containable or castrated by social forces, the outlaw—whatever his mode of transport— has always possessed tantalizing erotic power. Just as Maid Marion fell for Robin Hood, so have more contemporary women succumbed to the undeniable appeal of the motorized modern-day outlaw who refuses to bow to his boss's (or the police's) authority and who, thrusting his center finger up to all who would strip him of his individuality, his grace, his presence roars off into the horizon.

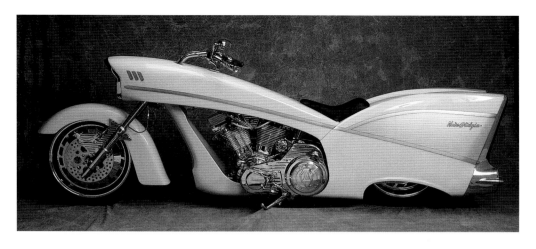

Fig. 8. Customized Chevy bike, 1995.

Primitive, unbridled, brave, uncomplicated, and ultimately romantic, the mythic outlaw biker offers a last, fleeting glimpse of that "real man" who appears to have been eradicated by our society's quest for politically correct compliance, middle-class respectability, and civilized conformity. No wimp, he has balls—even if "he" is a dyke on a bike. The more constraining and inhibiting our computerized, ever-more-regulated world, the more desirable this daredevil, dashing, and dangerous figure. And, best of all, he/she comes with no strings attached—for, come the morning, the outlaw biker of our dreams has always moved on without leaving a forwarding address.

Just look at him: the tough yet glossy leather adorned with zips, the hair wild as Samson's before his encounter with Delilah, the street credibility of the rough, worn denim, the gleam of chunky, esoteric rings and medallions, the tanned and tattooed display of flesh. The contrast with the almost invisible uniform of Mr. Respectable could not be more marked. In *The Psychology of Dress*, J. C. Fleugal plots the motivations and history of that "great masculine renunciation" of finery, adornment, and, ultimately, the male body itself. Fleugal reminds us that even in the Western world it was not until the aftermath of the French Revolution (as the bourgeoisie, especially in Britain, sought to distance itself from the excesses of the aristocracy) that men lost their peacock feathers.[18] Has there ever, in all of human history, been a less exciting male appearance than that which became the standard, shapeless, sexless, nondescript uniform of the middle-class man in the decade following World War II? Little wonder that it was this same period which saw the emergence of all manner of sartorially distinctive male subcultures—from the hipsters to the rockabillies, the Beats to the bikers.

While the image of the "tribal," "primitive" peacock male has been (in differing ways) adopted by hippies, punks, skinheads, new romantics, gothics, and a host of other subcultures, nowhere has it had a purer and more sustained realization than in the appearance of the outlaw biker.[19] Except for the Black and Hispanic hipsters (who, in their expansive, flamboyant zoot suits and accessories, were often physically attacked for their refusal to let wartime cloth restrictions finally force them to join in the great masculine renunciation), the bikers were the first Western men to reclaim their masculine status as peacocks. For while their gang uniforms may have been rough and ready, they were never devoid of either stylistic flair or flamboyant embellishment.

Like his immediate predecessor, the black-clad Wild West outlaw, the outlaw biker was never unaware of his image. Because the Beats could not bring themselves to emulate the sartorial flare of those Black hipsters whom they otherwise so admired, the outlaw bikers were the first white men to dismiss out of hand the absurd but accepted notion that a "real man" was ipso facto a visually restrained, unadorned, "invisible man."[20] In their tight-fitting leather and denim clothes, the rich visual iconography of their gang insignia, their refusal to

Fig. 9. Deadwood, South Dakota.

get a short-back-and-sides haircut, their flowing beards, and their chunky boots, they cut an appearance that was as stylish and sexy as it was threatening.

The outlaw bikers of America (and subsequently, Britain, Europe, and Australia) also displayed visual flair in their tattoo art. Long disgraced in the West (initially by the Catholic Church, which decreed that such adornment constituted a defilement of the human body; later as part of the renunciation of male adornment), tattooing had come to be seen as the definitive mark of delinquency and antisocial tendencies. More often than not, however, this judgment was simply a form of middle-class prejudice against the working men who had often continued to delight in this art form. The outlaw biker readily and proudly embraced the negative associations of tattooing, using the tattoo for all it was worth as a permanent badge of his outlaw status. And as the outlaw biker increasingly became a heroic, positive, mythic figure in his own right, tattooing also gained in popularity—its very permanence underlying its authenticity and street credibility.

That the "Tattoo Renaissance," like the outlaw biker, began in postwar California is surely no coincidence. And if today the tattoo has become an (almost) acceptable adornment, this must be seen, at least in part, as proof of just how effectively the image of the outlaw biker has shaped contemporary male sexuality. Even as recently as the mid 1960s, the desirable man could be identified by the refinement and elegance of his appearance, the capacity of his clothes to signal wealth and hierarchy. Think of James Bond in a suit, or Hugh Hefner in a silk dressing gown. Since the rise of the outlaw biker as male sex symbol, however, a completely opposite imagery has become de rigueur. Now, thanks to Brando, Hopper, Rourke, and all those real-life outlaw bikers who inspired their fictional characters, the sexy, desirable male needs a tattoo, a pierced ear, and denim or leather garments that look like they have survived many a wipeout.

A big, mean bike doesn't hurt either. "All that power between your legs"—it may be a cliché, but, like most, it no doubt gains its currency from a truth. While the automobile surrounds you in a womblike embrace, the motorcycle penetrates your physical form—and does so precisely at one's sex. In this, the motorcycle resembles a horse, another form of transport with a long and established erotic mythology. In addition, however, motorcycles offer the inducement of vibration, which female friends of mine who are cycling enthusiasts tell me shouldn't be dismissed.

In *Scorpio Rising* (1963), Kenneth Anger pointedly explores the erotic associations of motorcycling; the camera pans slowly over details of a custom bike as if showing the body of a porn star. Allen Jones' video project, *Manner, Wir Kommen* features a "Homage to Harley-Davidson" sequence developed from the following notes:

1) Woman leaning against Bardot poster.

2) Woman caressing pieces of unassembled machinery.

3) Close-up of woman's thighs astride shining gas tank.

4) Male arm slowly unscrews filling cap of tank.

5) Male hand brings petrol pump nozzle into picture.

6) Pump nozzle played around hole, then inserted.

7) Pump nozzle withdrawn to let drips be seen going into hole.

8) Female gloved hands could now restrain male arm and nozzle or have

helped to put nozzle in hole earlier.

9) Female booted foot caressing starter pedal.

10) Lips or finger tracing lines along complicated tubes on side of bike.[21]

Brigitte Bardot's homage to the motorcycle—"Harley-Davidson"—was at least as explicit in its conjugation of the bike and the erotic. Performing on French television in 1967, she straddled a motorcycle wearing skimpy black leather shorts, top, and thigh-high boots, her hair blowing in the studio-fan-generated wind, and sang:

Je n'ai besoin de personne in Harley-Davidson

Je ne reconnais plus personne en Harley-Davidson

Je vais à plus de cent

Et je me sens à feu et à sang

que m'importe de mourir les cheveux dans le vent.[22]

Every month, the photo spreads of magazines like *Easy Rider* make the same point, showing barely clothed women straddling or reclining on the featured custom bikes, their bodies fleshy accessories to the chromed and hand-painted motorcycles. In these photographs, the true erotic star is always the custom-built bike, not the woman in the bikini.

Marx decreed that in the industrialized, capitalist world, human beings become ever more objectified while consumer objects, "commodity fetishes," become the focus of our desires. Is there any more blatant example of this than a gleaming motorcycle devoutly polished to perfection? Bikers I've known have lovingly christened their bikes with women's names—"Lucy," "Sexy Sally," "Martha the Hog"—and our culture's imaging of the "perfect woman" has often striven to transmogrify the imperfections of flesh into the gleam of chrome and the smooth symmetry of the sex machine. The extraordinary, chillingly erotic female robot of *Metropolis* (1926); the piston-like limbs and buttocks of Dali's *Young*

Fig. 10. Daytona Beach, 1990.

Virgin Autosodomized by Her Own Chastity (1954); the obliging plasticity of Hans Belmer's dolls; the replication of identical female forms and their mechanical dance in Busby Berkely's movies; Paco Rabanne's and Courrège's metal-clad models; the hard-edged symmetry of Richard Linder's *Woman* (1970); Jane Fonda's see-through, plastic-coated breasts in *Barbarella* (1967); the flat flawlessness of Tom Wesselmann's *Nude* (1966); the half-flesh, half-chrome androids of Hajime Sorayama's pinups; or any of the "second skin" creations of fashion and fetishism that cover the body with a gleaming, hyperrealist patina—all render the human body more erotically powerful by allying it with the aesthetic qualities of a machine. Obviously, the motorcycle is only one of many inspirations of the aesthetic of the sex machine, but it plays a fundamental role in this erotic system.

In point of fact, our culture juxtaposes and oscillates between two seemingly contradictory and oppositional erotic constructs. On the one hand, the perfectly lubricated, pneumatic dynamo of the Sex Machine heralds a sci-fi future in which desire is unhindered by the friction of emotion. Conversely, the Animal—its beastly urges unconstrained by culture and civilization—harks back to a prehuman age when instinct ruled and hairy, sweating apelike men and women rutted with abandon in a jungle paradise.

In the contemporary iconography of the outlaw biker on his/her gleaming sex machine, these two erotic constructs are fused: the natural, uninhibited, instinctive, hairy, belching, groin-motivated, if-it-feels-good-do-it Animal astride a pneumatic, other-worldly, futuristic, emotionally oblivious, sublimely artificial, perfectly realized engine of desire. Man Ray once wrote: "Reality is fabricated out of desire." Jean Baudrillard has foreseen that the world is becoming one enormous theme park. Welcome to Biker-World, where, as Tom Waits put it, "all our dreams are made of chrome."

Notes

1. *Life*, July 21, 1947.

2. Hunter S. Thompson, *Hell's Angels* (Harmondsworth, England: Penguin Books, 1967), p. 67.

3. Frank Rooney, "The Cyclist's Raid," *Harper's*, January, 1951, cited in Maz Harris, *Bikers: Birth of a Modern Day Outlaw* (London: Faber & Faber, 1985), p. 23.

4. Due to censorship, *The Wild One* was not released in Britain until 1968.

5. One of these is wearing a black-and-white, horizontally striped T-shirt. Interestingly, in *The Wild One*, the arch-villain Chico wears a similar shirt and in the much later (1967) film *Rebel Rousers*, the evil Jack Nicholson character wears distinctive, black-and-white striped trousers.

6. *Life*, July 28, 1947, cited in Harris, pp. 17–18.

7. Quoted in Jan Hudson, *The Sex and Savagery of Hells Angels* (London: New English Library, 1967), p. 19, and Harris, p. 19.

8. Harris, p. 19.

9. The official insignia reads "Hells Angels" rather than "Hell's Angels."

10. See "The Western" in Edward F. Dolan, Jr.'s *History of the Movies* (Greenwich, Conn.: Bison Books, 1983), pp. 12–43.

11. Harris, p. 20.

12. In the mid '60s, Sonny Berger's Oakland chapter of the Hells Angels wrote to President Lyndon Johnson offering their services to fight in Vietnam. For some reason, Johnson failed to take them up on their offer.

13. Interestingly, even such comparatively late films as the 1967 *Rebel Rouser* and Russ Mayer's 1965 *Motor Psycho* still chose to portray bikers as jive-talking hipsters who, sans bikes, would have seemed more at home in a coffeehouse playing bongos. Such Beatnik/bikers were not a complete fiction: Hunter S. Thompson writes in *Hell's Angels* that both the Sacramento and San Francisco chapters of the Hells Angels "began with a distinctly bohemian flavor" (p. 135).

14. In Britain, something similar happened when the press persisted in labeling Rockers—the British term for bikers at the time—"Teddy Boys," despite obvious visual differences.

15. Thompson, p. 273.

16. For it is now impossible, at least in the public imagination, to divorce the motorcycle as object from its cultural connotations of rebellion and lawlessness. The statistics are irrelevant; the 1-percenter long ago became, at least in the mind's eye, the norm.

17. Consider the female biker exploitation films *Hell's Belles* (1969) and *Sisters in Leather* (1969).

18. J. C. Fleugal, *The Psychology of Dress* (London: The Hogarth Press, 1971).

19. Or, in British terminology, Rockers and, in the 1970s, Greasers.

20. In Britain, this role would be played by the Teddy Boys, and later by the motorcycle-riding Rockers and Greasers.

21. Allen Jones, *Projects* (London: Matthews Miller Dunbar; Milan: Edizioni O, 1971), p. 80.

22. Serge Gainsbourg, 1967.

Dennis Hopper

Bikes were always work for me

Crash and burn
outlaw glory
motorcycle mamas
tits to the wind
beer-drinking drug-taking and -dealing
lead-footed angels
not corporate tie-wielding execs from Wall Street
these angels were my models
they were scary dark tattooed riders
whose thunder shook our very foundations
The Wild One
Wild Angels
Hell's Angels on Wheels
The Glory Stompers
were the movies we made about our myths
Hells Angels
Satan's Slaves
the emblems of our times
the Devil's wheels burned and streaked our highways
crisscrossing our consciousnesses and lives
like the gingham-patterned oilcloth
that covered our kitchen tables
and hung from our windows
and the gingham chicken feed sacks that we wore
as shirts under our bib overalls
being born on a wheat farm in Dodge City, Kansas
not the black leather jackets, pants
stomping boots, chains, crosses, death's-head skulls
swastikas, daggers dripping blood, that the cigar-smoking
bearded dragons wore from the coast
The West Coast

My family moved West to San Diego when I was 13
saw my first Hells Angels in T.J. Mexico
having their pictures taken with a Donkey
sitting in a cart donning sombreros
stick matches bursting into flames
after a quick rub on the seams of their leather pants
cigar smoke billowing from behind their beards
the flashbulb pops the tequila bottle passed
one biker and his bike ram the cart
the Donkey lurches the camera on legs topples
the bikers scramble kicking their parked bikes
into a roar leaving us in a cloud of dust
and a hearty Hi Ho Silver
yelling they will return for the photo
after the Donkey show have it ready or else
Their heavy laughter and irreverence
stayed with me and helped form my attitudes
for nearly half a century

Then I saw *The Wild One* when I was 14
starring Marlon Brando
Every boy in America and half the world
would become "Sonny" Brando's character in the movie
James Dean had a motorcycle
but Jack Warner had made his agent
make Dean promise not to ride while he was shooting
Rebel and *Giant*
the two films I was in with Dean
(he only made three)
Dean had sat on his bike in the rain
watching Vic Damone and Pier Angeli coming out of the church
at their wedding
he was in love with Pier
she had asked him to marry her
while he was making *East of Eden*, his first film
he asked her to wait
because in his mind at that point
he had no career or money
she didn't wait
So we have Dean crying in the rain on his bike
at her wedding
so the story goes

Fig. 1. Biker, 1962.

Steve McQueen and I had our driver's licenses
taken away for too many speeding tickets
so we got Vespas to drive
thinking we would not get caught
on motorscooters without licenses
we used to race our Vespas on the dirt firebreaks
off Mulholland that we could take from
Coldwater Canyon all the way to the ocean
we had so many wrecks my Vespa looked
like a crushed beer can with wheels
after three years of suspension
and two weeks left to recover my license
I was driving my wife-to-be Brooke Hayward
on the back of my Vespa going to the Beverly Hills Hotel
to ask Leyland Hayward and his wife Pamela
(later to be Ambassador Pamela Harriman)
for Brooke's hand in marriage
I was ticketed on the way to the hotel
for changing lanes erratically
with someone on the back
another year without a driver's license
Steve went on to become an amateur national cross-country
dirt-bike champion I believe on a B.S.A.

Then I had a bad accident
riding down Sunset Boulevard
hitting an oil slick doing only 35 mph
The Vespa flipped over on me
breaking my ankle and her arm
(this was a young actress
that I had been working with on the film *Night Tide*
we had wrapped the film that night)
I ended up in the hospital for ten days
swearing I would never ride two wheels again
four-wheel drive and off the road for me
getting my kicks off Route 66
in the canyons and desert dirt roads
that dotted my universe
but then came *Easy Rider*

I had made a bike movie called *The Glory Stompers* that I starred in
at American International Pictures
Peter Fonda had starred in a bike movie called *The Wild Angels*
a big hit that made him a big star
Jack Nicholson was the star of *Hell's Angels on Wheels*
we were all at A.I.P.
the director Roger Corman made *The Wild Angels* with Peter
and then had Jack write a screenplay called *The Trip* about LSD
Corman had a way with picking subjects

Fig. 2. Biker couple, 1961.

that were current and controversial
A.I.P. made movies for the drive-in movie market
Peter and I promised each other
we would never make another bike movie
we didn't want to become
the John Wayne and Ward Bond of bike flicks

Peter had read *The Last Movie*
a screenplay that I had Stewart Stern write
from an original story by me
Peter wanted to produce it
then he and I wrote
a script called *The Yin and the Yang*
with a comedian named Don Sherman
then we went to New York to find financing for the films
Peter to produce and myself to direct
we found closed doors and Nos everywhere
we even had a meeting with Huntington Hartford who
because of my passion
about how I was going to win the Cannes Film Festival, etc.
said he would give us the money
if I would levitate in his office for him
I seriously thought about it
but decided not to try
I didn't want to be disappointed
I got up and said Peter let's leave

When we left I saw a pigeon in the street with a broken wing
I went to a Lucas Samaras show at the Green Gallery
Jim Rosenquist had left Dick Bellamy's gallery that day
I found Dick at this desk

Fig. 3. Still from Dennis Hopper's *Easy Rider*, 1969.

with Lucas' objects of broken glass and pins surrounding him
Jim had left Dick for Leo Castelli Gallery
Leo had given him a sizable money guarantee
Peter went to Millbrook
to see Billy Hitchcock and Tim Leary
I went back to L.A. in defeat
crossing the bridge to Kennedy airport
the Beatles were on the radio with "We Can Work It Out"
I remember looking back at the skyline of N.Y.
the taxi crossed the bridge
as we went under the steel girders suddenly
"We Can Work It Out" went to static
as had my trip to the Big Apple

Sometime later on
Peter went to Canada on a press junket
to promote *The Trip* with A.I.P.
he calls me in L.A. at 3 in the morning
and tells me that Sam Arkoff the head of A.I.P.
would give us the money to make a bike movie
if Peter starred in it
I could direct and Peter could produce
then Peter proceeded to tell me
about his idea of a couple of bikers

smuggling drugs from Mexico on dirt bikes
they sell the dope and get a couple of beautiful hogs
go across country to Mardi Gras
have a great time
go into Florida the next day
and are shot by a couple of duck hunters
Peter asked did I like it
I said Are you sure they said they'd give us the money
Yes he said
I said It sounds fine Peter fine
so this was the beginning of *Easy Rider*
back on a hog one more time

My greatest memory was riding across
Monument Valley chasing the dying sun
full bore and the crew following me
to catch the last rays of the sun from Inspiration Point
in John Ford country
thank God for that experience
it was the greatest moment of my life
chasing that light and recording it
it is the panning shot of Monument Valley in *Easy Rider*
just before the campfire scene
with Luke Askew the stranger Peter picks up hitchhiking
I was told it was too dark but we had a new kind of film
I pushed it two stops
the shot came out a beauty
so with the end of filming *Easy Rider*
so was the end of my riding a motorcycle
until the kidnapping of Jack some ten years later

The kidnapping of Jack Nicholson:
Jack was shooting *The Border*
a Tony Richardson film in El Paso
Paul Lewis my production manager on *Easy Rider*
and the producer of *The Last Movie*
and Chuck Bail my stunt coordinator
had written a script called *The Last Ride*
it was about some middle-aged bikers
who had become businessmen
they decide to go back to a town they had taken over
à la *The Wild One*
when they had belonged to a bad-ass bike gang
their leathers no longer fit
their bikes are covered in cobwebs, etc.
they meet some young bikers on the road
and wonder if they were ever that bad
when they arrive at the town
much to their surprise 1,000 bikers are there to celebrate

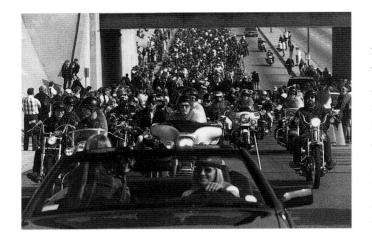

the 20th anniversary of their takeover
the National Guard gets called in
and the old bikers end up on the side of the National Guard
as a colossal bike war erupts in the finale
it was a cute idea
the hope was to get Jack to commit to act in it
and we could make *The Last Ride*
but Jack was working
and Jack doesn't read scripts when he's working
we needed to find another way to involve him

We hired a bike gang in El Paso where Jack was working
we used Warren Oates and Toby Rafelson as insiders
they were working on the film with Jack
they convinced him following our instructions
that the President of Mexico
would like a meeting with him in Juarez
we sent two Caddie limos
with Mexican flags and the Stars and Stripes
flying off the front fenders
and some big Mexican drivers and bodyguards
to pick up Jack after he finished shooting on the set
Unknown to us Jack had thrown his back out
and he decided to take his four-wheel drive
so he could lay down in the back
Warren and Toby went with Jack and Jack's driver
who was quickly informed about the plan by Warren
there was a limo in front and a limo in back of Jack's vehicle
supposedly heading for Mexico to meet the President
but as they hit the highway
they were surrounded by the bike gang
and diverted into a dark football stadium
Jack's motorcade pulled in surrounded by the bike gang
and there we were, five of us, sitting on our hogs
all former A.I.P. biker stars
Adam Rourke Earl Finn Jack Starrett myself
and I forget the fifth
As his truck stopped
the fireworks exploded
spelling out JACK'S NO. 1

A helicopter with searchlights came into the stadium
lowering a one-of-a-kind Harley-Davidson
with Jack's name engraved on the gas tank
they lowered it between Jack and us with rockets exploding in air
Earlier on the highway when Jack was surrounded by bikers
he had told Warren and Toby to jump and save themselves
that he couldn't move because of his back

when he saw me sitting on one of the bikes

he managed to get out of his truck and yelled HOPPER get over here

then the cheerleaders from the local university

ran toward him smothering him with kisses as we had instructed

he fell to the ground with excruciating back pain

this was not going well

naturally he turned down *The Last Ride:*

That's going to be our retirement man doing a bike movie

later man, much later on Hoppy, okay?

But what do you think about me keeping the bike?

I said Of course, why not, it's got your name on it

he kept the hog

Jack is still No.1 in my book

It was some twenty years later

before I got on a bike again

this time leading twenty-five thousand bikers

on The Love Ride, a charity for MS

Jay Leno and I were chairmen joined by

Dwight Yoakum, J.P. DeJoria and Peter Fonda

and on the back of my borrowed hog

sat my lovely wife Victoria Duffy

the courage of her conviction to stick with me

on the back of that bike as I drove her

going 80 mph those 60 miles to Lake Elsinore

where Dwight entertained us all at this giant biker picnic

cemented my heart to her forever

as I wobbled through stops and starts

her love and belief in me never did

So ends the ride until next time

I mount a bike

crash and burn

and piss out the fire

death before dishonor

when I get back from the Donkey show

you better have the photo ready or else

see how I remember that

thanks for the memory

valuable footnotes:

Harley-Davidson wouldn't comp us bikes

for *Easy Rider*

because the protagonists were outlaws and they thought

it was bad for their image

Cliff Voss a black civil-rights activist

chopped and rebuilt the Harleys for *Easy Rider*

Fig. 5. Hopper and Duffy on the Love Ride, 1993.

Art Simon

Freedom or Death: Notes on the Motorcycle in Film and Video

Fig 1. Still from Kim Wood's
Advice to Adventurous Girls, 1996.

"Hurrah for the poetry of machines," Dziga Vertov wrote in 1922, "propelled and driving; the poetry of levers, wheels, and wings of steel; the iron cry of movements; the blinding grimaces of red-hot streams."[1] In his *Man With a Movie Camera* (1929), there, amid the automobiles and the streetcars, the locomotives and the airplanes—all the modern means of mechanized transport—is the motorcycle. Knowing Vertov's conception of the *Kinok*, his ideal revolutionary documentarist who moves through the world recording film facts, one would think the motorcycle might be his preferred vehicle. Its slender frame enables access to the world at large, and its open construction permits the camera to shoot from unobstructed angles. How better to capture the rhythms of daily life and "bring people into closer kinship with machines" than to film sitting atop one, to straddle an engine and let its pulse vibrate through to the hand that cranks the camera?[2]

Practical reasons, of course, placed the *Kinok* more often in a car than on a motorcycle—the camera operator needed room to work and a driver to navigate the course. Indeed, Vertov wrote specifically of the "film car," modeled on the agit-train, a mobile *Kinopravda* in which "the projector is operated by the car's motor kept idling."[3] Still, it is the motorcycle that best embodies some of the principles of Soviet avant-garde art. Its exposed engine stands as the literal site of production, and simultaneously appears as a geometric abstraction. Design coexists with function, spoke and wheel like a Rodchenko line composition set in motion by the combustion engine. But in *Man With a Movie Camera*, Vertov is less interested in the bike for its Constructivist profile than for its contribution to the world of mechanized motion. It takes its place alongside the spindles and factory cranks that turn throughout the film, figuring the "revolutions" that have come to industrial and cultural production. Moreover, the images of motorcycles offer a mechanized pun for a film largely structured around "cycles"—human, labor, and urban. Given Vertov's penchant for hailing the body as machine, one could also imagine his celebration of their proximity as located in the motorcycle, the *Kino*-eye supported by motorized limbs. Specifically, Vertov intercuts shots of motorcycle racing with those of a merry-go-round, and then briefly, images of track-and-field athletes. In a couple of shots, we even see the *Kinok* riding behind the racers, the movie camera resting atop the handlebars. Vertov does not let these shots linger on screen, but instead subjects the movement of bikes to the pace of his montage. As with so much of the film, Vertov severs events and actions—athletics, urban locales, labor, and the motorcycles—from their immediate spatial and temporal contexts so as to insert them into the more profound contexts of parallel motion or dialectical collisions. He writes: "The geometrical extract of movement through an exciting succession of images is what's required of montage."[4] As extracts, the motorcycles are divorced from any narrative having to do with the races being filmed and are utilized as icons of movement, their right-to-left screen direction juxtaposed with the left-to-right movement of the merry-go-round. Rather, the bikes work more abstractly to draw (or drive) a line across the frame and motivate the lateral movement of the spectator's eye. These brief images of the motorcycle synthesize the optical and kinetic properties mobilized throughout the film.

Toward the end of *Man With a Movie Camera*, Vertov uses stop-motion photography to create the impression that the movie camera is assembling itself. It climbs out of its box, mounts the tripod, then spins and tilts to display its components before walking out of the frame on its wooden legs. The sequence allows Vertov to illustrate how cinematic technique can further animate the machine, and also to fantasize about a technology that no longer needs human assistance. Vertov cuts between the camera and the audience watching it in the film within a film that functions as the movie's framing device. The spectators are amused and impressed with the camera's autonomy, and suggest Vertov's wish of mass approval for the dynamism characterizing the early 20th century.

Five years earlier, in *Sherlock Jr.* (1924), Buster Keaton had offered a quite literal presentation of self-driven technology featuring the motorcycle. Playing the master detective of the film's title, Buster must save his love, the kidnapped young woman, from the clutches of crime. The climactic rescue scene begins as he jumps upon the handlebars of a motorcycle driven by his assistant, Gillette. But within seconds, Gillette is knocked off by a bump in the road, leaving Buster unaware that he is now perched on a bike that has no driver. Through intersections of city traffic, across country roads, on top of two trucks, over a collapsing bridge, between an exploding log, under a passing tractor, in front of an approaching train, a tense but unsuspecting Buster and the motorcycle miraculously survive the trip. Along the way Buster speaks to the absent driver, and only after he has discovered his predicament does the motorcycle begin to weave unstably. Still, it only comes to a stop after running smack into a pile of wood outside the criminal's hideout, throwing Buster through the window with a force that helps him subdue his lady's captor.

While Vertov set his camera atop the handlebars, fully participating in the new mobility, Keaton placed himself atop the handlebars, suggesting the possible peril accompanying the motorized '20s. Keaton's ride takes him from city streets to mountainous country roads, tracing the route of highway and road construction that dominated the decade after World War I as the automobile transformed American culture and its landscape. Indeed, at one point Buster rides past a roadside work crew and is struck in the face by dirt flying off their shovels. In *Sherlock Jr.*, the inherent instability of the two-wheeled machine and its lack of a protective shell underscore the dangers of mechanization. Cars sink underwater, bridges collapse, a train almost crushes Buster. The perilous encounter between man and modern times informs much of early film comedy. Physically slight but extraordinarily adroit comics would have to employ ingenuity and good fortune to survive any given day.

Like Vertov, Keaton used the film-within-a-film structure for *Sherlock Jr.*, explicitly identifying the cinema as a contributing force to the new mobility. Here too, though, Keaton envisions danger where Vertov saw sheer dynamism: when Buster dreams he is stepping onto the screen and into the frame, the radical changes in time and space produced by

editing create an unstable and hazardous world. If the pace of the 20th century was going to be set by the "poetry of levers, wheels, and wings of steel," as Vertov suggested, the American comic screen was less than confident about its charitability. But Keaton and his contemporaries insisted that danger could be funny, and given the historical setting that conditioned their work, this often resulted in some image of technology.

In *Love, Speed and Thrills* (1915), a motorcycle and sidecar allow Mack Sennett to send various characters flying heels over head during an extended chase through the countryside. In *Girl Shy* (1922), Harold Lloyd enlists the motorcycle, along with the automobile, fire truck, streetcar, and horse-drawn wagon, en route to saving the girl he loves; each vehicle proves more hazardous than the last. In the Marx Brothers's *Duck Soup* (1933), the motorcycle and sidecar represent the humiliation of being left behind, a fear fueled by the era of mechanized mobility in which the movie was made and fully realized by the economic failures of the decade that followed. On three separate occasions, Groucho, as Rufus T. Firefly, is left sitting while either his motorcycle or its sidecar drive off with Harpo (fig. 2). Like the motorcycle in *Sherlock Jr.*, Firefly's machine seems almost prepared to drive itself, a symbol for runaway technology.

The Wild One

The post–World War II period would redefine the image of the motorcycle, adding to this symbol of mobility a powerful degree of menace. Jean Cocteau's *Orpheus* (1950) used motorcycles to carry Death's leather-clad henchmen—the faceless riders who speed into or out of a scene to assist Death herself (fig. 3).

Laslo Benedek's *The Wild One* (1954) gave that menace a personality, more outlaw than evil, helping to forge an image of the American biker that would be imitated and subtly revised for the next quarter century. The film was roughly based on a 1947 incident in which thousands of bikers turned a July 4th celebration in Hollister, California, into a three-day public disturbance. *The Wild One* suggested that one aspect of American youth was experiencing an ambiguous sense of alienation, an aimless ennui that was defined as rebellion. When one of the local residents asks Marlon Brando's character, "What are you rebelling against, Johnny?" He responds: "What have you got?"

Johnny and his friends define community in terms of the leather-jacketed bike gang rather than the traditional home and marriage. They seek the pleasures of kicks—music, dancing, and speed. Brando's Johnny affixed to the motorcycle a cluster of meanings that appealed to restless youth—it was an image suited to the roads that wound far from the cities and well beyond the suburbs where postwar Americans were settling.

The very structure of the motorcycle could be read as antifamily: Affording room for one and possibly two, the bike cuts a figure antithetical to the Airstream mobile home of the '50s. And while the family depended on a contained and procreative sexuality, the motorcycle came to function both as object of desire and symbol of unrestrained Eros. This sexualized image of the bike is implied by the failed seduction in *The Wild One*. Johnny and Kathy, the young woman of his immediate affection, embark on a moonlit ride through the countryside. A series of close-ups reveal the motorcycle's transformative effect. With the wind in her hair and her arms around Johnny's leather, Kathy is seduced. The speed and movement of the bike symbolize her hopes for personal freedom and the wish to escape her small-town entrapment. But when the ride stops and Johnny tries to kiss her, Kathy seems no longer interested. She lusts after the motorcycle, not Johnny (fig. 4). When Kathy says "I wanted to touch you," the camera pans slowly to the left, showing the bike between Kathy and Johnny. Kathy then gets down on one knee and caresses the bike, her chin to the chrome. "I've never ridden on a motorcycle before," she says. "It's fast. It scared me, but I forgot everything, it felt good. Is that what you do?" Johnny appears to recognize that Kathy desires his bike more than him and responds: "Now I'm going to leave, that's what you want me to do, isn't it?"

Fig. 4. Still from Laslo Benedek's *The Wild One*, 1954.

The motorcycle as object of desire is intimately linked with the way it signifies sexual power. The proximity of the engine and the rider's genitals offer a rather transparent expression of sexual energy. Unlike the automobile, in which the interior and design distance the driver's body from the engine, the bike appears to offer little mediation between the force of the driver and the direction of the motorcycle. To ride is to imply that one can wrestle a heavy machine into submission. Still, the relationship is always a bit precarious, and the threat of the motorcycle resides partly in its potential to break out on its own. This fear is realized in *The Wild One*. While fleeing angry townspeople who suspect he has just molested Kathy, Johnny gets knocked off his bike, only to have it continue down the street until it strikes and kills Jimmy, an old man. The threat of an out-of-control sexuality is also suggested during the scene in which the gang circles Kathy on their bikes, as if the machines themselves had molestation on their minds.

The Wild One elaborated on the Hollister event and drew upon the subsequent barrage of reporting and publicity to establish an image that confirmed the postwar identity of the biker. Outlaw biker Preetam Bobo, a lifetime member of the San Francisco Hells Angels, recalled, "We sat up there in the balcony and smoked cigars and drank wine and cheered like bastards. We could all see ourselves right there on the screen. We were all Marlon Brando. I guess I must have seen it four or five times."[5] Bobo's return trips to the movie theater suggest how much of the film's attraction was founded upon image rather than narrative, more on display than diegesis. It hardly mattered if you knew how the story turned out. And although *The Wild One* has a tighter construction than the biker films of a decade later, it still pivots more on the fashions, sounds, and pleasure-seeking posturing of its biker/hipsters than on the narrative conventions of classic studio product. In fact, the movie functions both as Hollywood problem film and as founding ancestor for the cycle of biker films that would emerge in the mid '60s. Its rhetoric of moral gravity, its mise-en-scène and psychologized hero firmly locate the film within producer Stanley Kramer's oeuvre of social concern. But in its treatment of bikers as rebels for a vague individualism, potential outlaws, and sexual predators, as well as in its relaxing of narrative coherence, it anticipates the subsequent motorcycle subgenre.[6]

In *The Wild One*'s legacy to subsequent motorcycle movies there is a paradigmatic formal bequest—its opening shot. The camera is positioned in the middle of a highway, its point of view at the level of the blacktop. There is momentary calm. Then, from just over

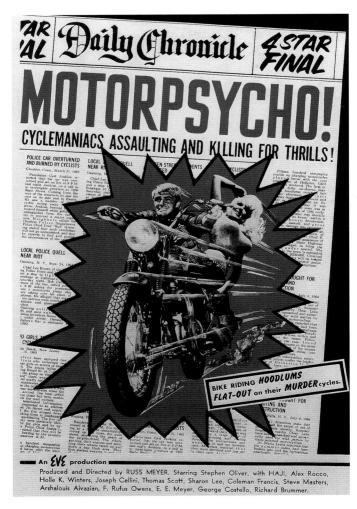

Fig. 5. Promotional material for Russ Meyer's
Motor Psycho, 1965.

Fig. 6. Still from John Rich's *Roustabout*, 1965.

the horizon, motorcycles appear and, as their engine noise builds on the soundtrack, they race toward and then past the camera. This shot is repeated early on in *The Wild Angels* (1966), the inaugural film of the biker cycle, and again in *Electra Glide in Blue* (1973) and *The Loveless* (1983). Its angle and framing make the camera—and thus our perspective—vulnerable, suggesting that the motorcycle is a danger to anything in its path. But it also establishes the road as privileged site, and mobility as a defining aspect of the biker's identity. No doubt this mobility served as the basis for why the biker appeared so threatening. He (and it was almost always a he) lacked a traditional home, and with it civic obligation or personal commitment.

This nomadic character was often translated into sexual promiscuity. Of course, in many films of the biker cycle, the leader of the club is granted the privilege of an attractive "old lady," but as Martin Rubin has pointed out, these films frequently display a "diffident and/or pessimistic treatment of romantic relationships." At the end of *The Wild Angels*, for instance, Peter Fonda's character tells his girlfriend, played by Nancy Sinatra, "Beat it. I don't want you."[7] This lack of attachment to place is often rendered through the biker's disregard for privacy and club members are frequently shown having sex near, next to, or in collaboration with each other. As with other aspects of the biker identity, the film cycle crafted the role of sexual predator from images circulating through the mainstream press. Just two years before the release of *The Wild Angels*, the Hells Angels had made headlines when several of its members were accused of raping two young women in Monterey, California. The charges, which attracted the attention of the national press, were followed by an investigation of the Angels by State Attorney General Thomas Lynch. Lynch's report and the media publicity it generated depicted the motorcycle club as a confederate of rapists, violent thugs whose pleasure came from terrorizing respectable and innocent citizens. Without being attached to some sort of home, at least as traditionally defined, the outlaw motorcyclist could be fashioned as the ultimate stranger, unknowable because of his transience, unassimilable because of his lack of origin.

Cinematic representations of the bike rider as predator were not confined to films about motorcycle gangs. Russ Meyer's *Motor Psycho* (1965) depicts the damage done by three bikers, embodying types often associated with motorcycles: the Vietnam vet, the leather-jacketed hipster of the '50s, and the absentminded, radio-toting Beatnik. Meyer's hyperdrama, combining mild sexploitation with elements of the juvenile delinquent picture, reinforces the image of the biker as nomadic rapist (fig. 5). Brahmin, the leader of the threesome, turns to murder and acts within a Vietnam War flashback, confirming the pun in the film's title. Psychos and cycles just seem to go together.

Hollow Rebels

But mobility could symbolize freedom as well as danger (fig. 6). *The Wild One* points toward an escape from middle-class commitments. The road offered an alternative to the synthetic environment of the suburbs and the counterfeit identities that populated the corporate world. And whereas, because of its '50s context, this form of expression and critique may have been primarily confined to the Beats, within a decade it became an essential ingredient of the emerging counterculture. In the American cinema of the '60s, the image of the road and the motorcycle carried multiple meanings. For the filmmaking industry, it symbolized an escape from the confines of the Hollywood studio and shifted the location of characters and events to "real" settings. In one of the *The Wild One*'s signature shots, Brando's character leads the Black Rebels Club as they roar down the highway. But the shot is composed with the help of rear projection, and the visual mismatch of foreground and background confines the apparent mobility of the motorcycles. Brando's next significant ride on a motorcycle, this time as a fleeing German officer in *The Young Lions* (1958), would also suffer from a similar visual confinement.

A decade later, films such as *The Wild Angels* and *Easy Rider* (1969) located the bike on the open road and employed traveling shots that integrated the motorcycles within the passing landscape. Thus, at a time when the commercial movie industry was undergoing significant reorganization, from the shift toward conglomerate ownership to strategies aimed at reclaiming a depleted audience, the biker film cycle was one way in which the movies tried to leave their old home behind. Indeed, the change came not only at the site of production but also when it came to exhibition as well. As drive-ins helped offset the declining box-office figures of traditional theaters, the independently produced biker films became a staple of "outdoor" cinema. And where better to project this image than on a huge outdoor screen where, just beyond its borders, actual highways and hillsides provided the illusion that the road was continuing as an extension of the cinematic frame.

But the open road suggested more than the liberation of the camera. It functioned as a recurring motif for a series of films from the '60s and early '70s which defined youthful alienation on the basis of mobility. In its purest Hollywood form, the road in *Two Lane Blacktop* (1971) figures literally as the dominant location of narrative action for a film that suggests there is no life without constant motion. In other films—*Five Easy Pieces* (1970), *Scarecrow* (1973), *Bonnie and Clyde* (1967), *Midnight Cowboy* (1969)—movement and flight define figures either unable or unwilling to find incorporation into mainstream society. It is *Easy Rider*, of course, which prominently placed the motorcycle alongside the cars, buses, and trains that carried these alienated figures across the country.

Legendary now for its rock-music soundtrack and its phenomenal return of over fifty million dollars on a production budget of under half a million, *Easy Rider* was produced by BBS, an independent production company under the auspices of Columbia Pictures. Unlike the outlaw bikers, their film kin from American-International, Captain America (Wyatt) and Billy are not violent MC gang members. In fact, they are the victims of a violent nation that interprets their long hair and motorcycles as threats to small-town, conservative values. "What you represent to them is freedom," George Hanson tells his companions by the fireside. But it is unclear whether Billy or Captain America are in any sense free of the self-centered individualism that informs American political thought and culture. Their goal (summed up near the end of the film by Billy) to get the big money and retire to Florida conforms nicely to middle-class aspirations. As critics have noted, the shot that frames the bikers changing a flat tire while, simultaneously, a horse is being shoed works rather blatantly to associate them with the image of the American pioneer. The point is repeated when the men ride through Monument Valley and are photographed climbing rocks against a dusk night sky. Throughout the west-to-east journey, Wyatt endorses national myths of self-reliance and a faith in the people. "It's not every man who can live off the land," he tells the rancher-farmer who, instead of fearing the riders, offers them a place at his table. "You should be proud." And it is Captain America who contradicts Billy's cynicism toward the agricultural efforts of the commune, telling him, "They are going to make it." His vision of a preindustrial America permits the rebel to adorn his bike and his jacket with the Stars and Stripes as well as to borrow the name of his country.

In *Easy Rider*, the motorcycle journey serves to express a vague discontent. The sim-

ple act of cross-country wandering expresses the film's ambiguous sense of resistance. The bike itself comes to represent the fantasy of freedom. Every time the riders exit the highway or get off their motorcycles they meet up with trouble—they are ignored by a motel proprietor, denied service and taunted at a small town café, and subjected at their campsite to a beating that takes George's life. Moreover, the rock songs that comprise the film's soundtrack are almost exclusively coupled with shots of the motorcycles in motion. Although they meet death while riding, the film is shot to emphasize less the murder of Captain America than the violence done to his motorcycle, which is torn apart in slow motion. If the motorcycle had come to signify in some biker films a form of homelessness, a life spent in transit, then *Easy Rider* can be read as a procession of alternative homes—the family ranch, the youthful commune, jail, the New Orleans house of prostitution—none of which Billy and Wyatt can settle down to (fig. 7). It makes sense that their final resting place is at the side of the road.

Fig. 7. Still from Dennis Hopper's *Easy Rider*, 1969.

Fig. 8. Still from Sidney J. Furie's *Little Fauss and Big Halsy*, 1970.

In their studies of the biker series, both Frank Arnold and Martin Rubin identify the loose narrative construction of these films, situating them in the context of an American cinema undergoing the influence of the European New Wave, which included strategies such as episodic structure, improvised performance styles, and a detached approach to the spectator's sympathetic identification with the characters.[8] Biker films of the '60s emphasize the capacity of film to accent motion, allowing action, such as "the biker run," to break free of the conventional demand that events ultimately submit to the logical coherence of the plot (fig. 8). The bike once again comes to signify the uncontainable. Throughout its appearances in the storytelling cinema, from the image of a driverless machine to its escape from the studio to its refusal of narrative integration, the motorcycle has stood for autonomy. Not even the apocalypse can contain it: The motorcycle survives into the violent futurist worlds of *Rollerball* (1975, fig. 9), *Mad Max* (1979), *The Terminator* (1984), and *Terminator 2: Judgment Day* (1991).

But the two-wheeled image of autonomy should not be confused with the idea of revolution, at least in its American context of the turbulent '60s. Most of the bikers in these films were hollow rebels, defying standards of taste and good manners perhaps, but unable to formulate any stance beyond a vague and conformist individualism. Membership in the gang was only one of the ways in which outlaw bikers rode in formation with such American values as violence, sexism, and patriotism. The visual as well as verbal rhetoric of freedom can hardly mask the conformity inscribed in these films. Their brutality towards women, endless macho posing, and subservience to a charismatic leader are hardly at odds with American structures of power. Its most extreme articulation is found in the array of Nazi regalia and symbols the bikers wear as they fashion an identity around the will to shock (fig. 10). In *The Wild Angels*, Peter Fonda's character, Blues, stands up to answer the question what do bikers want: "We want to be free to do what we want to do. We want to be free to ride. We want to be free to ride our machines and not be hassled by The Man." But so long as the bikers refrain from accosting The Man's daughter, The Man probably could not care less about the bikers quest to do what they want to do. Offscreen, of course, real Hells Angels were demonstrating their political affiliations by beating up peace marchers. As Hunter S. Thompson noted in his 1966 saga of the gang, "When push came to shove, the Hells Angels lined up solidly with the cops, the Pentagon, and the John Birch Society."[9]

Lindsay Anderson offered a more explicit representation of revolution in *If. . .* (1968). The film portrays the oppressive conditions at an English boarding school where students are subjected to the brutal whim of upperclassmen and administrators.

Fig. 9. Still from Norman Jewison's *Rollerball*, 1975.

Here, the institution of learning serves as a training ground for the military and the church as it seeks to instill a sense of duty and loyalty to the sons of a fading empire. However, several sons choose to resist the orders and humiliation and take up arms against the school. Lead by Travis, played by Malcolm McDowell, and armed with munitions found stored in the school basement, the youthful resisters take up rooftop positions and open fire on fellow students, teachers, clergy, and assorted British dignitaries. Travis's, and his fellow student Johnny's, will to freedom is suggested about midway through the film when they borrow a motorcycle to escape the school grounds.

Juxtaposed with the claustrophobic space of their dormitory, the ride to the Packhorse Café where they meet the Girl, their future co-revolutionary, wordlessly expresses liberation. Their subsequent ride over a grass field is like a dance of freedom. But the motorcycle does not appear again. Indeed, the escape it symbolizes, not only here but in many films of the period, is rejected in favor of the violent engagement of armed retaliation.

Men in Blue

By 1973, the biker film series had come to an end. Taking its last drag too was the counterculture from which the biker series had borrowed some of its regalia and rhetoric. When *Electra Glide in Blue*, directed by James William Guercio, appeared that year, it positioned its protagonist, motorcycle officer Johnny Wintergreen, in self-conscious

Fig. 10. Still from Roger Corman's *The Wild Angels*, 1966.

alienation to both establishment and counterculture. Indeed, *Electra Glide* presents the motorcycle cop as lonely man (fig. 11). His bike does not represent freedom so much as stagnancy—an occupational cul-de-sac—an assignment and a uniform that he longs to trade in for the status of a detective's Stetson. The solitude of the motorcycle is reinforced by the film's setting in the Arizona desert. Johnny denies the fraternal favors asked first by a Los Angeles detective and then by a fellow Vietnam vet whom he pulls over, demonstrating loyalty only to what his patrol partner Zipper calls "PPP"—Proper Police Procedure. But Johnny's faith in upward mobility, and his access to the upper echelon of the police force, is thoroughly eroded by his brief tenure as driver for detective Harv Poole. The Western-style suit, the Stetson, and the comfort of a car turn out to be little incentive when paired with Harv's unharnessed ego

and brutal procedures. The alternative culture of the hippie commune is also closed off to him. And although Johnny eventually returns to his motorcycle assignment with his integrity intact, it is a return that not only signals loneliness but points him toward death. Johnny Wintergreen cannot be comfortably integrated with his generic ancestry, and the film consciously situates him inside and outside the biker film tradition. He not only shares the first name of Brando's character, but he also owns a duplicate of the racing trophy that Brando steals and gives to Kathy in *The Wild One*. As Johnny Wintergreen puts on his policeman's jacket, Guercio montages close-ups of zippers being pulled across leather, echoing Kenneth Anger's shots from *Scorpio Rising*. But Johnny does not have his friend Zipper's dream of the ultimate bike and, in fact, kills Zipper in self-defense just after the fantasy two-wheel chrome machine is unveiled. Moreover, Johnny does not identify with the *Easy Rider* myth. He does not ride through Monument Valley as a tourist, but works its lonely stretches of highway every day. In addition, he uses a poster of Billy and Captain America as a target for pistol practice. The film's ending offers a stunning reversal of the ending to Hopper's film. Narrative closure comes in the form of death on the highway, but this time it is the hippies in the painted VW van who pull the trigger, sending Johnny Wintergreen flying off his motorcycle.

Cops on motorcycles would come to television just a couple years later with *CHiPs* (1977–83), a mildly dramatic series featuring John and Ponch, two members of the California Highway Police. But on the Reagan-era Los Angeles freeway, motorcycles are vehicles of order, their riders maintaining a strict upright posture. Here the roles seem reversed: cars defy the law, tanker trucks catch on fire, and police bikes are the means by which danger and criminality get contained. The montage that accompanies the opening credits sequence isolates parts of the motorcycle—the headlights, front wheels, and side bags—and intercuts them with close-ups of the police insignia worn by the riders. Cutting from the bike to a gun tucked into its holster makes the point clear—the motorcycle is standard issue. It is an extension of the uniform. These bikes may be on the highway, but they are hardly on the road. They contribute to a type of static mobility, taking their riders not on a personal journey but on a circumscribed routine of patrol and pursuit.

Housewives and Ex-Felons

Subsequent motorcycle gang films had hardened the image of the biker as outlaw for his own cause into a cliché. Hollywood narratives such as *The Loveless* (1983) and *Streets of Fire* (1984) hardly reworked this image beyond self-conscious caricature. However, video documentaries produced within the biking subculture labored to retool the identity of the motorcyclist. Videos such as *Women and Motorcycles* (1990), produced by Courtney Caldwell, founder of the American Woman Road Rider Alliance, and Dave L. Perry, function primarily to debunk the male outlaw image. Caldwell's mission is twofold: Make the case that women are among motorcycling's greatest enthusiasts and redefine the female rider from biker chick to motorcycling professional. Her video begins with Wayne Thomas, founder of the California Motorcycle Association, describing the "typical" woman rider as "a housewife and maybe a parent, [but] probably also vice president of the bank or a school administrator." But as if to underscore the crucial link between remaking the biker's image and strategies of corporate marketing, a giant banner for the Harley-Davidson corporation is visible behind Thomas. Caldwell and her cast frequently invoke the terms *independence* and *freedom,* seeking to give political substance to what is in essence a recreational activity. Ultimately it is Caldwell who most explicitly reduces the meaning of the bike and the concept of independence to a banal and market-friendly cliché: "I want people to realize that it doesn't matter if you are a man or a woman. If you want to get out and do something—do it."

Alice Stone's *She Lives to Ride* (1994, fig. 12) provides a nice antidote to *Women and Motorcycles*, as it seeks not only to change the image of the woman rider but also to historicize it. Stone's documentary integrates profiles with personal and social history to suggest that these women carry on a tradition of female sporting. Between profiles, Stone uses archival footage to deliver brief history lectures. A voice-over tells of the Van Buren sisters, who rode their motorcycles from New York to San Francisco in 1916, and Bessie Stringfield, a black woman who rode across the country eight times in the early '30s, including a number of trips through the segregated South. Some of the women in *She Lives to Ride* repeat the familiar phrases about the bike as freedom machine, and several tell of the empowerment derived from sitting directly behind the handlebars, rather than behind a man.

The film also restores to the motorcycle its association with sport, travel, and adventure, without the hyperbolic rhetoric about rebellion. For these five women, the bike is a vehicle for physical pleasure and access to a community of other women. The economic implications of this image makeover are hard to overlook though, especially since Malcolm Forbes is referred to during two of the profiles. Jacqui Sturgess's ride for Gay Pride is followed by her participation in Forbes's annual spring motorcycle ride, during which several riders wear shirts declaring themselves "Capitalist Tools." Indeed, here is yet another aspect of the motorcyclist identity in the post–biker film era—proud member of consumer society. These bikers not only seek to put The Man on the cover of their magazines, they insist on their motorcycles being a vehicle of the middle class.

Sturgis 90: 50th Anniversary Rally (1990), produced by Big Sky Video, documents the golden anniversary of the annual biker rally that takes place in Sturgis, South Dakota. Here, the message that motorcycling bridges otherwise disparate populations is balanced with the the outlaw appearance of the riders, who wear denim and leather. Biking as the unifying force between class and regional difference is suggested near the beginning, as a woman at the rally explains: "From all walks of life, from people who maybe don't work, maybe on unemployment, to millionaires that own construction companies and they all become real close friends when you've got motorcycles involved."

Hollywood offered its own version of this in 1984, with Peter Bogdanovich's *Mask*. The accepting friends of Rocky Dennis, a teenager whose face has been deformed by a rare disease, are a community of motorcyclists. While others are either horrified by Rocky's appearance or initially resist his presence, the biker friends provide unconditional support. In this film, the outcasts understand the outcast. Back in Sturgis, you will find recovering drug addicts and alcoholics, Vietnam vets, and the Christian Motorcycle Club. Several rally attendees discuss riding in strictly therapeutic terms, as a means of finding relief from the tense world of work and family. Despite the impression that the rally is a rehab center on wheels, *Sturgis 90* draws upon the familiar rhetoric of freedom; its soundtrack repeats the lyric, "Livin' free and rollin' on down the road." But just so that the "livin' free" does not appear too

menacing, the KHOG radio voice-over assures listeners the bikers are just "on vacation like anybody else."

The motorcycle club (MC) as a site of healing finds its most explicit expression in *He Would've Rode a Harley* (1996) directed by Marybeth Bresolin. The film profiles the Soldiers for Jesus motorcycle club, a group of evangelical bikers. Ex-felons describe how the club provided them with both a creed and a community after prison, while other members confess to drug and alcohol abuse and womanizing, behaviors they have replaced with the mission of sharing the gospel along America's highways and at biker rallies.

But like its Hollywood predecessors, videos produced within the biking subculture during the '90s also implied that biking was more than a hobby, motorcycle riding could become both a reflection and an integral aspect of individual identity. Bikes were part religion, part fetish, and as such the motorcycle was an object made over in the image of its rider.

Kenneth Anger's 1963 underground classic *Scorpio Rising* produced a different image of the biker. Thirty years before the Soldiers for Jesus, Anger's men in leather were soldiers for the Antichrist. Anger's bikers worshiped Lucifer, celebrated drugs and death, and desired men, not women. Film scholars have pointed out how Anger's collage strategies and the juxtaposition of hetero love songs with shots of gay bikers reverse the sexual values attached to pop-culture icons such as Brando (in images from *The Wild One*) and present Christ as an ancient ancestor to the film's gay partygoers. Anger's film anticipated several elements at the stylistic center of the biker film series—the incorporation of pop music, the impulse toward a cinema free from studio constraints and narrative coherence, the explicit linking of bikers with Nazi regalia. In *Scorpio Rising*, the motorcycle joins the Hollywood image, the comic strip, and popular music as yet another industrial product to be rearticulated to the purposes of a culture at the margins of American society. Anger's collaging of images from the film *The Road to Jerusalem* and his appropriation of songs such as "My Boyfriend's Back" are akin to the mechanic's work being done by the bikers at the beginning of the film.

Scorpio Rising begins with shots of a biker working on his motorcycle, fine-tuning engine parts. In his study of the Hells Angels, Hunter S. Thompson also describes the biker as a type of makeover artist, as *bricoleur*. He regards the factory product only in terms of potential: "a bundle of good raw material, but hardly a machine that any man with class would want to call his own."[10]

But in *Scorpio Rising* the motorcycle is not just a retooled factory product, it is an emblem of death. Its assembly is watched over by a human skull, and throughout the course of the film it is associated with fatal injury, torture, criminality, and genocide. The pace and tone of the film begin to shift during the sequence in which footage of a motorcycle race is introduced. These are not the bikes we had seen being rebuilt at the beginning of the film, and their presence on screen signals a shift to a different filmic register—a new public location, outdoor photography, and perhaps different film stock. This footage is then intercut with Scorpio atop a church altar, where his actions grow increasingly violent and the camera increasingly unsteady. The soundtrack also suggests an emerging loss of control as the lyrics sing out: "I'm at the point of no return and for me there'll be no turning back." Soon afterward, a photograph of Adolph Hitler is introduced. As the song switches to "I Will Follow Him," motorcycles, religious faith, and political extremism are cut into an ambiguous montage that proves both humorous and menacing. With the song "Wipeout," the editing reaches its point of frenzy, culminating in the bike crash, death, and pulsing red light that ends the film. This last sequence not only continues the association enunciated by Cocteau, a linkage between death and the motorcycle found not just in bike films such as *Easy Rider* and *Electra Glide in Blue*, but also in David Lean's *Lawrence of Arabia* (1962) and Michael Powell and Emeric Pressburger's *A Matter of Life and Death* (1946). But the death at the end of *Scorpio Rising* is hardly accompanied by sorrow. It is simply the end of one man's race, a cold casualty.

Ultimately, *Scorpio Rising* is more interested in the men than in their machines. After the opening mechanical sequences, its camera prefers to linger over the bikers styling themselves—putting on chains and leather bracelets, zipping up jackets and choosing rings (fig. 13). In the biker-produced videos that document more contemporary rallies, the focus shifts back to the motorcycles. Whereas the look of the rally-goers has become dictated by convention—leather jackets, jeans, chaps, bikini tops for many of the women—it is the bikes that have become the site of fashion, of stylistic overload. Close-ups and slow pans over and across the machines present the motorcycle as a form of personal sculpture, adorned with feathers, animal horns, flags, rhinestones. These shots, like the still photography that fills motorcycle magazines, privilege stasis over motion, defining the bike as display piece and not just vehicle of the road. Whatever freedom is implied in these shots refers solely to the aesthetic license to remodel the factory product. Their owners are therefore not only bikers but artisans. They redesign, they paint, they tinker. The bike becomes something to be performed upon rather than simply on which to perform.

Bruce Brown's documentary *On Any Sunday* (1971) suggests that, for motorcycle racers, studying the bike at rest is a necessary precondition of racing it; it is a craft in both senses of the term. *On Any Sunday* functions as an introduction to the varied world of motorcycle racing, pivoting around profiles of two champion riders—Mert Lawwill and Malcolm Smith. It removes the machine from the confines of the motorcycle club, replacing the image of the outlaw or hipster with that of the American sportsman. For the Hollywood biker, as for his counterpart in the MC subculture, the motorcycle is part of an overall look, a component of personal style. The status it lends the individual is available to anyone who can afford a bike and learn to ride. Brown's motorcycles are, for the most part, the property and province of a select group of men, but neither Lawwill or Smith cut a particularly dashing figure. Brown introduces Lawwill by telling us he is five foot six, one hundred and forty-three pounds. Brown describes the racers contending for Lawwill's championship, declaring, "Not the Hollywood image, but highly skilled professionals." Ironically, the film seeks to escape the Hollywood image by using one of its biggest stars— Steve McQueen. It was McQueen, in fact, who performed in what is perhaps Hollywood's greatest motorcycle scene. In *The Great Escape* (1963), as the character Cooler King Hilts, McQueen flees the Germans by jumping his motorbike over a series of barbed-wire fences (fig. 14). Offscreen, McQueen raced motorcycles, and throughout *On Any Sunday*, it is clear he prefers the rugged world of bike racing to Hollywood glitter. When McQueen runs in the Elsinore Grand Prix, he is but one of fifteen hundred riders in the hundred-mile race. The voice-over proudly states: "If the movie studio moguls realized what he was doing on a Sunday afternoon, they'd have a coronary." By using an actor who's not acting, *On Any Sunday* can suggest that the big-screen image is for show, and its own image of the motorcycle world is the authentic one. That world is made up of clean-cut young men who rather than being part of a club spend up to eight months on the road traveling the race circuit. Brown presents Mert Lawwill as a solitary figure, working late at night in his garage, spending a thousand hours a year meticulously refining his engines, shaving a few ounces off a gear or cutting additional tread into his tires to get a competitive edge.

On Any Sunday presents not just an alternative to the MC biker, real or cinematic, but to his bike as well. Here the "hog" is replaced by bikes adapted for a variety of trials and terrains. Yet here, too, the identity of the motorcycle as uncontainable machine continues, for throughout the film, the bike is primarily imaged as an off-road vehicle, something that constantly requires new settings or events beyond the typical stretch of highway. We see motorcycles negotiating muddy motor-cross trails, reeling around ice tracks set in ten-below temperatures, climbing steep hills, forced through the rough Spanish countryside, crossing the desert near Las Vegas, roaring around the Daytona Speedway, racing through the streets of Elsinore, California, and coasting over sandy beaches next to the Pacific.

The bike is defined as graceful yet rugged, liberating yet dangerous. Indeed, underlying its every move is potential danger. Motorcycles on film always carry the threat of a crash, and the crash represents the machine's ultimate, autonomous performance. Bike races are dramatic not just because of their speed or the surrounding stories of the individuals in competition, but because they occasionally display, if only for a moment, that point at which the driver has lost control, that moment when the machine reaches the limits of its independence and the bike no longer appears to be steering itself, its front wheel wavers, and it descends into its inevitable crash and slide. At this point, driver and cycle achieve an equal status, reduced to matter thrown out of balance by the force of speed. Here is the motorcycle as attraction, spinning free of the race and its own narrative, off course, making a spectacle of itself.

In the late '60s and through the mid '70s, this moment of danger was distilled and broadcast regularly on American television in the daredevil stunts of Evel Knievel. Perhaps no individual was more closely associated with the motorcycle, at least among the general public, than Knievel, and few pieces of sports movie footage would be repeated as often as that of his jump and crash at Caesar's Palace on January 1, 1968. In that footage, Knievel flies straight at us, the camera located parallel to the arc of his jump. When the rear wheel of his bike touches down, it does not quite make the ramp and he is immediately jarred loose, his hands coming off the handlebars, his body bouncing upward. Knievel flips over and lands on the back of his neck and then his back. He rolls over three times, all the while skidding and sliding toward and to the left of the camera. Meanwhile, the riderless motorcycle stays upright at first, as if it has successfully made the jump on its own. But eventually the front wheel begins to waver directionless, the bike falls on its right side and slides on the pavement in front of Knievel. The daredevil would remain unconscious in the hospital for thirty days. Knievel was, in fact, heir to earlier stunt riders who had performed in circuses or carnivals in attractions that played off the bike's image by trapping it within some type of enclosure. These stunts often featured a bike running upside-down loops inside a cage or driving centrifugally reinforced laps around a miniature wooden track. Hollywood produced its own versions, *Evel Knievel* (1972) starring George Hamilton, and *Viva Knievel!* (1977), but it is as singular phenomenon rather than biographical subject that Knievel is important. In fact, the latter film, which stars the daredevil as himself and locates him as the target of a murder plotted by drug dealers, only underscores the bad fit between Knievel the stuntman and the processes of narrative (fig. 15). The contrived scenario and ludicrously clichéd action and dialogue, painfully inflicted on costar Gene Kelly, testify to the bike jumper as attraction and not story.

However, it is the Caesar's Palace footage, shot by John Derrick and actress Linda Evans, that captures so precisely those aspects of the motorcycle that had come to define its identity on film: uncontainable still, as it floats through midair, its wheels still turning, defying gravity and even its definition as a machine of the road; a vehicle of peril, exposing its rider, be it Buster Keaton's Sherlock Jr., Marlon Brando's Johnny, or Evel Knievel, to danger and possibly death; giving the impression of autonomy as it descends the ramp and continues on its own. The only act in its own circus, the bike may look like Vertov's "poetry of levers, wheels and wings of steel," but it is a singular, individualized spectacle. It is the motorized offer of freedom or death.

Acknowledgement and notes

My thanks to Frank Arnold for his generosity in supplying numerous tapes for the writing of this essay.

1. Dziga Vertov, *Kino-Eye: The Writings of Dziga Vertov*, ed. and with an introduction by Annette Michelson (Berkeley: University of California Press, 1984), p. 9.

2. Vertov, p. 8.

3. Vertov, p. 30.

4. Vertov, p. 8.

5. Hunter S. Thompson, *Hell's Angels: The Strange and Terrible Saga of the Outlaw Motorcycle Gangs* (New York: Ballantine Books, 1967), p. 85.

6. The discussion that follows is indebted to two scholars who have written about motorcycle films. See Martin Rubin, "Make Love Make War: Cultural Confusion and the Biker Film Cycle," *Film History* 6, pp. 355–81; and Frank Arnold, "Ordinary Motorcycle Thrills: The Circulation of Motorcycle Meanings in American Film and Popular Culture," (Ph.D. diss., University of Southern California, 1997).

7. Rubin, p. 366.

8. Both Arnold and Rubin take recourse to film historian Tom Gunning's concept of the cinema of attractions; that is, the way in which early cinema was devoted more to displaying spectacle than integrating mise-en-scène and editing into the service of a dominating narrative. See Rubin, pp. 365, 371–72; Arnold, pp. 232–35.

9. Thompson, p. 313.

10. Thompson, p. 122.

Fig. 14. Still from John Sturges's *The Great Escape*, 1963.

Fig. 15. Still from Gordon Douglas's *Viva Knievel!*, 1977.

Ikuya Sato

Bosozoku
(motorcycle gangs)

Bosozoku *in Their Heyday*

Imagine a weekend night in the summer, the most popular and congested streets in metropolises across Japan exploding with sounds that startle and deafen pedestrians. Tens, easily hundreds, of *bosozoku*, members of Japanese motorcycle gangs, are terrorizing the cities. Motorcycles, their original appearance modified beyond recognition, and souped-up automobiles roar down the streets en masse at speeds twice those posted and three times those most drivers can manage in Japan's urban congestion. Some of the motorcycles that *bosozoku* use look like "chopped hogs," the customized Harley 74s favored by the Hells Angels, while the automobiles are similar to "low riders" in the United States. Yet, *bosozoku* themselves—young, well groomed, and carefully dressed in elegant if bizarre costumes, including some reminiscent of kamikaze party uniforms—do not at all resemble American gang members. Interestingly, however, *bosozoku* are also referred to as "Yankees." Dismounted from their vehicles and hanging around street corners, their hair permed and eyebrows and hairlines shaved, they look like *yakuza*, criminal gangsters. They prowl the streets in groups seeking "action," including occasional gang fights. But what these gangs live for is *boso*—high-speed and high-risk driving on city streets. That is why they became known as *bosozoku*, the tribe (*zoku*) of those who devote themselves to unlawful and often fatal racing (*boso*).

One frequently witnessed scenes such as the above in the mid 1970s through the early '80s. *Bosozoku* were one of the major youth problems in Japan. The 1981 edition of the *White Paper on the Police,* published from the National Police Agency, reflected the official view of the motorcycle gangs at that time. It included a feature article on *bosozoku*. Occupying about one-sixth of the issue, this article treated *bosozoku* as the first reserve of *yakuza*. Also in 1981, a major Japanese newspaper reported, erroneously, that *bosozoku* committed one-fourth of all criminal offenses in Japan and were responsible for making that year's record of juvenile delinquency the worst in the country's history. News reports of similar sort were fairly common during the '70s and '80s.

Information about the size alone of the *bosozoku* population was enough to cause moral hysteria among the citizens of Japan. In the ten-year period between 1973 and 1983,

Fig. 1. Image of the "picaro."

the number of young people associated with motorcycle gangs rose from about 12,500 to 39,000, involving an estimated 24,000 vehicles. During the same period, the number of arrests for *bosozoku* activity increased from some 28,000 to 54,819 cases, including 48,278 traffic and 6,541 criminal citations.

Several measures were taken to circumvent *bosozoku*, including the amendment of traffic laws and media and civil campaigns against gang activities. The most effective of those steps was the revision of the traffic laws in 1981 that reinforced penal sanctions against collective driving. From 1980 to 1983 the number of participants and vehicles in *boso* driving fell by more than half. The number of youths involved in gang fights in 1983 was less than one-seventh of that for 1980. Although the news media have occasionally reported *bosozoku*-related incidents since 1982, in most cases such occurrences have been treated as solitary incidents and not as symptoms of nationwide moral decay among Japanese youths. *Bosozoku*, once regarded as the most heinous of social evils, have been largely expelled from media reports and exorcised from the public mind.

Fig. 2. Intermission of a *boso* drive.

Precursors of Bosozoku: Kaminari-zoku and Circuit-zoku

The *bosozoku* are not a completely novel phenomenon. Motorcycle gangs have existed in Japan since the mid '50s. Advancing motorization and the emergence of affluent youths were the major catalysts of the first generation, and *bosozoku* are the third generation of motorcycle gangs in postwar Japan, following two antecedent tribes—*kaminari-zoku* (thunder tribe) and *circuit-zoku* (circuit tribe). Yet, it was not until the '70s, with the explosive growth of the *bosozoku*, that such gangs became a serious public concern, eliciting a unified societal reaction of nationwide proportions.

The motorcycle gangs that first appeared in the mid '50s were not comprised of members of clearly defined groups. Participants in these gangs often referred to themselves as *otokichi* (motorbike maniacs or sound freaks) and were, in most cases, either sons of wealthy families or auto mechanics who had access to motorcycles that were still too expensive for ordinary youths. A chance encounter among riders was enough reason for group driving. It was the public and mass media that imputed the assumed characteristics of collective enterprise by assigning the label *kaminari-zoku* to these impromptu gangs. This reference derived from the loud exhaust noise emitted by the youths' mufflerless motorcycles.

By the mid '60s, motorization in Japan had advanced further and vehicles became cheaper, and gangs came to use cars as well as motorcycles. Three names were applied to the gangs during this period: *thrill-zoku*, *Mach-zoku*, and *circuit-zoku*, the last being the most popular. A relatively large number of youths from various socio-economic backgrounds joined in gang activities. Toward the end of this period, several incidents occurred in which gangs attracted large audiences—varying from a few hundred to about a thousand—who congregated in parks and the streets. While these incidents were easily controlled by the police, several later events occurred between 1967 and 1972 in some western prefectures in which motorcycle gangs and their audiences grew into mobs that destroyed cars and stores. The most serious of these was the *Toyama Jiken* (Toyama Incident) in 1972, in which the mob numbered over 3,000 and 1,104 people were arrested. After that incident, the gangs attracted media attention, and the name *bosozoku* came into wide use to reflect their aggressive behavior. Many similar episodes followed throughout Japan, and the number of youths joining *bosozoku* groups increased. The gangs developed relatively articulated organizational arrangements, even forming intergroup confederations.

Fig. 3. *Boso* driving.

In the *kaminari-zoku* period (from the mid '50s to the mid '60s), motorcycle gangs were treated as a "bunch of noisy kids." Occasional traffic accidents, and the public's annoyance with exhaust noise, sometimes attracted media attention and led to calls for strengthened police regulation. But the gangs were often viewed as "victims" entrapped in behavior that emphasized "speed and thrills."

This perception was still predominant during the *circuit-zoku* period (from the mid '60s to the mid '70s): in fact, the term *kaminari-zoku* continued to be used as frequently as *circuit-zoku*. Even the mob outbreaks between 1967 and 1972 did little to change the relatively benign image of motorcycle gangs. News reports portrayed the groups involved as rioters or as a hot-blooded, disorderly crowd. Nonetheless, deviant behavior among the gangs was largely attributed to "crowd psychology," and spectators as well as gangs were blamed.

The situation changed dramatically during the height of the *bosozoku* period (from the mid '70s to the early '80s), when gang membership nearly tripled. Crimes committed by individual *bosozoku* youths, as well as *boso* driving and gang fights, began to appear in headlines. The expressions "criminals," "delinquents," and "criminal group" were frequently used in news reports. Motorcycle gangs were depicted as full-fledged villains or, indeed, as devils who should be "expelled" or "eradicated." During this period, the social drama featuring motorcycle gangs increasingly acquired the overtones of a morality play or sacrificial drama. The phenomenal growth of *bosozoku* in the '70s and early '80s is at least in part an artifact of the increased vigilance and census-taking effort by the police. Yet, the easy access to vehicles and the sheer momentum of numbers, characteristic of collective behavior, as well as the increased media attention to the gang activities shapes the general backgrounds of the actual increase in the number of Japanese youths taking part in these activities.

Boso *Driving*

The most distinctive activity of *bosozoku* is boso driving. What *bosozoku* call a *shinai boso* (*boso* driving on city roads) includes both driving at breakneck high speeds and showing off before passersby or onlookers on the busiest of city streets. A *boso* drive starts from a certain assembly point, usually a city park or parking lot. Members of a *bosozoku* group or several *bosozoku* groups come together at an appointed time. These arrangements are made at the previous *boso* drive or at a conference of *bosozoku* leaders called for that purpose. The number of participants in a drive varies from ten to over one hundred. Quite often its size expands in the course of the night through the recruitment of observers' vehicles.

A *boso* drive consists of several sessions of high-risk races throughout a night broken by intermissions. The length of each session varies from one to two hours. The speed of a *boso* drive depends on several factors, including the density of traffic and the condition of the road. Speeds usually vary from 70–100 km/h (43–62 mph) on city streets whose speed limits average 40–50 km/h (25–31 mph). Although the course of a *boso* drive is decided and transmitted to the participants beforehand, it is frequently changed according to the numerous contingencies that tend to accompany a drive: for example, an unexpectedly high number of police cars or the exceptional density of traffic. Changes in the course are indicated by the *sento-sha* (front vehicle), which maintains a position at the head of the band. The leader of the *bosozoku* group fills this role. When several groups join in a *boso* drive, one of the groups usually takes charge of sponsoring and coordinating the *boso* driving. In such a case, the leader of the sponsoring group occupies the front spot. A group flag flying from a motorcycle or a car indicates the name of the host group. The member who holds the flag is called *hatamochi* (flag holder).

Several measures are taken to prevent the band from becoming disorganized and to cope with various risks. While the participants are free to race each other, no one should pass the *sento-sha*. Also, a few automobiles are in charge of *shingo heisa* (intersection blocking), which involves blocking the traffic intersecting the course of the drive by making loud exhaust noises and sounding horns, as well as physically blocking the intersection. Automobiles in the front part of the band also clear out the course by intimidating ordinary motorists with their exhaust noises and horns. Motorcycles in the rear position of the band engage in *ketsumakuri* (tail wagging) to hinder pursuit by the police. When police cars reach the tail of the band, these vehicles step back and zigzag until the band gains sufficient distance on the police.

If the drive goes smoothly, *bosozoku* youths perform various acrobatic driving techniques for their fellow gang members and passersby. Techniques include *yonshasen kama* (zigzagging across four lanes), *hanabi* (fireworks; making sparks by striking an asphalt pavement with the kickstand of a motorcycle), and *raidaa chenji* (rider change; interchanging riding positions while driving a vehicle).

At the end of a *boso* drive, participants reassemble in a designated place. When the drive includes several gangs, each band regroups in its respective territory. Not all participants get to this point. Some may have dropped out and some may have been arrested during the *boso* drive. Among those who arrive at the reassembly point, some fall asleep as soon as they get there being relieved from the tensions of the high-risk driving, and some continue to engage in acrobatic performances or drag races. Eventually, the leader of each group announces that it is time to break up. The youths go home in the light of dawn.

Bosozoku *Paraphernalia: Customized Motorcycles and Costumes*

Boso driving causes a great hazard to city traffic and frightens citizens, but onlookers may also be shocked and annoyed by the outrageous paraphernalia *bosozoku* use during their drives. The unrestrained nature of *bosozoku* imagery, as well as *boso* driving itself, seems to testify to the public perception of *bosozoku* as diabolical figures. The paraphernalia include customized vehicles, costumes, and other artifacts.

For *bosozoku*, a factory motorcycle, which they call *nomaru* (normal), is nothing but raw material. They modify the *nomaru* vehicles into *kaizosha* (modified vehicles) of their own style. Motorcycles are usually called by nicknames. In most cases these are acronyms derived from the original manufacturer's model number, for example, *Pekejei* (Yamaha XJ400), *Efupeke* (Kawasaki FX400), *Jiesu* (Suzuki GS400), and *Zettsu* (Kawasaki Z750F).

To outside observers, *bosozoku* motorcycles appear to be quite alike. Indeed, informants' answers to questions about their modification procedures were very similar. The following response was typical: "Well, first of all I put on a *shugo* [custom header pipe]. Then, I painted the body and made the handlebars *shibori* [created the effect of squeezed handlebars]. You may want to put in a *sanren* [three-trumpet horn]. Some may use a Beet's point cover. I also put on a *hotaru* [lightning bug]."

Fig. 4. Modified motorcycle.

A *shugo* is an exhaust system that consists of a multiple-tube header and a single collector pipe connected to one muffler. A *shugo* may increase horsepower and improve acceleration, even if the engine itself is not custom-made. But it is for greater sound rather than increased power that *bosozoku* youths install their own exhaust systems. A *shugo* generates a high-pitched exhaust noise. While driving, *bosozoku* youths often race their engines two or three times in rapid succession. When this is done twice, the exhaust creates a sound like *hon, hoon! Bosozoku* call this procedure *daburu akuseru* (double acceleration). Done three times—then called *toripuru akuseru* (triple acceleration—the sound is like *hon, hon, hoon!* Bike riders usually take the diffuser pipes and the fiberglass packing out of the mufflers in order to further "improve" the sound.

The horn also contributes to these sound effects. The names *sanren* (three-trumpet horn) and *yonren* (four-trumpet horn) are derived from the number of horns connected vertically to each other. The horns are different lengths and make sounds of different pitch. They are fitted in combination with small air compressors on the backs of the bikes. *Bosozoku* youths call them music horns because they play specific melodies by relay. (In the United States such devices are called musical air-blast horns or air horns.) The number of horns varies from one to ten; bikes are usually equipped with three or four. Some automobiles are also outfitted with music horns, one large horn that plays various melodies from a computer chip.

Some modifications are aimed specifically at visual appeal. Many *bosozoku* paint the bodies of their bikes in primary colors. In particular, they write and draw figures on the gasoline tank. There are also many varieties of accessories (for example, decorative mirrors, custom-made covers) of different shapes and colors. Accessories allow for extreme specialization, especially those with definite visual impact, such as fenders, side (frame) covers, and point (distributor) covers. Beet, mentioned in the quote above, is one of the most prestigious brand names for accessories of this sort. Other well-known brands include Napoleon, Moriwaki, Yoshimura, and Select. Brand names are often clearly shown in relief or as emblems on parts.

Because *boso* driving takes place at night, lights are important for visual attraction. There are as many varieties of headlights and turn signals as there are choices of other accessories. Turn signals can be connected with "high flashers," relays that regulate flickering of the lights. A *hotaru* (lightning bug) is a tiny blue lamp that can be fitted to the back of a bike. Used for its visual appeal, it is purely ornamental and does not serve as a tail lamp.

There are some modifications that affect drivability. A *shibori* is a set of handlebars that are bent almost double. While other motorcyclists also use custom-made handlebars, though less extreme, *shibori* are illegal and used almost exclusively by *bosozoku*. Some motorcycles are also power-jumped by increasing the size of the bore and the length of stroke. This modification is called *boa appu* (bore up). Harder suspension coils and shock absorbers, tires with special tread patterns, and racer seats also enhance the sensation of driving: that is, they communicate the motion of the vehicle more directly to the rider.

A strong visual impression is made by the *bosozoku* themselves as well as by their vehicles. Two salient characteristics of *bosozoku* costumes and other artifacts are their extreme expressiveness and apparent affinity with nationalist symbols. One of the items that displays both these qualities is *tokkofuku*, the costume of the kamikaze bombers. While the classic and more orthodox combination of leather jacket and jeans has been prevalent throughout the history of Japanese motorcycle gangs, *tokkofuku* came into wide use during the *bosozoku* period. *Tokkofuku* literally means the uniform of kamikaze bombers.

However, whereas the original suicidal military group wore coveralls, the customary uniform for pilots on fighter-bombers, the *tokkofuku* of *bosozoku* are working clothes, chiefly a dark blue or black jacket and pants. Therefore the connection between original kamikaze uniform and *bosozoku tokkofuku* is often more from psychological association than from actual similarity in shape and color. *Bosozoku* youths even wear pink, white, or red *tokkofuku*.

A group name is usually sewn with gold or silver thread on the backs of *tokkofuku* jackets. It may also be stitched into the upper sleeves or onto the upper left pocket. Other symbols used on *tokkofuku* include the rising sun, the Imperial chrysanthemum crest, and words or phrases suggesting nationalism, such as "patriot," or "Protection of the Nation and Respect for His Majesty." Military ranks (e.g., "Captain of the Kamikaze Corps," "Maximum Leader") and personal names are also used.

Sentofuku as well as *tokkofuku* are often worn by *bosozoku*. *Sentofuku* means "combat uniform." The *bosozoku* version is a dark blue coverall made of cotton. Originally such a coverall was standard dress for right-wing organizations. As in the case of *tokkofuku*, group names and nationalist symbols are sewn into *sentofuku*, which are frequently worn with leather lace-up boots.

Hachimaki (headbands) and surgical masks are often used in combination with *tokkofuku* and *sentofuku*. The rising sun or the Imperial chrysanthemum crest is usually printed or embroidered in the middle of the *hachimaki*. Group names or nationalist slogans are sometimes written on the masks with pen.

The psychological association of nationalism with *bosozoku* arising from the outfits and symbols mentioned thus far may be strengthened if one perceives the group flag *bosozoku* use as the most important sign of collective identity during a *boso* drive. It is usually held by the *hatamochi* on the pillion seat of a motorcycle. The group name or emblem, sometimes both, are displayed on the flag. *Bosozoku* youths may use a national flag swiped from others' homes; often, however, they have group flags made to order. Custom-made flags frequently display the rising sun or the Imperial chrysanthemum crest. Group flags have strong visual appeal, and thus works about *bosozoku* by journalists often have pictures of gang members showing their flags. During intergang fights, *bosozoku* often steal and tear up their opponents' flags. Sometimes flags are turned in to the police when groups are dissolved. *Bosozoku* youths also may hold a sort of ceremony to commemorate their "graduation" from gang activities. These ritual performances attest to the temporally circumscribed nature of the gang activities, which we will see shortly.

The Attraction of Bosozoku

The extreme physical risks involved in *boso* driving and the outrageous nature of *bosozoku* paraphernalia seem to be good grounds for imputing irrationality and pathology to *bosozoku*. Indeed the Japanese mass media have portrayed *bosozoku* youths either as juvenile delinquents or as dropouts suffering from chronic inferiority complexes arising from their poor academic pedigrees. In this portrayal, the seemingly irrational behavior of motorcycle gangs is explained as being a way of evading frustrations, or a way of expressing frustrations inherent in the role of dispossessed youths.

But studies of *bosozoku* suggest a quite different picture of *bosozoku* youths and their activities. Field research based on participant observation over a year shows that the activities involved in *boso* driving provide positive reasons for participation. *Boso* driving turns out to be a creative dramaturgical form, cleverly crafted to provide a temporarily heightened sense of self to the participants through the enactment of a heroic role in front of the public. The outrageous paraphernalia are important stage props to present the *bosozoku* as special types of heroes (or antiheroes), who are also referred to as "tricksters" or "picaros" in literary studies and anthropological literature. Nationalist symbols serve as convenient ready-made props. On the one hand, *bosozoku* can gain attention and shock people by using these symbols, which are associated with fanaticism and violence. On the other hand, the connection to discipline and order implicit in nationalist symbols appeals to *bosozoku* youths.

In addition, the high thrills of *boso* driving provide a euphoric sense, or what Mihalyi Csikszentmihalyi[3] calls "flow." At the peak of such a euphoric experience, one has a sense of belonging to a community and a shared feeling of collective effervescence, similar to the euphoria induced by certain carnivals or ecstatic rituals. A female *bosozoku* described her experience as follows:

> I . . . I understand something, when all of our feelings get tuned up. . . . At the start, when we are running, we are not in complete harmony. But if the *boso* drive begins going well, all of us—all of us—feel for each other. How can I say this? When we wag the tail of the band. . . . When our minds become one. At such a time, it's a real pleasure. . . . When we realize that we become one flesh, it's supreme. When we get high on speed. At such a moment, it's really super.

Bosozoku activities are, therefore, fundamentally playlike activities. Their intensity derives from the limit on adolescence imposed on Japanese youths. Most *bosozoku* members, indeed, graduate from gang activities by their early 20s to settle down as "ordinary

Fig. 5. Menacing poses by "Ladies," female *boso* riders.

citizens." There are strong age norms shared by peer groups, which proscribe the continuation of "childish" activities beyond certain ages. Such age norms also encourage disengagement from the action-oriented life style of the street. While many ex-*bosozoku* members maintain a love for vehicles after leaving their gangs, very few of them would consider riding on a customized and heavily decorated motorcycle again.

Bosozoku *in the '90s*

The influential age norms of peer groups and the reinforcement of penal sanctions against *boso* driving and other gang activities are two major factors that led to the sharp decline of *bosozoku* activities in the early 1980s. The heightened violence of gang activities simply became too risky to be playlike and was not worthy of pursuing any longer. The situation has not changed much in the 1990s. Each year the *White Paper on the Police*, which tends to overemphasize the seriousness of various types of crimes and exaggerate the police's efforts to contain them, estimates the number of youths associated with *bosozoku* activity to be over thirty thousand. However, even the *White Paper* acknowledges that the majority of those *bosozoku* youths are not members of tightly organized gang groups.

Nowadays, the heroic image of *bosozoku* survives mainly in the popular media, especially in youth-oriented comic magazines. In such publications, *bosozoku* youths are portrayed as "good guys"—stoic and chivalric heroes who are contrasted with law-abiding, but hypocritical, "ordinary citizens." It is telling that the *bosozoku* heroes in fictive representations, in the majority of cases, ride on motorbikes rather than automobiles, while actual *bosozoku* youths use cars as well. The themes of masculinity and bravado associated with motorcycles have great appeal to those Japanese youths who have few other ways of self-dramatization.

It is unlikely that *bosozoku* or any other form of motorcycle gang activities will mobilize a sizable number of youths in Japan in the foreseeable future. Yet the bodily sensations characteristic of motorcycle riding and the promise of an action-oriented life style implicit in certain styles of motorcycles may generate another cultural myth, one that can satisfy the urges of Japanese youths for novel types of collective behavior, expressed through the medium of motorcycles.

Fig. 6. Modified automobile.

Notes

1. This essay is based on the ethnographic research detailed in Ikuya Sato's *Kamikaze Biker: Anomy and Parody in Affluent Japan* (Chicago: University of Chicago Press, 1991).

2. *Bosozoku* use automobiles as well as motorcycles, but for brevity's sake I will concentrate on motorcycles here. For typical modifications added to *bosozoku* automobiles, see *Kamikaze Biker*, pp. 43–45.

3. Mihalyi Csikszentmilhalyi, *Beyond Boredom and Anxiety* (San Francisco: Jossey-Bass, 1975).

Melissa Holbrook Pierson

To the Edge: Motorcycles and Danger

On motorcycles, up the road, they come:
Small, black, as flies hanging in heat, the Boys,
Until the distance throws them forth, their hum
Bulges to thunder held by calf and thigh.
In goggles, donned impersonality,
In gleaming jackets trophied with the dust,
They strap in doubt—by hiding it, robust—
And almost hear a meaning in their noise.

. . . .

A minute holds them, who have come to go:
The self-defined, astride the created will
They burst away; the towns they travel through
Are home for neither bird nor holiness,
For birds and saints complete their purposes.
At worst, one is in motion; and at best,
Reaching no absolute, in which to rest,
One is always nearer by not keeping still.

—Thom Gunn, "On the Move" (1967)

In Jean Cocteau's *Orpheus*, the black-clad, helmeted emissaries of Death ride motorcycles. They are at once wraiths from the other side, so quick you are not even sure you've seen them, and young hipsters straight out of the 1950 café scene. The ominous buzz of their motors precedes their materialization at the edge of the frame, and they racket off the scene at the same wild speed with which the beautiful Death herself appears and disappears, unbidden but imperative.

Perhaps because they are so apparently fragile—unable to stand by themselves, relatively small and light, and visually nothing but mechanical doilies—motorcycles are the ideal vehicles for danger. Both are sudden to arrive, quick to consume, and perverse in their ways. Neither is a stranger to paradox—the deceptive motorcycle least of all, for a huge power hides in its fragility.

It is not necessary for motorcyclists to know this; just because we are loath to admit something doesn't mean it isn't so. Anyway, they say that love is blind. But this play between danger and security, light and dark, is the very electrical current that animates this machine love of ours.

What the biker feels, and what she will readily admit to, is that she loves to ride for the joy of it—unpasteurized, undiluted, straight-from-the-can joy. This is the state of happy innocence in which most riders ride. It encloses them in a glossy bubble of pleasure, soaking them in a warm bath of endorphins. Then someone invariably comes along, pop, and lets fly the deflating dart: "But bikes are so dangerous!"

What could be more dangerous, however, than the statement itself, given that it, too, is an unexamined response? "Danger" is a loaded concept for a species as beset by fears of all kinds as ours is. So beset—by the foreknowledge of mortality, by various devils, by the possibility that our buried sadnesses will rise up to haunt us—that we have become masters of displacement. There is no more artful example of this skill than the story of how motorcycles came to be synonymous with danger.

Fig. 1. Still from Jean Cocteau's *Orpheus*, 1950.

The tale is confused: the motorcycle is dangerous to the rider; its pleasures are a danger to morality; the biker is dangerous to society. People tend to say the first, but they imply the latter two.

Motorcycle riders have long been seen as caring little about spilling their own blood, and so by extension have been feared as bloodthirsty. Bike racers and the bikers who like to watch them are considered altogether outsized characters, whether intrepid or uncivil. In a 1935 short story about dirt-track racing, Horace McCoy described the fans the sport attracts: "The majority came out just to hear somebody's skull crack (you may not think you can hear a skull crack with all those exhausts popping, but you can, you most certainly can) or to see somebody's brains spilled in the dirt."[1]

But the great majority of motorcyclists are not in fact murderous. Nor are they suicidal. They are, instead, like experienced climbers, who, as Yi-fu Tuan writes, in *Landscapes of Fear*, "abhor danger while welcoming risk, because risk presents difficulties that can be estimated and controlled."[2]

People who ride are not fundamentally masochistic or gripped by a death wish; one doesn't get much more normal, really. Rather, although motorcyclists may not know it, they are seeking "eustress," the scientific term for that pleasurable stress found in the mastery of risky sports. The term recalls a snatch of verse that in hundreds of popular appearances is always attributed though never with a precise citation to Apollinaire, making it an epigraphic counterpart to the urban legend whose factual origin can never be found. In this form it has been thoroughly colonized by parachutists and New Age banner men:

> Come to the edge, He said.
> They said, We are afraid.
> Come to the edge, He said.
> They came.
> He pushed them . . .
> And they flew.

Fig. 2. Still from Peter Bogdanovich's *Mask*, 1985.

One suspects, however, that people who choose to go up in Piper Cubs, or conquer icy mountains, or jump off bridges with elastics tied to their ankles don't hear that annoying, "But what you're doing is so dangerous" business half as often as motorcyclists, who justifiably perceive the warning as something more than mere observation. (Pilots, mountain climbers, and the rest are also more likely to be lionized as heroic or brave.) One hears this sort of comment so often, in part because seemingly every other person on the planet has personally known someone who has been crushed, dismembered, or grated like a carrot by a bad spill from a bike. But one hears it also because the denunciation of the vehicle stands in for a denunciation of its owner, who has engaged in the immoral (and illegal) act of putting his own life at risk. Any tendency to self-injury is seen as an assault on the cult of the sacredness of life, which we loudly profess but to which we only sporadically adhere.

Here, I think, is the other part of the story. Bikes have many virtues, prime among them, their high bang-for-the-buck ratio. They are much faster than cars, sinuously fun, and cheap. Thus their riders, already selected from the small pool of those for whom safety (often a code word for civility) is second to thrill, come largely from the bottom half of the socioeconomic pile. That is also where society locates, either in fact or fiction, its criminals, sinners, or time bombs. In this sense, the debasement of motorcycles is just another symptom of how little we have progressed from the 19th-century notion that financial poverty mirrors spiritual corruption. Even the idea of a threat from this vicinity is so toxic that its taint can spread to anything it contacts, so that a black leather jacket alone can strike fear in the heart of the beholder.

Neither is the sense of joyful abandon conferred by riding a bike above moral suspicion—especially when the other activity to which it is most commonly compared is often still considered proper only between married partners. The cause is not further advanced by the predilection for two-wheeled conveyance of such high-profile groups as the Hells Angels, or the frequent use of urban Jap-bike screamers as little more than boom boxes with rearview mirrors.

The word *bad* shadows the heels of, and in fact is often interchanged with, danger in the minds of those who behold the modern age's fearsome centaur. (Certainly, motorcycles' actual sound often makes them seem menacing. This makes bikes especially attractive to thuggish types, no less than to those on the other side of the law.) The long line of exploitation movies triggered by *The Wild One* (1954) cemented this alliance into a cliché so obdurate that the only thing left to do was to flip it over to create the expectation-reversing *Mask* (1985), in which the biker heroes are largely good, compassionate human beings.

Let us not forget, though, the very real allure of perversity, however minor its manifestation. Our linguistic reversals often display our truest feelings, as when *bad* becomes good, which it always does in the imaginations of those for whom the slightly dangerous character is the most luscious one of all. Thus in the slang of the '70s, "She's so *bad*" unequivocally meant, "Would you feast your eyes on that!"

The statement that motorcycles are dangerous also seems incomplete. What's missing? Perhaps a prepositional phrase describing to whom they pose a threat. Are they dangerous to the arbiters of morality? To us? To the perennially fearful? Or to those who equate wealth with virtue? Only one conclusion is possible: Since that which is distasteful to say can be made palatable by displacement, as any good psychotherapist will tell you, here the dangerous motorcyclist becomes the dangerous motorcycle; the rider becomes his mount. (This may well explain the otherwise inscrutable chorus to the Storey Sisters' minor hit of the early '60s: "He's a bad motorcycle.")

Given the enticing flirtation with danger that is essential to riding, the conflation is even more understandable. You might even go one step further, all the way to the primal scene, since it is how closely you bind with your machine that determines how close you can get to "the edge"—and thus how good it feels.

I have never meant to imply that the reputation of motorcycles as dangerous is a complete accident of circumstance. Only a fool would deny the fact that it is quite easy, should one wish, to ride off the road, at 80 or a 100 miles per hour, a machine whose sole protective covering is air. It is also fairly easy, by taking such hardly onerous measures as wearing a helmet, driving while sober, and enrolling in rider-education classes, to mitigate exponentially the peril. Sense dictates that an unlicensed teenager wearing flip-flops and dodging highway traffic on a vehicle that is about to lose a brake caliper bolt is in a different risk class from the rider who wears full leathers and always does a safety check before mounting.

There are indeed many avoidable dangers associated with riding motorcycles—including the lure of romanticizing them into nothing less than the chariots of hell, or the vehicle that slips the bonds of mortal earth; including the trap of getting lost forever in those 174 pages entitled "Motorcycle Accident Cause Factors and Identification of Countermeasures."[3]

But a culture with an inborn taste of blood in its mouth is naturally drawn only to the most lurid possibilities; we are rarely in the mood for minor crack-ups with happy endings, and we are hostile to reasoned explanation. Cut to the chase! Far better to believe—as do some bandannaed bikers in strange concert with their upstanding-citizen antagonists—that the flaming skull on the "Ride Hard, Die Free" bumper sticker tells some primal truth about life and how it can be lived. This notion frankly says more about the most primal anxiety of all—whether we have any say in the matter. In the meanwhile, by throwing caution and its attendant sense of responsibility to the wind, we sedate our anxiety. The price for this numbing relief comes, oddly enough, in the form of physical pain. Road rash has this funny way of showing up on those who least expect it.

I mean, if danger is something that always comes along for the ride, what's the point in carefully wording the invitation?

Certainly, as several studies show, often enough it is the other guy who is at fault—but he causes a very predictable sort of accident. So common is the car turning left into the path of the bike that it has become an exceedingly stale bad joke. More often, though, motorcyclists need no assistance to do themselves in: Collisions with stationary objects or simply the berm are the most popular. With apologies to the NRA, perhaps motorcycles don't kill motorcyclists—motorcyclists kill motorcyclists. This might seem to solve the problem: If riders learn better braking and cornering skills, bikes will at last lose their dangerous mien.

On second thought, don't hold your breath.

Speed unfairly takes the rap for motorcycling's greatest peril, because it is seen as

its greatest pleasure. But do a double check at the race track, the place where motorcycling's quiddity is best displayed. There, on the straightaway, home to blazing-hot speed, the racer actually gets to relax for a moment. His heart rate increases only when he applies the brakes before gearing down to enter turn one again. Every part of the scene must be attended to, none forgotten: The curve's radius and camber, the entrance speed, the lean angle, the state of the tires, the road, the suspension. . . . Motorcycling is like nothing so much as an extended mathematical formula: Add this, subtract that, multiply them

Fig. 3. Motocross jumps at sunset, British Moto-Cross Championships, Canada Heights, England.

together, and get an answer your life might literally depend upon—not quite the algebra you learned in high school.

Intense focus is both necessary for success and the gift of that success. You can imagine that a good game of Scrabble might provide the pleasure of total concentration, but only something that wagers life against death could lead to ecstasy.

Perhaps our addiction to this ecstasy is the legacy of our prehistoric past, when the feel of dying was bred permanently into our bones. Now, when we have reached the industrialized apex of assured safety from myriad harms, the challenge becomes how to put ourselves in danger again.

But let us face it: Motorcycling is not exactly running with the bulls in Pamplona, nor is it attempting to reshingle the roof yourself. Both of these are dreadfully perilous, and god forbid that you should decide to become a farmer. A recent British tabulation found that riding a motorcycle is not really too much worse than walking, which in turn is a bit more dangerous than bicycling (deaths per billion kilometers traveled: bicycle, 50; foot, 70; motorcycle, 104)—inviting us, once again, to reconsider our preconceptions.

If risk requires an expenditure, a good financier always demands maximal return on the dollar. A good financier, these days, gets a motorcycle. The fashionableness of danger in especially safe times has created a significant bubble in biking's sales chart, like the rise of cigars and attempts on the record for hot-air-balloon flight. All are examples of an analog to conspicuous consumption: conspicuous endangerment.

This facet of biking's popularity comes from a different sector of its defining qualities—the suggestive surface rather than the elemental wellspring—but is no less genuine a use than any other for a motorcycle's possibilities. One generates pleasure by making it possible to associate with bikes' devil-may-care renown (this symbolic use is confirmed by the fact that it works just as well when a bike is at a standstill). The other satisfies by providing escape into the heart of movement and that blessedly all-consuming ecstasy of total concentration, which is opposed to being associated with anything by anyone at all. The folk singer David Wilcox wrote of this use, and spoke for a million others like him, on the back of his first album: "I grew up a mile from the mall in Mentor, Ohio. I used to spend all my minimum wage on motorcycles to ride the trails along the high power lines because every once in a while it felt like getting free." Yet even this homespun use of a motorcycle can push you a little too close to the deep abandoned well of mythmaking; Wilcox falls in with a splash with one of the songs on this same record, a fable about a girl who buys the farm on a Honda Hurricane: "She wants to run away but there's nowhere she can go / Nowhere the pain won't come again. / But she can hide, hide in the pouring rain: / She rides the eye of a hurricane."[4]

The idea that embracing death is a purgative act (perhaps the ultimate one) is a cliché as old as the hills, and as true as it is false. It is true when we fabricate narratives about motorcycles, aggrandizing them and ourselves, when all they ask us to do is shut up and listen. It is true when we ride them simply to feel fear transformed to pleasure, or to avoid feeling the fear that remains itself.

In the end, there is nothing else to know but that motorcycles' joys are inseparable from their treacheries.

Cocteau knew this, and so the viewers of *Orpheus* in the dark room know *this*: When the motorcycles appear, someone is bound to be gone soon. But the cause merely exists in loose proximity to the effect, so it may not in fact be a cause at all. The perfume is faint, barely a suggestion. And the movie, all about death, is a joy to watch.

Notes

1. Horace McCoy, "The Grandstand Complex," in *On Two Wheels*, ed. Don McKay (New York: Dell, 1971), p. 21.

2. Yi-fu Tuan, *Landscapes of Fear* (New York: Harper and Row, 1979), p. 202.

3. Harry Hurt, "Motorcycle Accident Cause Factors and Identification of Countermeasures." Hurt, a researcher at the University of Southern California, released this exhaustive report in 1979. It was widely reviewed in the motorcycle press at the time.

4. David Wilcox, "How Did You Find Me Here," 1989, A&M Records.

Inventing the Motorcycle

1868
1919

Inventing the Motorcycle: 1868–1919

The 19th century spans an impressive period of invention, one notable for its preoccupation with time, space, and the notion of invention itself. The year 1825, for example, saw the first railroad locomotive; in 1879, Thomas Edison, an obsessive patentee of his own experiments, harnessed electricity to provide electric light; and, in 1888, Etienne-Jules Marey built the first camera to use flexible film, a crucial step in the creation of motion pictures. Edison was also an early pioneer of cinema, and his shorts, such as *Sandow* (1894), demonstrate early film's fascination with capturing physical movement. The influence of these technological advancements was profound. Indeed, they could be said to be responsible for fundamental alterations in the manner in which we perceive our environment, even live our lives, today. The railroad isolated us further from a spatial relationship to the landscape; electricity released us from those quotidian routines dictated by natural light; cinema, with its illusion of occurring in "real" time, changed traditional notions of temporality and mortality.

These particular inventions share more than a continued resonance. They also demonstrate the restlessness of human nature since the industrial age—the desire for more speed, more time to work, more entertainment, the demand for "different and better" as quickly as possible. It is this love affair with dynamism that inspired the invention of the motorcycle.

Certain early experimental motorcycles are fascinating in terms of the transparency of their inventors' intentions: namely, how can we move *faster*? The Michaux-Perreaux (fig. i), created in France in 1868, took a small commercial steam engine and attached it to the bicycle, which had existed since 1840. Use of steam-powered two-wheelers continued until late in the century, as evidenced by the Geneva (1896, fig. iii). In other early motorcycles, like the De Dion–Bouton (1899, fig. iv), the Orient (1900, fig. v), and the Thomas (1900, fig. vi), the designers began experimenting with petrol power while maintaining basic bicycle design. Gottlieb Daimler, the German engineer who earned the nickname "Father of the Motorcycle," was actually using his 1885 wooden "boneshaker" (a term often used to describe early cycles, with their wooden frames and wheels, fig. ii) to test a gasoline engine intended for a four-wheeled carriage. Finally, in Germany a decade later, the Hildebrand & Wolfmüller (cat. no. 1) became the first powered two-wheeled vehicle to be offered to the public on a series production basis. The Hildebrand was crucial in its move away from the foot pedal as a source of engine power. The motorcycle was no longer a

Michaux-Perreaux Steam Velocipede • 1868 • France
Bore x stroke: 22 x 80 mm • Power output: not applicable •
Top speed: 19 mph (30 km/h) • Musée de l'Ile de France, Sceaux

Daimler Einspur • 264 cc • 1885 (replica) • Germany
Bore x stroke: 58 x 100 mm • Power output: .5 hp @ 600 rpm •
Top speed: 7 mph (12 km/h) • Deutsches Zweirad-Museum,
Neckarsulm, Germany

Geneva •1896 • United States
Bore x stroke: 1½ x 1½ inches • Power output: .5 hp •
Top speed: 16 mph (26 km/h) • Collection of Peter Gagan

hybrid, but a machine with its own essential qualities.

Great diversity and competition characterized the pioneer years of motorcycling in the United States, and such companies as Indian, Harley-Davidson, and Henderson thrived. The spirit of exploration of those early years encouraged breakthroughs in engineering and feats of invention. An early manufacturer of motorcycles, the Pierce Cycle Company, for example, was founded by the son of a famous car manufacturer. And Glenn Curtiss, who became better-known as an airplane engineer, used a dirigible engine to power his record-breaking V-8.

Even the more traditional arts of architecture, sculpture, and painting turned to dynamism as a compelling subject matter at the dawn of the new century. Almost concomitant with Gottlieb Daimler's first test run of his Daimler Einspur was Gustave Eiffel's fantastic achievement, the Eiffel Tower, completed for the 1889 Paris Exhibition. The Eiffel Tower succeeds in making a radical, absolute equation between architecture and technology. The structure is precisely the sum of its engineering; there is no aesthetic embellishment other than the lively, graphic quality of the industrial materials of which it is composed. Over the past century, the tower has remained a symbol of the dawn of the worship of technology and of the dominance of the dynamic urban center.

Later, in Paris, one of the most celebrated examples of artistic experiments with space and time was the Analytic Cubism explored by Georges Braque and Pablo Picasso between 1908 and 1912. By simultaneously examining the dimensions of an object from many views, Cubism revolutionized the very concept of perspective on a two-dimensional surface. Marcel Duchamp was briefly under the direct influence of Cubism, and his *Nude (Study), Sad Young Man on a Train* (*Nu [esquisse], jeune homme triste dans un train*, 1911–12) dissects the movements of both train and figure. Duchamp also chose to show a blurred landscape through a window, presenting speed as the destroyer of what critic Wolfgang Shivelbusch refers to, in his book *The Railway Journey* (1977), as the "close relationship between the traveler and traveled space."

The Italian Futurists were also intensely interested in speed, technology, and the fragmentation that went hand-in-hand with such progress. Like the Cubists, the Futurists believed in demonstrating how the nature of vision produces the illusion of a fusing of forms. Umberto Boccioni's *Dynamism of a Speeding Horse + Houses* (*Dinamismo di un cavallo in corsa + case*, 1914–15), for example, is a sculptural configuration of intersecting planes, manifesting how an object is redefined by the space it traverses.

Meanwhile, the motorcycling world's method of immortalizing its continuing obsession with speed was through racing events and record keeping. The Isle of Man TT, the world's oldest continuously run race, was founded in 1907, though other annual events, like the Speed Carnival in Ormond, Florida, had been held years before. Some of the most dangerous racing was done on board tracks, where the wooden surface allowed for exhilarating speeds. By the 1920s, speeds averaged over 100 mph, and many accidents occurred, including spectator injuries caused by splinters flying up from the track as bikes raced past.

As the first phase of motorcycle development came to a close with the beginning of World War I, motorcycle manufacturers sought to put their machines to uses beyond the achievement of ever-higher velocities. Companies such as Indian supplied the U.S. Army with motorcycles, sidecars, and delivery cars in bulk, and military concerns were reflected in their marketing strategies. The priority in the postwar years shifted to increasing the public's accessibility to machines that had been largely available only to specialists until then. Harley-Davidson was extremely successful in targeting their 1919 Sport model to a mass market. As a result of the Sport's smooth ride and easy handling, a new age and new audience was primed to embrace the motorcycle. —*Vanessa Rocco*

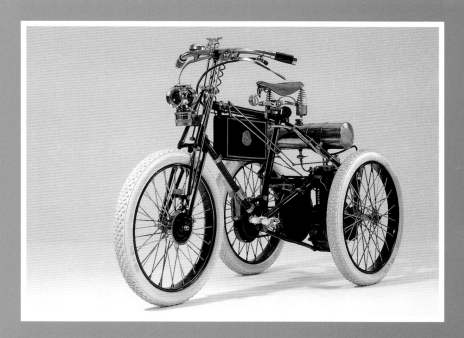

 iv

De Dion–Bouton • 240 cc • 1899 • France
Bore x stroke: 66 x 70 mm • Power output: 1.8 hp •
Top speed: 20 mph (32 km/h) • Collection of Reed Martin

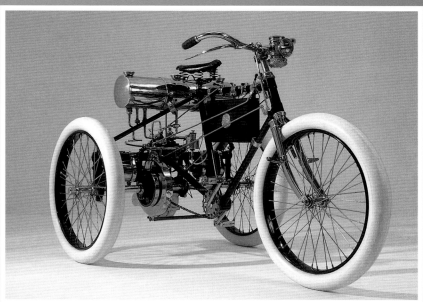

 v

Orient • 20 ci • 1900 • United States
Bore x stroke: $2\frac{15}{16}$ x 3 inches • Power output: 2.5 hp •
Top speed: 25 mph (40 km/h) • Collection of Reed Martin

vi

Thomas • 1900 • United States
Bore x stroke: not applicable • Power output: 1.8 hp •
Top speed: 25 mph (40 km/h) • Collection of William Eggers

101

Hildebrand & Wolfmüller

1,489 cc • 1894 • Germany
Bore x stroke: 90 x 117 mm • Power output: 2.5 hp @ 240 rpm •
Top speed: 28 mph (45 km/h) • Deutsches Zweirad-Museum,
Neckarsulm, Germany

The honor of producing the world's first series production motor-cycle goes to the German brand Hildebrand & Wolfmüller. The men behind the Munich-based company were Heinrich and Wilhelm Hildebrand, Alois Wolfmüller, and Hans Geisenhof. Not only was their 1894 machine the first to be referred to as a *Motorrad* (German for motorcycle), but it also featured the largest engine fitted to any production motorcycle during the first 90 years of biking history.

Each bore and stroke of the horizontal twin-cylinder engine was 90 x 117 mm, giving a total displacement of 1,489 cc. The pistons were linked by long connecting rods, as in a steam loco-motive. There was no flywheel—the solid-disc rear wheel served this function—and fuel was supplied by a surface carburetor. The bike had automatic inlet valves, and its pair of exhaust valves were separated by long rods and a cam on the rear wheel. The rear mudguard was used as a water tank for engine cooling, and one of the frame tubes acted as an oil tank. The Hildebrand & Wolfmüller was also the first motorcycle to employ pneumatic tires.

The bike's huge engine turned 2.5 hp, producing a maxi-mum speed of almost 30 mph—sensational performance in 1894. Orders totaled over 2 million deutsche marks in only a few weeks. Soon the machine was being built in France as well, through a license agreement. In May 1895 a pair of the German motorcycles finished second and third in Italy's first car and motorcycle race, which ran from Turin to the village of Asti and back, a distance of 62 miles.

Elsewhere, however, problems were beginning to surface. The hot tube ignition was proving both unreliable and difficult to operate, and customers began asking for their money back. In addition, both the German and French factories discovered that the selling price was less than the cost of manufacture. In early 1897, both ventures collapsed—an early indication of the dangers fac-ing motorcycle companies whose enthusiasm outweighed their business sense. —*Mick Walker*

Indian Single

16 ci • 1901 • United States
Bore x stroke: not applicable • Power output: 1.8 hp •
Top speed: 30 mph (48 km/h) • The Otis Chandler Vintage Museum
of Transportation and Wildlife, Oxnard, Calif.

Bicycles interested nearly everyone at the turn of the century, and bicycle racing inspired greater public awareness of the available makes and their varied potentials. As riders went for record runs, something faster was needed to pace them. In June 1898, Waltham Manufacturing Co., the makers of Orient bicycles, announced plans to market a version of their heavyweight bicycle with a single-cylinder De Dion gas engine attached. Other manufacturers quickly followed suit, including former racer George Hendee, who made bicycles called Silver King and Silver Queen.

In 1899, Carl Oscar Hedstrom, a Swedish machinist working in Brooklyn, New York, bought a De Dion engine and modified it to improve reliability. He fitted it to a tandem bicycle used for pacing racers at Madison Square Garden. Hendee, impressed, asked him to design a salable motor bicycle. Hedstrom produced his own patterns for crankcases and cylinder barrels; he designed and built a carburetor that improved combustion and simplified engine control; he set the single-cylinder engine within Hendee's diamond-frame bicycle as a stressed member, replacing part of the seat tube; he devised a rear-fender, "camel's hump," two-section tank for gasoline and oil; and he placed three dry-cell batteries into a canister behind the front down tube, connecting them to a spark coil for ignition timed off the crankshaft, De Dion–style. Unlike most manufacturers, who used leather belts (which tended to slip), Hedstrom used a chain drive.

The result weighed just 98 pounds. After testing this prototype, the two men formed Hendee Manufacturing Co. to produce the machine they called the Indian. Recent research suggests that Hendee assembled only two production Indians in 1901. Hedstrom showed one of these throughout New England on the velodrome circuit. Hendee shipped the other, shown here, to England for the Stanley Bicycle Show. It was bought by a Scottish mechanical engineer named McDermott, who later emigrated to California. After his death, it changed hands several times before it was acquired by Gordon Bennett of Oakland, who restored it inexpertly, painting it a blue that was darker than that of the original. The motorcycle world thought the Indian had disappeared, but his widow Viola Bennett held on to it for years after his death.
—*Randy Leffingwell*

Catalogue for Indian, 1902. Collection of George and Milli Yarocki.

Curtiss V-8

265 ci • 1907 • United States

Bore x stroke: 3⅝ x 3¼ inches • Power output: 40 hp @ 1,800 rpm • Top speed: 136 mph (219 km/h) • National Air and Space Museum, Smithsonian Institution, Washington, D.C.

Photograph of Glenn Curtiss on his V-8, 1907. Glenn Curtiss Museum, Hammondsport, New York.

"No such speed was ever made by anything but a bullet," announced the *Chicago Daily News* following the record-breaking accomplishment of Glenn Hammond Curtiss and his experimental V-8 motorcycle. The landmark event took place on January 23, 1907, when Curtiss surprised the world with his 26.4-second dash through a measured mile on the hard-packed sand of Ormond Beach, Florida, achieving a new land-speed record of 136.36 mph.

Before Curtiss could officially enter the record books, however, his machine was seriously damaged; the universal joint on his driveshaft broke while he was traveling at an estimated 90 mph. The wildly flailing driveshaft damaged his machine's chassis and threw the drive gears out of alignment, preventing Curtiss from making an officially timed corroborating run. Nevertheless, the New York engine builder's unique achievement was widely reported by the press, earning him the title "the fastest man on earth."

The engine with which Glenn Curtiss set the land-speed record was originally designed to power a dirigible. Like his earlier V-twins, Curtiss's V-8 is air-cooled and employs splash lubrication for oiling, and dry-cell battery ignition. The intake valves are automatic, operated by changes in atmospheric pressure, whereas the exhaust valves operate mechanically via pushrods from the camshaft. It was calculated that the engine produced 40 hp at 1,800 rpm.

Curtiss began his historic timed run with a push start from two men positioned on either side of his machine. The judges at Ormond Beach had agreed upon a 2-mile run to get up to speed, 1 mile for the actual test, and a final mile in which to stop the motorcycle. The February 1907 issue of *The Motorcycle Illustrated* reported that, after the time trial, the 28-year-old Curtiss "looked over each watch that had been held on him before he could be made to believe that he had actually sent a world's record shimmering." With this unique performance, Glenn Curtiss set a new land-speed record for all vehicles, which he held until 1911. He retained the motorcycle-speed record until shortly before his untimely death in the summer of 1930. —*Daniel K. Statnekov*

FN Four

498 cc • 1908 • Belgium
Bore x stroke: 78.7 x 69.9 mm • Power output: 9 hp •
Top speed: 28 mph (45 km/h) • Collection of Chris Le Sauvage

The first motorcycles were essentially bicycles with primitive single-cylinder engines. These engines vibrate severely; hence, the cycle's body must be heavy in order to avoid breaking apart.

A far better way to deal with vibration, developed by the FN's designer Paul Kelecom, is to make it self-canceling. Kelecom adopted four cylinders for this FN's engine. As the inner pair of pistons rises, the outer pair falls. The primary shaking forces cancel, and the engine does not rock fore and aft.

Belgian armaments maker Fabrique Nationale d'Arms de Guerre added bicycles to its line in 1901. Before joining the FN team, Kelecom gained design experience working on the Ormonde, a simple, single-cylinder, belt-driven, 3-hp machine, one of which competed in the celebrated Paris-Madrid race of 1903.

Belts slip, single-cylinder engines vibrate, and bicycle chassis fatigue and break. Kelecom adopted shaft drive (the same used today on BMW and other machines) and designed his chassis around the engine, rather than the other way around. The engine hung between split-bottom-frame rails, while the bevel-driven, ball-bearing-supported driveshaft was integrated into a rear-frame stay. Like the Ormonde and other pioneer engines, the 350-cc engine had atmospheric intake valves—that is, the piston's suction stroke pulled the valves open against light spring pressure. But the absence of a multispeed gearbox limited the machine's speed range.

The unit projecting in front of the engine is the magneto. The carburetor, located behind the cylinder block, is connected to the intake ports by a branched manifold. The oil pump is rider-operated. This bike, like most early motorcycles, was started by vigorous pedaling. (By 1911, the promoters of the Isle of Man TT road races would prohibit pedaling gear. They deemed it an unseemly reminder of the motorcycle's humble origins, the bicycle.)

With its displacement increased to 493 cc for the European market and 498 (shown here) for the American, and with the addition of a two-speed gearbox and an automotive-style clutch, the FN Four was produced for another 20 years. But as it emerged from its initial status as a novelty, the motorcycle became unprofitable. After Kelecom left FN in 1926, the machine was replaced by conventional chain-driven singles and twins. FN left the business in 1957, a time when reviving European small-car production again rendered the motorcycle a luxury item. —*Kevin Cameron*

Catalogue for the FN Four, 1904. National Motor Museum, Beaulieu, England.

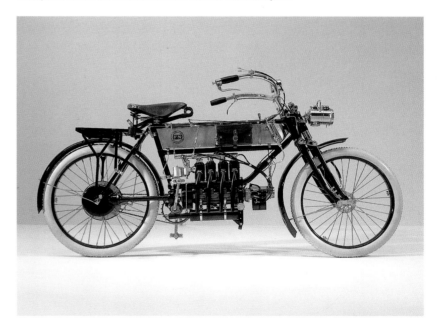

Pierce Four

43 ci • 1910 • United States
Bore x stroke: 2⁄₁₆ x 2¼ inches • Power output: 4 hp •
Top speed: 60 mph (97 km/h) • The Otis Chandler Vintage Museum
of Transportation and Wildlife, Oxnard, Calif.

Brochure for Pierce, 1909. Collection of the Gilbert family.

In 1909, the Pierce Cycle Company of Buffalo, New York, introduced the first four-cylinder motorcycle manufactured in the United States. From its inception, the Pierce Four was intended to achieve the same standard of excellence as the Pierce-Arrow automobile. Percy Pierce, son of the founder of the motorcar company and owner of the Pierce Cycle Company, was inspired by the successful design of the four-cylinder FN, which was manufactured in Belgium by Fabrique Nationale. Using the European machine as a departure point, Pierce company engineers built their own version of an inline four-cylinder motor, and, along with it, designed a state-of-the-art motorcycle.

Advertised as the "Pierce Vibrationless Motorcycle," the Pierce Cycle Company claimed that their motorcycle would "give motorcar comfort, and travel comfortably from a mere walking pace up to the speed of the motorcar." As with his father's automobile company, Percy Pierce insisted that his motorcycle be manufactured to the highest standards of workmanship and utilize the finest materials.

The 43-ci Pierce four-cylinder engine is inherently smoother than a V-twin or a single-cylinder power plant, and the motorcycle's enclosed drive shaft was a significant engineering advancement over the leather belt typically employed in 1909 by most manufacturers. As in contemporary motorcycle design, the drive shaft on the Pierce also functions as a structural component of the frame. Another notable feature introduced by the New York firm is the use of 3½-inch-diameter tubing for sections of the machine's chassis, enabling the frame to serve a second purpose as the motorcycle's fuel tank.

Priced at $350, the 1910 Pierce Four was the most expensive motorcycle of its time. Two years later, it rose to $400, but even at the higher price, the company was unable to cover fully the cost of building a motorcycle to such a high standard. In 1913, the Pierce Cycle Company declared bankruptcy and production came to a close. It is estimated that approximately 3,500 four-cylinder machines were built in the five years that they were produced. —DKS

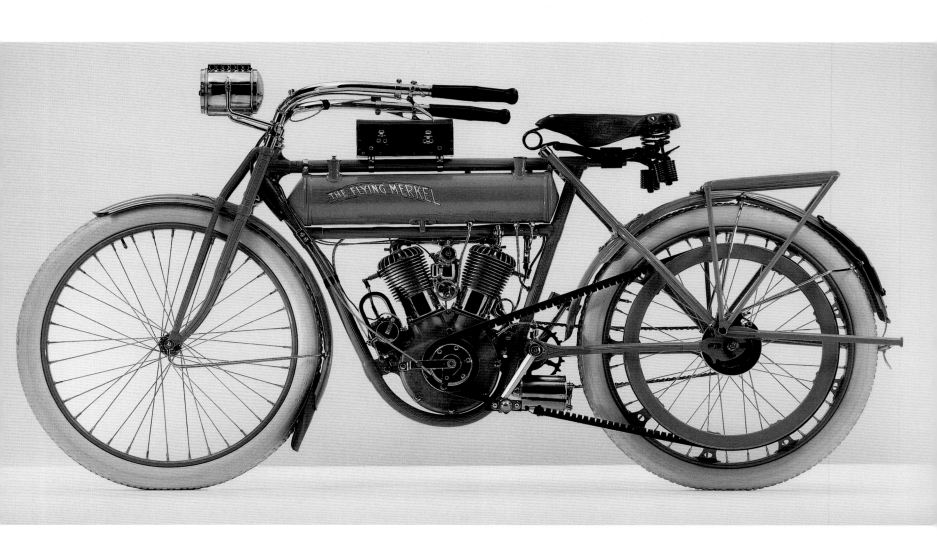

Brochure for the Flying Merkel, 1912. National Motor Museum, Beaulieu, England.

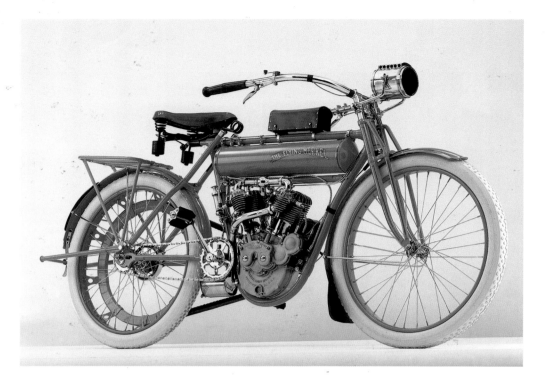

Brochure for the Flying Merkel, 1913.
Collection of the Gilbert family.

Flying Merkel Model V

54 ci • 1911 • United States

Bore x stroke: 3¼ x 3¼ inches • Power output: 6 hp • Top speed: 60 mph (97 km/h) •
The Otis Chandler Vintage Museum of Transportation and Wildlife, Oxnard, Calif.

The 1911 Flying Merkel Model V is a curious blend of early mechanical features and farsighted technical innovations. The transmission of power to the rear wheel is still by means of a belt, but the chassis of the machine is a showcase for the ingenuity of its designer. Unlike most early motorcycles with chassis suspension, the Merkel spring frame is designed so that the up-and-down movement of the rear wheel does not change the tension of the drivetrain. Merkel also patented a spring fork that is considered the forerunner of the modern "telescopic" fork.

In contrast to its primitive intake valves, which operate by atmospheric pressure, the 1911 Flying Merkel uses precision-ground ball bearings in place of the bronze bushings that were typically used by engine builders of the day. Another significant innovation is the machine's throttle-controlled oiler. Lubrication was a continuing problem in the early days of the industry, but Merkel's system for oiling the engine preceded by nearly two decades both Indian's as well as Harley-Davidson's adoption of this feature.

In 1911, the only color available for the Flying Merkel was bright orange, but the customer for a twin-cylinder model did have a choice of power plants. The Model V, with its 54-ci motor, was rated at 6 hp; the high-performance VS model featured a 61-cubic-inch motor that was rated at 7 hp. The price tags for the two motorcycles were $300 and $325, respectively.

A general decline in motorcycling in America, as well as legal and service difficulties connected with a poorly designed self-starting mechanism and the country's imminent involvement in World War I, were all factors in the firm's decision to go out of the motorcycle business. In 1915, production of the Flying Merkel came to a close. —DKS

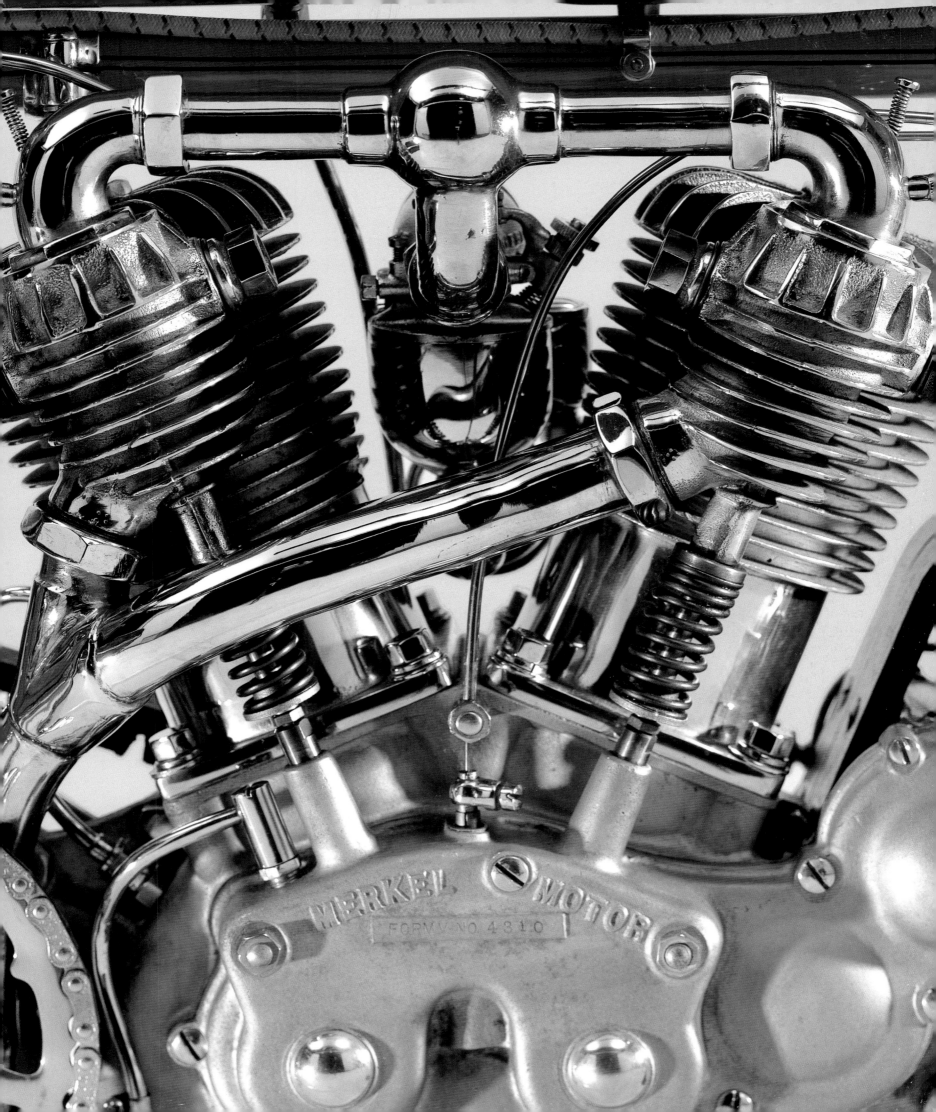

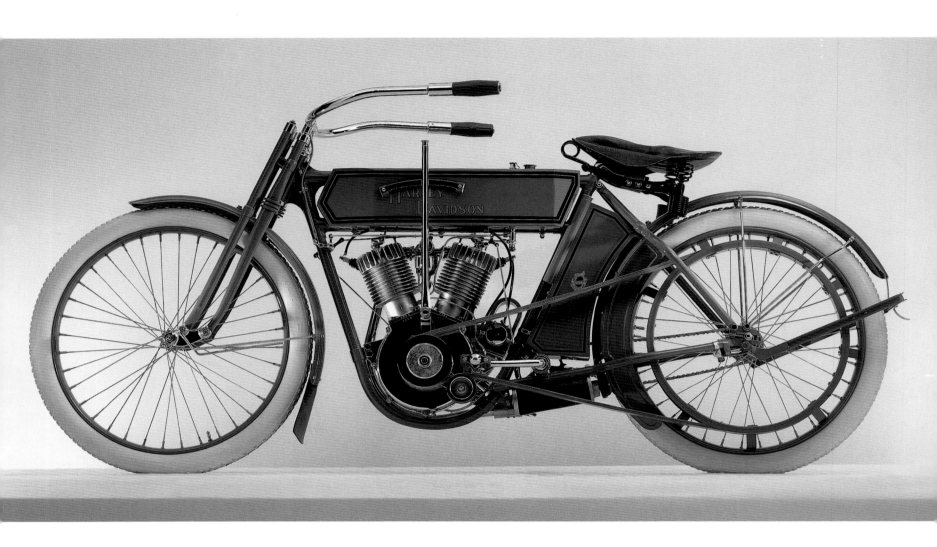

Harley-Davidson Model 7D

49 ci • 1911 • United States
Bore x stroke: 3 x 3½ inches • Power output: 6.5 hp •
Top speed: 60 mph (97 km/h) • The Otis Chandler Vintage
Museum of Transportation and Wildlife, Oxnard, Calif.

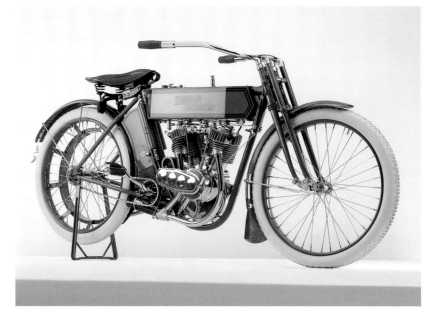

The first Harley-Davidson V-twin engine appeared in 1909, but the initial design was flawed, and only a few machines were produced. The Milwaukee manufacturer did not offer another twin until 1911, when the firm expanded their product line beyond the rugged single-cylinder model that until then had been their sole product. Catalogued as the Model 7D, the revised V-twin was the first in an uninterrupted succession of V-twin engines that would remain the hallmark feature of the Harley-Davidson motorcycle.

The 1911 Harley-Davidson twin engine has a displacement of 49 ci and is rated at 6.5 hp. The mechanically operated intake valves allow for a controlled influx of fuel and a higher engine speed, a significant improvement over both the earlier twin and the company's single-cylinder model. Lubrication on the first Harley V-twin is by a drip system, with oil metered to the engine through a needle valve. The machine's well-designed muffler makes for a quiet-running motor; the company advertised this motorcycle as "The Silent Gray Fellow."

The machine's chassis is fairly typical. Suspension is provided by long coil springs in the front fork tubes and smaller springs attached to the saddle. Although the leading brand of motorcycle (Indian) and most racers were equipped with a chain drive in 1911, transmission of power to the rear wheel on the first Harley-Davidson twin is effected by a 1¾-inch flat leather belt. A simple belt-tensioning device serves as a primitive clutch, and a bicycle-type pedal mechanism is employed for starting the engine. Top speed is estimated at 60 mph; the two-cylinder model cost $300.

In 1911 the Harley-Davidson Motor Company built 5,625 motorcycles. Detailed factory records are incomplete, however, and it is not known how many twin-cylinder machines were manufactured in the first year of production. Harley-Davidson's landmark Model 7D is treasured by collectors. Less than half a dozen examples are known to have survived. —*DKS*

Brochure for the Cyclone, 1914 (reproduction).
Collection of the Gilbert family.

Cyclone

61 ci • 1914 • United States
Bore x stroke: 3⁵⁄₁₆ x 3½ inches • Power output: 45 hp @ 5,000 rpm • Top speed: unknown •
Collection of the Gilbert family

Perhaps the most legendary of all pioneer motorcycles produced in the United States was the overhead-cam Cyclone, manufactured by the Joerns Motor Manufacturing Company of Saint Paul, Minnesota. First offered for public sale in the summer of 1914, two models were catalogued: a standard road bike and a stripped-stock version. Following industry practice, the Joerns company also built racers to showcase their innovative engine design.

The hallmark feature of the 61-ci V-twin Cyclone engine is its shaft-and-bevel-gear-driven overhead-cam and valve arrangement. The motorcycle also contains a number of other important features that presage modern high-performance engine technology: a near-hemispherical combustion chamber, the extensive use of caged-roller and self-aligning ball bearings, and a precise, recessed fit of the crankcase, cylinders, and heads all contribute to the engine's exceptional performance. Even with its modest compression ratio of 5.5 to 1, it is estimated that the Cyclone engine produces 45 hp at 5,000 rpm.

The Cyclone made its first major appearance at a 1914 Labor Day race meet in Stockton, California. The overhead-cam engineering was an immediate success; the cyclone demonstrated an unequivocal speed advantage, winning the 5- and 10-mile national championships. For the next eighteen months, the "yellow speed demon" continued to break records, causing a sensation whenever it appeared on American racetracks.

Its exceptional speed, however, was not enough. The machine needed more development, and in several long, important track races, the Cyclone failed to finish because of mechanical breakdowns. It also became apparent that the motorcycle was too expensive to build and sell at a competitive price, and by the end of 1915, production was discontinued.

The bike shown here is a hybrid Cyclone, constructed by a privateer racer in 1926. The machine's chassis was taken from a Harley-Davidson. Period photographs document this machine as having raced in the 1920s with the Harley-Davidson paint scheme and nameplate. In the 1960s, the machine was restored, and the Harley-Davidson chassis was cosmetically refurbished with the Joerns bright-yellow paint scheme and Cyclone decal. As originally constructed, this hybrid racer is an example of the innovation that often takes place within the milieu of racing. —*DKS*

Peugeot Paris-Nice

345 cc • 1914 • France
Bore x stroke: 56 x 70 mm • Power output: 2.5 hp •
Top speed: 43 mph (70 km/h) • Collection of Alain Cortot

Early motorcycles—like the racing cars of the time—quickly evolved into intimidating giants powered by huge engines. The emphasis on power and speed limited the motorcycle's customer base, since what most riders wanted was a light, manageable, reliable machine. In order to reach this wider market, Peugeot launched a series of experiments, calling their machines "Light Motorcycles."

Their first, driven by a Zedel single, lacked power. Next came a Peugeot V-twin, but it too had to be powered up to meet the competition. Both engines suffered from flaws in their automatic intake systems. While the exhaust valves had to be mechanically driven to open against cylinder pressure, intakes were provided with light springs so that the engine's suction stroke could pull them open automatically. This worked well enough at the prevalent low rpm, but the action of the valves was sudden. As the throttle was opened, they remained largely closed until adequate vacuum was generated. Then they came on with an abrupt rush.

By 1913 owners knew enough to begin calling for refinements such as smooth acceleration. Accordingly, Peugeot added mechanical operation to the intake valves, resulting in a side-valve engine with smoothly controllable power across the whole range.

Meanwhile, the company had gone racing, albeit discreetly. Because the public was frightened by bikes like Fournier's "*le Monstruosité*" of nearly 2,500 cc, it wouldn't do to admit that the new "Light Motorcycle" from Peugeot was successful in racing. Hence, Peugeot raced strictly for the engineering value, making no promotional use of it. A souped-up version of this new twin won the 1913 GP de France, but the catalogue model was innocuously named the Paris-Nice, after the road rally. It could be ordered with belt drive, declutcher, or a three-speed hub gearbox and clutch.

Simultaneous with these innocent entertainments, the armies of Europe were mobilizing. World War I began before the Paris-Nice could fulfill its potential, though the engine survived to power postwar models until 1921. Peugeot's motorcycle production ceased in 1959. — *KC*

Brochure for Peugeot, 1914. Collection of Bernard Salvat.

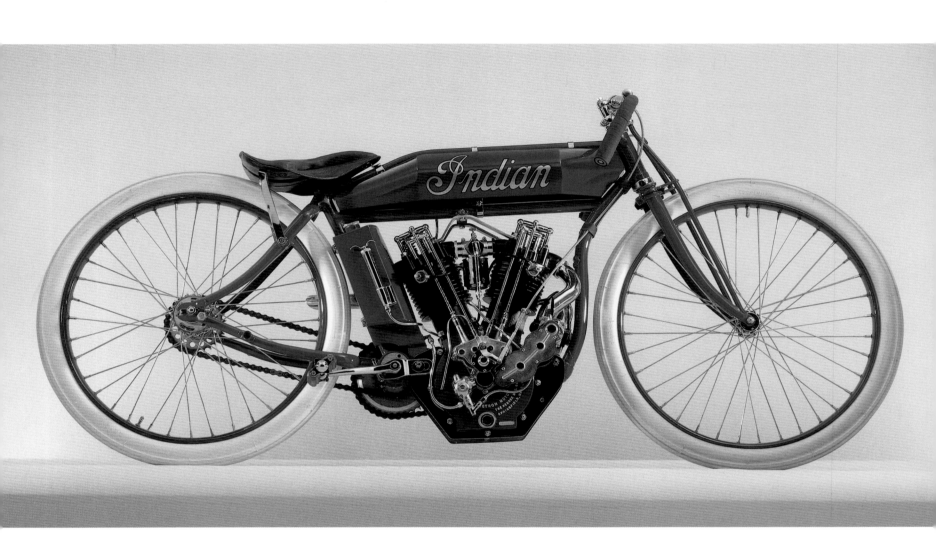

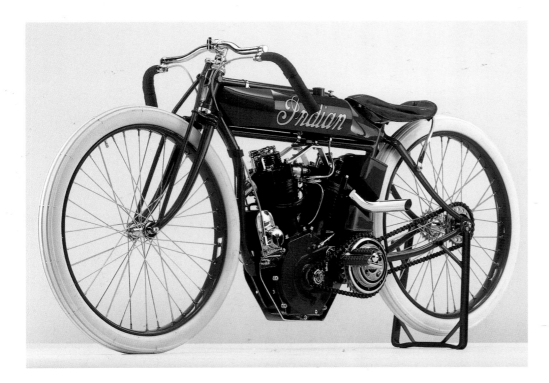

Catalogue for Indian, 1915.
Collection of George and Milli Yarocki.

Indian 8-Valve Board Track Racer

61 ci • 1915 • United States
Bore x stroke: 3¼ x 3⁴³⁄₆₄ inches • Power output: unknown • Top speed: 132 mph (212 km/h) •
Collection of Daniel K. Statnekov

By 1910, rival companies had started to overtake the Indian entries on the circular wooden speedways that served as the principle venues for motorcycle racing in America. Oscar Hedstrom (who had designed the Indian motorcycle in 1900) returned to his drawing board. His goal: to design a new motor capable of regaining the lead for Indian. The result of the engineer's effort was an overhead-valve design, but this posed a problem: valves in the overhead position within the combustion chamber could not withstand the extreme temperatures of a high-speed race.

Hedstrom's solution was to decrease the size of the valves and add more of them. Instead of the usual two valves in each cylinder, Hedstrom calculated that four smaller valves would be better able to dissipate the heat. The Indian engineer's theory turned out to be correct, and the overhead-valve configuration also proved to be more efficient. When engine tuners learned to take advantage of the increased valve area afforded by multiple valves, they discovered that not only had Hedstrom solved the problem of valve breakage due to excessive heat, but also that the new motor was faster as well.

The Indian 8-valve debuted in 1911 and was immediately successful on the pine-board tracks. From 1911 on, Indian's multi-valve racer garnered valuable publicity for the company by winning numerous championships and setting new track records. In 1920 an Indian 8-Valve set an official world record for the mile, achieving a speed of 114.17 mph, and in 1926 an updated version of Hedstrom's landmark design was clocked at 132 mph, setting another world record, which would remain unsurpassed for the next 11 years.

Initially, the Indian 8-valve motor was not offered for sale to the public; it was retained by the company for use on their professional racing equipment. Beginning in 1916, however, a production 8-Valve Racer was catalogued as the Model H and sold for $350. It is not known how many Indian 8s were produced, but approximately six are known to have survived. The example included in *The Art of the Motorcycle* features a prototype racing frame. It was originally obtained from the Indian Company by a former factory rider. —*DKS*

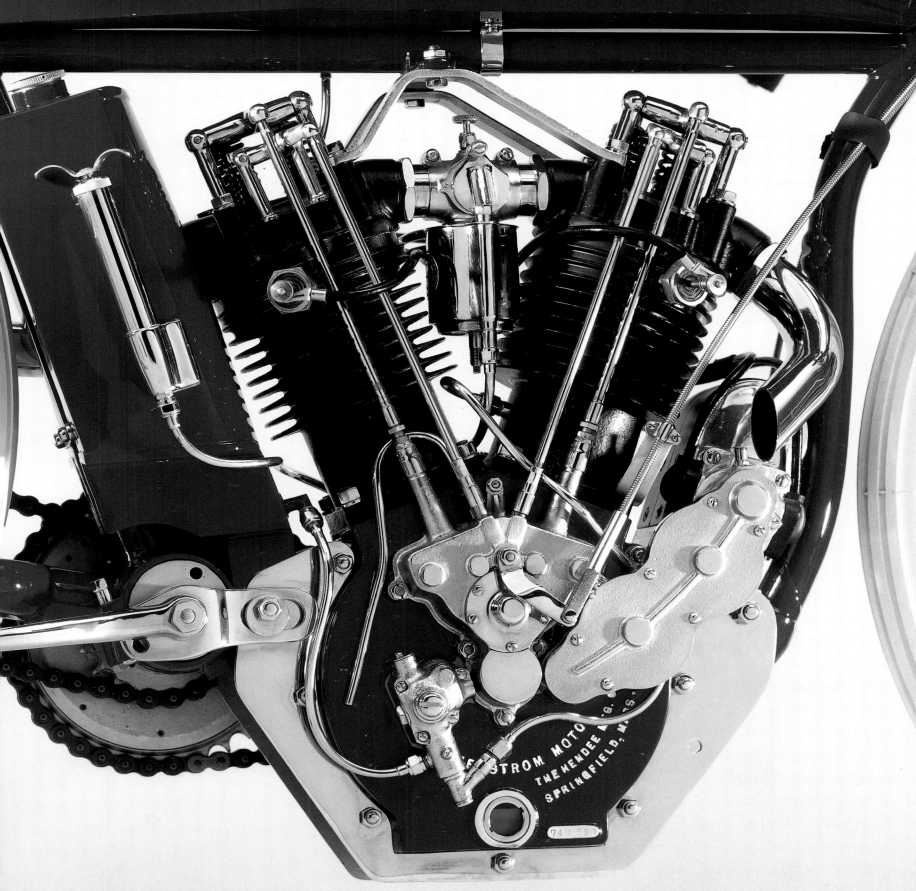

Brochure for Iver Johnson, 1914.
Collection of George and Milli Yarocki.

Iver Johnson Model 15-7

62 ci • 1915 • United States
Bore x stroke: 3¼ x 3¾ inches • Power output: 7 hp • Top speed: 60 mph (97 km/h)
The Otis Chandler Vintage Museum of Transportation and Wildlife, Oxnard, Calif.

The Iver Johnson motorcycle was produced by the Iver Johnson Arms and Cycle Works of Fitchburg, Massachusetts. A successful manufacturer of firearms, Iver Johnson entered the bicycle business in the 1880s, and in 1910 began to manufacture a single-cylinder motorcycle. In 1913 the firm expanded their line to include a V-twin. Proud of their reputation for working to the highest standards, the company affixed their founder's name to the new product and adopted the slogan "Mechanically Perfect" for their motorized two-wheelers.

There are similarities between the company's motorcycle and the bicycle that preceded it. The graceful arch in the frame member above the engine closely follows the truss-bridge design that Iver Johnson pioneered with their popular bicycle. This frame geometry gives rise to the sculpted fuel tanks that are a distinctive feature of the marque. The understated elegance of its gray-and-black enamel paint scheme (accented with a soft sheen of polished nickel) furthered the image of the Iver Johnson as "the aristocrat among motorcycles."

Mechanically, the Iver Johnson's 62-ci engine is notably different than the other V-twins of its day. The most significant variations are in the flywheel assembly and the ignition sequence. An arrangement of two separate crankpins enables the pistons to travel in a synchronized manner, each piston reaching the top of its cylinder simultaneously with the other. Ignition is evenly spaced and (like a vertical twin) accomplishes a smooth delivery of power to the rear wheel.

By 1915, all of the leading manufacturers offered a kick start and a three-speed transmission on their top-of-the-line machines. Under-geared in terms of the competition (and still using the old-fashioned pedal-start arrangement), the Iver Johnson motorcycle was at a significant disadvantage in the marketplace. It had also become evident that, despite its "aristocratic" reputation, the mechanical complexity of the Iver Johnson was beyond the repair skills of the average rider.

Suffering a decline in sales, the Iver Johnson Arms and Cycle Works discontinued production of their motorcycles in 1916. It is estimated that fewer than six examples of the twin-cylinder machine have survived. —DKS

Harley-Davidson Model W Sport Twin

36 ci • 1919 • United States
Bore x stroke: 2¾ x 3 inches • Power output: 6 hp •
Top speed: 50 mph (80 km/h) • The Otis Chandler Vintage Museum
of Transportation and Wildlife, Oxnard, Calif.

In the spring of 1919, Harley-Davidson introduced a horizontally opposed, middleweight twin; this was catalogued as the Model W and was known to the American public as the Sport Twin. The new model represented the Milwaukee company's bid to attract a larger number of entry-level riders as well as to expand the market for motorcycles in the United States.

Patterned after a contemporary British machine (the Douglas), the 36-ci opposed-twin motor was a significant departure for those American riders who had developed an affinity for the V-twin. From a consumer's perspective, the new Harley-Davidson entry was a contender for a share of the market. The little bike was easy to start and smooth-running (because of the inherently good balance of the opposed twin design), and its low center of gravity made for a machine that was easy to control.

The Sport Twin also incorporated features that were designed to keep both rider and motorcycle cleaner than had been possible in the past. The transmission and clutch assembly were integral with the engine crankcase, thus reducing the number of oil compartments; a dust-proof case made of sheet metal completely enclosed the drive chain, eliminating the potential for excess chain oil to find its way to the exterior of the machine or onto its rider's clothing.

The Sport Twin had a top speed of only about 50 mph. Nevertheless, the 257-pound motorcycle was successful in timed distance contests, and it earned the distinction of being the first motorized vehicle of any kind to reach the 10,114-foot summit of Mount San Antonio (Old Baldy) in Southern California. Despite these achievements, the new middleweight opposed twin did not enjoy a wide acceptance with American riders, nor did it attract a significant number of new riders to the sport.

The comparably sized Indian Scout proved to be much faster than the Sport Twin, and the Indian significantly outsold the midsize Harley-Davidson. Production of the Model W Sport Twin was discontinued in 1922. In all, approximately 6,000 machines were built, the majority of which were exported to overseas markets, where the opposed twin design had already received acceptance. —*DKS*

Cover of *The Harley-Davidson Enthusiast*, 1919.
Collection of George and Milli Yarocki.

The Machine Age

The Machine Age: 1922–1929

The 1920s was an age of euphoria and sobriety born on the heels of the first global war in modern history. The devastation caused by World War I was unprecedented—10 million dead and nearly 20 million wounded—and technology, in the form of airplanes, tanks, machine guns, and bombs, was responsible, unleashing unspeakable damage and transforming the complexion of modern warfare forever. The aftermath of this far-reaching conflict ushered in an era celebrated as "the Roaring Twenties" and "the Machine Age," a decade in which a return to order on the political front was offset by social liberation and an outburst of artistic creativity. Characterized by carefree expression on the one hand and sober, utopian visions on the other, the cultural spirit of the 1920s was both freewheeling and deliberate, bound by a desire to wipe away the horrors of war and to rebuild society according to new values and ideas.

In the popular postwar imagination, the machine had come to be known as potentially destructive and uncontrollable, a view propagated by artists of the international Dada group, who lampooned the machine as a contorted, dysfunctional jumble of gears and metal. But technology did not lose its allure as the leitmotiv of modern culture. Both visual and performing artists sought to distill the features and characteristics of mechanization as a positive, forward-looking creative force. The syncopated rhythms and polyphonic melodies of jazz music echoed throughout the cabarets and nightclubs of 1920s Europe and America, along with dance crazes like the Charleston, whose clipped, energetic movements echoed the measured patterns of an automated gear. The notion of dance and choreographed movement as mechanical rhythm bore an even more distinct relationship to industrial process. In Russia, theatrical pioneer Vsevelod Meyerhold's studies in "bio-mechanics"—the reduction of an actor's movements to their most essential means of expression—were based upon Frederick Taylor's ideas earlier in the century for making factory workers on a production line more efficient.

The era also gave birth to the phenomenon of "mass ornament," the almost military-like subjugation of individual expression in synchronized, collective display: spectacles such as parades and other public performances, which were commemorated through film and photography. The most famous example of this was the popular American dance troupe known as "The Tiller Girls," whose identical-looking members performed high-kicking chorus-line routines to widespread acclaim in cabarets and theaters across Europe.

In the newborn Soviet Union, the upheavals of the Bolshevik Revolution gave way to an era of planning and restructuring, defined by the promise of technology, to form the foundation of a socialist utopia. While the government sought to link the country's widespread agrarian regions through expansion of a modern rail system and the establishment of mass communications through broadcast radio, Russia's artists dreamed of a new civilization where art would be a means toward social transformation. Known generally as Constructivists, artists like El Lissitzky, Alexander Rodchenko, Varvara Stepanova, and Vladimir Tatlin perceived themselves as engineers rather than fine artists, eschewing easel painting at a certain point for design, typography, architecture, and photography. They abandoned realist representation in favor of the abstract language of geometry, creating forms that served as metaphors for a New World order of harmony and precision. Materials like steel and glass were celebrated for their qualities of solidity and transparency. They signified the values of stability and honesty that informed their plans for Modern buildings intended to stand in stark juxtaposition to the oppressive, fortresslike architecture of Russia's czarist past.

This new direction in Modern architecture came to be known as the "International Style," so-called because of its widespread adoption and its seemingly universal visual language. Among the most eloquent voices of the movement were Le Corbusier in France and Walter Gropius, founder of the Bauhaus in Germany. In his 1923 treatise *Towards a New Architecture*, Le Corbusier extolled grain elevators, steamships, automobiles, and airplanes, drawing a parallel between their sleek, mechanical forms and the sober virtues of Classical architecture. His landmark Pavilion de l'Espirit Nouveau, a two-story apartment built for the 1925 *Paris Exposition Internationale des Arts Décoratifs*, exemplified his principle of the building as machine, constructed from modern materials like concrete, steel, and glass, and a design language culled from a hybrid of Classicism and Modern engineering. The exhibition was also a watershed for Modern design, serving as the foundation for Art Deco, the quintessential Machine Age style defined by its combination of streamlined forms and use of industrial materials like chrome and plastic.

But perhaps the most far-reaching influence of the machine aesthetic can be traced to Germany's Bauhaus, the landmark school founded in 1919, where crafts, design, and fine arts were taught under one roof. Under the directorship of Gropius, the Bauhaus espoused social change through architecture, functional objects, and works of art crafted in cool, sleek forms based on a universal visual language—geometry—capable of being mass-produced through the use of inexpensive, industrial materials. Its emphasis on practicality and efficiency achieved through a reductive vocabulary of forms epitomized the ethos of the Machine Age: clean, lean, and devoid of ornamentation. —*Matthew Drutt*

DAS MEGOLA-ZWEIRAD-AUTO

Leaflet for the Megola, n.d. Classic Bike, Kettering, England.

Megola Sport

640 cc • 1922 • Germany

Bore x stroke: 52 x 60 mm • Power output: 14 hp @ 3,600 rpm • Top speed: 68 mph (109 km/h) •

Deutsches Museum, Munich

The long history of the motorcycle has seen some weird and wonderful machines, but the Megola is perhaps the most remarkable of them all. Designer Fritz Cockerell built the first prototype of the Megola in 1920, mounting the engine's five cylinders in a star formation within the rear wheel. The concept of fitting the power unit into the wheel hub was not new, yet fitting the engine to the front wheel, which he did in 1922, was. This was the first—and one of the only—motorcycles in the world to locate it there.

Each of the bike's five air-cooled cylinders had a displacement of 128 cc, with a bore and stroke of 52 x 60 mm. There was no clutch or gearbox; instead, while the engine and wheel rotated forward, the crankshaft, which operated via the gear train, functioned six times as quickly in the opposite direction, which meant that the driving forces were equally distributed. The engine produced 14 hp at 3,000 rpm, and, at its maximum of 3,600 rpm, it turned the front wheel at no less than 600 rpm, giving a top speed of over 60 mph, an impressive achievement for its day.

Cockerell incorporated a host of other unusual features, including two fuel tanks. The main tank was hidden under the extensive bodywork, and the fuel from it was taken to a much smaller tank above the engine via a hand pump. Because the engine occupied most of the front wheel area, Cockerell used two independent brakes for the rear wheel. The Megola also came well-equipped: a fuel gauge, tachometer, and ammeter were all standard equipment.

The Megola was available in either touring or sport variants. While the former featured a sprung rear wheel and soft saddle, the latter came without rear suspension, but with a more powerful engine. In just under five years, the company sold approximately 2,000 motorcycles. The Megola ceased production in 1926, in the midst of Germany's rampant inflation and general economic instability. — MW

Monet & Goyon Moto Légère

117 cc • 1922 • France
Bore x stroke: 52.5 x 59 mm • Power output: 1.5 hp •
Top speed: 25 mph (40 km/h) • Collection of Michel Gagnaire

Initially, French motorcycle innovation was supreme, its engineers rapidly elaborating on the new internal combustion engine. As a result, early British or American motorcycles usually had French De Dion or Peugeot engines. The four-valve, double-overhead-cam cylinder head found on almost every motorcycle engine today is the invention of three racing drivers and a draftsman, all of them working in France in 1912.

But ideas were more plentiful than money. Between the wars, undercapitalized French motorcycle makers usually bought their engines from domestic or foreign specialists. More ambitious machines attracted intense interest in the prototype phase, but too often failed to become financially viable products.

Monet & Goyon began by marketing the strange Wall Auto Wheel under their own name in 1917. This was a lawn mower–sized engine, built into a third wheel, with an accompanying fuel tank. It was designed to attach to one side of a bicycle's rear wheel, and the resulting contrivance could lean to the right or the left in conventional fashion.

By 1922 Monet & Goyon had sensibly rearranged the elements in this scheme to make a very practical little motorbike. The four-stroke engine had a single vertical air-cooled cylinder and was located beneath the rider's seat. The machine had an open frame, like that of a scooter, which afforded the driver useful weather protection in the form of a legshield and a floor. The fuel tank was located above the rear wheel.

The motorcycle took the nickname "Priest's Bike" because a frocked clergyman could have operated this machine without bespattering his clothes. French practicality in transportation is legendary, and the spartan Citröen 2CV is not its sole manifestation. A representative of one of the Japanese makers has remarked that the French market is the only one that does not require the motorcycle to have any specific form. The French, he said, will gladly accept a machine with a roof, a floor, or even side-curtains, if it will economically get them to work and keep them dry, year-round.

In the last 20 years, the French tendency to work from first principles has reasserted itself, leading to a variety of unconventional chassis concepts from the likes of Eric Offenstadt, Claude Fior, and Andre de Cortanze (the ELF experiments). And, since horsepower is hardly elusive any more, the chassis defines the capability of today's racing and sports motorcycles. —*KC*

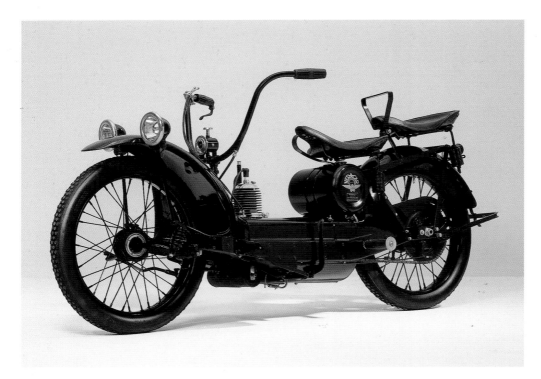

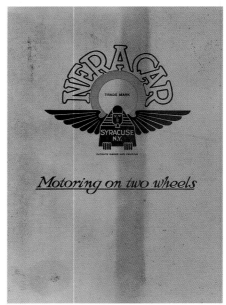

Owner's manual for the Neracar, 1922.
Collection of Kurt and Maxine Ritthaler.

Neracar

14 ci • 1922 • United States
Bore x stroke: 2½ x 2¾ inches • Power output: 2.5 hp • Top speed: 35 mph (56 km/h) •
Collection of Maxine and Kurt Ritthaler

The Neracar was an oddity in the field of two-wheeled motorized transportation. Before its appearance in 1921, nothing quite like it had ever been seen before on American roads. Developed by Carl A. Neracher and manufactured in both Great Britain (beginning in 1921) and Syracuse, New York (beginning in 1922), this unusual vehicle possessed design characteristics that allowed for a comparison between it and the automobile.

Indeed, there were plenty of features (aside from its name) that invited the comparison. The chassis of the Neracar was constructed from steel members that enclosed the bottom portion of the vehicle's engine and its novel drive train. Unlike most motorcycles' motors, the Neracar engine was turned sideways, so that its crankshaft was in line with its frame. This enabled the motor's exposed flywheel to turn at right angles to a friction-operated "drive wheel" that transmitted the power (by means of a chain) to the rear wheel.

The box-frame construction allowed the 175-pound machine to have a very low center of gravity; the Neracar consequently exhibited outstanding handling characteristics. Salesmen commonly demonstrated the motorcycle's ease of handling by riding while standing upright on the machine with their hands in the air. Photographs from the era depict a variety of unorthodox riding positions, including a man riding down the road, steering with his feet while his hands were handcuffed in front of him!

The 13-ci, two-stroke Neracar engine was capable of propelling the vehicle to a top speed of 35 mph, and the Syracuse company claimed that their machine would travel 85 to 100 miles on a single gallon of fuel. The Neracar even enjoyed some success in competitive events. In the 1923 National Six-Day Trials (which called for a sustained low speed over a 1,400-mile course), Neracar-mounted riders claimed the first three places and the team prize.

Despite its economy, ease of handling, and modest price, the Neracar did not sell in sufficient quantities to make it financially viable. In 1926 the investors who had financed the company halted production of the vehicle in Syracuse; in the same year, manufacturing ceased in Great Britain. —*DKS*

BMW R32

494 cc • 1923 • Germany
Bore x stroke: 68 x 68 mm • Power output: 8.5 hp @ 3,200 rpm •
Top speed: 62 mph (100 km/h) • Collection of David Percival

At the outset of World War I, BMW's forerunners, Eisenach, Otto, and Rapp, were all separate companies. Then, in March 1916 the Otto and Rapp aircraft factories merged to form Bayerische Flugzeugwerke AG (BFW). Due to the rapid growth of the fledgling German Air Force, BFW's reputation as an airplane engine builder of the highest order flourished. Their alliance was cemented in 1917, when the company went public and the name was changed to Bayerische Motoren Werke GmbH (BMW). Later, in 1927, BMW acquired the Eisenach automobile manufacturing concern.

At its wartime peak BMW employed over 3,500 people, but with Germany's defeat the company foundered and was forced to turn its hand to anything to remain in business. Materials originally intended for airplane-engine production were diverted into a vast number of new uses, including, in 1920, motorcycles. BMW's first attempt, the Flink, which had a proprietary Kurier 148-cc two-stroke engine, was not a success. In 1921 engineer Martin Stolle designed the M2B15, a 494-cc flat-twin side-valve engine that was sold mainly to other manufacturers, such as Victoria and Bison.

The next year, airplane-engine designer Max Friz, one of the original directors of the company, designed what was to be hailed as a masterpiece, the R32. When the R32 was unveiled at the Paris Motorcycle Salon in 1923, it created a sensation. Although it retained a 494-cc flat-twin engine, this was now transversely in unit with a three-speed gearbox and a shaft drive to the rear wheel. The frame was of a full-twin triangle design, and the front fork, with short arms, had a quarter-elliptical leaf spring. It was the beginning of a design concept that was modern enough to last throughout the rest of the 20th century.

There were 3,090 R32s constructed between 1923 and 1926, and its success launched BMW in the two-wheel world. — *MW*

BMW works in Munich, c. 1923. Courtesy of BMW AG, Munich.

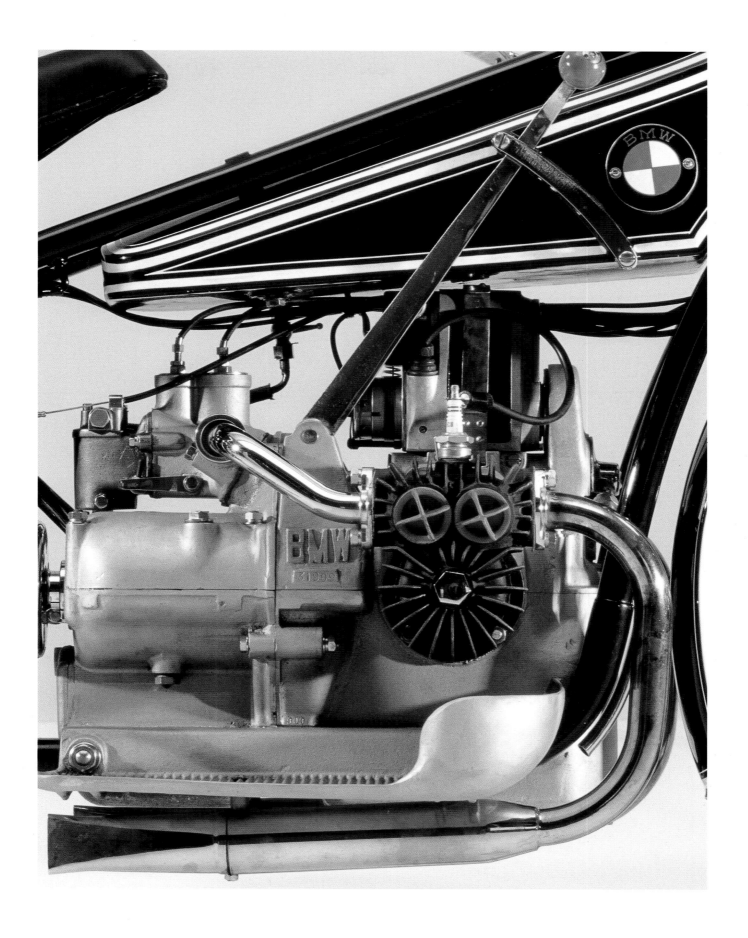

Harley-Davidson 8-Valve Board Track Racer

61 ci • 1923 • United States
Bore x stroke: 3⁵/₁₆ x 3½ inches • Power output: unknown •
Top speed: 109 mph (175 km/h) • Collection of Daniel K. Statnekov

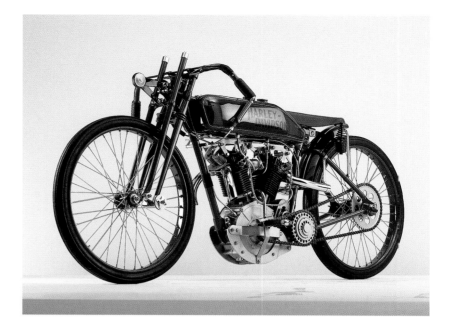

Unlike the founders of the Indian Motorcycle Company, William Harley and the three Davidson brothers did not have backgrounds in bicycle manufacturing. Nor did they have their competitors' experience with respect to the publicity benefits that were derived from winning races. Consequently, more than ten years elapsed from the inception of the Harley-Davidson Motor Company before the Milwaukee firm committed itself to a factory-sponsored race effort.

By 1915, however, factory-team riders were victorious in two highly publicized events, including the important 300-mile race held on Independence Day in Dodge City, Kansas. The publicity that ensued from this nationally recognized victory had an immediate effect on sales. Bolstered by their initial success, the founders of the company agreed to underwrite the development of an eight-valve motor intended solely for competitive events.

Drawing upon state-of-the-art aeronautical engine technology, Harley-Davidson engineers designed an overhead-valve V-twin with four valves per cylinder and hemispherical combustion chambers. With its efficient porting and combustion chamber design, the 61-ci 8-Valve outdistanced the competition, and in 1916 the Harley brand was again victorious at the prestigious Dodge City event. The 8-Valve motor continued to evolve, bringing even more success and publicity to its manufacturer.

Harley-Davidson reached a noteworthy milestone in 1921, when an 8-Valve piloted by the company team captain became the first motorcycle in the world to win a race at a speed in excess of 100 mph. The following year the machine captured a new world's record for the mile, attaining a speed of slightly over 109 mph. In the international arena, the company's specialized race motor won important European championships, including the inaugural Grand Prix at Monza, Italy.

Five Harley-Davidson 8-Valves are known to have survived to the present. All were originally shipped abroad for international competition. Examples have been discovered in England, Austria, New Zealand, and Italy. The 8-Valve exhibited in *The Art of the Motorcycle* was obtained from the estate of the English competitor, Fred Dixon, who achieved fame with it in 1923 when he was awarded a Gold Star by the British Motorcycle Racing Club for his 100-mph performance at the Brooklands race course. —*DKS*

Moto Guzzi C4V

498 cc • 1924 • Italy

Bore x stroke: 88 x 82 mm • Power output: 22 hp @ 5,500 rpm •
Top speed: 93 mph (150 km/h) • Courtesy of Moto Guzzi SpA,
Mandello del Lario, Italy

Squadron life in the Italian Air Service during the last stages of World War I was instrumental in creating what is now regarded as Italy's most famous motorcycle, the Moto Guzzi.

During off-duty hours, two pilots, Giovanni Ravelli and Giorgio Parodi, along with their young mechanic/driver, Carlo Guzzi, concocted an advanced design for a motorcycle, which Guzzi sketched out. Sadly, Ravelli was killed in a flying accident shortly after the end of hostilities, but Parodi and Guzzi, with backing from Parodi's father, a wealthy Genoa shipping magnate, began work in 1919. The result was the GP (Guzzi-Parodi), debuting late in 1920. The founders soon changed the motorcycle's name to Moto Guzzi, and they adopted a company trademark, an eagle with its wings spread in flight, in honor of their fallen comrade.

The prototype design was revolutionary for its time. Its 498-cc single-cylinder engine was laid horizontally and featured an overhead cam driven by shaft-and-bevel gears. Perhaps even more interesting were the four-valve head layout and the engine's oversquare (short-stroke) dimensions of 88 x 82 mm. The first production model, the Normale, closely followed the original layout, but the overhead cam was ditched in favor of pushrod-operated valves, with two instead of four valves.

Guzzi's first racing model, the Corsa 2V debuted in 1923; it was replaced in 1924 by a much improved model, the C4V, which returned to many of the features of the original GP prototype, such as overhead cam and four valves. Producing 22 hp at 5,500 rpm, and reaching a maximum speed of 93 mph, the C4V made its debut at the famous Lario event (often called the Italian TT), winning at an average speed of 42.2 mph. This speed may seem low, but the race was run over unsurfaced roads and the course had numerous hairpin bends.

Although it was updated from time to time, the basic design of the Guzzi single—with its giant outside flywheel, semi-unit-construction gearbox, magneto ignition, and original 88 x 82 mm engine dimensions—remained viable and in production as late as 1976. —*MW*

Böhmerland

598 cc • 1925 • Czechoslovakia
Bore x stroke: 79.8 x 120 mm • Power output: 16 hp @ 3,000 rpm •
Top speed: 60 mph (97 km/h) • Collection of D. J. Light

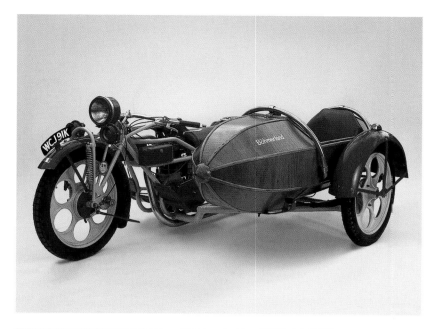

In 1924, Albin Liebisch began manufacturing motorcycles at a factory in the northern Bohemian town of Krasna Lipa. These machines, along with the Neracar and the Megola, were some of the most unconventional in the history of motorcycling. Only 1,000 were built between 1924 and 1939, when production ceased. In Germany they were marketed under the name of Böhmerland; in Czechoslovakia they were called Cechie.

All versions employed an air-cooled, 598-cc, overhead-valve, single-cylinder, long-stroke engine with a hemispherical combustion chamber. Initially, the power output was 16 hp at 3,000 rpm; it was later increased to 24 hp at 3,600 rpm. However, it was not the power unit that was the most interesting feature of the design, but the low, duplex, tubular frame, which seated two passengers on an extra long dual saddle and a third on a tandem seat above the rear wheel. Some versions were almost 10 feet long.

Drive to the rear wheel was transmitted via a hand-operated three-speed Sturmey Archer or Hurth gearbox. The disc wheels were manufactured from cast aluminum. Some bikes even had two gearboxes, the second operated by either passenger, to provide additional ratios for mountainous terrain. Dual fuel tanks, each with a capacity of 5 liters, were located on each side of the rear wheel. Another unusual aspect of this motorcycle was the heavy and complicated front fork assembly, which featured friction dampers; there was no form of rear suspension. The Liebisch design also relied on bright color schemes—yellow and red, yellow and black, or yellow and green—at a time when most vehicles were finished in a single shade, and a conservative one at that.

These machines, which reached a maximum speed of 60 mph, proved to be long-lasting and reliable. But Albin Liebisch's stubborn belief that he knew best what the customer wanted meant that few of his motorcycles sold. In commercial terms the venture was a failure, but today, with only a handful remaining, the motorcycles have become supremely collectable. — *MW*

Brough Superior SS100
Alpine Grand Sport

988 cc • 1926 • United Kingdom
Bore x stroke: 85.5 x 86 mm • Power output: 45 hp @ 5,000 rpm •
Top speed: 100 mph (161 km/h) • Collection of Jack Silverman,
Silverman Museum Racing, Aspen, Colo.

The years between the end of World War I and the Great Depression constituted the golden age of British motorcycling. Production was high and innovation, constant. According to a tongue-in-cheek theory, when the most popular motorcycle reaches 1,000 cc, an economic crash is imminent. The Brough Superior was that machine.

Beginning in 1919, George Brough's Nottingham firm assembled large, capable motorcycles for the relatively affluent. They were built largely from bought-in components, which reduced tooling costs, but placed the maker at the mercy of suppliers. This 988-cc air-cooled JAP V-twin was built in the style of the time, with overhead valves operated by exposed pushrods and rocker arms. This arrangement was possible when engine speed and power were low enough to do without pressure lubrication of each moving part. Internal function is externally explicit: when the engine runs, you see the valve gear in motion. The same was true in aviation—the J5 Wright Whirlwind engine that Lindbergh used to cross the Atlantic in 1927 also had an exposed valve gear.

Earlier Broughs set records at England's great Brooklands racetrack. They were capable of sustaining high speeds and able to climb hills without shifting, but their length and weight denied them rapid maneuverability.

The SS100 Alpine Grand Sport appeared in 1924, and each machine was sold with a written guarantee that it would reach 100 mph. Because the weight and speed were too much for the girder forks of the time, in 1925 the "castle" fork (seen on this machine) was adopted. Its moving element is supported at both top and bottom, rather than just by links at the top, as with a girder. Although later SS100s would have rear springing, this chassis is rigid. The star-shaped device on the fork, just above the level of the fender, is a friction damper designed to prevent bouncing of the suspension when the bike hits a bump.

The Brough derives a certain fame from the fact that T. E. Lawrence owned a succession of seven SS100s, and eventually met his death on one in 1935.

In time, the exclusive machines Brough wanted to build became too expensive for the market to bear. The company switched to war manufacturing in 1940 and never resumed production of motorcycles. —KC

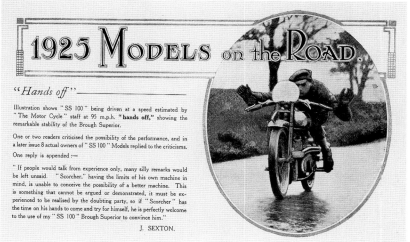

Brough Superior owner's manual, 1926. Collection of Jack Silverman, Silverman Museum Racing, Aspen, Colo.

Scott Squirrel Sprint Special

620 cc • 1929 • United Kingdom
Bore x stroke: 74 x 68 mm • Power output: 25 hp @ 5,000 rpm •
Top speed: 85 mph (137 km/h) • The Barber Vintage Motorsports
Museum, Birmingham, Ala.

With their two-stroke engines and bridge-like open chassis, Scotts were thoroughly unconventional machines. Alfred Angus Scott built a prototype of the prescient two-stroke, liquid-cooled, 180-degree-firing twin as early as 1898, ultimately developing it into a motorcycle power unit.

A two-stroke engine fires twice as often as the four-stroke type that powers most bikes and cars today. Because of this, its pistons receive double the heat exposure and therefore need more intensive cooling. This can be achieved by surrounding each head (and, later, cylinder) with water cooled by a radiator.

The triangulated chassis is another example of Scott rationality. It attains maximum stiffness from a minimum weight of material. Although the rear of the machine was rigid, the front suspension was cushioned by way of telescopic elements. The telescopic fork displaced girder and bottom-link forks only after World War II.

TT racing success came to Scott in 1912, and the machines continued as an unusual minority alternative to the conventional four-stroke, air-cooled mainstream. The example featured in *The Art of the Motorcycle* was raced by George Silk in 1929 at a displacement of 498 cc, before its later adjustment to 620 cc. Road-going Scotts produced about 14 hp at 3,200 rpm—a leisurely output equal to the task of gentlemanly travel.

The Scott thrived in the 1920s, when its good pulling power, smoothness, and excellent cooling made it superior. It was a product of the first, diverse flowering of the motorcycle, and not of its subsequent commercialization. Having found its niche, the Sprint Special then failed to develop as rapidly as its four-stroke competition in the vigorous era of British motorcycling after World War I. As the two-stroke principle lagged behind, it came to be associated mainly with low-priced "poor-man's specials" and was looked down upon. This situation was reversed after 1960, when German and Japanese engineers developed the two-stroke engine to achieve remarkable heights in racing. Today a 500-cc four-cylinder two-stroke racing motorcycle engine is capable of producing up to 200 hp. —KC

New World Orders

New World Orders: 1930–1944

The free-spirited character of innovation and experimentation that flourished during the 1920s underwent a sea change in the next decade. Whereas the machine aesthetic of the '20s was realized through a prevailing tendency toward abstraction, based on a reductive, geometric vocabulary and a utopian political agenda, the ethos of machine culture in the 1930s assumed an altogether different scale and demeanor. Ushered in by a wave of conservative, even totalitarian, political ideology that overswept Europe, the cultural landscape shifted toward social realism, a state-controlled ideology of popular, classically inspired art and architecture that celebrated national identity through grandiose themes in works on a commensurate scale. Ironically, social realism incarnated many of the principles and ideals of the prior decade: a belief in technology's potential to transform society and a desire to communicate through a universal form of visual expression. Only now, mammoth industrialization became the leitmotiv, mediated by a belief in the human form as the most powerful and effective means to communicate with a mass audience.

Italy initially led the way. The Fascist Party assumed power there far earlier than in other European countries, taking control in 1922 following its celebrated "March on Rome." By the time Mussolini had garnered absolute power in 1928, he had effectively deployed a popular campaign to create a reborn, modernized Italy through reclamation of the glories of ancient Rome. Driven by a desire to instill civic pride and maintain social order in a country that had lost its way in the aftermath of war, Mussolini initiated large-scale civic projects such as the decongestion of the cities, dissolution of the ghettoes, and industrialization of the farmlands. Even the railway system was overhauled, earning a well-deserved reputation for punctuality.

Among Mussolini's earliest ventures was the symbolic restoration of classical monuments from the era of Roman supremacy, such as the Coliseum, which had become hemmed in by overcrowded low-income slums. As the landmarks of Italy's vaunted past were rejuvenated, new monuments were planned to celebrate the glories of the present, among them the imposing Esposizione Universale di Roma. A dehumanizing complex of classically inspired buildings, planned for completion in 1942, it was to have been the site of the Olympic games and stand for the new Rome. Above all, monuments to Mussolini himself became commonplace, replicating the ancient Roman ideal of state power residing in the body of an individual leader, and establishing the cult of personality that would characterize other totalitarian governments of the period.

In Germany, the Weimar Republic's short-lived experiment in parliamentary democracy was buried under the weight of high inflation and unemployment. Demoralized by the loss of World War I, Germany had been further humiliated by the Treaty of Versailles, which exacted a high price from the country in the form of reparations, demobilization of its armed forces, and concessions on territorial claims. Thus, by the time Adolf Hitler became chancellor in 1933, Germany was ripe for transformation.

Blaming Germany's ills on a loss of identification with its cultural heritage and contamination by foreign influences, the Nazis initiated a campaign of purification, turning the celebration of Teutonic culture and the Classical ideal into an ideology of terror and xenophobia. European Modernism was a primary target, and in 1937, the infamous "Degenerate Art" (*Entartete Kunst*) exhibition presented hundreds of artworks by Modern masters, including Max Beckmann, Ernst Ludwig Kirchner, and Pablo Picasso, which had been confiscated from German museums. The exhibition lampooned the works as expressions of a deranged psyche. In a sweeping condemnation of all that the Bauhaus had stood for, Hitler declared that "the German roof is not flat," consigning Walter Gropius and his colleagues to a temporary dustbin of German history. The 1936 Olympics held in Berlin became an international showcase for the Third Reich's vision of a new society, its monumental, classicizing pavilions built to the stifling, sober specifications of Albert Speer's new architecture.

The irony of this era is that communism, the arch enemy of fascism, embraced many of its ideals. Steeped in the same cults of personality and celebrations of national identity, Stalin launched Soviet Russia into a new era of bold industrialization that was to be achieved through a series of harshly ambitious Five Year Plans. As in Italy and Germany, the ideology of modernization was propagated through large-scale planning and classical ideals of physical strength, continuity, order, and stability. The first Five Year Plan yielded one of the world's most powerful hydroelectric plants—the 810,000-horsepower Dniepr Dam—which was completed in 1933 and served as a symbol of the transition from revolutionary socialism (a society in flux) to industrial socialism (economic and social stability).

Monuments were an inevitable outgrowth of this ideology of scale, and perhaps the most outrageous expression of the ideal was the never-realized Palace of the Soviets. A government structure planned for Moscow as the seat of power for Soviet Russia, it was the symbolic antithesis of the Kremlin. A neoclassical wedding cake of startling size and unfathomable engineering was, at one point, to be topped by a statue of Lenin taller than the Empire State Building. With arms stretched toward the heavens, the statue was to have signified the limitless potential of communism.

The legacy of these ideological dictatorships is now a matter of history. Having placed their own houses in order, or in some cases due to an inability to do so, they set out to change the rest of the world, each seeking to establish a new paradigm based on its own political philosophy. Technologies developed for social transformation became weapons of destruction, and as a similar wind blew in the East, the world suddenly found itself at war again. —*MD*

Majestic advertisement from *Moto Revue*, 1929.
Collection of Bernard Salvat.

Majestic 350

349 cc • 1930 • France
Bore x stroke: 75 x 79 mm • Power output: 11 hp @ 4,000 rpm •
Top speed: 56 mph (90 km/h) • Collection of Alain Petitjean

In the optimistic spirit of France's machine age, everything had to be streamlined. The Majestic 350's bulletlike design was unlike any other, with mechanical details concealed under louvered sheet metal.

Under the direction of Georges Roy, the Majestic's transformation was more than cosmetic. While mainstream machines steered like a bicycle—a fork holding the front wheel, pivoting high on the front of the frame—the Majestic made use of hub-center steering, a persistent design alternative throughout the development of the motorcycle. Hub-steerers locate the steering pivot inside the front wheel. Thus, only the wheel and brake are steered, creating, in theory, the reduction of steered mass and increased stability. But in fact, this design has yet to prove superior over conventional forks. Further, the design has proved unappealing to most traditionalists.

As with many other French machines, a variety of proprietary power plants were used by Majestic—Train, Chaise, and the English JAP. The example included in *The Art of the Motorcycle* is powered by a single-cylinder overhead-valve Chaise, in unit with a three-speed transmission and chain final drive. The machine is steered by a horizontal rod, visible on the right, that extends from the front axle rearward and is linked to handlebars. A similar arrangement may be seen on contemporary automobiles, where a front axle exists between two prominent vertical members on either side of a wheel to provide suspension movement.

The impulse to de-mechanize, tame, or civilize machines with an outer skin seems to be a persistent one. In the postwar period, Vincent built the Black Prince, which had curving black fiberglass panels, and notable recent examples include Ducati's Paso and Honda's Pacific Coast. In these self-contained designs, the rider's presence may seem like an unwelcome afterthought. —*KC*

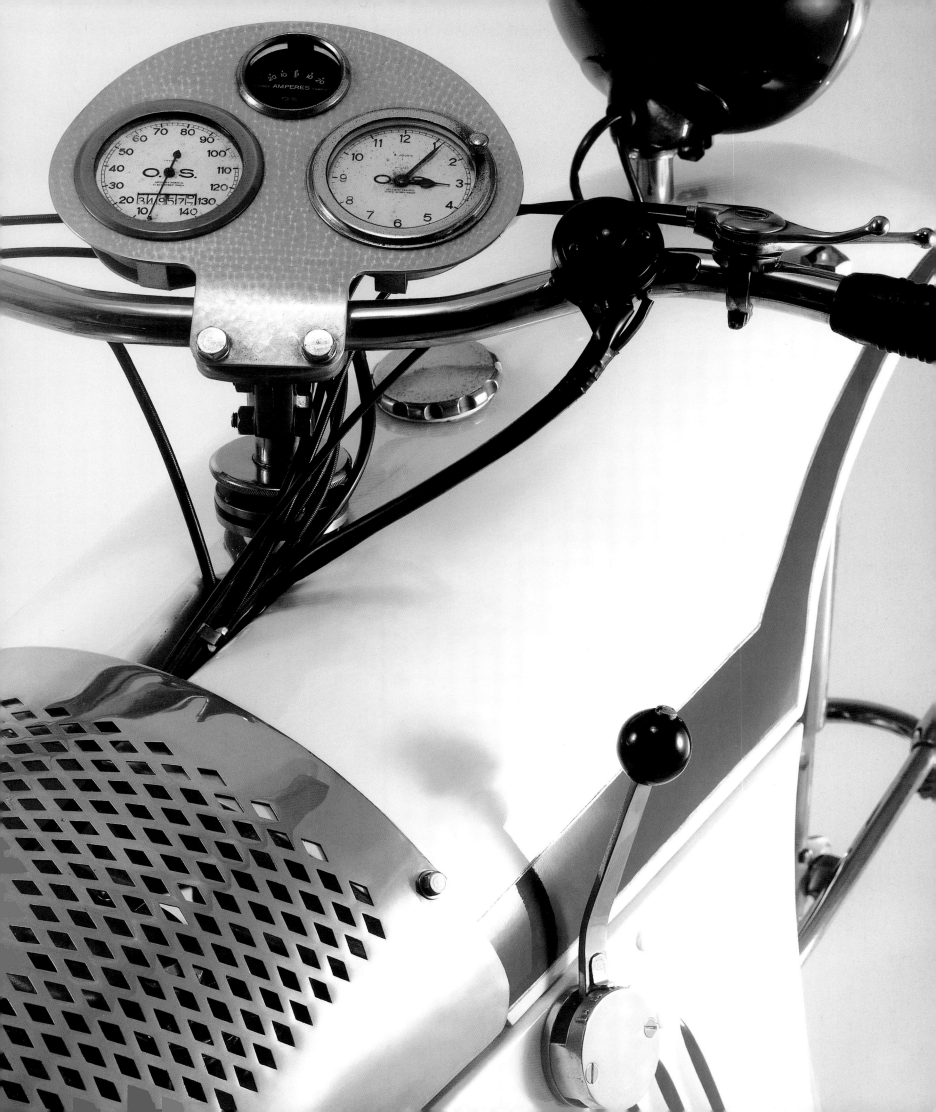

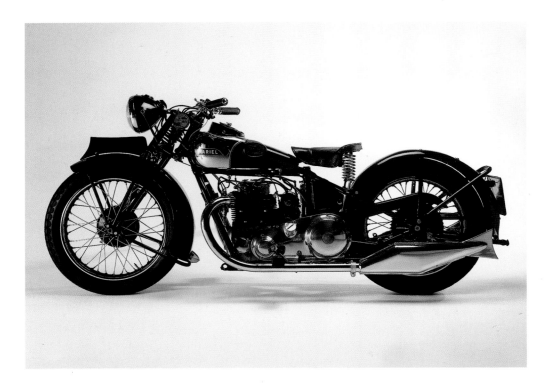

Catalogue for Ariel, 1931.
Collection of Jeremy P. Mortimore.

Ariel Square Four

497 cc • 1931 • United Kingdom
Bore x stroke: 51 x 61 mm • Power output: 24 hp @ 6,000 rpm •
Top speed: 85 mph (137 km/h) • Collection of W. Eric Oddy

Like so many motorcycle makers, Ariel evolved from a bicycle business at the turn of the century. Combining French engines with cycle-style chassis, Ariel's early specialty was the motor tricycle.

A motorcycle dealer and amateur engine builder with a special interest in four-cylinder engines, Edward Turner designed this unusual machine after joining Ariel in 1928. Its valves are operated by a camshaft placed above the cylinder head (hence "overhead camshaft," or "ohc") and driven by a chain, thus doing away with pushrods and minimizing the number and weight of parts between cam and valve. This, in turn, allows the valve mechanism to operate accurately at a higher speed, and enables the engine, at least potentially, to generate more power.

The resulting 497-cc engine had two 180-degree cranks, geared together. The overhead cam was noisy (just listen to a modern Honda RC30 to confirm how real the problem is), and the engine was later redesigned with conventional pushrods and rocker arms. The gearbox was a built-in unit with the engine rather than mounted separately as was usual at the time. Because the four-cylinder engine had smaller, lighter flywheels than a single, it accelerated rapidly, giving a sporty feel. Later versions of this machine became the favored choice for sidecar work, since the engine's "plonk," or ability to pull from lower rpm, was excellent. But attempts to increase the power of this engine only accentuated the heat distress of its rear cylinders.

Ariel joined BSA in 1958 (forming BSA Ariel) and switched to making mass-market, two-stroke-powered bikes. Meanwhile, the evolving Square Four continued in production until 1959. BSA Ariel ended its enterprise in 1965.

Commercializing the four-cylinder engine was only partly successful, because British industry remained craft-based, depending on experienced fitters rather than Fordist mass production. Only in 1969, with Honda's CB750, did the four-cylinder achieve mainstream success.

Despite its limitations, the Square Four incorporates adventuresome features and remains an outstanding example of individual design. Sadly, market forces tend to weed out such inspirations, and we are left with conventional designs. — *KC*

Brochure for MGC, 1931. Collection of Bernard Salvat.

MGC N3BR

245 cc • 1932 • France
Bore x stroke: 62.5 x 80 mm • Power output: 14 hp @ 5,500 rpm •
Top speed: 81 mph (130 km/h) • Collection of Dominique Buisson

Little more than a novelty when it first appeared in 1912, aluminum was widely adopted after World War I for its light weight, good heat conductivity, and shine. A motorcycle dealer named Marcel Guiguet grew obsessed with casting as a single piece many of the theretofore-separate parts of the motorcycle. He proposed to enclose engine and gearbox between an upper member constructed out of the tank, steering-head, and chassis beam, and a lower member embodying the engine's oil tank, joined by steel struts. The material was one of the Alpax series of high-silicon alloys made by Lightalloys of London.

But pouring sound castings of such size and thinness was almost impossible at that time. Part after part suffered cold shorts, shrinkage cracks, and porosity. (Close inspection of Constantin Brancusi's *Bird in Space* reveals evidence of the same problems.) Guiguet sealed the pores with heat and drying oils, and eventually usable parts were devised. The first MGC (Marcel Guiguet et Cie.) appeared at the Paris Salon in 1928.

Since the power plant was a proprietary British-made JAP 500 single, attention centered on the cycle parts, stunningly different as they were. This first model was dubbed "The Creamer" because of the tubby, potlike shape of the fuel-containing part of the upper chassis member. In 1930, Guiguet, knowing the infinite plasticity of the casting process, refined it, giving it the more graceful shape shown here.

Aluminum—especially cast aluminum—lacks steel's ability to survive vibration fatigue. It would require years of progress in the foundry arts, and much refinement of the internal combustion engine, before cast aluminum could be widely used in motorcycle chassis. Today, examples abound. Examine any aluminum-framed sportbike and you will see such refined castings. Guiguet's few successful parts (only two hundred or so machines were built) are isolated freaks—albeit fascinating ones—in the evolution of aluminum.

As demonstrated during the 1980s by Antonio Kobas, large aluminum beams offer much greater rigidity than an assembly of small steel tubes. The MGC offered exceptional handling and stability. This N3BR model was a racer. With its stiff chassis, good brakes, and modern drivetrain, it achieved the beginnings of success before it was priced out of existence. Only two were built.— *KC*

Dollar V4

748 cc • 1933 • France
Bore x stroke: 62.6 x 60.8 mm • Power output: 22 hp @ 4,000 rpm •
Top speed: 68 mph (110 km/h) • Collection of Gérard Gruschwitz

In addition to the series of attractive prototypes with which Dollar made its debut after World War I, the company produced numerous small displacement machines. Very few of these capable-looking 750s were built, however, and only the example in *The Art of the Motorcycle* survives.

The compact, narrow-angle V4 engine and driveline are not its only features of interest. Despite having the conventional suspension of the time—a girder fork at the front and a rigid rear—the chassis is constructed entirely of triangulated straight members. Unusual in motorcycles, this design has been favored in aircraft due to its light weight and stiffness (see, for example, the use of curved tubes in the Norton Manx). It is surely no coincidence that Dollar's owner, Maurice Chaise, had previously worked as manufacturing director of the giant wartime aero-engine maker, Gnôme et Rhône. And, while proprietary engineer at Dollar, Chaise built an aircraft engine that was quite similar to the Dollar.

The Dollar 750 has the four cylinders considered essential for smoothness, but in a much more condensed package than the usual in-line arrangement. The cylinders are in a narrow V of 14 degrees, with the pairs offset and staggered. A similar plan is used today by Audi. Four pushrods at each side of the engine operate the exposed valve gear on the cylinder head. The gearbox makes a compact unit with the engine, sending power to the rear wheel through shaft and bevel gears. This is a successfully integrated design: the goals of a short wheelbase, a powerful engine, and the convenience and reliability of a shaft drive are all achieved by making the engine fit into the assigned space rather than define the structure of that space (as in the Brough SS100).

The four air-cooled cylinders and the upper crankcase half are cast in one piece—a remarkable feat for the time, since the casting technique was far from reliable. (Curtiss in the U.S. and Rolls-Royce in Britain tried to make their V-12 aircraft engines this way and failed.) One-piece construction affords the rigidity needed for high-rpm dependability. The technique was perfected by Honda in the early 1960s for their four-cylinder racing engines. Such *monobloc* engines are now the norm for production motorcycles.

France, devastated in every way by World War I, was more agricultural than commercial in outlook between the wars and did not encourage the production of high-performance motorcycles. The year 1939 marked the end of Dollar. —*KC*

Gnôme et Rhône M1

306 cc • 1934 • France

Bore x stroke: 69 x 82 mm • Power output: unknown • Top speed: 55 mph (89 km/h) •
The Barber Vintage Motorsports Museum, Birmingham, Ala.

How do swords become plowshares? During World War I, the French company Gnôme built engines for biplane fighters, but that line of production ceased with the armistice. Money grew scarce. Gnôme started licensing the manufacturing of British-developed engines. Making motorcycles seemed like a good idea, as well. Production began in 1919 and continued past the Great Depression and through World War II, after which point Gnôme was absorbed by SNECMA, the nationalized aviation complex.

The chassis of this M1, like that of larger G-R models, is made of pressed steel, as are the fork girders. Previously, motorcycle chassis were usually made by brazing bent steel tubing into forged or cast lugs that joined the tubes—a slow, costly process. But, by the 1930s, aircraft were quickly evolving away from kite-like wooden affairs into sheet-metal structures, and motorcycle designers followed suit. Hence, the elements of this M1's chassis were stamped from sheet metal, then seam-welded into a well-braced structure. The bigger the box you can make out of a given weight of metal, the more rigid it becomes. The ultimate in this respect is an aircraft fuselage: a very large tube made of very thin metal. The M1's pressed-steel frames were a step towards today's stamped-and-welded twin-beam aluminum sportbike chassis.

There is nothing remarkable in the side-valve single-cylinder M1 engine, or in its rigid-mounted rear wheel and front girder fork. This model and many other G-Rs were chain-driven, though larger shaft-drive models were also produced.

Immediately after World War II, bicycles and motorcycles were easier to put into production than cars, and hundreds of thousands were built. It took time to get cars into production, and more time to replace expensive human labor with machinery. But when the change did happen, there was little price difference between a cheap car and a capable motorcycle. Bike makers fought back in the mid-to-late 1950s, cutting costs where they could by using pressed steel and other automotive simplifications, but the cheap car always defeats the motorcycle, and the surviving bike makers must earn their bread selling fewer, fancier machines.

Throughout this century, the motorcycle has alternated between two roles: the personal rocket, as exemplified by the Dollar, Brough, or Vincent; and the pragmatic, if unexciting, conveyance, as embodied by this G-R M1. —*KC*

BMW World Land-Speed Record

493 cc • 1937 • Germany
Bore x stroke: 66 x 72 mm • Power output: 95 hp @ 8,000 rpm •
Top speed: 174 mph (280 km/h) • Courtesy of BMW AG, Munich

During the interwar period of the 1920s and '30s, the ultimate prize for many of the leading motorcycle factories was the world land-speed record. At first American and British teams dominated the proceedings, but in September 1929, a new contender appeared on the scene in the shape of BMW, and its star rider, Ernst Henne. Together, they set a new record speed of 137.58 mph on Germany's first autobahn at Ingoldstad, establishing a pattern of achievement that would last for almost a decade.

At first BMW employed a specially prepared 736 cc overhead-valve version of its famous flat-twin four-stroke design, with a bore and stroke of 83 x 68 mm. Then, in 1936, BMW technicians decided to decrease the engine's displacement from 736 to 493. This might have appeared to be a backward move, but there was a sound basis for this technical change. Although previous machines that Henne had driven looked crude and were reminiscent of 1920s designs, the BMW newcomer was different. While the motorcycle still featured a flat-twin engine and shaft final drive, everything else was new. The engine was a 493 cc double-overhead-cam with a bore and stroke of 66 x 72 mm, a Zoller supercharger mounted on the front of the crankshaft, and rearward-facing inlets of long pipes passing over the cylinders. With a power output of 105 to 108 hp at 8,000 rpm, the running gear was suitably uprated. The motorcycle had a tubular du-plex frame with telescopic front forks and a plunger rear suspension. The entire machine and its rider were encased in an aluminum body with a detachable top section that allowed the driver to get in and out. This supercharging technology had been under development since 1929, when a production R63 model had been fitted with a positive displacement blower that was mounted atop the gearbox and driven by the magneto shaft.

After Henne broke his own record in 1936 with a speed of 168.92 mph, two teams surpassed his new mark. But within weeks of an Italian team's triumph, Henne and BMW were back on top for the seventh and final time in eight years. On November 28, 1937, the German pair clocked an amazing 173.57 mph, a record that remained unbroken until 1951. — *MW*

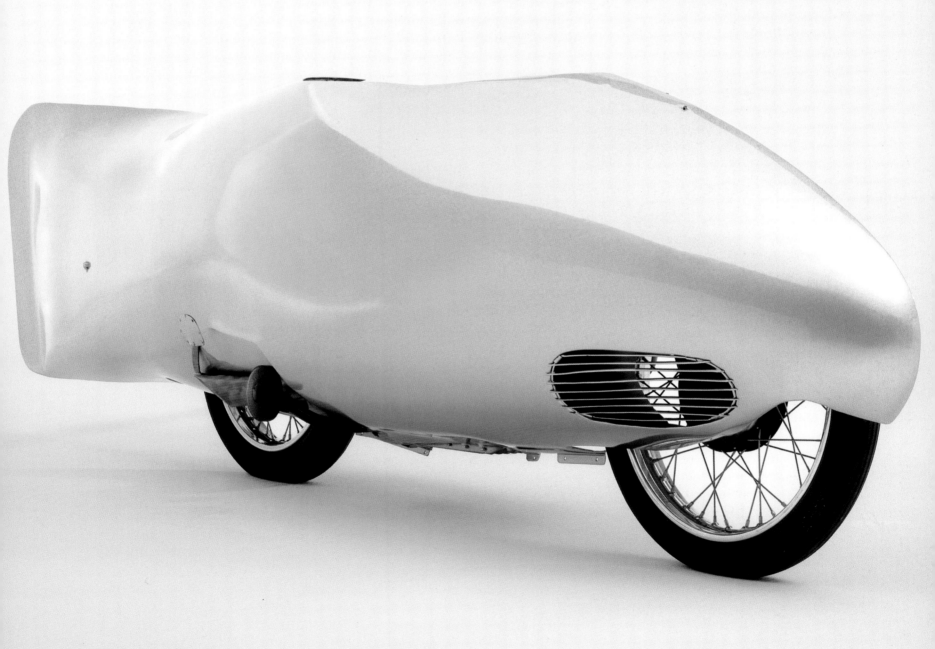

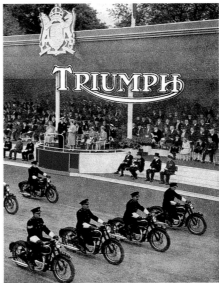

Catalogue for Triumph, 1947.
Collection of Charles M. Falco.

Triumph Speed Twin

498 cc • 1938 • United Kingdom
Bore x stroke: 63 x 80 mm • Power output: 23 hp @ 6,000 rpm • Top speed: 75 mph (121 km/h) •
The Barber Vintage Motorsports Museum, Birmingham, Ala.

The Triumph Speed Twin is the first and definitive parallel-twin design. This concept dominated British motorcycle production during the postwar period, when BSA, Matchless, AJS, and Norton all produced bikes with similar engines. Veteran engineer Doug Hele notes that this engine type was the only one Great Britain could then afford to produce in quantity.

Triumph entered the motorcycle business in 1903, building singles for many years. The Speed Twin represents a cost-effective compromise between the market's desire for something smoother and more powerful than a single, yet less complex and expensive than multicylinder engines. Why not just make the engine bigger, as George Brough did, or as American makers had done? The answer is that fuel cost and vehicle tax structure pushed most development towards smaller, harder-working engines.

Legend has it that Val Page saw an Ariel Square Four engine running on a test stand, minus its front crankshaft, and noticed its moderate vibration. He thought it might be an alternative to the more complex V-twins, flat-twins, and multis, and the Speed Twin is the result. As part of Turner's program of simplification, he abandoned traditional roller bearings for the twin's con rods, replacing them with pressure-lubricated plain bearings. The Speed Twin was actually lighter than the single-cylinder designs it replaced. The characteristic bulbous crankcase encloses a large central flywheel. The overhead valves are operated by fully enclosed pushrods and rocker arms. The chassis is conventional—rigid at the rear with a girder fork at the front.

Since its two pistons move up and down together, the engine shakes like a single, but the vibration is less severe because the twin's stroke is shorter. Firing on every revolution, its propulsion is twice as smooth as that of a single, yet it runs well with a single carburetor. It is potentially able to generate more power than a single by virtue of its shorter stroke (making possible higher rpm) and greater valve area (allowing the cylinders to be filled even at high speed).

Thousands of Speed Twin Triumphs were sold, and the design was later elaborated to 650 and then 750 cc. American riders discovered that a light, handy alternative to the heavy Indians and Harleys they already knew did exist. — *KC*

Crocker

61 ci • 1940 • United States
Bore x stroke: 3¼ x 3⅝ inches • Power output: 55 hp @ 3,600 rpm •
Top speed: 120 mph (193 km/h) • The Otis Chandler Vintage Museum
of Transportation and Wildlife, Oxnard, Calif.

Regarded by many as "the Duesenberg of motorcycles," the over-head-valve, V-twin Crocker was almost immediately recognized as an American classic. Designed by Albert Crocker and Paul "P. A." Bigsby, the hand-crafted sporting motorcycle was first offered for sale to the public in 1936 by the Los Angeles–based Crocker Motorcycle Company. From the very beginning, the California heavyweight was a sensational performer.

In its first competitive appearance (in 1936 at Muroc Dry Lake in Southern California) the Crocker factory entry was 10 to 15 mph faster than the competition. Company advertisements claimed that "the Crocker motorcycle . . . is ideal for those who like to tangle on the highway," and Al Crocker never had to make good on his advertised offer to return the full purchase price to any Crocker rider who was beaten by a stock Indian or Harley-Davidson.

The Crocker engine is a 45-degree V-twin with a standard displacement of 61 ci and a 7-to-1 compression ratio. Extra-thick cylinder walls enabled the customer to specify a larger displacement engine, and the company advertised that "every Crocker motor is a bench job." The initial batch of motors was of hemi-head design and produced 60 hp at 4,000 rpm. After 1936, the company produced engines with vertical-valve heads, rated at 55 hp at 3,600 rpm.

Every major component of the Crocker motorcycle was manufactured in the firm's machine shop. Numerous aluminum castings (including gas and oil tanks) were also made in the company foundry. The Crocker gas tanks had a capacity of 2.5 gallons; however, the design of the motorcycle changed in 1939, and a larger tank allowed for an additional gallon of fuel. The paint scheme and choice of colors were optional.

As a limited-production motorcycle, hand-built to an ideal rather than a price, the Crocker never achieved commercial success. Nevertheless, the big boulevard cruiser represents a milestone in motorcycle design; it was a forerunner of the postwar custom motorcycle as well as the modern superbike. Of the estimated 70 to 90 Crocker motorcycles that were built between 1936 and 1942, 49 complete machines are known to have survived. —*DKS*

Cover of *Indian Motorcycle News*, April–May 1942.
Collection of George and Milli Yarocki.

Indian Sport Scout "Bob-Job"

57 ci • 1940 • United States
Bore x stroke: 2²⁹/₃₂ x 4¹⁵/₃₂ inches • Power output: 40 hp @ 5,500 rpm • Top speed: 110 mph (177 km/h) •
Collection of David Edwards

After the war, many young veterans who settled in Southern California bought used motorcycles, not auto-mobiles. Inspired by the hill-climb motorcycles of the 1930s, they began removing any weight that hindered acceleration or handling. They shortened, or "bobbed," rear fenders, and they removed front fenders completely.

California offered a year-round riding climate; its aircraft industry also had a significant influence on biking culture. Workers translated machining and metal-working techniques used on air-cooled airplane engines to their bikes. On the nearby dry lake beds (including Muroc Lake, now Edwards Air Force base), countless experiments flew or failed across the hard sands. The "Bob-Job" was the antithesis of the fully dressed cruiser bikes of the early 1940s. Speed was everything now, and it dictated the bikes' form. People spent money on bigger carburetors or hotter magnetos; they discarded instruments, which carried weight as well as information. Buddies who pushed or bump-started the bikes replaced heavy kick-start mechanisms, and owners bent up rear-fender-mount loops to give pushers a handle. Riders ignored the holes that remained after parts came off. Appearances had never mattered in a foxhole or a bomb bay.

Many of these veterans thought of their day jobs as annoyances that interrupted work on their bikes and their trips to the dry lakes. Yet a pay raise might send an owner to an air-brush artist to personalize the bike. Re-creations of bomber nose art were popular on gas tanks, as were flames. With the increasing affordability of chrome plating, "Bob-Jobs" evolved into Choppers (for chopped-off fenders and trim), bikes customized for both performance and appearance. The "Bob-Job's" fender-loop push bars were chromed and stretched into Chopper sissy bars. "Bob-Jobs" used raised front ends to increase cornering clearance. Choppers lowered theirs, raking and extending front forks, making them more difficult to turn. Both had big engines, modified frames, and abbreviated fenders. But the "Bob-Jobs" raced the dry lakes, hoping to set speed records, while Choppers cruised the boulevards, looking for attention. —RL

Zündapp KS600

597 cc • 1941 • Germany
Bore x stroke: 75 x 67.6 mm • Power output: 28 hp @ 4,700 rpm •
Top speed: 84 mph (135 km/h) • Collection of Matthew Janquitto,
Vintage Imports

Zünderland Apparatebau GmbH, better known as Zündapp, was founded in Nuremberg, Germany, in 1917, at the height of World War I. The company was a joint venture between three established firms to produce fuses for artillery guns. At war's end, Zündapp was under pressure to find a suitable peacetime occupation, and it started building motorcycles in 1921.

Over the next 63 years, the company manufactured more than three million machines. The first model to enter series production was powered by a 211-cc, British-designed, Levis single-cylinder two-stroke engine. By the end of 1924, new models, powered by engines of Zündapp's own design, were added to the range. In 1929, the company opened an entirely new factory, which was hailed as the most modern in the world. Zündapp survived the Great Depression, and by 1933 the company was producing its first flat-twin, four-stroke models, with capacities of 398 and 498 cc, designed by Richard Küchen. All were characterized by an unconventional, but very successful, chain-and-sprocket gearbox.

On the eve of World War II, Zündapp introduced several new models, including the 597-cc KS600 flat twin, which had a bore and stroke of 75 x 67.6 mm. Although the KS600 retained the chain-operated gearbox, the newcomer sported overhead-valve rather than single-valve cylinder heads and was clearly developed from the KS500, sharing its pressed-steel frame and blade-type girder front forks, which featured a central spring. Other notable features included shaft final drive and a four-speed gearbox operated by hand or foot.

In March 1940, all supplies to civilian customers were discontinued. Exactly two years later, Zündapp built its 250,000th motorcycle, a KS750. After the war, an improved version of the KS600, the KS601, entered production; nicknamed the "Green Elephant" after the bike's paintwork and size, this model was the last of the Zündapp flat-twin series, and was available until 1959. The Elephant Rally, the famous winter motorcycle gathering that had its heyday in the 1960s and '70s at the Nürburgring race track, was named after this bike. — *MW*

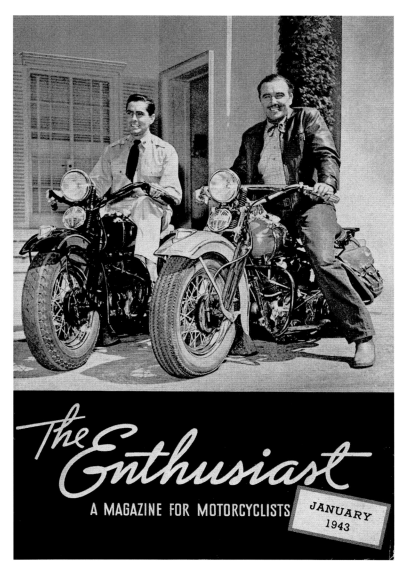

Cover of *The Enthusiast*, January 1943. Collection of George and Milli Yarocki.

Harley-Davidson U.S. Military Model U

74 ci • 1944 • United States
Bore x stroke: 3⁵⁄₁₆ x 4⁵⁄₃₂ inches • Power output: 34 hp @ 4,000 rpm •
Top speed: 87 mph (140 km/h) • Collection of Chris Le Sauvage

With the onset of World War II, the U.S. Government was forced to replace its horse cavalry with motorized transportation. Since the Jeep hadn't yet been invented, the motorcycle was the logical choice for this new "mechanized cavalry." In 1939 Harley-Davidson engineers began development on a number of models designed to meet the changing criteria.

The 1944 74-ci V-twin motorcycle produced by Harley-Davidson for the Navy differed only slightly from the heavyweight side-valve model the Milwaukee manufacturer had been cataloguing ever since 1930. But, as with all military issue, the Military Model U boasts various features found on neither civilian nor police machines, including "black-out" lights, an oil-bath air cleaner, a special carburetor, a heavy-duty cargo carrier, military-type fenders, and non-gloss, lusterless gray paint.

In addition to its optional gray paint scheme (olive drab was standard military issue), the machine shown here features a Thompson sub-machine gun; the motorcycle's storage compartment holds a maximum of ten clips (300 rounds) and one drum (50 rounds) of .45 caliber ammunition. The Model U, which was used primarily for shore patrol, was produced in very small numbers. Of the 18,688 motorcycles that Harley-Davidson manufactured in 1944 for the military, only 366 machines were 74-ci V-twins.

Rubber shortages necessitated several changes on all military models at the end of the 1941 production run: plastic handgrips were substituted for rubber grips; the kick-start pedal with rubber cleats was replaced by a simple tube; and metal floorboard pads were substituted for rubber pads embossed with the Harley-Davidson name. The change to metal floorboards brought the company into compliance with the military directives that prohibited exhibiting a civilian brand name on military equipment.

During World War II, Harley-Davidson produced more than 88,000 military-issue motorcycles, distributing them to the various branches of the armed forces. One postwar benefit of Harley-Davidson's massive participation in the war effort was that the thousands of returning servicemen who had learned to ride a Harley-Davidson while in the service now formed an expanded pool of potential civilian customers for the motorcycle company. —*David Sarafan*

Freedom and Postwar Mobility

1946
1958

Freedom and Postwar Mobility: 1946–1958

On the afternoon of August 16, 1945, a group of war-weary combat veterans sailed into New York harbor aboard a U.S. Navy cargo ship. The afternoon silhouettes of skyscrapers and the distant bang of the parade drums brought the ship's two thousand soldiers up on deck. Soon horns and hoots and waving banners cheered the men, who, days before, had been embroiled in one of the bloodiest battles in human history. As they approached the docks, the veterans were able to make out their wives, children, mothers, and a certain tune. The band was ever-so-patriotically playing "Here Comes the Navy."

The homecoming of the GIs was bittersweet, and their adjustment was uneasy. They were glad to be home, but the country that welcomed them had vastly changed during the years they had been away; it seemed not always to have a place for them on their return. Kay Starr, a former singer with the Glenn Miller Band, remembers:

> My husband came back. He was the first trumpet player for NBC. And they had promised all the musicians who left that when they came back they would have their jobs. Well, it was not true. And my husband became very angry, as so many men did. . . . They had gotten so used to those people, young minds, the energy of young people, that they were hesitant to take back these so-called "war-torn souls." My husband was so angry and he was so mad all the time that I couldn't live with him. So I had to divorce him. Now that was another tragedy of the war.

The world the veterans had experienced during the war was one of adrenaline overdrive and a daily confrontation with death; the new peacetime world they returned to was one of unbridled suburbanization and a rage to conform. The dissonance between the two fostered a disgruntlement among many World War II vets which was to match that of the bewildered soldier just home from the hell of Vietnam two decades later. The motorcycle—specifically, a juiced-up army bike with the everyman-sounding moniker "Bob-Job"—became the symbol and vehicle of this discontent. Attempting to mimic the rush and paradoxical freedom of wartime, thousands of combat vets were soon roaming America's roads in cohesive groups, forerunners of motorcycle gangs like that led by Marlon Brando in *The Wild One* (1954).

To help the returning veteran adjust, the U.S. government enacted the GI Bill of Rights, a landmark piece of legislation that enabled thousands of former servicemen to fashion better lives for themselves and their families through loans and access to education. The GI Bill greatly benefited the country, and it assured the creation of the most educated and productive middle class the U.S. had ever known. But the roar of the "Bob-Job" continued to echo around the edges of this production-line society, a phenomenon that was symptomatic of the unease brewing below the blissful surface of the new America.

The counterpoint to the "Bob-Job" was the Vespa. Born amid the chaos of postwar Italy, in response to a heightened need for cheap personal transportation, it zipped into the collective American cultural psyche, as seen in the movie *Roman Holiday* (1953), starring Audrey Hepburn. In the scheme of cinematic symbolism, it was Hepburn in a billowing skirt against Marlon Brando in black leather. The Vespa epitomized suburbia's embrace of the motorbike. Socially acceptable yet still romantic, plebeian yet sexy enough for the plutocrats, the motorcycle was now adopted by the burgeoning American middle class.

Postwar prosperity fostered a love for possessions, and the boom at the end of the 1940s yielded a range of inventions that middle-class consumers collected with a keeping-up-with-the-Joneses zeal. By the spring of 1947, the purchasing power of the average American family was more than 30 percent higher than it had been in 1939. And purchase they did. The catalogue of American consumerism encompassed a wide range of totally new items, including everything from Henry Dreyfuss's classic Model 500 telephone to automatic bowling-pin spotters, from curvaceous and colorful electric typewriters to reclining chairs, from radio-phonograph consoles to frozen fish, from automatic washers ("breakfast with the family while the clothes wash super clean") to Modernist collages in advertising. In 1948, General Motors sold one million Frigidaires, and Cadillac offered the first car with tail fins. Pan Am began showing movies during its flights, Milton Berle hosted the first 24-hour telethon, raising over one-hundred-thousand dollars for the Damon Runyon Cancer Fund, and 172,000 television sets were sold in the United States. By comparison, in 1950, Americans bought five million TVs.

Through this rush of innovation and the deepening penetration of the American media, mainstream culture began to co-opt the postwar fringes. Inherent in American innovation was a quintessentially American demand to conform. That paradox would inform the cultural foundation of the age called "Atomic." The euphoria with which America greeted the end of World War II was not only a reaction to the end of the war itself but a response to 31 years of global conflict. The first fifty years of the 20th century were defined by war. A recent estimate of the century's deaths puts the toll at 187 million, and the vast majority of these occurred in the first half of the century. As the historian Isaiah Berlin said, "I have lived through most of the 20th century, I must add, without suffering or hardship. I only remember it as the most terrible century in Western history."

But the end of warfare did not mean the end of conflict. A new term, *cold war*, rapidly supplanted the phrase *world war*. Linguistically, it had the same ring; psychologically, it gave off perhaps an even greater cultural reverberation. *Nuclear* became society's operative word. And the anxiety provoked by the perils of nuclear war spawned a fixation with the nuclear family. The resulting insularity, perhaps best characterized by such planned, homogeneous communities as Levittown, followed a pattern—the disintegration of the traditional, more extended models of human social relationship, and with it, the snapping of the links between generations. As the historian Eric Hobsbawm writes, "The values of an absolute asocial individualism became dominant, both in official and unofficial ideologies." Preoccupation became neurosis as war planning, family planning, and economic planning sucked all spontaneity out of the postwar world. And with the insidious widespread paranoia that accompanied the threat of communism and the witch-hunts that ensued, political and social conformity became law.

In this context, the GIs' uncomfortable homecoming emerged as all the more jarring, suburbanization all the more unavoidable, and social rebellion all the more predictable. The motorcycle emerged as the ideal vehicle for all shades of rebellion—from the vigilantism of hard-core biker gangs to the softer, almost sexy poses of suburban housewives daring to mimic Hollywood starlets. Fine machines—from daunting Harleys to dainty Vespas—became the metaphor on which America would ride into one of the most tumultuous eras the young country had ever known. The preoccupations of postwar society forecast the chaos of the '60s, and the motorcycle became the cultural icon that tracked the societal meltdown. —*Greg Jordan*

Gilera Saturno

499 cc • 1947 • Italy
Bore x stroke: 84 x 90 mm • Power output: 22 hp @ 5,000 rpm •
Top speed: 85 mph (137 km/h) • The Otis Chandler Vintage Museum
of Transportation and Wildlife, Oxnard, Calif.

Gilera is one of the great names in Italian motorcycling. In 1909, at the age of 22, Giuseppe Gilera built his first motorcycle, a 317-cc single-engine model with a bore and stroke of 67 x 90 mm. With the outbreak of World War I, he transferred his efforts to the production of bicycles for the Italian military. Gilera was unable to capitalize on the massive postwar demand for motorcycles in Italy until 1920, when he relocated to a larger factory; this new plant was outside of Milan, not far from Monza park, where the famous race circuit was soon to be constructed.

Over the years, Gilera built a series of single-cylinder four-stroke machines, including the Turismo (1920–24); the Sport (1923–28); the Gran Sport (1929–31); the L-SS (1931–36); the Sei Giorni (1931–34), named for the bike's success in the ISDT, or International Six Days Trial; and the VT (1935–41). The VT's class-leading performance and pushrod-operated valves made it the forerunner of Gilera's most famous production model, the Saturno.

The Saturno was created in 1939 by Giuseppe Salmaggi, from a 1933 design by Mario Mellone; the prototype won the last Targa Florio (the classic Sicilian road race) just prior to Italy's entrance into World War II. During the war, the company built motorcyles for the Italian Army. In 1946, the Saturno, one of the company's first peacetime bikes, entered production. Its 499-cc single-cylinder engine with a bore and stroke of 84 x 90 mm sported an alloy cylinder head and pushrod-operated valves. The design was of semi-unit construction, with a four-speed gearbox and multi-plate clutch. The original model used girder forks and Gilera's own rear suspension; it had a swinging fork with horizontal compression springs. In 1950, the Saturno Sport appeared, featuring oil-damped telescopic front forks; in 1952, all models received a new swinging arm and twin-shock rear suspension.

The Saturno was highly successful in every field it entered. Like its British counterpart, the BSA Gold Star, the Saturno was developed over a number of years and also saw service as a racer, a trials bike, and a motocrosser. Gilera built some 6,450 Saturnos (including 170 racers) before production ended in 1959, in favor of smaller motorcycles. —*MW*

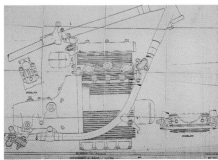

Blueprint diagram of the Sunbeam S7 engine mounting, 1950. Collection of David Holyoake.

Sunbeam S7

487 cc • 1947 • United Kingdom
Bore x stroke: 70 x 64 mm • Power output: 21 hp @ 5,800 rpm •
Top speed: 70 mph (113 km/h) • The Barber Vintage Motorsports Museum, Birmingham, Ala.

This was designer Erling Poppe's version of that perennial industry theme, the "car on two wheels." It offered the comfort of a fully sprung frame (most prewar machines had only front suspension), large soft tires, and a stylized engine. Although some 10,000 of these machines were sold through 1956, what British postwar motorists turned to, once it became available, was the low-priced motorcar.

With its roots in a 1932 BSA project called "line-ahead twin," the 1946–47 S7 was a radical conception, with its 70-x-64-mm single-overhead-cam engine built in unit with a four-speed gearbox and mounted in rubber to isolate the rider from its considerable vibration. Unlike the Speed Twin and its clones, the S7 carried its crankshaft longitudinally, as an automobile does. The chassis incorporated the best suspension concepts developed in prewar racing—a telefork with hydraulic damping, and plunger rear suspension.

Despite its postwar financial crisis and the rationing of food and fuel, England had big plans for resumption of motorcycle production. Innovation was certainly plentiful, but scarce money and a worn-out production system proved fatal. Though English designers were as prolific as ever, none but the simplest ideas could be profitably realized. Ultimately, it wasn't enough. The death of the British motorcycle industry has been blamed on Japanese competition, but its demise was more a result of suicide than murder.

Flooded as we are by equipment from Japan and Italy, it's tempting to dismiss Britain's part in motorcycling as the dead hand of the past. But British design was strongest during its last days. A culture of innovation takes time to develop, but it can be destroyed in an instant.

Sunbeam began motorcycle production in 1913 and was bought and sold several times before becoming part of BSA Group in 1943. In their early days, Sunbeams were considered England's best-finished singles. The name continued on Sunbeam-badged BSA scooters, which were sold until 1964. —*KC*

Indian Chief

1,206 cc • 1948 • United States
Bore x stroke: 82.6 x 112.7 mm • Power output: 40 hp @ 5,000 rpm •
Top speed: 85 mph (137 km/h) • Collection of Doug Strange

The Indian Chief debuted in 1922, 21 years after the Springfield, Massachusetts, company produced the first Indian motorcycle. During the 31 years that it was produced, the Indian Chief was Harley-Davidson's main sales competitor in the V-twin heavyweight class.

Over the years, riders of the two marques perennially debated the various improvements introduced by the manufacturers. Throughout the passing decades and the different models that it faced in the marketplace, the original side-valve design persisted, and the Indian Chief not only continued to sell, but it was often the first to introduce new features that were later adopted by its Milwaukee rival.

The statistics for Indian's flagship model were imposing. The 1948 Chief had a 1,206-cc V-twin motor, rated at an estimated 40 hp, that was capable of propelling the 550-pound machine and its rider to a top speed of 85 mph. With special cams and a little tuning, the Chief could achieve a speed of 100 mph on the open road, and, depending on riding conditions, the Chief traveled between 35 and 45 miles on a single gallon of fuel.

E. Paul duPont took control of the Indian Motorcycle Company in 1930, and, a year later, the full range of DuPont Duco (later Dulux) colors were available on Indian motorcycles. From then on, two-tone paint schemes, elegant pinstripes, and striking decals graced the sheet metal and fuel tanks of the Indian heavyweight. The most important cosmetic feature distinguishing the late-model Chief from other motorcycles of its era, however, was the long, graceful sweep of its deeply valanced fenders, which were first introduced on this model in 1940.

Production of the Chief was discontinued in 1953, when the Massachusetts-based company ceased manufacturing. In recent years, aficionados of the marque have restored hundreds of derelict Chiefs to better-than-new condition, and pristine examples now sell for upward of $25,000. The example included in *The Art of the Motorcycle* was restored from a "basket case," and in 1990, it received the Grand National award from the Antique Automobile Club of America for best-restored motorcycle of its class. —*DKS*

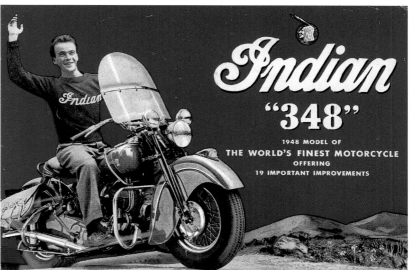

Catalogue for Indian, 1948. Collection of George and Milli Yarocki.

Curé on a Solex Vélosolex, 1966.
Collection of Bernard Salvat.

Solex Vélosolex

45 cc • 1948 • France
Bore x stroke: 38 x 40 mm • Power output: .5 hp @ 2,200 rpm • Top speed: 17 mph (30 km/h) •
Collection of Franck Meneret

Trailing smoke from its two-stroke engine and dripping unburned oil onto the pavement, the Solex was for decades a ubiquitous feature of the streets of Paris and other French cities. The rider pedaled the machine to life and then let the tiny engine push him on his way. Steep hills often required more pedaling. With its front, fork-mounted engine, which drove the front wheel by friction roller, this Paul Mennesson design is the motorcycle returned to its minimalist origins.

More specifically, the Solex moped is a throwback to the original Werner of 1897, whose engine was located in the same position. Surely Soichiro Honda saw these machines on his first European trip and understood their meaning: his 50 Super Cub step-through was just a more practical version of the Solex. It became the foundation of his industrial empire. The safety bicycle is truly an enduring form, in as little need of R&D as the knife, fork, and spoon. Attaching a small engine to the cycle remains as natural today as it was 100 years ago.

In the 1960s there was such interest in the sportier European mopeds that a Grand Prix road-racing class was created for the 50-cc engine size. In its final days, this class was distinguished by 20-hp, 50-cc engines capable of propelling 120-pound racing motorcycles at 120 mph. But as national governments have set more stringent exhaust emissions standards, two-stroke-powered machines like the Solex have fallen out of use. Motobecane, another French manufacturer, took over Solex production in 1974, and the bikes are still built in Hungary. — *KC*

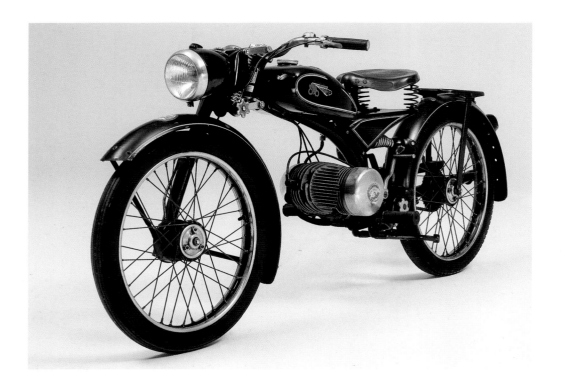

Imme R100

99 cc • 1949 • West Germany
Bore x stroke: 52 x 47 mm • Power output: 4.5 hp @ 5,800 rpm • Top speed: 47 mph (75 km/h) •
Deutsches Museum, Munich

For some 50 years, motorcycle design clung tenaciously to the theory of a diamond frame with forks supporting each side of the front- and rear-wheel spindles. But in 1949, the Imme, one of the most talked-about, ultralightweight motorcycles of the immediate postwar era, broke with tradition. The machine's layout was ingenious. The 99-cc single-cylinder, two-stroke engine was egg-shaped and efficiently arranged. Often referred to as "the German Hobby-Horse," the Imme was designed by Norbert Riedel and built in the small southern Alpine town of Immenstadt in Bavaria, a place where visitors might have expected to hear the jangle of cow bells rather than the sound of cutting-edge motorcycles.

The Imme's 52-mm piston and 47-mm stroke gave it a high engine revolution. Mounted on a single steel tubular member, which acted both as an exhaust outlet and rear-fork support, the ultracompact unit transmitted the final drive by chain to the rear wheel. The wheel itself was of a conventional pattern, but could be detached quickly by removing three nuts, leaving the sprocket and brake assembly in place. The three-speed, twist-grip-controlled gearbox, shaft, and spindle centers remained equidistant from each other, regardless of the action of the spring frame, which meant that the chain tension stayed constant. The front wheel, too, was quickly detachable, thanks to its single-sided mounting. The frame was sprung by a massive pivotal bearing in a lug between the rear and central frame members, and movement of this point was controlled by a barrel spring situated beneath the single saddle. Auxiliary damping was provided by a rubber block, housed within this spring, and the rider could further control the degree of frame movement with an adjustable friction damper.

Although the machine was publicized in both America and Great Britain, very few examples were ever imported to these countries. Riedel also designed and built a 148-cc twin-cylinder model along the same lines, but produced it only in very small numbers before he closed Riedel Motoren AG in 1951. Nevertheless, the Imme introduced a number of innovative features, many of which, including the single-sided front and rear forks and cantilever rear suspension, were later adopted by other manufacturers. —MW

Jackson-Rotrax JAP Speedway

490 cc • 1949 • United Kingdom
Bore x stroke: 85.5 x 85 mm • Power output: 40 hp @ 6,000 rpm •
Top speed: 50 mph (80 km/h) • The Barber Vintage Motorsports
Museum, Birmingham, Ala.

Speedway racing is a short, loud, intense affair that consists of sliding sideways around tight oval tracks of dirt or grass. An import into Britain from Australia, speedway racing flourished because of its combination of close competition and a rapid succession of short, decisive, spectacular races.

Bikes for speedway racing have to be lightweight, and they have to accelerate hard. The light chassis and rudimentary front fork have been specialized for this environment. Speedway engines burn alcohol, whose refrigerating effect as it enters the engine is such that little cooling fin area is necessary. This gives alcohol burners their short-finned, "crew-cut" look. Alcohol fuel tolerates a high compression ratio, which allows for rapid acceleration. Because race follows race in quick succession, engines must be strong— they have to survive with little moment-to-moment maintenance.

The advent of longer continental tracks in the 1960s changed the nature of these engines, but this example would retain the moderate-valve timing that gave such a wide power spread on English tracks. These are rightly called "racing tractor engines."

In contrast with the Norton Manx, the JAP speedway engine has valves operated by pushrods and rocker arms rather than by overhead camshafts. The sustained high speeds of road racing require an engine to turn at a high rpm, which necessitates placing the fewest parts between cam and valve. But in speedway, compactness benefits from less machinery atop the engine, since engine speed seldom exceeds 5,000 rpm.

The extreme forward engine position—the same bias found in contemporary sport and pavement racing motorcycles—is necessary to prevent these bikes from flipping up during starts and hard acceleration.

The JAP speedway engine was designed by S. M. Greening for John A. Prestwick. It first appeared in 1932. This design, since updated, won races until more modern four-valve engines appeared in 1975. —*KC*

DKW RT 125 W

122 cc • 1952 • West Germany
Bore x stroke: 52 x 58 mm • Power output: 4.8 hp @ 5,000 rpm •
Top speed: 47 mph (76 km/h) • Collection of Karl-Heinz Mutschler

Along with BMW and NSU, DKW was one of the primary forces behind the rapid growth of the German motorcycle industry in the first half of the 20th century. The company's name stood for *Dampf Kraft Wagen* (steam-powered engine), but people also referred to it as *Das Kleine Wünder* (the Little Miracle), or *Der Knabische Wünische* (the Schoolboy's Dream).

Jorgen Skafte Rasmussen established DKW in 1919, when he was just 21. The fledgling company's first major achievement came in 1921, with the Hugo Ruppe–designed 122-cc auxiliary engine, which could be clipped to a conventional pedal cycle and drove the rear wheel by a belt. By mid 1922, these miniature two-stroke engines had gained a reputation for reliability, and DKW had sold some 25,000 of them. The company expanded rapidly, and by 1928 it had become the largest motorcycle producer in the world.

In 1929, DKW formed Auto Union AG with Audi, Horch, and Wanderer, with each company retaining its separate identity. By the mid-1930s, DKW was making extraordinarily fast 250-cc racing motorcycles with supercharged, double-piston, twin-cylinder engines. In 1939, from the motorcycle world's largest racing department—employing some 150 technicians—DKW launched its most famous model, the RT 125. Designed by Hermann Weber, this lightweight motorcycle was powered by a unit-construction, 122-cc piston-port, two-stroke, three-speed engine with a bore and stroke of 52 x 58 mm.

The RT 125 was an instant hit with the German Army, and was produced in huge numbers during the war years. But the model's main claim to fame was that it became the most copied motorcycle of all time. The British BSA Bantum, the American Harley-Davidson Hummer, the Soviet Moska, and even the original Yamaha YAI (Red Dragon) all revealed DKW design influences. After the war, when Germany was partitioned, DKW's Zschopau plant found itself in the Russian sector. This factory went on to make motorcycles for the Warsaw Pact countries, while DKW itself relocated to the West, which meant that for years the RT 125 was built on both sides of the Iron Curtain. —*MW*

Poster for DKW, 1953. Archiv Auto Union, Ingolstadt.

AJS E-95

499 cc • 1953 • United Kingdom
Bore x stroke: 68 x 68.5 mm • Power output: 45 hp @ 8,500 rpm (est.) • Top speed: 115 mph (185 km/h) •
The Barber Vintage Motorsports Museum, Birmingham, Ala.

By 1938, British single-cylinder road racers had exhausted the virtues of ease of handling and reliability. Continental makers Gilera and BMW reigned because of the horsepower their engines gained by supercharging, in which a fuel-air mixture is forced into the engine with a blower. During World War II, British designers planned to redress this imbalance. The design of the AJS Porcupine was conceived by Joe Craig (famed for his Norton engine development), Harry Collier, Vic Webb, and Matt Wright. Gear-driven overhead cams, unit-engine/gearbox construction, and plain bearings were advanced features of the motorcycle.

From the start, the designers planned to boost power by supercharging. The two-cylinder layout presented its hottest part—the cylinder head—foremost. The cylinders were almost horizontal. Casting problems made it easiest to cool the head not with conventional fins, but with the spikes that gave the machine its name: Porcupine. This E-95 500 Road Racer is a redesigned version of the Porcupine.

The suspension of the Porcupine was impressively modern in concept: a swing arm at the rear was controlled by hydraulic dampers, while a telescopic fork was used at the front. The chassis was a wide-twin loop design. When this machine appeared in the first postwar Isle of Man TT races in 1947, it was the only completely new 500 cc. Unfortunately, it had problems that would require continuous redesign throughout its life, although it did win a single World Championship in 1949.

The Porcupine was confronted in the fall of 1946 by a sudden FICM ban on superchargers. Engines are designed for specific conditions. Having been designed for supercharging, the reconfiguration for unsupercharged operation took time and money. The E-95 was the answer to the supercharge ban on Porcupines.

Not all of AJS's problems were technical. Parent company AMC forbade the use of any streamlining, and when engine-airflow pioneer Harry Weslake (responsible for the Jaguar XK120 cylinder head) proposed applying his methods to the engines, company director Donald Heather declined. There was wrangling over suspension choices—corporate policy required use of the proprietary "jampots" you see here, while the riders wanted to use the best available.

Having reached a power level somewhat above that of the top factory singles, the Porcupines and their offspring, including the E-95, retired, along with the rest of the British race team, in 1954. —KC

Brochure for AJS, 1952. Classic Bike, Kettering, England.

Vincent Black Shadow Series C

998 cc • 1954 • United Kingdom

Bore x stroke: 84 x 90 mm • Power output: 55 hp @ 5,700 rpm • Top speed: 125 mph (201 km/h) •

The Otis Chandler Vintage Museum of Transportation and Wildlife, Oxnard, Calif.

The Vincent Black Shadow, a big-engined machine intended to deliver maximum performance at a considerable price, is the spiritual forefather of today's "open-class" bikes. It continued the role previously defined by the Brough SS100, but its implementation was considerably more thoughtful.

    The Vincent-HRD first appeared in 1928. With its patented, triangulated swing arm at the rear, it pre-dated Yamaha's very similar 1975 Monoshock considerably. After World War II, steel tubing—the usual frame material—was in short supply. In order to do without, designer Phil Irving planned the atrophy of the frame. A stiff sheet-metal spine, doubling as an oil tank, joined the steering head to the engine's two cylinder heads. Rear suspension loads were fed into the rear of this box, while the engine itself completed the chassis structure. There was no other frame. The triangulated swing arm pivoted from the back of the engine. These structural ideas are mirrored in the modern Britten V-twin, but with a carbon fiber member substituted for the Vincent's steel spine/oil tank. High-quality aluminum casting alloy was then available only from scrapped aircraft engines (notably the RR Merlin, star of the Battle of Britain), and it was from these that the first postwar Vincent crankcases were cast.

    Contrast the wheelbase of the Vincent and the Brough SS100. One of Irving's design goals was rapid direction–changing ability, which requires a short wheelbase. To achieve this despite the extra length of a V-twin engine, the normal front-chassis downtube—so prominent on the Velocette—had to be elim-inated, taking with it three inches of excess chassis length.

    Frameless design, multiple functions in many parts, the adjustability of controls, quickly detach-able wheels—with these developments the Vincent explores what the motorcycle could be, rather than merely elaborating what it has been.

    Sadly, this machine was like an author who receives critical success only to go out of print. Admirable though a design may be, the public vote with their checkbooks, and the austerity of postwar Britain proved inhospitable to the Vincent's cost and purity of purpose. Production ended in 1954, but enthusiasts and stu-dents of the marque will never permit it to perish. — *KC*

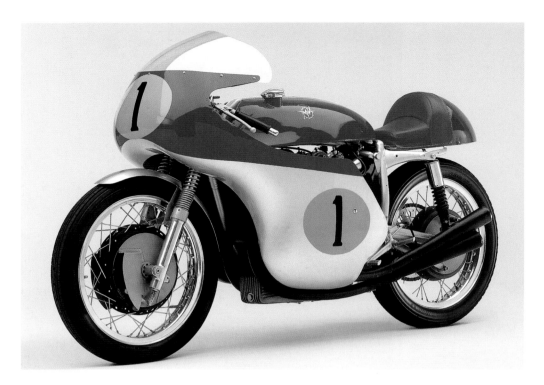

Sir John Surtees winning the 1959 German Grand Prix.
Classic Bike, Kettering, England.

MV Agusta 500 Grand Prix

497 cc • 1956 • Italy
Bore x stroke: 53 x 56.4 mm • Power output: 56 hp @ 10,500 rpm •
Top speed: 145 mph (233 km/h) • The Barber Vintage Motorsports Museum, Birmingham, Ala.

Giovanni Agusta was one of Italy's aviation pioneers; he flew his own prototype airplane in 1907, and the company he founded was a major force in aircraft construction from the period between the wars on through the end of World War II. After the war, Agusta specialized in helicopters, and the company established a motorcycle division, MV (Meccanica Verghere), in 1946.

MV's first motorcycle, featuring a 98-cc two-stroke single-cylinder engine, appeared that year, and was quickly followed by a racing version. The first four-stroke, a 249-cc overhead-valve single-cylinder engine was built in 1947. But it was the company's first four-cylinder Grand Prix Racer that really grabbed the head-lines. The prototype made its debut at the 1950 Milan Trade Fair—a rare instance in which a racing machine was exhibited to the public before it appeared on the circuit. The bike, designed by former Gilera chief engineer, Pietro Remor, had several features not normally found in racing designs, including shaft drive and torsion-bar suspension. Its first race was the Belgian Grand Prix in July 1950, where Areiso Artesiani rode it to a highly respectable fifth-place finish.

Always a speedy machine, the MV's main problem was road holding, and the following year it was equipped with conventional telescopic front forks. In 1952, MV built a heavily modified version with new bore and stroke dimensions of 53 x 56.4 mm, to produce 497 cc. With larger valves, hotter cams, the gear-box uprated from four to five ratios, the drive shaft replaced by a chain, and four instead of two carbs, power rose to 56 hp. A new frame completed the picture. MV experimented with Earle's-type front forks, but after team leader Les Graham's fatal accident in the 1953 Senior TT, these were replaced by the tele-scopic type.

MV's breakthrough came in 1956, when it signed the rising British star John Surtees, who rode the bike to its first 500-cc world title. Surtees went on to win six more titles (three in the 500-cc class) be-fore retiring at the end of 1960. By the time MV quit the sport at the end of 1976, it had won over 3,000 international races, 38 individual world championships, and 37 manufacturer's titles, making it the most successful team ever. —*MW*

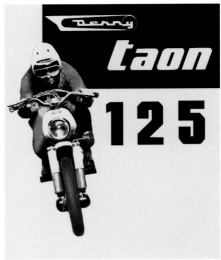

Catalogue for the Derny Taon 125, 1957.
Collection of Bernard Salvat.

Derny Taon

124 cc • 1957 • France
Bore x stroke: 54 x 54 mm • Power output: 6 hp @ 4,500 rpm • Top speed: 56 mph (90 km/h) •
Collection of Jean Malleret

From the late 1920s to the '50s, the elements of the automobile—body, fenders, headlights, trunk—were fused together to form smooth, aircraftlike shapes. Attempts to do the same with the motorcycle have been stoutly resisted by those who believe its functional elements should be separate and distinct. This is not the sort of difference in design philosophy that seems likely to be resolved even today.

The Derny Taon, a thoroughly modern little sports two-seater designed by Roger Tallon, made its first appearance in 1957. Proprietary French engine maker AMC supplied the 124-cc two-stroke engine, which hangs beneath the integrated headlight-tank-chassis-fender unit for all to admire. The bike's front suspension was fashionable—a leading-link Earle's fork, the type briefly popular in road racing at that time. Front and rear suspension units are telescopic-coil, spring-over-damper. This kind of suspension unit was rare before the war, but proliferated rapidly on cars and bikes thereafter. Early makers included companies like England's Dowty, which gained experience working with the technology on aircraft landing-gear struts.

Note that the front fork passes through the headlight/tank unit as a single shaft, a feature of the very successful Moto Guzzi racers of the mid-to-late 1950s. Tallon was known to be an admirer of the highly refined Guzzis designed by Giulio Carcano (who was later to design sailboats as well). Tallon's machines also had horizontal single-cylinder engines and leading-link forks. Is it an accident that this Taon reminds us of another phenomenon of the 1950s—the chromed steel dinette set? Modernist forms do seem to lend themselves to parody and debasement.

The French market at this time was shaped by a taxation system that favored machines under 175 cc, and so this category grew at the expense of larger machines. Even Gnôme et Rhône, which had produced bigger bikes before World War II, built mostly simple, sub-175-cc two-strokes during the 1950s.

Derny began production in 1949, focusing on mopeds and two-seaters as well as scooters—all powered by proprietary engines. The company declared bankruptcy in 1958, when French youth were otherwise occupied with defending the empire in Algeria or recovering from Dien Bien Phu. Motorcycling would return to wide popularity in France in the late 1970s. —*KC*

Harley-Davidson KR

750 cc • 1957 • United States
Bore x stroke: 69.9 x 80.6 mm • Power output:
50 hp @ 6,000 rpm (est.) • Top speed: 130 mph (209 km/h) •
The Barber Vintage Motorsports Museum, Birmingham, Ala.

In 1937, the American Motorcycle Association established Class C, for "same-as-you-can-buy" motorcycles, quieting amateur racers' complaints about unaffordable, factory-built or -backed models. Class C bikes had to begin life as stock machines purchased through the front door of any dealership. Harley sold its Model WLDR road-ready, with brakes and headlights. AMA rules limited Class C to 45-ci (737 cc), side-valve, twin-cylinder engines, or 30.5-ci (500 cc) overhead-valve singles. Because the sanctioning organization was generously supported (some would say owned) by Harley-Davidson and Indian, Class C favored the models of these companies over European and English high-performance, overhead-valve, two-cylinder models. Competition intensified after the war, when the U.S. virtually eliminated duties on imported machinery and manufactured goods. By then, Triumph, Norton, and BSA were making 500-cc bikes that were legal according to Class C requirements and cost less than Harleys or Indians.

In 1950 Harley-Davidson began developing its Model K, planning a KR race version in tandem with it. The engineering of the motorcycle adopted ideas from English competitors, using a swing-arm rear suspension with shock absorbers to improve handling. A foot-operated, four-speed transmission with hand clutch made better use of its greater horsepower. By midsummer 1952, after a few troubles with early versions, Harley-Davidson KRs were winning. Harley rider Joe Leonard won five national events in 1953, and in 1954, KR racers won 13 of 18 races.

Class C racing leveled the track between privateers and factories. In 1949, the AMA added two rules. One required manufacturers to produce 25 or more examples of models entered, which meant that makers couldn't race prototypes. The second allowed any bike to be claimed within 30 minutes of the finish for $1,000 in cash or a certified check, which discouraged individuals from investing heavily in modifications. Still, Harley-Davidson shop owners and tuners like Tom Sifton, working with riders like Joe Petrali and Paul Goldsmith, often humbled factory efforts. Sifton's improved engine breathing, high-rpm lubrication, and high-speed handling became legendary, especially when he wouldn't share secrets with the factory. His successes inspired countless others to go racing, including 1960s factory team riders Mert Lawwill, Bart Markel, Cal Rayborn, and Illinois Harley-Davidson dealer Roger Reiman. Reiman won the inaugural Daytona 200 Speedway on this KR in 1961. —RL

Roger Reiman in the 1961 Daytona Speedway.
Photograph courtesy of the Harley-Davidson Motor Company Archives.

Harley-Davidson Sportster XL

883 cc • 1957 • United States

Bore x stroke: 76.2 x 96.8 mm • Power output: 40 hp @ 5,500 rpm • Top speed: 101 mph (163 km/h) •
The Otis Chandler Vintage Museum of Transportation and Wildlife, Oxnard, Calif.

The 1950s were tough on American motorcycles. European motorcyclists raced down narrow lanes, over hills, and through valleys, prizing handling and braking, while Americans raced from one stop sign to the next, favoring brute horsepower over cornering ability. Still, some Americans, drawing on their wartime riding experiences, preferred European bikes.

In *The Wild One* (1954), Marlon Brando gave a recognizable face to antisocial motorcycling, riding a stock Triumph into the place where fear lived in most Americans. (In fact, outlaw riding groups reinforced the negative public perception of motorcycles to a degree completely disproportionate to their small numbers.) In 1950, the British manufacturer of Royal Enfields bought the Indian Motorcycle Company, and in May 1953 they assembled the last of the Indian Chiefs. Harley-Davidson was now the only American bike left. The AMA, who had the most to gain from promoting wholesomeness and responsibility in motorcycling, fought internally.

Into this unsteady marketplace, Harley-Davidson brought the 30-hp, 45-ci (737 cc) flat-head Model K in 1952, introducing Harley's hand clutch and foot-pedal gear shift. However, English motorcycles offered overhead valves, quicker acceleration, and greater speed. In response, Harley-Davidson lengthened piston stroke from 98.6 to 115.8 mm, enlarging displacement to 883 cc. It produced a 38-hp KH with this new engine in 1955, and a 40-hp KHK in 1956.

But even these didn't catch the public's interest. Harley-Davidson's answer was the 1957 Sportster XL. The XL retained the 883-cc engine displacement, but it enlarged bore from 69.9 to 76.2 mm, using larger valves to improve breathing. The engineers returned stroke to 98.6 mm, permitting higher rotating speeds to create more power, a favorite large-bore/short-stroke combination of English makers. The engineers also designed new cylinder heads to accommodate valves above the pistons, rather than on the side. Rocker arms lay in a valve cover resembling an overturned spoon or shovel.

This was the first of the Harley engines to be nicknamed "Shovelhead." The bike itself was also named, with the word cast into the gear-case cover. It wasn't the first time Harley-Davidson had titled a product, but Sportster buyers had to talk to their grandfathers to learn about the "Silent Grey Fellows" of the beginning of the century. —RL

Advertisement for the Harley-Davidson Sportster, 1957.
Photograph courtesy of the Harley-Davidson Motor Company Archives.

Triumph Twenty-One

350 cc • 1958 • United Kingdom
Bore x stroke: 58.3 x 65.5 mm • Power output: 18.5 hp @ 6,500 rpm • Top speed: 80 mph (129 km/h) •
The Barber Vintage Motorsports Museum, Birmingham, Ala.

This machine lays claim to two noteworthy features: the first Triumph unit-construction engine, and a scooter-like, enclosed rear wheel, encased in a sheet-steel "bathtub." It was dubbed the Twenty-One because it had an engine displacement of 21 ci, and because 1957, the first year in which the bike was produced, marked the 21st anniversary of the Triumph Engineering Company. A cautious compromise between traditional fenders and the idea of full-machine enclosure, the "bathtub" was actually the brainchild of famous Norton racing tuner Francis Beart, who used it to keep wheel-thrown grit from entering the carburetors of his bikes.

Prior to this, British manufacturers had bought their gearboxes from specialist makers. Hence, in the past, it was natural for the gearbox to be a separate unit from the engine. Triumphs, too, had always had separate gearboxes. The Twenty-One was a first. Adjustments of primary chain tension involved moving the gearbox in the engine plates, which in turn required adjusting drive-chain tension. Switching to unit construction eliminated this antique task, simplified manufacturing, and made leakage less likely. The gearbox itself was redesigned to allow all of its shafts and gears and its shifting mechanism to be assembled on the gearbox endplate.

The "bathtub" was made of right and left pressed-steel halves joined at a rubber strip; it had a scooter-like, modular appearance. The hinged seat covered a toolkit, the battery, oil tank filler, and ignition parts—a kind of centralizing of auto service tasks under the hood. This inexpensive machine served well for touring and commuting. It began a process of design-for-manufacturing that Triumph and other British makers could not, unfortunately, pursue sufficiently to make truly profitable. The Model Twenty-One was produced from 1957 to 1966. — *KC*

Popular Culture / Counterculture

1960
1969

Popular Culture/Counterculture: 1960–1969

In the 1960s, motorcycles became fashion. Co-opted by suburbanites and their hippie children, bikes were now as relevant to the cultural iconography of the decade as miniskirts, LSD, and street protests. With packs of angry rebels cruising on their Harleys and nuclear families puttering around on Honda Super Cubs, the motorcycle took its place as a fixture on both the new American superhighways and the old, middle-American backroads. The speed, sexiness, utility, and custom design of the motorcycle satisfied a society that was roiling amid a decade of movement and change.

A catalogue of cultural and political events summons the awesome range and magnitude of cultural innovation and political upheaval that occurred during the decade. In 1961, John F. Kennedy became the first Catholic elected to the U.S. presidency, and Joseph Heller wrote *Catch-22*. In 1963, Martin Luther King, Jr., led a massive civil rights rally, the March on Washington, and there were race riots in Birmingham, Alabama; Betty Friedan's *The Feminine Mystique* was published, and the Beatles's song "I Want to Hold Your Hand" got extensive air play. In 1965, Malcolm X was assassinated; Bob Dylan released his song "Like a Rolling Stone"; and Pop art began to shake up the art world. In 1966, the Cultural Revolution in China began. The year 1967 saw the Six-Day War in the Middle East; the publication of Gabriel Garcia Marquez's *One Hundred Years of Solitude*; and the opening of Arthur Penn's film *Bonnie and Clyde*. King and Robert F. Kennedy were assassinated in 1968, and students at Columbia University took over the university. In 1969, the year that Neil Armstrong walked on the moon and Richard Nixon was elected to the presidency, Dennis Hopper directed and co-starred in *Easy Rider*, and the first exhibition of Conceptual art opened at the Seth Siegelaub Gallery in New York.

Night after night the evening news was a veritable mirror of the themes that preoccupied Lyndon Johnson's Great Society: the Vietnam War, the Cold War, the civil rights movement, women's liberation, the sexual revolution, and rock 'n' roll. The Vietnam War provoked grave questioning of the legitimacy of the same state that, only a decade before, had been universally lauded by its citizenry. In spite of this, throughout the '60s and into the '70s, American politicians kept trying to force the Vietnam War to fit the World War II mold: American activism in defense of American, or even global, values. In her 1994 essay, "The American State and Vietnam," Mary Sheila McMahon wrote: "American policy-making elites acted as though the existence of the American state itself rested on the outcome of a rebellion in a small, remote country that (almost everyone in the government agreed) was peripheral to the core material interests of the United States."

And so the state grew tyrannical, and the American population, especially its young, revolted—against the Establishment, against the university, and especially against the Vietnam War, which increasingly became the focus of student discontent. The student movement had its roots in the civil rights struggle, as thousands of college students traveled south to participate in education and voter registration drives. By 1965, the New Left, advocating the idea of "participatory democracy," had become a mass movement: the first march against the war took place, CBS did a piece on draft resistance, and Congressmen called for a crackdown on the anti-draft movement, which was accused of sedition and Communist sympathies. Despite FBI harassment of student protesters, over one hundred thousand demonstrators participated in the March on the Pentagon in October 1967.

Parallel to the national identity crisis over the war in southeast Asia, another sort of world war, the Cold War, continued to nag at the collective consciousness with a psychological effect rivaling the physical toll of the previous world wars. Its potential consequence—total annihilation—made the Vietnam War seem, at times, but a prelude of the chaos to come, and the only adequate response was the idiom of the absurd, brilliantly epitomized in Stanley Kubrick's 1964 film, *Dr. Strangelove or How I Learned to Stop Worrying and Love the Bomb*.

As the decade unfolded, militance increased among both students and blacks. Stokely Carmichael called for Black Power in September 1966, writing, "Integration is a subterfuge for the maintenance of white supremacy, and reinforces, among both black and white, the idea that 'white' is automatically better and 'black' is by definition inferior." Black nationalism expressed its frustration with the societal status quo through social protest, social strife, even fashion. Based on both racial and economic discrimination, the civil rights movement exposed schisms in American society that only years before had seemed invisible. Was this not the land where, in the '50s, "everyone" had prospered, "everyone" owned a home, "everyone" suppressed his or her tiny disenchantments in the name of the national creed, patriotism?

Changes in attitudes toward sexuality in the '60s made the departure from the status quo of the '50s seem even more shocking. As late as 1957, America's favorite TV couple, Ricky and Lucy Ricardo, slept in separate beds. As late as 1962, June and Ward Cleaver never appeared together in the same bedroom. Soon, however, the increased availability of the birth control pill allowed a sexual revolution to be actively, if self-consciously, proclaimed. Young people were using sex not only for the pleasure of the deed but for the heft of its politics. The sexualization of culture was next, and *Playboy*, *Cosmopolitan*, and *Esquire* followed the cultural suit. Women, especially, attempted to shed the taboo of sexual promiscuity, battling with vigor to show that sexual liberation had less to do with sex than with power. From the workplace to the kitchen, from the bedroom to the boardroom, women transformed Eros from recreation to politics.

The '60s was both a decade of idealism, a real, if naive, belief in the possibility of social change; and a decade of chaos, giving rise to fear that, like Weimar Germany, years of assassination, antiwar protest, drug use, and free love would lead to anarchy or fascism. In March 1969, the Chicago Seven—Dave Dellinger, Tom Hayden, Abbie Hoffman, Jerry Rubin, and Bobby Seale among them—were indicted on charges of conspiracy to incite a riot in Chicago during the Democratic National Convention. The revolution had devolved into theater, but its cultural effects would be felt for years to come. —GJ

259

BSA Gold Star Clubmans

499 cc • 1960 • United Kingdom
Bore x stroke: 85 x 88 mm • Power output: 42 hp @ 7,000 rpm •
Top speed: 110 mph (177 km/h) • The Barber Vintage Motorsports Museum, Birmingham, Ala.

Those who lapped Brooklands' outer circuit at 100 mph or better received a gold star. Walter Handley received one in 1937 on a new BSA Empire Star 500, and the next year a model with an aluminum-alloy head and cylinder went on sale, renamed the Gold Star.

BSA had always been a quantity producer of solid transportation machines, so the high-performance Gold Star was a new venture for them. A 350 Gold Star won the Clubman's TT in 1949, and added a BSA 500 to the line in 1950. In 1952 the company further updated the chassis with swing-arm rear suspension and a twin-loop frame. The engine received continuous detail improvement.

The original Gold Star demonstrated the value of aluminum's high heat conductivity in the cylinder and the head. These parts were of cast iron, a durable material where mechanical friction is involved, but with only one-third of aluminum's ability to transmit heat.

A high-performance model such as this could survive in the market only because BSA's production know-how kept costs down. Unlike the pure racing Norton Manx, with its double-overhead-cam cylinder head, the Gold Star offered a simpler, cheaper-to-make pushrod-and-rocker-arm engine. In time, independent tuners were able to get as much or more power from the Gold Star's engine as from the "purer" overhead-cam engines.

A vigorous aftermarket made a wealth of special sporting/racing parts for both engine and chassis. Many Gold Stars were ridden on the highways or competed in scrambles or other off-road events. In its prime, between one and two thousand machines were produced annually. Moderate price and accessibility made the "Goldie" the vehicle of imagination for a generation of riders and tuners, both in the United States and in England. The last Gold Stars were produced in 1964, when they were replaced by the off-road-oriented 441 Victor. BSA parallel twins took over the high-performance road bike role from the Gold Star single.

Gold Star bikes brought the qualities and capabilities of true racing machines to street production motorcycles, demonstrating that the racing look can attract nonracing buyers. In this they foreshadowed today's sportbikes. —*KC*

Honda CB92 Benly Super Sport

125 cc • 1960 • Japan
Bore x stroke: 44 x 41 mm • Power output: 15 hp @ 10,500 rpm •
Top speed: 81 mph (130 km/h) • The Motorcycle Heritage Museum,
Westerville, Ohio, extended loan of Mark Mederski

During the economically strapped years in Japan following World War II, 200 or so motor-bicycle makers sprang up to meet the increased demand for inexpensive transport. Honda was among them. Although the company's founder, Soichiro Honda, loved racing (he was injured in 1936 in a racecar of his own making), his business partners and ensuing sales experiments guided him towards the utilitarian Super Cub step-through. Millions were sold, and the company prospered, bankrolling its research capabilities. The Benly 125 cc was the first step towards the creation of a worldwide market for Japanese sporting motorcycles.

Whereas European and especially American motorcycles generated their power through big pistons and a relatively low rpm, the Benly and later Hondas reversed this ratio. They compensated for their small size by operating at much higher rpm—the Benly developed its peak horsepower at a then exceptional 10,500 rpm. Operation at such a high speed made it necessary to work the valves as directly as possible via camshafts located directly above them in the engine's cylinder head. Such "overhead cams" and the chains, gears, or shafts that drive the valves gave this and subsequent Japanese engines their complicated appearance.

The Benly also introduced a civilizing innovation: reliable electric starting. Starting a motorcycle had previously been an exercise in tough-guy theater, something that eliminated many potential customers.

The Benly's chassis parts and styling were responsible for rekindling the dying embers of Europe's postwar motorcycle boom. Key to the design were the money-saving pressed-steel chassis and swing arm. Elements from the German NSU motorcycles also appeared—the leading-link fork (also pressed steel), and monobeam chassis in particular. Other Honda models had Germanic flaring and deeply valanced fenders as well. The shape of the Benly engine's cylinder head and its single-overhead camshaft derived from the German Horex twins of the 1950s.

In later years, Honda's sporting motorcycles abandoned the pressed-steel frame for more fashionable tubular steel, and, more recently, they have adopted from racing the much stiffer and lighter chassis made from paired large aluminum beams. — *KC*

Advertisement for the Honda CB92 in *Motorcyclist*, 1961.
American Motorcyclist Association.

NSU Supermax

247 cc • 1961 • West Germany
Bore x stroke: 69 x 66 mm • Power output: 18 hp @ 7,000 rpm •
Top speed: 78 mph (126 km/h) • Collection of John Mishanec

NSU (Neckarsulmer Strickwaren Union) was one of the pioneers of the motorcycle. The company built its first machine in 1901, using a single-cylinder Swiss Zedal engine. Later NSU produced machines with its own engines, including a line of V-twins ranging from 496 to 996 cc.

In 1929, leading British designer Walter Moore joined NSU from Norton, and during the 1930s, Moore was responsible for a series of rapid single-cylinder models. During World War II, NSU built thousands of motorcycles and bicycles, including the Kettenrad, or chain-track motorcycle, a small, tracked personnel carrier powered by a 1,478-cc Opel car engine. Albert Roder became chief designer in 1947, and, under his leadership, NSU enjoyed unparalleled success. His two most important and successful models were the Max motorcycle and the Quickly moped. (The company sold an amazing 1.1 million of the latter between 1953 and 1965.)

The very unorthodox 247-cc Max, with a bore and stroke of 69 x 66 mm, debuted in September 1952. Its frame-and-fork design had the pressed-steel chassis and leading-link front forks of NSU's Fox and Lux models, but the Max's overhead-cam engine was completely new and featured a type of valve gear unique among motorcycle engines. Known as the Ultramax system, the drive to the overhead valve gear was powered by long connecting rods housed in a tunnel, cast integrally on the left-hand side of the cylinder. At their ends, these rods carried eye-encircling, counterbalanced, eccentric discs connected to the half-time pinion and the overhead camshaft. As the engine revolved, the eccentrics imparted a reciprocating motion which was transferred to the valve gear. Roder also used hairpin valve springs and enclosed the entire mechanism.

Production of the Max hit its stride in 1953, when NSU built 24,403 bikes. In 1955, the company introduced a racing version, the Sportsmax, and Hermann Peter Müller scooped the 250-cc world road-racing title on a semiworks version. That year, the Special Max went on sale; and in 1956 the definitive Supermax hit the streets. The last Supermax rolled off the production lines in 1963, and NSU stopped making two-wheelers in 1965. In 1969, they merged with the Volkswagen Group, becoming Germany's largest automobile complex. In just over a decade, NSU had sold over a hundred thousand Max-based models, and the Max is acknowledged to be one of the best motorcycles ever to have reached series production. —MW

Leaflet for NSU Max, 1957. Classic Bike, Kettering, England.

Ducati Elite
204 cc • 1962 • Italy
Bore x stroke: 67 x 57.8 mm • Power output: 17 hp @ 7,500 rpm •
Top speed: 85 mph (137 km/h) • Collection of Guy Webster

Italian motorcycle manufacturer Ducati Meccanica rose from the ashes of the Societa Scientifica Radiobrevetti Ducati immediately after World War II. The original company, which was founded in 1926 by Antonio Cavalieri Ducati and his three young sons, had specialized in the production of radio equipment, and prospered between the wars, thanks to the Fascist Party's propaganda machine.

Although World War II virtually destroyed Ducati's Bologna plant, Aldo Farinelli, a Turin-based engineer, managed to create the Cucciolo (puppy)—a 48-cc four-stroke engine with clipped-on conventional pedal cycles—soon after the war ended, saving Ducati from extinction.

A larger, 60-cc version of Farinelli's engine powered Ducati's first complete motorcycle in 1950. From this, a whole series of pushrod lightweights evolved, heralding a new era that would see the marque gain great success, both in the showroom and on the international trials stage.

In 1954, Fabio Taglioni joined Ducati, and shortly thereafter a new breed of single, which had a camshaft driven by bevel gears and shafts—the 98-cc Grand Sport racer—debuted in 1955. Eventually, this model became a class winner in both the Milano-Taranto and the Giro d'Italia long-distance road races. In the following year, Ducati developed the twin-cam 124-cc Grand Prix and three-camshaft Desmo racers, together with one of the marque's most important street bikes of all time, the 175 Monoalbero (single camshaft).

The 174.5-cc engine was first displayed to the public at the Milan show in November 1956. It had a bore and stroke of 62 x 57.8 mm, and it closely mirrored the engine of the 98GS. Its alloy cylinder, with cast-iron liner, inclined slightly forward. Driven by a pair of bevel shafts and gears on the offside of the engine, its single-overhead-cam valve gear had enclosed rockers (they were exposed on the 98GS) and hairpin valve springs. The geared primary drive and multi-plate clutch, which were on the left-hand side, transmitted power to a four-speed gearbox. The full-circle crankshaft featured a roller big-end bearing, with a bronze small end bush. Lubrication was wet-sump, with a gear-type oil pump. Ignition was by battery/coil; the engine acted as a stressed member for the steel, tubular frame.

The first version, the 175T (Turismo) went on sale in 1957, soon followed by Sport and Formula 3 variants. In 1958, Ducati premiered its 204-cc Elite, which had a bore and stroke of 67 x 57.8 mm. Production ceased in late 1963. Thereafter came a vast array of overhead-cam bevel singles, culminating with the 436 cc in 1969. —*MW*

Honda CR110

50 cc • 1962 • Japan
Bore x stroke: 40.4 x 39 mm • Power output: 8.5 hp @ 13,500 rpm •
Top speed: 85 mph (137 km/h) • The Barber Vintage Motorsports
Museum, Birmingham, Ala.

In 1963 the International Federation of Motorcyclists (better known by its French initials, FIM) decided to give the 50-cc class of bike world status in the racing schedule. The move helped bring new blood into the sport, as privateers would now be able to afford to participate in the competitions.

Honda had just the machine for this new niche, an easily obtainable production-racing model, the CR110. By competition standards this racer was both fast and inexpensive—it cost less than $1,000. The CR110's engine was an air-cooled single cylinder, with a wet sump; the crankcases split vertically. From the crankshaft, three intermediate gears rotated to drive the double-overhead camshafts. The cams worked four valves, arranged in parallel pairs for better fit in the tiny combustion chamber. The engine was almost square, with a bore and stroke of 40.4 x 39 mm; with its race-ready 10.3 to 1 compression ratio, the motorcycle generated 8.5 hp at 13,500 rpm—emitting a healthy noise through the megaphone exhaust. The spark came from a crankshaft-mounted generator, although often this was dispensed with in favor of a battery and coil.

To be able to keep the revolutions high, the transmission had eight speeds and used a dry clutch. The motorcycle's maximum speed depended on gearing, but with stock sprockets, it could approach 90 mph. A street-legal version was also available in some countries, its engine detuned to 7 hp at 12,700 rpm.

The engine unit was suspended from a double-tubular backbone, or spine frame. The cylinder was canted forward about 45 degrees, with the double-hanger front mount attached to the forward part of the cylinder head. Suspension was effected by telescopic forks and a dual-shocked swinging arm. It had a 2.00:18 tire in front, a 2.25:18 at the rear, and single leading-shoe drum brakes in light alloy hubs on both. The motorcycle weighed a modest 134 pounds, and only small riders could fit behind the fairing.

However, this little single just could not win at the Grand Prix level, falling behind the two-stroke engines of both Suzuki and the German Kreidler. So the factory went back to the drawing board to design the two-cylinder, double-overhead camshaft, eight-valve RC112.

But that wasn't the end of the CR110. On Japanese and European amateur clubman circuits, the CR110 held its own quite well for a number of years. And Honda has recently reissued the CR110 for nostalgia buffs. —*Clement Salvadori*

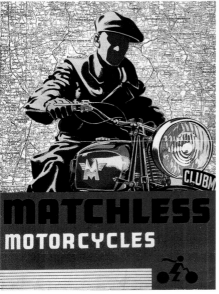

Brochure for Matchless, 1938.
Classic Bike, Kettering, England.

Matchless G50

496 cc • 1962 • United Kingdom
Bore x stroke: 90 x 78 mm • Power output: 48 hp @ 7,200 rpm • Top speed: 135 mph (217 km/h) •
The Barber Vintage Motorsports Museum, Birmingham, Ala.

The 1958 Matchless G50, big brother to the 1948 350-cc AJS 7R, was created in response to the failure of the fragile, street-based G45 twin to prove itself a satisfactory racer.

The great British tradition of single-cylinder power was becoming ever more refined, until it existed mainly within the realm of racing, where reliability is prized above all; the fewer the parts, the less frequent the failure. The British single personified this rule. On the continent, more prosperous companies were experimenting with racing twins and fours, as well as with supercharging. The English replied by elaborating on their existing strengths, developing, for example, the ability to assist cylinder filling by means of tuned intake and exhaust-wave action. This advancement gave the British singles their characteristic long intake and exhaust pipes, often equipped with intake funnels or exhaust megaphones.

Denied the luxury of pure horsepower, the developers of the single concentrated on ease of handling, light weight, and wide-range acceleration. On race courses with many slower turns, the direction-changing prowess and powerful acceleration of singles frequently won races against much more powerful machines.

Whereas the Norton Manx was a factory racer, later produced for private entrants, the 7R and G50 were designed with robust simplicity in mind. A single-overhead cam was used; it was driven by a chain that operated the valves, which worked via roller-tipped rockers. This eliminated much of the complexity of the shafts, bearings, and gears that characterize the Norton. Like the Norton Manxes, G50s soldiered on for years after they were no longer produced, continuing to fill top placings in the Grand Prix. During this period they were further developed, and they served to school an outstanding cadre of British riders. The availability of closely matched, eminently raceable motorcycles such as the Matchless G50 and Norton Manx made this possible.

The evolution of the 7R and the G50 was to be a model for the future. Jack Williams developed methods of measuring engine airflow, fuel distribution, and valve action that are in use to this day. His emphasis on raising average horsepower rather than peak power is as valuable in today's superbike racing as it was in 1958. — *KC*

Norton Manx

498 cc • 1962 • United Kingdom
Bore x stroke: 86 x 85.8 mm • Power output: 47 hp @ 6,500 rpm •
Top speed: 130 mph (209 km/h) • The Barber Vintage Motorsports
Museum, Birmingham, Ala.

The Norton Manx 500 motorcycle was a production road racer that was sold to private entrants in quantities of about 100 a year. Norton folded its own factory racing team after the 1954 season, but continued to build these machines until October of 1963. The Manx 500 and the Manx 350 are two of the finest expressions of the British single-cylinder engine ever produced. In private hands, these machines continued to place well in Grand Prix racing throughout the 1960s, schooling young British riders such as Mike Hailwood, who went on to world championships riding Italian and Japanese machines.

Norton's prestigious race department absorbed most of the company's development resources. It tested such innovations as a lay-down single, a desmodromic engine, and a rotary-valve engine. Valve control proved seminal, sprouting the growth of the machinery visible atop the engine's cylinder head. And the long intake and exhaust pipes exploited power-boosting pressure waves.

Painstaking development made the Manx singles successful. A spring frame was adopted in 1936, and telescopic forks soon after. In 1950, the brilliant Irish engineer Rex McCandless designed and built the twin-loop, swing-arm frame for Norton that you see here, later dubbed "the Featherbed." The most copied of all motorcycle chassis, it worked because it combined the best suspension ideas available with a forward placement of both rider and engine weight. This makes it possible to steer accurately even when the machine is accelerating rapidly out of a turn. Although this innovation helped even the score against the power of the Italian fours, it was a losing struggle. When it became clear that Norton would not replace the hard-worked singles with a four-cylinder engine of their own, McCandless left.

A failing Norton was absorbed by Amalgamated Motor Cycles (AMC) in 1953. When Norton relocated in 1963, the contents of the Bracebridge Street race shop were sold for £1,000. The Norton-Villiers group stayed in business until 1977, producing such parallel twins as the Atlas. —*KC*

Parilla GS

247 cc • 1962 • Italy

Bore x stroke: 68 x 68 mm • Power output: 21 hp @ 8,800 rpm • Top speed: 110 mph (177 km/h) • Collection of Guy Webster

Giovanni Parrilla emigrated to southern Italy from Spain in the 1920s. During World War II he found himself in Milan, where he opened a small business specializing in the repair of agricultural diesel pumps and injectors.

At the end of the war, much of northern Italy, including Milan, was economically shattered, and Parrilla made an early decision to transfer his attention to motorcycles. Parrilla's first design, a single-overhead-cam 247 cc, made its debut as a racer in October 1946. The Parilla 247 cc (the second "r" was deleted) quickly became the company's first production roadster, much admired in the Italian press as the first new design to come out of Italy during a postwar period in which rival makers were mainly building hoards of cheap, cheerful two-stroke commuter motorcycles and scooters.

In 1948 Parilla developed the Biaberro (twin camshaft) racer with a power output at a bore and stroke of 66 x 72 mm (a dimension it shared with its roadster brother) and a healthy 18.5 hp, giving a maximum speed of almost 100 mph. More Parillas followed, including both four and two-stroke bikes, but the model that was to have the most effect on the company's future appeared at the end of 1952, in the shape of the unorthodox 175 Fox, with a high-camshaft engine.

The valves operated via short, splayed pushrods on the left-hand side of the cylinder. With a capacity of 174 cc and a bore and stroke of 59.8 x 62 mm, the ultrashort pushrods were operated from a single chain-driven cam, mounted at the top of the timing case, and kept in adjustment by a Weller-type tensioner.

The "hi-cam" concept, the invention of two notable motorcycle designers Giuseppe Salmaggi and Alfredo Bianchi, was often adapted for the Parilla street bikes and racers. During the mid-to late 1950s, the 175 hi-cam appeared in a wide range of models, including the GS (Gran Sport), and by 1960, the MSDS, built under Italian Formula 3 racing regulations, could achieve 100 mph with open exhaust. The following year, Parilla upped the motor to 199 cc (64 x 62 mm) and then 247 cc (68 x 68 mm), the latter mainly for the American market, both in tourist and GS forms. Parilla ceased production of motorcycles in 1967 to concentrate on the manufacture of kart engines. —*MW*

Vespa GS

146 cc • 1962 • Italy

Bore x stroke: 57 x 57 mm • Power output: 7.8 hp @ 7,500 rpm •

Top speed: 62 mph (100 km/h) • Collection of Ron Bussey

When the Piaggio company was founded in Genoa in 1884, it produced woodworking machinery for the local shipbuilding industry. In 1901, it turned to railway rolling stock, then in 1916, to aircraft, and in 1924, to car manufacturing. By 1939, Piaggio was playing a leading role in Italian aviation. Its most famous wartime airplane was the P108—the nation's only four-engined heavy bomber to attain service status during the hostilities.

By 1944, nothing was left of Piaggio's production facilities but bombed-out buildings, a few machine tools, and a huge workforce. Factory owner Enrico Piaggio called a management meeting, after which his chief designer, aviation specialist Carradano d'Ascanio, began work on what emerged as the Vespa scooter, which used a a small, two-stroke auxiliary engine.

Along with its rival Lambretta, the Vespa put Italy back on wheels. It embodied the latest motorcycle, automotive, and aviation technology; today, over 50 years later, the machine is still being manufactured, using the same general design concept. Production began in 1946, using a 98-cc two-stroke single-cylinder engine with a bore and stroke of 50 x 50 mm. One hundred examples of this original Vespa were constructed; later that year, a simplified version entered mass production. In 1948, Piaggio replaced it with the first 125-cc (56.5 x 49.8 mm) Vespa. By the early 1950s, the Vespa was a familiar sight not only in Italy, but around the world. The Grand Sport, with a cc of 146 and a bore and stroke of 57 x 57 mm, was introduced in order to cater to the sportsmen's market for scooters. The greater power of the GS allowed it to compete successfully in racing events.

Throughout its first 20 years, the Vespa fought for supremacy in the scooter sales war with Lambretta (owned by Innocenti). By the mid-1990s, Piaggio had built over ten million scooters, while Innocenti had produced four million. Piaggio effectively created the industry, and its Vespa played a huge part in postwar European youth culture. Today Vespas are also manufactured under license agreements in many countries. —*MW*

Still from William Wyler's *Roman Holiday*, 1953.

Honda C100 Super Cub

49 cc • 1963 • Japan
Bore x stroke: 40 x 39 mm • Power output: 4.5 hp @ 9,500 rpm •
Top speed: 43 mph (70 km/h) • Collection of Jerry Tamanini

This little 49-cc step-through, often referred to as the 50 Super Cub, was responsible, to a large degree, for establishing Honda's reputation in the United States. It was inexpensive and easy to ride; it required minimal maintenance; and it looked sharp.

Soichiro Honda had been marketing a 50-cc, no-pedal motorbike on the home front long before he tackled the American market. A four-stroke aficionado, Honda had built a small 49-cc overhead-valve engine, but here the single cylinder was lying flat and pointing forward; it was an excellent, extremely reliable motor, putting out a maximum 4.5 hp at 9,500 rpm.

Primary drive gears connected the crankshaft to a three-speed transmission, which used an automatic centrifugal clutch to relieve the rider from the chore of clutching. A fully enclosed chain ran to the rear wheel, and large leg protectors kept road grime off the rider's trousers.

Perhaps the Cub's greatest contribution was its use of plastic for the front fender and the leg shields; plastic did the job just as well as metal, at a considerably lower cost. The frame, leading-link forks, and swinging arm were all made of inexpensive pressed steel, which also helped to keep the Cub's price down.

Honda's market was the new rider; this little machine was designed to attract the nonmotorcycling crowd, which was an ingenious plan. Although the rider, man or woman, had to kick-start the engine to life, cranking a 50 was not at all difficult—you had only to start it up, roll the bike off the center-stand, put it into gear, twist the throttle, and away you went. If you shifted to second, then third, on a good downhill, the Cub might get all the way up to 50 mph—the aerodynamics were, in a word, nonexistent. The Cub was not intended as a speedster, but as transportation around town.

Today, Honda factories in a dozen countries around the world continue to turn out tens of thousands of C100 descendants, a basic means of transportation in many Asian, African, and South American countries. At last count, approximately twenty-six million of these extremely utilitarian machines had been produced over the years. — *CS*

Advertisement for Honda, 1963. Collection of Jerry Tamanini.

Velocette Venom

499 cc • 1963 • United Kingdom
Bore x stroke: 86 x 86 mm • Power output: 34 hp @ 6,200 rpm •
Top speed: 105 mph (169 km/h) • Collection of Harry Lindsay

Velocette, the last of the independent British motorcycle producers, went into liquidation in 1971. Although they had been longtime makers of high-quality sporting singles, after World War II they
found themselves under-supplying the demand for their singles while
striving to mass market other products. Despite Velocette's strong
ideas, the company was out of tune with its markets.

Velocette evolved out of Veloce, Ltd., an outgrowth of the
Paul Kelecom (see FN) partnership with Ormonde, in 1905. The
marque was always close to sport, developing its singles through
practical experiments conducted in a familial, rather than a corporate, atmosphere. Designer Harold Willis was a former TT rider
who invented the modern positive-stop foot shifter while at
Velocette in 1929. Later, in 1936, he added aircraft-type hydraulic
suspension dampers to the bike. Velo development was a matter
of item-by-item refinement, a process in which men like Willis
came to know their machines extremely well.

It is hard to convey to a modern reader the informality of
motorcycle design and development in the era of big singles. The
nearly vertical-front down-tube of this Venom's chassis was the result of a particular day of testing in the autumn of 1935. Lumps
of lead were placed ahead of the engine to determine whether the
machine held its line better when accelerating out of corners with
its weight farther forward. It did. The engine was moved to where
you see it here. The arc-shaped slots at the back allow rear suspension stiffness to vary according to load.

The Thruxton model, introduced in the mid '60s but based
upon many previous racing and production singles, was a tuned
sports version of the Venom. It derived its name from a race for production machines held at the Thruxton circuit. About 1,100 were
built over six years.

The company had reached for the future in 1950, beginning
work on a four-cylinder 500-cc racer. The plan was that it would
have disc brakes, develop 70 to 75 hp, weigh 300 pounds, and
achieve a top speed of 175 mph. All this would come to pass, although not in Velocette's hands. —*KC*

Brochure for Velocette, 1932. Classic Bike, Kettering, England.

Bultaco Sherpa T

244 cc • 1965 • Spain

Bore x stroke: 72 x 60 mm • Power output: 19.8 hp @ 5,500 rpm •
Top speed: unknown • The Sammy Miller Museum,
Bashley Manor, England

The original Bultaco Sherpa T, the most successful trials motorcycle of all time, was built and developed by Ulsterman Sammy Miller in 1964. Ironically, the marque only exists because another manufacturer pulled out of racing. In May 1958, the directors of Montesa ended their involvement with Grand Prix, and Francisco Xavier, one of the founders of the company, departed to start his own endeavor. Within days, work started on a 125-cc single-cylinder two-stroke at a small industrial unit near Barcelona.

The new bike didn't have a name until Bulto's close business associate—and top-flight road racer—Johnny Grace came up with Bultaco, a contraction of Bulto and Paco, Francisco's nickname. The "thumbs-up" gas tank emblem was designed by Bulto after he noticed British riders giving the signal to show that all was well as they flashed past the pits.

In May 1959 the Bultaco team entered their first road race, the Clubman class of the Spanish GP. Grace finished inches behind the winning Montesa. But in an astonishing coup, seven Bultacos were among the first nine finishers. Still, by 1963, although Bultaco was producing nearly 12,000 motorcycles a year, four-stroke singles from Royal Enfield, AJS, and Ariel dominated the trials scene. Bulto decided to expand his range and make a trials bike.

The obvious choice to build the prototype was Sammy Miller, who had long dominated the sport on an Ariel that would have been hopelessly outclassed if it hadn't been for his development work and unsurpassed riding skill. Miller selected an experimental 244-cc, two-stroke engine with a radial-finned head and put it in a modified, Sherpa N trail-bike frame; he changed the steering head angle, bringing it closer to his old Ariel's ideal; he fabricated triple clamps to reduce tiller action; and he fitted a long-travel front fork with Miller-modified bottom castings, positioning the wheel spindle further forward. Miller then announced at the December 1964 British Experts Trial that he was signing up with Bultaco.

The trials world did not expect much of Miller and the new Bultaco, however. One respected journalist wrote, "I do not expect to see Miller winning in his first rides on the new machine. A good time and place to judge his progress on the Bultaco will be in 12 months' time at the next British Experts." But Miller won Bultaco's first event the very next day. And a few weeks later, at the 1965 Colmore Trial, he produced the first-ever win by a foreign bike at a British championship round. Miller went on to win the championship outright, and the prestigious Scottish Six Days Trial as well. Before the end of the year, Bultacos made up a third of most British trials entries. This was an auspicious beginning to Bultaco's domination of the sport, which would last for 15 years. —*Phillip Tooth*

Brochure for the Bultaco Sherpa T, 1969. Classic Bike, Kettering, England.

Brochure for the Kreidler Florett, 1966.
Classic Bike, Kettering, England.

Kreidler Florett

49 cc • 1965 • West Germany
Bore x stroke: 40 x 39.5 mm • Power output: 3 hp @ 5,500 rpm • Top speed: 43 mph (69 km/h) •
Deutsches Zweirad-Museum, Neckarsulm, Germany

Kreidler Fahrzeugbau, originally a metal factory near Stuttgart, holds the honor of winning six 50-cc world road-racing titles, more than any other motorcycle manufacturer in the world. The company only built ultralightweight motorcycles, but their quality is superb, and the Florett is considered the best 50-cc bike ever manufactured.

Kreidler Fahrzeugbau's first motorcycle designs were the much praised K50 and K51 mopeds developed in 1951. The success of these early models led to the introduction of the Florett (meaning "foil," as in a fencing saber) in early 1957. This bike would dominate the company's motorcycling future for the next quarter-century.

For its era, the Florett was an exceptionally modern-looking machine, one which would prove popular and long lasting. At the heart of this newcomer was a brand-new horizontal (the first such layout by a German manufacturer since the Imme) 49-cc piston-ported, three-speed unit construction engine, with a bore and stroke of 40 x 39.5 mm. To escape strict German moped speed restrictions, the Florett was marketed from the start as a motorcycle, albeit one with flyweight proportions. The Kreidler factory owners were so confident about their product that they presented customers who completed 100,000 kilometers (62,500 miles) on the bikes with solid-gold tiepins bearing the Kreidler emblem.

The sport-race-equipped Floretts made their debut in 1959, and in 1960 Hans Georg Anscheidt, Kreidler's factory rider and later a world champion with Suzuki, won the factory's first gold medal in the International Six Days Trial in Austria. In 1962, Kreidler won the first ever 50-cc Grand Prix race in Spain, but not until 1971 did the German marque, in association with the Dutch Van Veen team, win the first of its six record-breaking world racing championship titles. —*MW*

Triumph T120 Bonneville

650 cc • 1967 • United Kingdom
Bore x stroke: 71 x 82 mm • Power output: 46 hp @ 6,500 rpm •
Top speed: 112 mph (180 km/h) • The Barber Vintage Motorsports
Museum, Birmingham, Ala.

After World War II, American riders took readily to Triumph's Edward Turner–designed light twins. Compared to the heavy American Indians and Harley-Davidsons, the Triumph Speed Twins were agile and quick. Modern sportbikes, as capable as they may be, are not yet as light as these simple, effective machines.

The Bonneville has its roots in the Triumph 500. In 1949, more power was deemed necessary for the bike, and it was expanded first into the Thunderbird, and eventually, in the mid '50s, into the T110 650. When, in 1958, the single carburetor of the T110 650 needed help, twin carburetors were added. These defined the Bonneville, a bike that continued to evolve, adopting the unit construction of the 1957 3T in 1963. The name Bonneville derives from the Utah salt flats where speed records are set. It was intended to play into the bike's decidedly American sales orientation—and it succeeded. Countless young men walked into U.S. dealerships, sat on the Bonneville, liked its feel, and laid out a handful of one-hundred-dollar bills on the spot.

The bigger an engine's pistons, the stronger its vibration. At idle, the front wheel of a Bonneville whipped cyclically forward and back, driven by the motion of large crank counterweights. Today, such a vibration would be considered unacceptably harsh, but at the time it was embraced as part of the bike's charm.

Triumph, however, failed to appreciate its buyers' loyalty and conservatism. Although this motorcycle defined high performance on two wheels for 20 years, when the bikes were restyled in the early 1970s—with megaphonelike mufflers, aluminum fork bottoms, and larger fuel tanks—riders were highly critical of the changes. When it came to a new Bonneville, they didn't want Triumph to match Japanese features; riders wanted the time-honored King James version. Harley-Davidson, by contrast, understood the iconic value of their designs, and has been very careful not to repeat Triumph's mistake.

Production ceased in 1973, although it was later restarted, and continued in a lame-duck fashion for a number of years. Today's Triumph motorcycle is made by an entirely new company and according to new designs. —*KC*

Catalogue for Johnson Motors, 1965. Collection of Charles M. Falco.

Still from Dennis Hopper's *Easy Rider*, 1969.

Harley-Davidson Easy Rider Chopper

1,200 cc • 1969 (1993 replica) • United States
Bore x stroke: 80.9 x 96.8 mm • Power output: 61 hp @ 6,000 rpm (est.) • Top speed: 100 mph (161 km/h) •
The Otis Chandler Vintage Museum of Transportation and Wildlife, Oxnard, Calif.

After Peter Fonda secured funding for *Easy Rider* (he had conceived both the movie and the motorcycle four years before he started making them), he bought several used Los Angeles Police Department Harley-Davidsons at auction. These were low-compression 1,200-cc 1962 Model FLs. Fonda had two of these bikes dismantled and heavily chromed before reassembly. He had the front forks raked to a nearly 45-degree angle and lengthened 12 inches. He mounted "ape-hanger" handlebars on the Wide-Glide front end. Years later, Fonda recalled that after the first few days of filming, his arms ached from maneuvering the bike.

In 1993, with a commission from Otis Chandler, Glenn Bator and Jerry Sewell set out to reproduce the Captain America bike for Chandler's Vintage Museum. Sewell put in 100 hours of research while Bator began gathering parts for chroming. They examined photos, wore out a videotape of the film, and interviewed dozens of people associated with the production of the Captain America bike. When Fonda first saw the replica, he threw a leg over it and said, "Boy, does this bring back memories."

One motorcycle was crashed and destroyed on film (a requirement of the script). During the completion of filming, Fonda put the second motorcycle, used for close-ups, into storage. But several men broke into the storage facility, terrorized the family living there, and stole the Captain America bike as well as other motorcycles belonging to Fonda and his friends. Because these bikes were never found, Fonda and the L.A. Police and Ventura County Sheriff's departments are certain they were dismantled and parted out. "The film wasn't out yet," Fonda explains. "To them, it was a chromed chopper. None of us imagined the bike would become an icon for a way of life. That bike got scattered." He added, "But I like the idea that in a variety of places around the country, folks are riding parts of that bike. Underneath some metal-flake-painted tank somewhere, there are stars and stripes. And the owner doesn't have a clue." —RL

Getting Away from It All

1969
1978

LAVERDA

Getting Away from It All: 1969–1978

The year 1969 marked the end of one era, which reached its peak with Woodstock, and kicked off another, with Dennis Hopper's iconic film *Easy Rider*. Jack Nicholson's rebel, tasting freedom and marijuana for the first time, was a better icon of the future than Dennis Hopper's freakish pothead or the cool motorcycle guru Peter Fonda, with whom he rode. The advertising campaign for *Easy Rider* proclaimed, "A man went looking for America and couldn't find it anywhere," a sentiment that could be expanded to embrace the entire decade. In 1970 the Beatles disbanded, and Jimi Hendrix and Janis Joplin self-destructed, as did Jim Morrison and Duane Allman. A much-mythologized period was over.

Protest remained a defining element of the early '70s, and there were plenty of issues to protest. While Nixon was pulling soldiers out of Vietnam and bringing them home as heroes in the "retreat with honor," he continued to plot devastating acts of aggression, bombing villages (Haiphong) and cities (Hanoi) as well as vast coastal areas of Vietnam. The violence wasn't restricted to the war abroad; Nixon threatened martial law at home, and, in 1970, at Kent State University in Ohio, the National Guard fired on a thousand antiwar protesters, killing four students. Even Hollywood spoke up: Jane Fonda traveled to Hanoi, and Marlon Brando went to the Pine Ridge Reservation in South Dakota for the trial of Dino Butler and Bob Robideau, following the shoot-out deaths of two FBI officers.

At the same time, Congress finally responded to growing public pressure to act on environmental and public health issues. The Environmental Protection Agency was formed to enforce the Clean Air Act of 1970, pollution testing began in the Atlantic Ocean, the Endangered Species Act and the Safe Drinking Water Act were passed, and the National Cancer Institute linked cancer to pollution. Antinuclear protests were organized, though they were yet to be taken seriously despite the Three Mile Island nuclear accident in Pennsylvania. In 1973, *Roe v. Wade* made abortion legal—a triumphant, landmark decision in favor of a woman's right to chose.

On the global stage, in retaliation for U.S., European, and Japanese support of Israel during the Arab-Israeli conflicts of the previous decade, the Arab oil-producing countries in 1973 formed the Organization of Petroleum Exporting Countries (OPEC). The resultant oil embargo and doubling of oil prices precipitated an energy crisis that had tangible effects in the U.S., leading to widespread panic. At around the same time, the House Judiciary Committee initiated televised impeachment hearings against Richard Nixon, who was charged with conspiring to obstruct justice in the Watergate cover-up and with failure to uphold his oath of office through flagrant abuses of power. Then, in 1976, official charges were leveled against the CIA for "dirty tricks" both at home and abroad.

The result was a widespread loss of faith and trust in U.S. institutions, as well as growing feelings on the part of the American public of insecurity and powerlessness in the face of crises on the domestic and international fronts. Many people responded by seeking escape from life's uncomfortable realities by any means possible. Experimentation with alternative religions and lifestyles was widespread, as the disaffected searched for life's meaning through transcendental meditation, yoga, mysticism, Eastern religion, the writings of Carlos Casteneda, communes, and hallucinatory drugs. This experimentation reached extremes with the mass weddings of over two thousand couples, presided over by the Reverend Moon, and the mass murder/suicides of 911 devotees of the Reverend Jim Jones, in Jonestown, Guyana.

Disco, immortalized in the 1977 movie *Saturday Night Fever*, was arguably the most pervasive symbol of the era. It emerged initially as the music of a true underground society, whose denizens wore wild fashions and makeup, expressed an outrageous sexuality, and danced till morning to frantic nonstop music plied by "dee-jays" using two turntables. But disco soon became a studio-manufactured product with a wide commercial market. Concurrently, punk and new wave, two forms of music diametrically opposed to disco began to surface, each exhorting a call to anarchy and rebellion that suggested a more dissonant, if slightly more politically charged, response. If the means were different, the ends were the same—oblivion, a state that could be obtained through the use of pot, cocaine, and heroin as well. Feeding on the public's appetite for fear-induced thrills, Evel Knievel became one of the highest-paid entertainers of his time, making stunt-riding an industry unto itself. In 1974, he negotiated a fee of between eight and nine million dollars to jump the 1,600 feet across Idaho's Snake River Canyon, dressed like a Confederate Captain America. (The attempt failed.) A more accessible form of escape could be found in the movies, with their preoccupation with large-scale disasters and outer space. Steven Spielberg's *Jaws* (1975) and George Lucas's *Star Wars* (1977) were two of the most popular movies of the decade, defining a new genre of moviemaking that was as interested in spectacle as in story or character development.

Motorcycles have always offered riders escape through speed, but, in the 1970s, manufacturers learned to apply the technology of the racetrack to the creation of super-speedy bikes for the road. Honda, for example, transformed both motorcycle design and habits with its CB750 Four. Harley-Davidson and Triumph made noble attempts to compete, offering their own sporty superbikes, and a type of U.S./British cultural exchange occurred. While Harley-Davidson's XLCR, a smaller-bodied café racer, tempered classic Harley design components and took inspiration from Europe, Britain's Triumph made a last-ditch marketing attempt by crossing the Atlantic with styling that made direct reference to a classic "American" (i.e., Harley-Davidson) look. Both were market failures. Although nothing could be further away from Captain America's *Easy Rider* Chopper, it was the Ducati 750SS, the product of masterful Italian design, that captured the era's zeitgeist. In the '70s, this bike was the ultimate escapist vehicle. —*Sarah Botts*

BSA Rocket 3

740 cc • 1969 • United Kingdom
Bore x stroke: 67 x 70 mm • Power output: 60 hp @ 7,250 rpm •
Top speed: 122 mph (196 km/h) • Collection of Andrew Sturgeon

As the U.S. motorcycle market developed, a demand for machines that were bigger and more capable than England's bread-and-butter twins emerged. As early as 1961, Triumph/BSA engineer Bert Hopwood proposed a three-cylinder 750 engine. Doug Hele (previously at Norton) recalls sketching the crank in 1962, and one evening in Hele's office, the two men drew the layout. It was prototyped three years later at a bore and stroke of 63 x 80 mm, with an iron cylinder, and was later changed to 67 x 70 mm. Small bores seemed a good way to limit engine width.

The project moved along slowly, and the Triumph Trident, with its famous "ray-gun" exhaust pipes, reached the market in 1969, the same year as did the Honda CB750, and only three years before the 903-cc Kawasaki Z1. The Rocket-3 was a Trident with slightly sloping cylinders. The hitch was that, compared to the new Japanese fours, the BSA/Triumph triple, which had seemed smooth in 1965, now felt rough. The bike, essentially Triumph's 500 twin with an extra cylinder, was already almost obsolete when it entered production. Although the triple-based racers that were prepared and campaigned in 1970 did in fact achieve a number of excellent performances, including a 1971 Daytona 200 win.

But sales were falling in the home market—motorcycle registrations had peaked in the summer of 1959. This shift was due to the arrival of low-priced autos such as the 1959 BMC Mini. Between 1960 and 1965, British bike production dropped from 194,000 to 95,000 and, by 1970, it had fallen to 70,000. In 1971, senior engineers Bert Hopwood and Doug Hele proposed a modular production system, based on a 200-cc cylinder size. Bikes from 200 cc to 1,000 cc could be produced so as to share many common parts—almost exactly as is being done by the new Triumph Company in England today. The company collapsed as this proposal was going to the directors. BSA's version of the triple, the Rocket 3, was discontinued in 1972.

As with other British motorcycle makers, there was never a shortage of ideas or technology. In BSA's case, projects underway at the time of the collapse included a four-valve-per-cylinder Commando, a 500-cc overhead-cam twin, a Commando with a balancer shaft, a single-overhead-cam Trident, an Isolastic Trident, a 900-cc T180 triple, and the four-cylinder Triumph Quadrant. —*KC*

THERE'S NEVER BEEN ANYTHING LIKE IT BEFORE!

Catalogue for the BSA Rocket 3, 1969. National Motor Museum, Beaulieu, England.

Brochure for the Kawasaki Mach III, 1973.
Classic Bike, Kettering, England.

Kawasaki Mach III

498 cc • 1969 • Japan

Bore x stroke: 60 x 58.8 mm • Power output: 60 hp @ 8,000 rpm • Top speed: 118 mph (190 km/h) •
The Otis Chandler Vintage Museum of Transportation and Wildlife, Oxnard, Calif.

Power to weight—that ratio was the key to Kawasaki's 498-cc two-stroke triple, the Mach III. The three cylinders, each enclosing a mere 166 cc, generated 60 hp, and the whole motorcycle, with a gallon of fuel in its tank, barely reached the 400-pound mark.

When Kawasaki's research and development department decided to build this midsized muscle machine, they knew exactly what they were after: the market in America, where most of the racing took place from stoplight to stoplight. There were three pistons in a row on the Mach III, firing at 120 degrees, with port-controlled carburetion using 28-mm Mikunis, Injectolube oiling, and a new capacitive-discharge ignition system that could hit a spark plug with 25,000 volts to guarantee ultraefficient combustion.

The factory bolted this engine, and five-speed transmission, into a double-cradle frame with a 56.3-inch wheelbase—hoping that some irresponsible owner would not flip the whole thing over backwards. But quite a few did. Up to 5,000 rpm, nothing much happened—but from 5,000 to 8,000 rpm the rider had to hold on and try very hard to keep his weight forward.

This was one of the least useful motorcycles available on the market, but the Mach III sold like proverbial hotcakes. The late 1960s were the heyday of the massive American muscle-car V-8s, which put out huge amounts of horsepower, and here was a motorcycle that could blow just about anything else off the road—for less than $1,000.

At a reasonable rate of speed, the Mach III handled like other good motorcycles. But in 1969, the ability to cover 1,320 feet from a standing start in the shortest time was considered the truest measure of power. The limits of the Mach III's engine went well beyond the limits of the softly sprung suspension. If a corner came up, the rider slowed down and then accelerated into the next straight.

The Mach III would not have received much in the way of style awards, although its projectile-type gas tank and long flat saddle did give it a certain sleek look. You didn't buy this Kawasaki for its looks, however; you bought it if you wanted to have the fastest wheels in town. And as it could make that standing quarter-mile in the range of twelve seconds, it was respected.

The Mach III was a phenomenal seller, especially to young people; it was cheap and extremely fast. Motorcycle lore has t that very few original owners of the Mach III survived. — *CS*

Norton Commando 750 Fastback

745 cc • 1969 • United Kingdom
Bore x stroke: 73 x 89 mm • Power output: 58 hp @ 6,800 rpm •
Top speed: 117 mph (188 km/h) • Collection of Peter Swider

Following Triumph's lead, Norton produced its own parallel-twin-powered bike, the 500-cc Model 7, in 1948. While Triumph and BSA aggressively attacked the U.S. market, Norton kept to a more leisurely pace. Over time, their twin was enlarged and upgraded. The company failed in 1953, and was absorbed by AMC, which became Norton-Villiers in 1966. This new entity undertook a thorough revision of its twins for 1967.

Parallel twins vibrate on a single plane, so the engine, gearbox, and rear swing arm were joined together as a unit, then coupled to the rest of the frame through rubber mounts whose flexibility existed only within that plane. The concept was given the name Isolastic, and its purpose was to allow the existing engine design to soldier on—despite its natural heavy vibration—into an era increasingly dominated by more sophisticated Japanese machines. Norton-Villiers could not afford to design and retool for an all-new engine.

Previous Norton twins had a severe vertical look, now considered stodgy. This was derived from the original 1950 racing Featherbed (consider the Norton Manx) as well as a long history of vertical single-cylinder engines. In the new Commando, the engine's cylinders were sloped forward like those of Japanese engines, with the emphasis falling on length and grace.

With vibration quelled by Isolastic, Norton-Villiers was free to increase performance by enlarging and powering-up the engine. Unfortunately, the company's manufacturing equipment was incapable of maintaining the accuracy necessary for endless upgrades.

Big Japanese machines were still just a rumor, and British bike fanciers adopted the capable new Nortons with enthusiasm. Even when the Japanese fours did arrive, their abysmal handling made British and European alternatives seem brilliant. But as more and more power became necessary, problems developed.

In 1972, a special Norton factory racer appeared, cleverly designed by rider/engineer Peter Williams. Many other innovative projects, both for racing and production, were in the works. But when Norton-Villiers added electric starting to the Commando, the result was shoddy. Powered-up engines with high compression wore out their lower ends in as few as 1,000 miles.

Meanwhile, Norton-Villiers-Triumph was formed out of what little was left of the industry. In 1975, it too went into receivership. A few more Nortons were assembled from parts up to 1978; the rest was silence. — *KC*

Catalogue for the Norton Commando, 1970.
Norton Owners Club, England.

Derbi 50 Grand Prix

49 cc • 1970 • Spain
Bore x stroke: 38.7 x 42 mm • Power output: 15.5 hp @ 15,000 rpm •
Top speed: 106 mph (170 km/h) • Courtesy of Derbi-Nacional
Motor SA, Barcelona

Angel Nieto's tiny frame—more sparrow hawk than biker hero—perched atop an even tinier motorcycle, his 49-cc Derbi, might have made it hard for the casual viewer to consider him a serious competitor. But anyone racing against Nieto and the Derbi knew that this brilliant Spanish combination was virtually invincible in the most junior of all Grand Prix classes.

When, in the 1950s, Derbi, Spain's longtime leading maker of bicycles, decided to manufacture bicycles with engines, it was natural for the company to concentrate on a range of lighter mopeds and motorcycles. Derbi quickly became dominant in the Spanish moped and light motorcycle market with a series of inexpensive and reliable designs—a position they retain today.

It wasn't until the late 1960s that Derbi's motorcycles made their mark on the world racing stage. During Derbi's early years as a motorcycle manufacturer, its riders sped their little bikes around the racetracks of Spain and France. Then, in 1969, after having narrowly lost two 50-cc world championships to the German Kreidler and the heavily funded Suzuki teams, Derbi reversed the results dramatically. Suzuki withdrew from 50-cc racing to concentrate on the larger classes, and Derbi won the championship after an extremely close battle with perennial rival Kreidler. In 1970, Nieto and the Derbi 50 Grand Prix streaked to their second 50-cc World Championship, leaving Kreidler trailing.

The Derbi 50 Nieto that was ridden in those championships is a marvelous piece of minimalism. The tiny Derbi engine is a watchmaker's delight: a disc-valved, water-cooled, single-cylinder two-stroke that develops 15.5 hp at an astonishing 15,000 rpm. (In a rather unfair comparison, the Honda C100 Super Cub, also 50 cc, develops 4.5 hp at 9,500 rpm!) Revving like a sewing machine and sounding like a mechanical banshee, the Derbi was also virtually bulletproof. Nieto retired his Derbi only twice during the entire 1970 season, a remarkable record for a motorcycle engine so highly tuned. Its chassis, crafted with an economy of design worthy of a '90s Ducati, made the Derbi 50 the perfect motorcycle for the job, and the bike is secure in its place, along with its brilliant rider Angel Nieto, in the motorcycle racing annals of fame.
—*Ultan Guilfoyle*

Honda CB750 Four
736 cc • 1970 • Japan
Bore x stroke: 61 x 63 mm • Power output: 67 hp @ 8,000 rpm •
Top speed: 124 mph (200 km/h) • Collection of David Edwards

The Honda CB750 stands as one of the pivotal motorcycles of the past 50 years. Powered by Honda's novel transverse-mounted, overhead-camshaft, in-line 750 four, it introduced an engine design that is not only still being manufactured but is the most popular design in use today.

While Edward Turner's 1937 original overhead-valve vertical twin was produced and marketed for more than 30 years, the overhead-camshaft in-line four will certainly be current for far longer. But, even in 1969, when the CB750 came out, the idea of a transverse overhead-camshaft four was nothing very new; the Italians had been racing such engines since before World War II, and in 1965 MV Agusta marketed a rather unattractive and expensive 600-cc street model with an electric starter and manual disc-brakes.

The CB750, however, was good-looking, had the design sophistication of an electric starter and hydraulically operated disc brakes, and was for its quality quite inexpensive—$1,500. Traditionalists groused about the machine being too complex and possibly unreliable, but anyone familiar with Honda's products knew of their dependability. After all, Honda had been racing multicylinder Grand Prix bikes in the '60s, and the engines of those bikes had been stressed considerably more than the CB750's engine ever would.

The CB750 was a prime example of the innovative construction techniques at which the Japanese excelled. There was nothing miraculous about the engine itself, just four slightly undersquare (61-x-63-mm) cylinders with a modest 9 to 1 compression ratio, able to rev freely to more than 8,000 rpm due to the lightened valve train, generating appreciable power. The CB750 did not introduce engineering breakthroughs; its technology adhered to the standards of the day: one carburetor and two valves per cylinder; chain-driven primary and final drives; and a double-cradle frame with 57.2 inches between the axles.

Not everyone liked the looks of the CB750. The tank and side panels still had the angularity typical of other Japanese models, and, to many, the four exhaust pipes seemed unnecessarily elaborate. For a lightweight bike, it was heavy, weighing more than 500 pounds.

In the machine's favor, the engine produced the advertised 67 hp and ran extremely smoothly. The transmission had the advantage of possessing five speeds. The bike could tear off a standing quarter-mile in 13 seconds and stop on a dime. The CB750's popularity and performance dealt the final blow to the vertical twin, and ushered in a new era in motorcycling. —*CS*

Advertisement for the Honda CB750 Four, 1969.
Courtesy of American Honda Motor Company, Inc., Torrance, Calif.

All new for 1971:
Super Glide

Shown here in optional
"Sparkling America" paint style

Advertisement for the Harley-Davidson Super Glide, 1971.
Photograph courtesy of the Harley-Davidson Motor
Company Archives.

Harley-Davidson Super Glide "Night Train"

1,200 cc • 1971 • United States
Bore x stroke: 87.3 x 100.8 mm • Power output: 65 hp @ 5,400 rpm • Top speed: 117 mph (188 km/h) •
The Otis Chandler Vintage Museum of Transportation and Wildlife, Oxnard, Calif.

In 1969, the American Machine and Foundry Corporation, a vast organization that cast, formed, assembled, and manufactured heavy machinery, acquired Harley-Davidson. AMF brought Harley its up-to-date management techniques, inventive promotional ideas, and sharp advertising—as well as engineering expertise from its manufacturing and production divisions. But Harley's new owners had little money for new product research and design.

William G. Davidson, a grandson of one of Harley-Davidson's cofounders, was the company's design chief. Willie G., as he is known, frequented weekend rides and races to listen to loyalists and new riders alike. Drawing on what he heard, and knowing he could not re-engineer, Willie G. raided parts bins to revise the look of the bikes, playing on Harley's established legends. He pulled styling cues from the machine-age design of the Flatheads of the 1930s, and from opulent body work of the Knuckleheads of the 1940s, all the while realizing he couldn't build bikes that were merely retro.

In 1971, the company introduced the Super Glide. It was an enthusiast's machine, influenced by the independent chopper shops of the late 1960s. Searching in Sportster options bins, Willie G. found a single-piece fiberglass seat and a rear fender that tapered to a recessed taillight, recalling the Packard and Duesenberg custom Boat-Tail bodies of the 1930s. He fitted an oversized front wheel into a Sportster front fork and topped it with the smaller XLCH headlight. He attached these components to an FLH frame, added rear suspension, engine, and transmission, and eliminated the starter and battery.

The Super Glide had the look of a bike that had been assembled, not manufactured, and it caught the attention of customers and journalists. Harley sold 4,700 Super Glides in 1971, and 9,200 in 1974. By then the new electric-start FXEs outsold the purist kick-starters two-to-one, but Willie G. didn't mind. Magazine reviewers loved the Super Glide's streamlined bodywork, and praised the engine as pulling like the locomotive the motorcycle's design evoked. The Super Glide was a success during the dark days of the Vietnam War, and the bike spoke loudest in a red, white, and blue combination called "Sparkling America," as if to say, "Harley-Davidson, love it or leave it." —RL

Harley-Davidson XR750

750 cc • 1972 • United States
Bore x stroke: 79 x 76 mm • Power output: 82 hp @ 7,600 rpm •
Top speed: 115 mph (185 km/h) • Collection of Glenn M. Bator

The AMA rules for 1969 effectively declared open season on Harley, finally allowing other makers to compete fairly. Japanese and English bikes—Yamaha 650-cc twins, two-stroke Kawasaki 500-cc and Suzuki water-cooled triples, BSA Rocket 3s, and Triumph Tridents and X75 Hurricanes—all performed better. Their two-stroke engines, and those with three or four smaller pistons, transferred power and torque to the dirt more efficiently than Harley's four-cycle big twins. Suddenly, few competitive riders wanted a Harley.

Harley's racing manager Dick O'Brien and designer Pieter Zylstra set out to build a better racer. They started with cast-iron 883-cc Sportster engines. Zylstra shortened the stroke to reach 750 cc, but the early production engines generated too much heat, and the bike was heavy and slow.

O'Brien and Zylstra then produced heads and barrels of one-percent silver alloy, which better dissipated heat, and they incorporated larger fins that virtually eliminated the cooling problems racers experienced under full power load. For flat-track racing, a brakeless version of the 1972 XR750 weighed 295 pounds. Road-racing versions weighed 324 pounds with brakes, fairings, and a larger fuel tank. Engines produced 90 hp and more at 7,600 rpm.

By the end of 1972, XR750 racer Scott Berelsford had the AMA class championship. But in 1973, three great Harley riders—Cal Rayborn, Jarno Saarinen, and Renzo Pasolini—all died in racing accidents. Yamaha took the championship and Triumph knocked Harley back to third. In 1974, Harley finished second, behind Yamaha's TZ700.

At this juncture, Honda made a strong move for the championship. The 1968 AMA regulations had specified that every manufacturer had to produce 200 of each 1970 racing model; they could hold a few for their team, but they had to offer the rest to the public. Taking advantage of this rule, Honda bought an XR750, dismantled it, copied it, and rebuilt it, adding overhead camshafts and four valves per cylinder. It is said that imitation is the highest form of flattery. When Honda brought their RS750 to the United States, it flattered Harley to death. —RL

Evel Knievel on a Harley-Davidson XR750, ca. 1974.

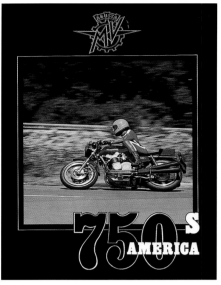

Brochure for the MV Agusta 750S America, 1975.
Collection of Creighton Demarest.

MV Agusta 750S

743 cc • 1973 • Italy
Bore x stroke: 65 x 56 mm • Power output: 69 hp @ 7,900 rpm •
Top speed: 125 mph (201 km/h) • Collection of Guy Webster

Although MV Agustas were ridden to unparalleled success on the race circuits of the world, the company never had the same success with its standard production models. In 1950, MV displayed a road-going version of their illustrious GP double-overhead-cam four-cylinder bike at the Milan show. But while the public was treated to occasional tantalizing glimpses of this sole prototype at various European shows over the next several years, MV never put the bike into production. Customers were only able to buy less exciting one- or two-cylinder lightweights.

Finally, at the 1965 Milan show, Count Domenico Agusta, the eldest son of founder Giovanni Agusta and the company's driving force since his father's death in 1927, displayed a 592-cc four-cylinder model with a bore and stroke of 58 x 56 mm. The following year the engine went into production. Enthusiasts still craved a road-going version of the 500 GP, but this bike was very much a touring mount, and its engine size was obviously intended to thwart attempts to create a replica of the factory racer. Finished in a sombre black instead of the racers' Italian red, and displaying a combination of strange humps and angles and garish chrome, it was also arguably the ugliest motorcycle of the postwar era. Just 135 examples were built for sale between 1967 and 1972.

But MV scored a hit at the 1969 Milan show when it launched the new 750S, which went into production in 1971. Like the MV 600, the 750's engine used 1950s Grand Prix technology, which meant expensive gears, bearings, and shims, and the high production cost meant that it sold for over four times the price of a Honda CB750. But unlike its predecessor, the 743-cc (65 x 56 mm) double-overhead-cam four-cylinder S (for Sport) was stylish and exciting—a Ferrari on two wheels.

The roadster's main function was to generate publicity and glamour. Other versions followed, including the largely unsuccessful America and Monza, before production ceased in late 1977. Production of four-cylinder models was always limited. In over 10 years, MV sold fewer than 2,000 four-cylinders, compared to Honda's sales of over 61,000 CB750s during its first three years in the U.S. alone. —MW

Triumph X75 Hurricane

750 cc • 1973 • United Kingdom
Bore x stroke: 69 x 65.6 mm • Power output: 58 hp @ 7,250 rpm •
Top speed: 115 mph (185 km/h) • The Barber Vintage Motorsports
Museum, Birmingham, Ala.

After the demise of BSA in 1973, Triumph had 1,200 BSA Rocket 3 engines left over. Those engines went into the X75 project at a time when the "Easy Rider" chopper look was popular in the United States.

Though made in England, the X75 is a fusion of American themes. Craig Vetter, a U.S. designer/builder, interested Triumph in building this combination of hot rod, chopper, and dirt-track styling. Vetter's signature is the one-piece tank/seat unit (now seen in the Harley-Davidson VR road racer). The three exhaust pipes routed to the right side reflect the bike's roots in dirt-track racing, in which ground clearance is essential on the left side only.

The chopper look, with its extended and raked front end, rigid rear end, and mechanical simplicity, emerged in the U.S. as a result of popular reaction to the unique appearance of bikes built for drag racing and dry-lake speed runs. Motorcycle chassis of the 1950s could be unstable at very high speeds, and to fix this, dry-lake and drag racers raked their front ends—that is, increased the piviot angle of the front fork. This gave bikes a long, low look that was compounded by the low engine placement—necessary to make an accelerating bike go forward instead of standing up on its back tire. Competition bikes were simple because they had to be light, and they carried small fuel tanks for the same reason. Dirt-trackers had no front brake because rules prohibited it.

People liked these design elements, and custom builders adopted them. But craftsmanship in hot-rodding must be seen as a product of the ready availability of highly skilled craftsmen in the California aircraft industry, a community that gave rise to the term "super-sano Cal custom."

Until relatively recently, the shape of motorcycles has mainly been determined by the manufacturer's own tradition. Then, in the aftermath of a near-collapse in 1980, Harley-Davidson began to promote themes of tradition, nostalgia, and manly robustness. However one might feel about the integrity of this approach, it is one that been hugely successful.—*KC*

Ducati 750SS

748 cc • 1974 • Italy
Bore x stroke: 80 x 74.4 mm • Power output: 65 hp @ 8,800 rpm •
Top speed: 135 mph (217 km/h) • Collection of Laurence L. Forstall

V-twin engines have been around since the dawn of the motorcycle, but rarely have they been seen in the L-shaped configuration chosen by Ducati's chief designer Fabio Taglioni when he created the 750GT prototype in 1970. Despite the layout's advantages, including smooth running, excellent cooling, and a low center of gravity, the need to accommodate the horizontal cylinder within the frame could easily lead to an over-long wheelbase and poor handling.

However, Moto Guzzi and Aermacchi singles had ably demonstrated that a horizontal engine need be no disadvantage, and Taglioni partly solved the problem of length by sticking the front cylinder between the two front downtubes of the frame. The result was a package that handled extraordinarily well; and so a bike that originally set out to capture the grand touring market quickly became a sportster and racer par excellence.

One of the biggest racing upsets of all time occurred at the international Imola 200 in April 1972, when Paul Smart and Bruno Spaggiari, riding specially prepared Desmo versions of the Ducati 750 V-twin, finished first and second. They defeated the cream of the big league—Honda, Suzuki, Kawasaki, Moto Guzzi, Triumph, BSA, and MV Agusta—and the company cashed in by offering replicas of the Imola machines for sale, which it called the 750SS, or Supersport.

Four hundred fifty of these bikes were built in 1973 and 1974. The SS engine shared the dimensions of the 750GT touring model—748 cc, a bore and stroke of 80 x 74.4 mm—but a number of improvements were made to that of the SS. In addition to Desmo valve operation, the 750SS had a higher compression ratio, double-webbed connecting rods for extra strength, a special camshaft, and larger carburetors. The engine revved to 8,800 rpm, and the standard five-speed gearbox was in unit with the engine. For riders who wanted even more powerful performance, Ducati sold a kit to transform the bike into a full Formula 750 racer.

In its day, the round-case 1974 750SS was the ultimate sportbike. It boasted the best handling, the best brakes, and the most beautiful lines, and its twin Conti mufflers emitted a truly wonderful sound. —*MW*

Brochure for Laverda 750 models, n.d.
Classic Bike, Kettering, England.

Laverda SFC

744 cc • 1974 • Italy
Bore x stroke: 80 x 74 mm • Power output: 75 hp @ 7,500 rpm •
Top speed: 130 mph (209 km/h) • Collection of Guy Webster

Laverda's first motorcycles were humble 75-cc pushrod singles, which debuted at the end of the 1940s. Success in the Italian long-distance road races of the 1950s helped establish the company's sporting credentials. But what really attracted international attention was its prototype engine, a 654-cc (75 x 74 mm) parallel twin with a four-bearing 180-degree crankshaft and a duplex chain-driven single-overhead-camshaft with triplex chain for the primary drive, along with a multi-plate clutch and five-speed gearbox.

At the 1967 Milan show, Laverda announced that its new big production twin would be a 750. The company decided to re-enter the racing arena to publicize the bike, as it had years earlier with its tiny singles, and, by 1970, it had won the first 500-km race for production motorcycles at the Monza circuit.

The SFC (the C stood for *Competizione*), was launched in 1971 as an endurance racing version of Laverda's SF series. It won its first event, the grueling Barcelona 24-hour race at Montjuic Park. Although derived from the touring SF, the 744-cc SFC incorporated a number of important differences. Its engine was more highly tuned, and it had a larger oil pump and bigger bearings. Although the frame employed the same basic design geometry as the touring SS, with a spine of four 40-ml tubes from which the engine was slung, visually it was very different from the SS. Its chassis incorporated a revised frame and a racing-style half-fairing, seat unit, and controls. In 1974, a second-generation SFC made its debut. It was notable for its triple-Brembo disc brakes (the SFC had initially been equipped with Laverda's own drum front brake), stronger fork tubes, a magnesium rear-wheel hub, and revised styling.

The bike's racing origins did not deter road riders from using the motorcycle on the street, and the SFC was one of the fastest machines on the road in the early 1970s. Although it was expensive, demand always exceeded the output of 100 or so in each of the first three years of production. During the SFC's six-year production span, Laverda built only 549 of them, making the bike extremely valuable today. — *MW*

Honda GL1000 Gold Wing

999 cc • 1975 • Japan

Bore x stroke: 72 x 61.4 mm • Power output: 80 hp @ 7,500 rpm • Top speed: 124 mph (200 km/h) •
Courtesy of American Honda Motor Company, Inc., Torrance, Calif.

The public reacted cautiously after this unusual motorcycle appeared at the Cologne motorcycle show in late 1974. Honda's GL1000 Gold Wing was large and long, and neither utilitarian nor sporty. Little was really innovative about the bike's technology. Other flat fours had occasionally appeared on the motorcycle scene over the years, and liquid cooling, shaft drive, and electric starting were common. The engine ran a belt drive to the two camshafts, one atop each pair of cylinders; while this was a breakthrough concept for a motorcycle, belts had long been used in the automotive world.

The 999-cc engine had a one-piece crankshaft, running on three main bearings, and each half of the vertically split crankcase was integral with its two cylinders, leaving no base gaskets to worry about. Each of the four combustion chambers—with a 9.2 to 1 compression ratio—had its own individual carburetor, which breathed through a big air-box beneath the panels of the false gas tank. The Gold Wing weighed 650 pounds when fueled and ready to travel, which was a great deal for a rider to hold up at the gas station and stoplight. Honda had worked diligently to keep the center of gravity as low as possible, and had placed the 5-gallon tank under the saddle, necessitating a fuel pump. The bike had wire wheels and three disc brakes, with a stable wheelbase of 60.6 inches. Overall, the Gold Wing was as complicated as a car.

But the machine was so well put together that it attracted a whole new class of rider, often people who had never ridden motorcycles before. It was reliable, comfortable, and smooth; it went fast, stopped quickly, and handled reasonably well. At the time the yen was weak against the dollar, and at $2,899, the Gold Wing was affordable in the United States. Honda had taken a serious look at the U.S. consumer, and they understood that a sizable percentage of riders wanted to get on a big motorcycle and cruise from coast to coast, stopping only now and then to put in a little gas. Honda built this single-track convertible for just that clientele. It was regarded by some as stodgy-looking, but owners learned to love its appearance.

The Gold Wing got off to a slow sales start in the year it was introduced, but, once it took off, its popularity was remarkably consistent. It became a success and remains so to this day—although the latest, the GL1500, has two more cylinders, 521 more ccs, a longer wheelbase, more weight, and, of course, a much higher price—$17,899—than the original. —*CS*

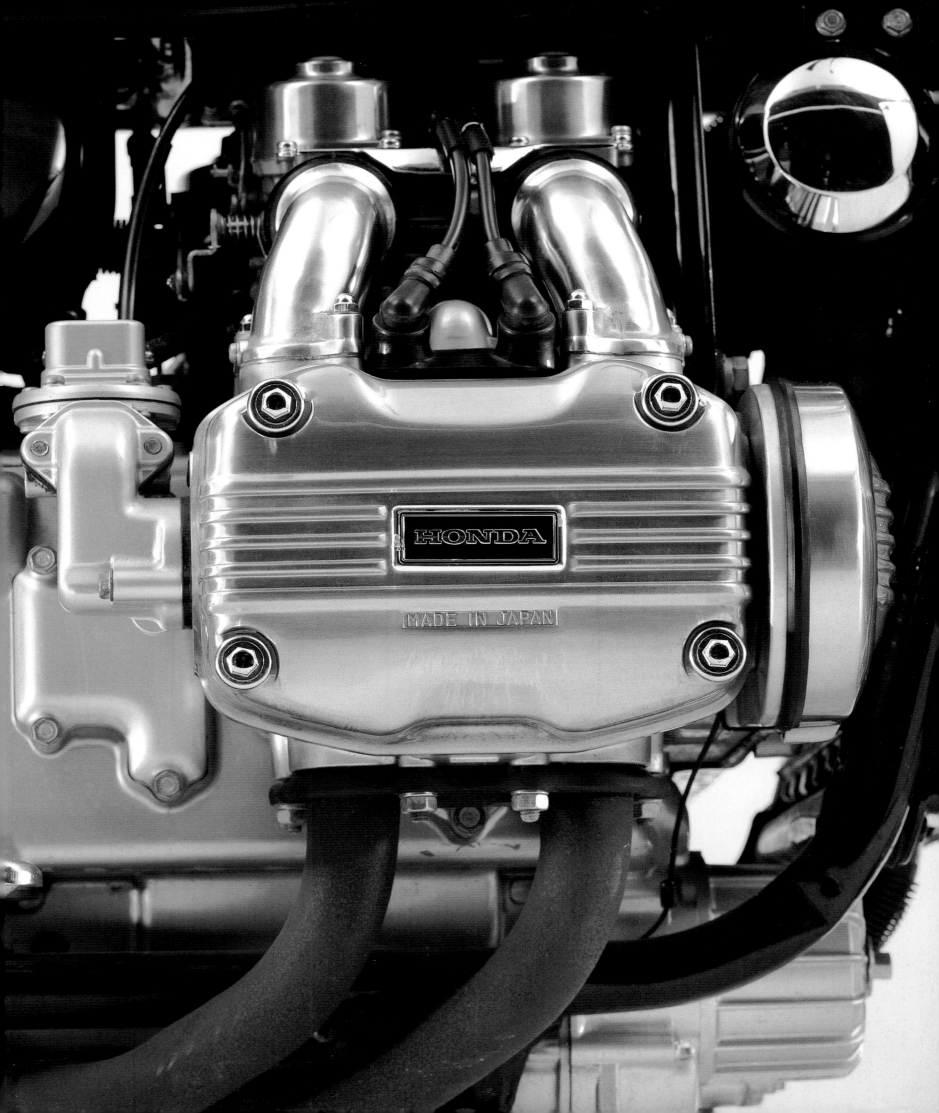

BMW R90S

898 cc • 1976 • West Germany
Bore x stroke: 90 x 70.6 mm • Power output: 67 hp @ 7,000 rpm •
Top speed: 125 mph (201 km/h) • Collection of David Percival

The press called the R90S "Germany's sexiest superbike"—an apt description of what was probably BMW's best-loved postwar street bike, the machine that hurled BMW to the top of the Superbike stakes.

The R90S, along with the rest of the Stroke 6 series (which included 600- and 750-cc versions as well), was launched in a blaze of publicity at the October 1973 Paris show, the venue where 50 years earlier BMW had presented its very first motorcycle, the Max Friz–designed R32. It used a version of the famous flat-twin engine with 898 cc and a bore and stroke of 90 x 70.6 mm, and, as with all the Stroke 6 series models, saw a switch from a four- to a five-speed gearbox. Compared to the standard R90, the S put out an additional 7 hp. The bike weighed 441 pounds dry and could top 125 mph.

For the first time, BMW had employed a stylist, Hans Muth, for one of its motorcycles, and the R90S's styling represented its biggest milestone, featuring a dual "racing-style" seat, a fairing cowl, twin hydraulically operated front brake discs, and an exquisite airbrush custom paint job in smoked silver-gray (and later in orange) for the bodywork, which meant that no two machines were ever absolutely identical. The small fairing not only provided a surprising degree of protection for the rider, but also housed a voltmeter and an electric cock.

During its three-year life span (production ended in 1976), BMW made almost no changes to the R90S, and its success led the company to build the fully faired R100RS, a best-seller for well over a decade. The R90S also proved popular in sports production racing events, winning at the Isle of Man and Daytona. The American importers for BMW at the time, the New York–based Butler and Smith Company, even constructed a special one-off racer based on the roadster, to prove that a BMW could win on the track as well as the street. The R90Ss that survive today represent the nearest BMW came to building a real sportbike, and are hence eagerly sought by collectors. —MW

Catalogue for 1975–76 BMW models. Courtesy of BMW AG, Munich.

Harley-Davidson XLCR

1,000 cc • 1977 • United States
Bore x stroke: 81.4 x 96.8 mm • Power output: 61 hp @ 6,200 rpm •
Top speed: 100 mph (161 km/h) • The Otis Chandler Vintage Museum
of Transportation and Wildlife, Oxnard, Calif.

By the mid-1970s, AMF knew it had made a mistake in acquiring Harley-Davidson. The conglomerate had planned to transform the ailing motorcycle maker into a success by increasing market share while improving manufacturing facilities, but it realized too late that Harley made obsolete motorcycles for traditionalists. The new generation of riders, with no loyalty to magnetos, kick-starters, and self-sacrifice, found Japanese makes less expensive and more modern.

At this stage, AMF hired Vaughn Beals, an MIT engineering graduate, to head Harley-Davidson's engineering department. Beals snatched Jerry Bleustein, a Columbia engineering Ph.D., from AMF's staff, and together they supplemented the one secret weapon the company still had: William G. Davidson, grandson of one of the company's founders. Beals knew from Willie G.'s "Night Train," the Super Glide he introduced in 1972, that Davidson's efforts did not sell as well as traditional models, but that his ideas got Harleys into magazines and people into the showrooms. Clearly Harley couldn't compete with the Japanese or the Italians head-on; but they could make effective end runs.

Willie G. knew that many urban riders patterned themselves after racers and bought bikes that resembled the ones their heroes rode. He was also familiar with the Sunday-morning treks many owners took to breakfast cafés hidden away on country back roads. These high-speed, nonalcoholic pub crawls were often the only opportunity the riders had to use their bikes.

In 1977, Willie G. introduced his XLCR, a 1,000-cc Sportster Café Racer fitted to a new lightweight, triangulated space frame. Available only in black, it ran on cast-alloy spoked wheels and was topped with a small Italianate fairing and windscreen. The bike drew journalists' attention, but it never caught the public's imagination. Like the Super Glide, few XLCRs sold—only about 3,100, until the bike was dropped in 1978. But its effect, like that of the "Night Train," was long-lasting. The XLCR's menacing allure brought riders into the stores—and some of them rode home on a more traditional Harley. —RL

Catalogue for Harley-Davidson, 1977.

Photograph courtesy of the Harley-Davidson Motor Company Archives.

Moto Guzzi Le Mans 1

844 cc • 1978 • Italy

Bore x stroke: 83 x 78 mm • Power output: 71 hp @ 7,300 rpm •
Top speed: 125 mph (201 km/h) • The Barber Vintage Motorsports
Museum, Birmingham, Ala.

In the early 1960s, the Italian government invited Moto Guzzi to bid for new motorcycle contracts for the army and police forces. Moto Guzzi answered this call with the V7. Work began on this design in 1964, and the company soon realized that it had developed a machine destined to be a success in the wider field of everyday riding. The first civilian prototype appeared in December 1965 at the 39th International Milan show.

The V7 was named after the engine's transverse 90-degree V-twin layout and its capacity of 704 cc (80 x 70 mm). This layout gave superb accessibility, and its simplicity and uncomplicated pushrod-operated valves provided the expectation of a long, relatively maintenance-free life. In fact, the big Guzzi's transmission system—its shaft final drive, large-capacity dry clutch, and electric starter—was closer to an automobile's. The whole power-drive assembly was mounted in a substantial set of cycle parts, which made it very much a touring, rather than a sports, bike. The engine capacity was increased to 844 cc (83 x 78 mm) in 1972. But perhaps more significant was the new chassis, designed by Lino Tonti, which, with a 750 engine, was launched in 1972 as the V7 Sport.

In 1976, Guzzi introduced the 850 Le Mans 1, which took advantage of all the best features of the earlier models. Named after the famous French racing circuit, the Le Mans 1 marked a milestone: it was a civilized sports bike. Its modified and tuned version of the 844-cc unit was fitted into the sports chassis of the 750S3. Its triple-disc brakes, sure-footed handling, and high performance made it a sportster at the top of the 1970s Superbike league.

The Le Mans 1 was built between the spring of 1976 and mid 1978. Equally successful on road and track, it became a legend in its own lifetime. In standard form it put out 71 hp and was good for 125 mph. A race kit added 10 hp and 10 mph. Moto Guzzi built later versions of the Le Mans, but none captured the original bike's unique combination of style and speed. The last Le Mans (the Mark IV) was produced in 1991. —*MW*

Poster for the Moto Guzzi Le Mans 1, 1978. Collection of Creighton Demarest.

The Consumer Years

1982
1989

The Consumer Years: 1982–1989

The 1980s was characterized by extremes. The decade began with the Iranian hostage crisis and ended with Operation Desert Storm. It opened with the proposal of the "Star Wars" space defense program and closed with the fall of the Berlin Wall and the crumbling of the Soviet Union. These years were witness to the attempted assassination of a pope and a president and the massacre of between three and four hundred Chinese students at Tiananmen Square in Beijing during a pro-democracy protest. President Jimmy Carter had declared a "national crisis of confidence" in the summer of 1979. By the beginning of the 1980s the country found itself in the throes of a full-fledged recession: unemployment in the U.S. was at its highest since the Great Depression; the Federal deficit exceeded $100 billion for the first time; inflation soared as a continuing result of the OPEC oil crisis; and economic growth had slowed almost to a standstill.

Dissatisfied with this state of affairs, the American public voted Carter out of office and elected Ronald Reagan as president. Reagan's presidency neatly spanned the decade; his government's fiscal policies came to define the uneven nature of the U.S. economic recovery during those years—a roller-coaster ride of proposed solutions to the crisis, including massive increases in government spending (particularly on defense), reductions in taxes, the silencing of trade unions and labor groups, and increases in interest rates.

By 1983, signs that inflation was being brought under control pointed to the beginning of an economic recovery that would transform the bank accounts and lifestyles of much of the American middle class. The booming stock market attracted both small-time investors and the untutored "barrow boys" who made it big brokering stocks and junk bonds, negotiating mergers and acquisitions, and dabbling in illegal insider trading.

Newfound economic power in Asia was manifested by the flood of cheap electric goods, cars, and motorcycles that came pouring into the United States. Honda, Kawasaki, Suzuki, and Yamaha were among the most heavily marketed and widely bought motorcycles of the '80s, and they came to define and eventually to symbolize the look and design of the motorcycle during that era. Speed capabilities and racing-type styling found its quintessential form in the "crotch rocket" and its market in the newly flush yuppie with a taste for the image of danger and the status of speed.

The lust for consumer goods extended to the art market, helping to radically inflate prices paid for art at auction. In 1987, for example, the same year as "Black Monday," the largest Dow Jones industrial average plunge up to that date, Vincent van Gogh's *Irises* was auctioned for a record $53.9 million at Sotheby's in New York. In the meantime, movies like Oliver Stone's *Wall Street* (1987) reflected both the heady excesses of mid-'80s postindustrial capitalism and the co-opting of art, particularly contemporary art, by commercial interests. In a defining moment of the film, Gordon Gekko (Michael Douglas) responds to a challenge from the young Bud Fox (Charlie Sheen) by offering a distillation of the money-mad society's concept of value in art:

> Money itself isn't lost or made, it's simply transferred from one perception to another. Like magic. This painting here, I bought it ten years ago for sixty thousand dollars; I could sell it today for six hundred thousand dollars. The illusion has become real and the more real it becomes, the more desperately they want it. Capitalism at its finest.

Art had become merely another commodity to be bought and sold in the marketplace.

Figurative painting on a heroic scale began to replace the hermetic Conceptualism of the previous decade, and the term "avant-garde" arguably ceased to have meaning. Practiced by such artists as Jean-Michel Basquiat, Eric Fischl, David Salle, and Julian Schnabel, neo-Expressionism became as much a paradigm of the art world of the early 1980s as did their swift and youthful rise to fame. In opposition to this trend, other artists and critics, influenced by both French structuralist theory and the example of the '70s generation, called for an art of critique that would question the dominant culture's aesthetic, cultural, and political assumptions. Artists such as Jenny Holzer, Barbara Kruger, and Cindy Sherman, using the tropes of mass culture, participated in distinctly feminist attacks on the ways in which identity, desire, and public opinion are manipulated.

But perhaps the epitome of the decade's sensibility could be found in the alternately praised and derided Jeff Koons. With his stainless-steel bunnies and floating basketballs, he seemed to wish to prove, with Gordon Gekko, that greed was not only good, it could also be fun. —*SB*

Suzuki Katana

997 cc • 1982 • Japan
Bore x stroke: 78 x 59 mm • Power output: 108 hp @ 8,500 rpm • Top speed: 140 mph (225 km/h) •
The Otis Chandler Vintage Museum of Transportation and Wildlife, Oxnard, Calif.

Suzuki's Katana was an exercise in style, pure and simple. Suzuki's marketing department took a look at its standard GS1100E and decided to give that motorcycle—a very good one even in its conventional shape—a brand new look; not just any clothes, but a costume one might wear to a *Star Wars* theme party.

The restyling job was given to Target Design, a European company whose designers Hans Muth and Jan Fellstrom had long been known in the automotive world for their daring and fantasy. The two men were given carte blanche to do as they saw fit with the motorcycle. Muth and Fellstrom turned out the most radical-looking production sportbike that the world had yet seen: the Katana, named after a Japanese sword that was supposed to strike mortal fear into those who saw it unsheathed. The quarter-fairing looked something like a shark—especially when seen in a rider's rearview mirror while moving along at a brisk pace.

The bits and pieces that cover up a motorcycle, starting with the necessary gas tank and saddle, had heretofore been more functional than aesthetic. On the Katana this equation was reversed: the entire body of the machine, from its mean-looking fairing, which flowed into the gas tank, and from the tank, which flowed on into the saddle, was one smooth and rather aggressive line. It was not the Katana's performance that set the machine apart from the others, it was its looks.

The basic 1,074-cc GS1100E engine had four cylinders in line, with double-overhead camshafts and four valves per combustion chamber; to meet the 1-liter racing limit, it was debored to 997 cc. It sat in a conventional cradle frame with new, trustworthy shock absorbers at the rear, and new forks with spring-preload adjusters and anti-dive on the front.

There were two good reasons for this new, radically styled Katana. First, Suzuki had been busily reinventing its own liter-plus sportbike, which had been around for over two years, and was becoming a bit outdated. Second, the market for sophisticated motorcycles in North America and Europe was floundering in a morass of too many bikes. Prices were being slashed, but there was always an opportunity for a "limited-edition" model.

Even in this flooded market, the Katana was an enormous sales success. It continues to give motorcycle designers and producers pause for thought, as its popularity was due entirely to its space-age looks, rather than its functionality. —CS

Honda VF750F "Interceptor"

748 cc • 1983 • Japan
Bore x stroke: 70 x 48.6 mm • Power output: 77 hp @ 10,000 rpm •
Top speed: 132 mph (212 km/h) • Courtesy of American Honda Motor
Company, Inc., Torrance, Calif.

In 1983, the American Motorcyclist Association changed the rules for superbike racing, limiting four-cylinder motorcycles to 750 cc, and the atmosphere in the serious sportbike world heated up measurably. Honda responded to the new rules that same year with the VF750F Interceptor.

Here was one of the most race-ready motorcycles on the market, a V-four displacing 748 cc, bolted into a very stiff frame, with sophisticated suspension in front and back, and excellent brakes—all in a relatively short 58.9-inch wheelbase.

The weight, with 5.8 gallons of gas in the tank, was slightly less than 550 pounds. And, measured at the rear wheel, 77 hp at 10,000 rpm was mildly astonishing. In general, Honda's machines were built to take the checkered flag, and the Interceptor was the motorcycle to do just that.

In 1982 Soichiro Honda had shown a willingness to trump his own ace—the 1969 in-line four—by introducing the Sabre's transverse-mounted, liquid-cooled, double-overhead-camshaft V-four engine. This was more of a generalist's motorcycle than the subsequent Interceptor, producing only 65 hp in a less powerful chassis, with a six-speed transmission and shaft drive.

For the Sabre to evolve into the Interceptor meant starting all over again with almost everything but the basic engine. The new steel square-tube frame's structural rigidity promised improved high-speed handling; the engine was canted back 15 degrees, allowing for a shorter wheelbase and better handling on corners. Final drive changed from shaft to chain, which allowed the Interceptor's gearbox to become a five-speed.

The front wheel was 16 inches in diameter, which made for quicker steering. The fork tubes, a fat 39 mm in diameter, had sturdy braces to ensure that flexing would not present a problem. The right fork leg held an antidive unit, and the left had variable rebound damping. At the rear was the adjustable Pro-Link mono-shock and cast-aluminum swinging arm, which extended back to an 18-inch wheel.

All these features gave the Interceptor a great boost in the sportbike world, and sales were high. The motorcycle was fast, agile, and, at $3,500, the right price for the market. Honda tried to capitalize on the Interceptor's success by quickly producing 500- and 1,000-cc versions, but by then the other motorcycle companies had brought their in-line fours up to par, and the transverse V-four Interceptor's rapid sales did not last. —CS

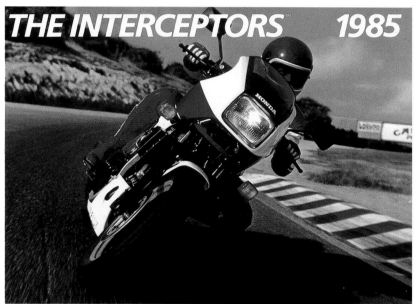

Brochure for the 1985 Honda "Interceptor," 1984. Private collection.

Benelli Sei

906 cc • 1984 • Italy

Bore x stroke: 60 x 53.4 mm • Power output: 80 hp @ 8,400 rpm • Top speed: 130 mph (209 km/h) •
The Barber Vintage Motorsports Museum, Birmingham, Ala.

The Benelli company, founded in 1921 by the six Benelli brothers, boasts a proud history that encompasses the winning of two 250-cc motorcycling world championships (in 1950 and 1969) as well as a diversification into gun manufacturing. Yet, by the late 1960s, the once-prosperous company was struggling, and in 1971 the family sold Benelli to Argentinean industrialist Alejandro De Tomaso.

The shift in ownership introduced a new era of Benelli street bikes. The flagship model was a six-cylinder, 750-cc bike produced as a blatant attempt by De Tomaso to upstage other manufacturers' superbikes. The Benelli Sei (Six) was a typical Italian luxury engineering creation. Its single-cam, six-cylinder engine was a logical, almost obvious choice, resembling the configuration of its four-wheeled, 12-cylinder counterparts such as Ferrari, Lamborghini, and Maserati. Like them, the 750 Sei was outrageously expensive. Unlike its glamorous peers, however, it didn't have the benefit of an amazing styling job. Aside from six mega-phone mufflers that crowded the rear wheel, the Sei's styling was traditional, even conservative.

The 750 Sei's engine design owed more to Tokyo than to Milan, but the prototype still created a stir when it was launched in 1972. Under close inspection, similarities to Honda's four-cylinder CB500 became apparent; identical bore and stroke dimensions seemed to demonstrate that expediency came before technical independence for Benelli. Top speed ranged between 110 and 120 mph. Benelli sources claimed 71 hp at 8,500 rpm from the 748-cc (56 x 50.6 mm) across-the-frame six.

By the time the 750 Sei entered production in 1974, Honda's development of its own six-cylinder model, the CBX, was well advanced. Benelli responded with the larger 900, featuring 906 cc and a bore and stroke of 60 x 53.4 mm. The was not merely a new styling job that included a six-into-two exhaust; the engine was updated to avoid the gearbox and crankshaft problems of the original 750 Sei. The result was a stronger and faster motorcycle, with a top speed of 130 mph. Production of this model ceased in 1987. —*MW*

Kawasaki GPZ900R Ninja

908 cc • 1984 • Japan
Bore x stroke: 72.5 x 55 mm • Power output: 115 hp @ 9,500 rpm •
Top speed: 151 mph (243 km/h) • Collection of John Hoover,
Courtesy of Kawasaki Motors Corp., USA, Irvine, Calif.

Despite first impressions, Kawasaki's Ninja GPZ900R is much more than just another in-line Japanese four. Kawasaki rewrote the sportbike rule book with the Ninja. While competitors continued producing air-cooled engines with two valves per cylinder, Kawasaki spent six years secretly developing the world's first 16-valve, liquid-cooled, four-cylinder motorcycle. The Japanese company had massive resources with which to devote to the Ninja development program; motorcycle production was, and still is, just a small part of industrial giant Kawasaki Heavy Industry's portfolio.

The design team concentrated instead on making the new engine more powerful, lighter, and narrower than that of the legendary Z1—the double-overhead cam, four-cylinder superbike Kawasaki launched in 1973. The slim width of the Ninja engine allowed it to be mounted lower within the bike's frame, which gave the new machine quicker handling.

Kawasaki unveiled the Ninja to the press in December 1983. Rave reviews ensured that production models were snapped up as soon as they hit the showrooms early the following year. Just three months after the bikes went on sale, a trio of dealer-entered GPZ900Rs trounced works-supported teams from rival manufacturers by finishing a convincing one-two-three in the Isle of Man Production TT, and the Ninja's status as an all-time classic was assured. Able to out-drag any contemporary 1,100-cc motorcycle, but lighter than some 750s (thanks to its new engine, an aluminum-alloy rear-frame section, and a 16-inch front wheel), the GPZ900R was the first stock road bike with a top speed in excess of 150 mph.

But the Ninja wasn't just some hairy-chested brute. Although the ultrasmooth 908-cc Kawasaki produced almost 115 hp at 9,500 rpm, and could rocket its rider a standing quarter mile in 10.9 seconds, it could be easily controlled in city traffic and ridden at a walking pace with both feet on the pegs. The full fairing—a standard fitting on the Ninja—kept wind and rain off both rider and passenger, making the Kwack a competent, mile-eating tourer as well as a super sportster. The Ninja also featured anti-dive front forks with Kawasaki's own automatic variable damping system, triple-disc brakes, a hydraulic clutch, and a six-speed gearbox. Though early Ninjas suffered from faulty camshaft hardening, this was soon rectified, and the GPZ900R remained in production for nearly 10 years. —*PT*

BMW K100RS

987 cc • 1985 • West Germany
Bore x stroke: 67 x 70 mm • Power output: 90 hp @ 8,000 rpm •
Top speed: 134 mph (215 km/h) • Courtesy of BMW AG, Munich

During the late 1970s the motorcycle division of BMW was in big trouble. Sales were still strong in Great Britain, but, due to an outdated model range, this was not the case anywhere else. In January 1979, BMW hired a new management team, which included three experts, Dr. Wolfgang Aurich, Karl Gerlinger, and Dr. Eberhardt C. Sarfert, who would recharge the famous German marque. Immediately, BMW took over distribution of its motorcycles in the U.S. from longtime importers Butler and Smith, and introduced a fresh new series of machines.

Previously, tests had been made on various three- and four-cylinder layouts. However, it was Stefan Pachernagg who would be responsible for developing the new breed of K100s. Introduced in October 1983, the unfaired (or "naked") K100, the half-faired K100RS sports, and the fully-faired K100RT touring models (which debuted six months later) all used a double-overhead-cam, 987-cc (67 x 70 mm), water-cooled, fuel-injected, four-cylinder with "brick-type" flat engine configuration.

The advantages of laying an engine on its side to drive a shaft to the rear wheel are certainly sound. The BMW-patented design, CDS (Compact Drive System), allowed the chassis to be built around the engine, while claiming three particular advantages: a low center of gravity, access for maintenance, and a longitudinally installed crankshaft, which permitted direct drive to the drive shaft, thus avoiding power losses as a result of deviations. Although the entire exhaust system was made from stainless steel (a first on a series production motorcycle), the four-sided muffler was, on aesthetic grounds, less well received.

The RS benefited from a wind tunnel–developed fairing that not only allowed for riding at a much higher speed without the wind pressure of the original unfaired K100, but also increased stability. Further developments included the three-cylinder K75 (1985), the K1100RS (1993), and the K1200RS (1997). —*MW*

BMW R80 G/S Paris-Dakar

980 cc • 1985 • West Germany
Bore x stroke: 94 x 70.6 mm • Power output: 71 hp @ 6,800 rpm •
Top speed: 112 mph (180 km/h) • Courtesy of BMW AG, Munich

With their trend-setting R80 G/S (the G stood for *Gelände*, or off-road), BMW pioneered the large-capacity, enduro-style, on-off road motorcycle. Since its introduction in 1980, many manufacturers have copied this concept, including Honda, Suzuki, and Cagiva.

Comprehensive triumphs at the ISDT (International Six Days Trial) in 1979 and success in the grueling Paris-Dakar rally of 1980 provided valuable prelaunch publicity for the bike. But the G/S was really intended to introduce dirt-bike style to the streets; the 797-cc (84.8 x 70.6 mm) flat-twin engine produced 49 hp and could catapult the lightweight bike to 107 mph.

Much of the interest surrounding the G/S was a result of its styling, which was radical for BMW and was conceived after close collaboration with the Italian motorcycle company Laverda. Another innovative feature was its reduced engine weight, which was achieved by using aluminum cylinders with a Galnikal bore coating and by paring dead weight from the single-plate diaphragm clutch assembly. Eventually, these improvements were introduced on other models.

But it was the rear drive and suspension layout that made the G/S stand out among production BMWs. A swing arm contained the drive shaft on the right, and the wheel was completely unsupported on the left, saving considerable weight without diminishing structural rigidity. The Monolever strut also proved a real boon—not only did it facilitate quick and easy removal of the rear wheel, but it was largely responsible for the newcomer's excellent handling—a point not lost on BMW, which by 1985 had standardized the feature throughout the model range.

The R80 G/S went on to win the Paris-Dakar event in 1981, 1983, and 1984, and this particular bike, with a capacity of 980 cc (94 x 70.6 mm), won the competition in 1985. To celebrate these successes, in 1984, BMW launched the limited-edition Paris-Dakar version of the bike, available either as a complete motorcycle or as a kit to convert an existing machine.

In 1987 BMW launched the 980-cc R100GS, which produced 60 hp. This was replaced in 1993 by the 1,085-cc, four-valve 1100GS. The company's success with these enduro-styled machines is reflected in its sales figures, which now total almost 100,000. —*MW*

Gaston Rahier winning the Paris-Dakar race on the BMW R80 G/S, 1985. Courtesy of BMW AG, Munich.

Buell RS1200

1,203 cc • 1989 • United States
Bore x stroke: 88.9 x 96.8 mm • Power output: 68 hp @ 6,000 rpm •
Top speed: 140 mph (225 km/h) • The Barber Vintage Motorsports Museum, Birmingham, Ala.

As an engineer at Harley-Davidson, Erik Buell had worked on projects such as the FXR rubber-mount system and the air antidive suspension. But imagination and ambition pushed him further. He left Harley-Davidson in December 1983 and subsequently founded the Buell Motor Company, under the auspices of which he produced two copies of a prototype race bike, the RW750, in the barn behind his home. In 1984, however, the AMA eliminated the class for which RW750s were conceived, so Buell soon focused his attention on street machines.

When Harley-Davidson ended the two-year production run of the XR1000s, it had 50 engines left. Buell acquired these and installed them in his 1987 and 1988 RR1000 Battletwins. Underneath this stylish and aerodynamically effective bodywork, he mounted a horizontal-shock-absorber rear-suspension system on a chrome-moly steel frame. Working from his newly established factory in Mukwonogo, Wisconsin, he then produced 75 RR1200s, using Harley's Evolution engines. In 1989, Buell introduced the RS1200 Westwind. Buell's bodywork now revealed Harley's handsome engines and his own visually interesting frames; the flip-up seat and storage area below hinted of things to come.

In 1993, Buell's success came full circle when he and Harley-Davidson formed Buell Motorcycle Company, giving him the capital to develop new models while providing Harley-Davidson with intriguing new products for its showrooms. The motorcycle boom of the early '90s was a double-edged sword for Harley. Suddenly, demand for its bikes far exceeded supply, leaving showrooms nearly empty. Foot traffic was necessary to keep franchise-owner revenue high through purchase of parts, accessories, and apparel.

Buell's S-2 Thunderbolts, which had developed a loyal following among those who prized sophisticated handling and braking, were a godsend to the company at this time. His 1996 S-1 Lightning, named one of *Cycle World*'s ten best motorcycles of the year, only advanced his less-bodywork-more-machine philosophy. The S-1 has been called a "hooligan bike" because of its riders' urban-guerilla style of riding. But the bike is at least as significant for its 1990s design engineering approach to the same problems the "Bob-Job" tackled in the 1940s. —RL

Yamaha Vmax

1,198 cc • 1989 • Japan
Bore x stroke: 76 x 66 mm • Power output: 120 hp @ 9,000 rpm •
Top speed: 150 mph (241 km/h) • The Barber Vintage Motorsports
Museum, Birmingham, Ala.

The Yamaha VMX 12 Vmax was intended to look *bad*, and it did. There was nothing sleek or refined about Yamaha's Maximum V, just a big chunk of engine sitting in a Bronze Age frame.

A fake tank cover sat on top, accompanied by a pair of odd-looking air scoops on the sides. Drag bars, short and straight, were bolted to the triple clamp, and the shiny speedometer was prominently displayed. A stepped saddle, silver side covers, a bobbed rear fender, and two fat megaphone mufflers finished the dressing.

But the styling was just a come-on intended to gain attention for the engine, a black, transverse-mounted, liquid-cooled V-four. Its 70-degree angle included the distance between the cylinders, with silver-toned highlights masquerading as fins. And four very conspicuous carburetors sat high in the V, pointing straight down.

Brochure for the Yamaha Vmax, 1988–89. Private collection.

The power of an engine is a direct product of the amount of fuel that can be burned in the combustion chamber; if more fuel can be forced in, more power can be forced out. Yamaha had originally developed this 16-valve V-four, with a 76 x 66 mm bore and stroke—giving a total of 1,198 cc—as a relatively benign engine to power its touring motorcycle. But when the market developed another model niche, best described as the pseudo-dragster motorcycle, with minimal frills and maximum power, Yamaha engineers decided that this engine was a natural. It just needed a lot more horsepower.

In anticipation of the power increase, alterations were made in the valves and the overhead camshafts, the pistons were lightened, and the connecting rods and crankshaft were strengthened. But the main feature was to be called "V-Boost." Four 35-mm constant-velocity carburetors fed the chambers, one per cylinder; as soon as the engine revved past 6,000 rpm, however, the dynamics changed. The manifold was split, so that each side fed a bank of two cylinders. Between the paired intakes was a butterfly valve with a tiny motor operated by a microprocessor. When the machine reached the magic 6,000 mark, the butterfly opened, allowing the fuel mixture from both carburetors to flow into the one chamber, actually forced in by the exhaust stroke of the non-firing cylinder.

This worked perfectly, with close to 120 hp at the rear wheel: the Vmax could clock a quarter-mile in 10 seconds. In fact, the design worked so well that Yamaha has not made major changes to the Max for 14 years. —*CS*

Retro / Revolutionary

1993
1998

Retro/Revolutionary: 1993–1998

The 1990s is the decade where niches have been identified, marketing has grown up, and the middle-aged have been allowed to feel young again. The '90s is the decade which has seen borne out the sentiment of Honda's '60s sales pitch of thirty years ago, "You meet the nicest people on a Honda." Simply put, motorcycling sells.

In design terms, the decade echoes the rapid-fire change of politics and culture throughout the world. Borders collapse in a blink. Old orders are swept aside, upstarts take their place and, surprisingly, they succeed. This is the decade in which you "just do it," whoever you are and whatever "it" might be. In the 1990s, as a generation of coffee-house grunge kids have reminded their boomer parents, it is officially cool to be a dude.

When the Argentinean Miguel Galluzzi was a student at the Art Center College of Design in Pasadena, California, he noticed what those young dudes were doing to their noisily styled race bikes—junking the fairings, the fiberglass, and the whizz-bang color schemes, and stripping their bikes bare. By exposing the delta-box frames and the engines, these designers-at-large were, he realized, creating a distilled vision of the suburban motorcycle life, grunge biking at its hippest.

Working at Milan's Ducati, Galluzzi got the idea to recreate these naked grunge guns in a production motorcycle, a notion that flew in the face of every contemporary motorcycle design rubric from Tokyo to Munich. The result was the M900, which he dubbed "The Monster." (His colleagues called him *Il Monstro*.) The Monster is a brilliant piece of pop-culture interpretation, a bike for the streets, rather than the fantasy racetrack that had inspired a previous generation of motoryclcles. With its wide handlebars and upright riding posture, the M900 can putter around at 10 mph, or do 100 when mood and circumstances allow. It is unmistakably sexy, with a practical androgyny that permits it to glide freely across gender barriers like no motorcycle since the Honda Super Cub. Unlike the ubiquitous little Honda 50, however, the Monster is not so much transportation device as fashion statement; it is Italian after all.

The '90s, in a way, has been Ducati's decade. Alongside the Monster, they produced the 916, which brought the chaotic '80s racetrack aesthetic to a sublime expression. This design was borne out of a marriage between the technical brilliance of Ducati's race-bike designers, led by former Bimota designer Massimo Tamburini, and an instinctive understanding of how a motorcycle could appeal to the rider now ten years older than the young buck who first threw his leg over an '80s Japanese speedster. Aspirational and inspired, the 916 is the motorcycle for the would-be Ferrari driver: Italian, fast, and, of course, red.

Then there are the bikes of Erik Buell. If ever there was a designer born and bred with racing in his blood, it is Buell, the brilliant individualist of the American motorcycle tradition. Early in 1991, Buell was virtually broke. A call came to his little Buell factory at

Mukwonogo, Wisconsin, from the bicycle manufacturer Schwinn. Their chief designer was working on a new mountain bike and he was considering using suspension, standard on motorcycles but at that time unimaginable on a bicycle. Mountain biking was, and remains, the life blood of Gen X sports, and Buell understood the need for some radical thinking. The prototype bike, with Buell's rear suspension, was entered in the World Championship in Italy that year. Seeded fifty-second, it astonished everyone by finishing third.

Buell's motorcycles are as individual as the man, taking their departure points from such diverse influences as Willie G. Davidson's '70s classic, the Harley-Davidson XLCR, and even from Galluzzi's Ducati Monster. But he has done something even more notable. By using only Harley-Davidson engines in his eponymous motorcycles, Buell has shown Harley that it is possible to be successful with a purely American design, without having to pander to the worst, retrograde tendencies of the cruiser ideal. At the same time, Buell's designs, while environmentally sensitive and technically brilliant, are also commercially successful, turning the received thinking about homebred American motorcycle design on its head.

In the drive to break the conceptual stranglehold held over '80s production by Japanese companies, with their stream of technically brilliant but stylistically challenged sportbikes, motorcycle manufacturers like Ducati realized that there was not simply one market for motorcycles but several. Others have looked to emulate Harley-Davidson's success in the so-called cruiser market, with styling harking back to the Crocker and Indian Chief, the prototypes of American motorcycling ideals. What drives the marketing of these cruisers is the wallet of the born-again Sunday morning biker, wherever in the world he (and it's always a "he") might ride.

When BMW decided to depart from their seventy-year script of reliable, quick, sporting tourers and plunge into the cruiser market, they could easily have made the same mistake as all of their competitors and aped the spurious Harley-Davidson cruiser style. That they didn't fall into any obvious traps was due to the brilliance of their director of motorcycle design, David Robb. Like Galluzzi, Robb is a graduate of the Art Center College of Design; like Buell, he is sharply tuned to the world outside his design studio. But where Galluzzi and Buell come straight out of a motorcycle tradition, Robb's design antecedents are more complex, deeply rooted in those of American automotive and product design.

With its extravagant use of chrome and its soft, flowing lines, the R1200 C cruiser seems to spring from the fertile ground of Harley Earl, Raymond Loewy, and Larry Shinoda, three of the great American car designers. (Robb actually worked briefly with both Loewy and Shinoda.) But the R1200 C, true to '90s imperatives, refers to those halcyon days of big fenders, big chrome—big hair!—without being at all "retro," a word pregnant with negative motorcycle associations. And, most successful of all, the bike is very clearly not a Harley-Davidson. On Robb's motorcycle, quiet and efficient, you can cruise at 55 mph while smelling the flowers. You can almost hear the birds singing. This is the soul of American motorcycling, with a heart that's all BMW efficiency: shaft drive, a proven Boxer engine, Telelever forks, and electronic engine management.

As the '90s draws to a close, it is as perilous to predict the near future as it is to articulate the recent past, since both are part of the swirl of the present. But some things stand out—the songs of Kurt Cobain, the rhymes and rhythms of hip-hop, the films of Quentin Tarantino or the Coen brothers, the motorcycles of Ducati, Buell, and BMW. Bruce Willis morphed from the slick comedy detective of '80s hit TV show *Moonlighting* into the double-crossing palooka of Tarantino's *Pulp Fiction* (1994), or even closer to the edge, the lucidly insane space traveler of Terry Gilliam's *Twelve Monkeys* (1995). In *Pulp Fiction*, he rides a motorcycle. What else? —*Ultan Guilfoyle*

Ducati M900 "Monster"

904 cc • 1993 • Italy

Bore x stroke: 92 x 68 mm • Power output: 66.6 hp @ 7,000 rpm •
Top speed: 128 mph (206 km/h) • Courtesy of Ducati Motor SpA,
Bologna

One of Ducati's most inspired moves of the last decade came at the Cologne show in September 1992, when the famous Bologna factory created a sensation by showing a motorcycle like no other, the M900. It was more commonly known as "The Monster," as a factory worker had dubbed the original prototype after seeing it for the first time—and the name stuck.

Even though its previous custom model, the Indiana, had bombed in the showrooms during the late 1980s, the new Monster was more of a street fighter in reality. Probably best described as a fashion statement, the M900 is equally at home cruising the boulevard or used for back-road fun—take it near a motorway at your peril. This is very much a bike to be seen on, for getting around the urban sprawl in style and comfort; but most of all for putting a king-sized grin on the rider's face.

At 408 pounds, the M900 is relatively light and compact—in stark contrast to the "Monster" tag—which is a plus for many, in particular, women. Technically, its 904-cc (92 x 68 mm), belt-driven, single-overhead-camshaft, 90-degree, Desmo V-twin engine is shared with the fully faired 900SS sports bike, which includes the same six-speed gearbox and hydraulically operated dry clutch. With an abundance of engine torque, the M900 has the ability to lift the front wheel at almost any time in the lower gears, while the sharp response gives the machine excellent urge at higher speeds. It's only above 80 mph that a lack of fairing comes into play.

This successful design resulted in smaller versions: a 600 (583 cc, 80 x 58 mm bore and stroke) in 1994, and a 750 (748 cc, 88 x 61.5 mm bore and stroke) in 1996. Various limited editions of the M900 have been produced for those customers with extra funds who wanted something different. First came the Special Edition in 1996, with 916SP braking components, a miniature fairing, and a Connolly leather saddle. Eventually the Azzalin model appeared in an edition of 20, with an almost endless list of goodies, including an oval-section chrome-moly frame! — *MW*

Yamaha GTS1000

1,003 cc • 1993 • Japan
Bore x stroke: 75.5 x 56 mm • Power output: 96.5 hp @ 9,000 rpm •
Top speed: 133 mph (214 km/h) • Courtesy of Yamaha Motor Corp.,
USA, Cypress, Calif.

For a hundred years engineers and crackpots alike have been fiddling with the front forks of motorcycles, trying to improve the handling. In the 1930s several European manufacturers introduced telescoping forks, which have been the norm in motorcycle design for the past 60 years. Yamaha's GTS1000 presented a divergence from that norm, proving that sometimes, when an original design works well, innovation may only present more complication at a higher cost.

There is always room for improvement. The telescoping forks that have been in use for six decades have two main problems: first, they can flex under duress, and second, as they compress, the steering geometry of the motorcycle is slightly altered. In 1985 an American inventor named James Parker patented a single-sided, swinging-arm design that allowed the motorcycle's front wheel to absorb surface irregularities by moving in a mostly vertical manner, without compromising the chassis, even on a bumpy corner. The rear wheel on a motorcycle has only to go up and down; the front wheel must also be able to turn. Telescoping forks do both the suspending and the turning, while Parker's Rationally Advanced Design Development (RADD) required the complication of separate steering hardware.

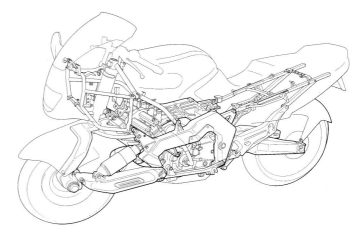

GTS1000/1000A OMEGA CHASSIS

Yamaha licensed the rights to the patent on a nonexclusive basis, and, in late 1992, the GTS1000 presented the results. Putting Parker's concept into a workable package required a brand new chassis, a costly risk on the part of the factory. The machine's frame resembled an inverted U, and was called the Omega Chassis Concept (OCC), after omega, the final letter of the Greek alphabet, for its resemblance to the letter's shape. The engine was tucked inside, with the rear-swinging fork pivoting off the back of the OCC and the new, front-suspension fork off the front.

To add to the exotic aspect of the GTS's forward end, a single disc brake with six-piston caliper was placed in the center of the wheel. An antilock braking system was included. The frame enclosed an in-line four-cylinder, 20-valve engine, borrowed (and detuned) from Yamaha's speedy FZR1000. Additionally, the GTS used Nippondenso Electronic Fuel Injection and a catalytic converter in the exhaust system.

The GTS was intended not as a race bike but as a sophisticated high-speed sports-touring machine, at the rather high price of $13,000. However, the GTS was a sales bust. Cost-effectiveness and the tried-and-true telescoping fork won that day. —*CS*

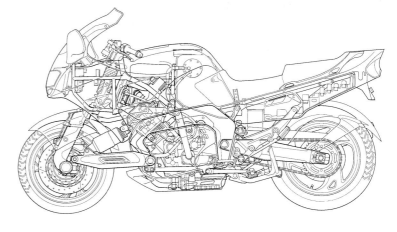

GTS1000/1000A SIDE VIEW

Line drawing of the Yamaha GTS1000 Omega chassis, 1992.
Courtesy of the Yamaha Motor Corporation, Cypress, Calif.

Britten V1000

985 cc • 1994 • New Zealand

Bore x stroke: 99 x 64 mm • Power output: 165 hp @ 12,400 rpm •
Top speed: 185 mph (298 km/h) • Collection of James M. Hunter

The Britten V1000 is proof that one man, with one idea, can construct an exceptionally fine motorcycle on his own, even in these closing years of the automotive century.

In the earliest days of motorcycling, virtually anyone who wanted to build an engine could make patterns for crankcases, cylinders, and the rest, take them to the local foundry, ram some sand, pour in molten metal, and make a motor. In the late 1980s, New Zealander John Britten, an engineer, designed and built his own two-cylinder, 1,000-cc race bike with a liquid-cooled 60-degree V-twin that fit within a short wheelbase. By 1991 his privateer efforts were making racing history, and several years later he began selling his motorcycles, though in very limited numbers.

The 1994 version of Britten's V1000 has a bore of 99 mm, and a stroke of 64 mm for 985 cc. Each combustion chamber is fed by two Bosch fuel injectors. Double overhead camshafts are driven by a belt with four valves per cylinder. The Britten produces 165 hp at 12,400 rpm, with usable power coming in a broad range. Lubricating oil is held in a wet sump.

The V1000's careful construction, balancing, and assembly resulted in an exceptionally smooth motor, so no counter-balancers were included. Primary drive is controlled by gears, followed by a dry clutch and a five-speed transmission.

The Britten V1000 has no conventional frame; its structure is made of carbon fiber and Kevlar composites. A beam is bolted to the top of the cylinders and stretched out to hold the saddle. Attached to the front of the engine is a modernized version of girder forks with an Ohlins shock; to the rear of the engine there is a swinging arm and another Ohlins shock, which sits upright, attached to the swinging arm by a long connecting rod. These suspension components have multiple adjustment possibilities, allowing the machine to be set up for individual rider preference and racetracks.

The wheels are Britten-made carbon composites, with Brembo brake discs and calipers to stop the vehicle. The price was high—more than $100,000—but the bikes were winners.

Sadly, Britten died in 1995. His achievements within a few years were astounding; had he had the opportunity for a full career, he might have gone on to produce more winning machines. The V1000 remains, however, a legacy to John Britten's extraordinary talent as a motorcycle designer. —*CS*

Advertisement for the Britten V1000 from *Riders Club*, June 1995. Collection of James M. Hunter.

Ducati 916

916 cc • 1994 • Italy

Bore x stroke: 94 x 66 mm • Power output: 109 hp @ 9,000 rpm •
Top speed: 165 mph (266 k/mh)• Courtesy of Ducati Motor SpA,
Bologna

For almost 30 years, chief designer Fabio Taglioni's talent had set Ducati on its course. He was responsible for a truly vast array of singles, twins, and even the occasional four-cylinder motorcycle for both road and track. But the maestro chose largely to ignore the development potential inherent in four-valve cylinder heads, however. This was left to his successor, Massimo Bordi.

The first prototype of Ducati's liquid-cooled, double-overhead-cam, fuel-injected, four-valves-per-cylinder V-twin made its introductory appearance at the 1986 French Bol d'Or 24-hour endurance race. Although the bike was retired after 18 of the 24 hours had elapsed, it showed great promise.

The Castiglioni brothers, who took over Ducati in May 1985, brought with them much-needed funding, which made it possible to develop a series of new bikes. The production model of the 851-cc (92 x 64 mm) superbike was unveiled to the public at the Milan show in November 1987. These superbikes went on sale early the following year in both Strada (street) and Kit (supersport) versions: a total of 500 of the motorcycles were built that year. In 1988 Marco Lucchinelli won the first round of the first World Super Bike (WSB) race ever held on a racing version of the 851 at Donington Park in England. Shortly thereafter, the factory built a racer for the general public; these bikes, which went on sale for the 1990 season, were outfitted with the larger 888-cc (94 x 64 mm) engine that had been pioneered on Lucchinelli's racer.

Subsequently, Ducati produced a relentless series of street, supersport, and racing models, including the SP (Sport Production), which also used the 888-cc displacement. The 851 was discontinued in 1993, and in 1994 the Corsa (Racing) model was increased in size to 926 cc, with a bore and stroke of 96 x 64 mm. But it was the arrival of the brand new 916 street bike that was the big news that year. Its displacement matched its code number—the stroke of the 888 was increased from 64 to 66 mm, and the bore remained unchanged at 94 mm. Not only was the maximum power of 109 hp an improvement over that of the 888, but also the engine was much stronger throughout the rev range. Another important element of the bike was its ram-air induction system, which was originally developed for the Cagiva 500 GP racer.

Other features introduced on the 916 included a single-sided swing arm, patented adjustable steering, an exhaust system with twin mufflers exiting just underneath the seat, and one of the most distinctive styling jobs ever seen on two wheels. Ever since the 916 was introduced, Ducati has not been able to produce the bike in large enough quantities to satisfy the enormous demand for it! —*MW*

Carl Fogarty winning the 1995 Australian Superbike title on a Ducati 916.

Aprilia Moto 6.5

649 cc • 1995 • Italy

Bore x stroke: 100 x 82.7 mm • Power output: 42 hp @ 5,500 (est.) • Top speed: 95 mph (153 km/h) •

The Barber Vintage Motorsports Museum, Birmingham, Ala.

In the past, car designers have been known to tackle the challenge of styling motorcycles, but no kitchen-ware and furniture designer had ever take on the task—until Aprilia hired Frenchman Philippe Starck. When the radically styled Moto 6.5 went on sale in 1995, its appearance prompted lots of column inches.

The 6.5 was painted silver and a subtle dusty grey from its brake hoses to its handlebar grips, from its coolant lines to its turn signals. Only the front of the fuel tank was either orange or cream; the rest of the bike was monochrome—apart, of course, from its seat, which was silver. But the Moto 6.5's veerings from the norm didn't just stop with its initial visual impact: the bike was dripping with the kind of details that drew the most casual of onlookers to the machine, eliciting a double-take even if the design was not to one's particular liking.

The radiator of the liquid-cooled, 649-cc (100 x 82.7 mm) five-valve, double-overhead-cam, single-cylinder engine wrapped around, rather than away from, the machine—bringing a sense of completion to the rounded center of the bike initiated by its oval frame and deep tank. (Its nearest competitors, the Ducati Monster and the Harley-Davidson 883, were both V-twins.) The rear tire, a big, fat 17-inch cross-ply, was in direct opposition to the low-profile sport radials of most of the other motorcycles produced during the 1990s. Emphasis was also placed on the 6.5's traditional spoked wheels and alloy rims.

What was strange was that a company like Aprilia, with its background of road racing and hi-tech, high-performance two-strokes, would even consider building a motorcycle whose appearance was so radical. But whereas many designers' pipe dreams don't translate into reality, the finished Moto 6.5 largely remained true to Starck's original concept. And, even more impressive, out on the street, Aprilia's racing expertise, together with only 331 pounds of dry weight, made it an easy machine to control. In fact it would be true to say that for a deliberately mold-breaking design, the Aprilia was reassuringly simple to ride. Its engine made the Moto 6.5 a well-thought-out city bike, and the low seat height and weight also combined to make it exceptionally easy to control.

Aprilia had built its first powered two-wheeler, a moped, in 1960. However it wasn't until the mid 1970s that it began producing motorcycles—motocross and trials bikes at first, then, later, racing and street mod-els. Currently, Aprilia is Italy's fastest growing motorcycle company, producing everything from trendy scooters to the new-for-1998 RSV Mille V-twin superbike. —*MW*

Honda EXP-2

402 cc • 1995 • Japan
Bore x stroke: 80 x 80 mm • Power output: 54 hp @ 7,000 rpm •
Top speed: 105 mph (169 km/h) • Courtesy of American Honda Motor
Company, Inc. , Torrance, Calif.

While the Honda EXP-2 may appear to be just another big off-road enduro bike, it conceals a revolutionary combustion system. Enduro design emphasizes ruggedness, high-ground clearance, long suspension travel, and the capacity to carry plenty of fuel and other necessities. It's not hard to see how it would be able to compete in the 1995 Grenada-Dakar (formerly Paris-Dakar) race in Africa.

The engine's virtue is that, from idle up to 50 percent power, it operates without need for ignition spark. Honda calls it ARC, or Activated-Radical Combustion. In effect, the fuel-air mixture in the engine's cylinder is made to self-ignite by a heat-driven chemical process, much as time and temperature will pop corn heated in a covered saucepan. It's the form of combustion experienced in the "run-on" of a car engine after the ignition has been switched off. Honda's achievement in the EXP-2 engine is to make such self-ignition controllable, and the results are large cuts in fuel consumption and exhaust emissions.

At present, two combustion systems dominate automotive transportation: spark ignition (the familiar gasoline engine) and compression ignition (the diesel engine), each with its strengths and weaknesses. Gasoline engines are light, but combustion knock limits their power. Fuel-efficient and immune to knock, diesels are heavy and expensive. Honda's ARC system offers a third way.

The concept behind the ARC has roots in German, Russian, and American research dating back to the 1930s. At present, when the need for lower emissions and reduced fuel consumption are forcing rapid change in automotive engineering, obscure concepts such as radical-initiated combustion have become attractive.

Aside from the technological achievements of the EXP-2, the look of Paris-Dakar machines has been highly influential, leading to the present crop of so-called dual-purpose (on-/off-road) motorcycles. Such machines can operate on the highway like any other, but can then competently go off-road at will. — *KC*

Bruce Ogilvie on a Honda EXP-2 at the Nevada Rally, August, 1995.
Courtesy of American Honda Motor Company, Inc., Torrance, Calif.

Beta Techno

272 cc • 1997 • Italy

Bore x stroke: 76 x 60 mm • Power output: 30 hp @ 11,000 rpm •
Top speed: 65 mph (105 km/h) • Collection of Ron Commo

Trials riding is a very particular sport, and the motorcycle that wins a world competition is perhaps the most narrowly defined instrument in the world of motorized two-wheelers. The basic idea of trials is that the rider must get himself and his machine over incredibly daunting obstacles without ever putting a foot to ground, or "dabbing," as this is known.

In 1997 the Englishman Dougie Lampkin won the number-one spot in the World Trials Championship on an Italian-made Beta Techno 250 that had been modified specifically for him.

The Techno's perimeter frame is made by the Italian company Verlicchi of extruded aluminum; it has excellent rigidity, is light in weight, and doubles as a 1.1-gallon gas tank. Extending down from the steering head are two arms that serve both to hold the front of the engine and to enclose the radiator. A large skid-plate protects the underside of the motor, with almost a foot of ground clearance. At the back, the swinging arm pivots through both the bottom of the frame and the engine cases.

The front forks, manufactured by Paioli, have adjustments for spring preload and rebound damping, while custom valves are used, and black chrome-carbon-titanium tube coating. At the back of the Techno, the specially modified Boge shock has preload and rebound adjustability. The motorcycle's wheels are 21 inches at the front and 18 inches at the rear, both with small, protected disc brakes.

The Techno's engine is a liquid-cooled two-stroke of 248 cc, with a bore of 72.5 mm and stroke of 60 mm. Horsepower is not the issue here—the mildly tuned engine generates only about 19 hp. The Technos made for Lampkin, like this one, on which he won the U.S. run of the World Championship, were increased to 272 cc, with an output of 30 hp. To suit his riding style, the engine has been shifted forward slightly from the standard placement, putting more weight on the front wheel. The 26-mm Mikuni carburetor has an enlarged float bowl, and breathes through a carbon-fiber air box. The fuel passes through a reed valve. Variable computerized ignition keeps the engine smooth at any rpm. A hydraulic clutch eases the effort for the rider. With a full tank, the Techno's weight is a mere 176 pounds.

The rider does not sit on this motorcycle—he stands, and his foot-peg placement is of utmost importance. There is no comfort in this machine, nor is there meant to be—but in the hands of an expert such as Dougie Lampkin, it can be made to defy the natural forces of the planet. —CS

Poster of Dougie Lampkin at the World Trials Championship, 1997.
Courtesy of Betamotor SpA, Florence, Italy.

BMW R1200 C

1,170 cc • 1997 • Germany
Bore x stroke: 101 x 73 mm • Power output: 61 hp @ 5,000 rpm •
Top speed: 104 mph (168 km/h)• Courtesy of BMW AG, Munich

When BMW decided it was time to enter the booming American "cruiser" market, David Robb, BMW's director of motorcycle design, had quite a few problems to solve. The most pressing challenge, right from the start, was to avoid the inevitable comparisons with Harley-Davidson. Harley had, after all, more or less defined the cruiser ideal: retro, if not downright retrograde, with a design lineage that, without shame, harkened all the way back to the Indian Chief, the prototypical American cruiser.

But Robb faced a whole bevy of more subtle obstacles as well. A BMW motorcycle means three things: utility, reliability, and technical excellence. Its style, however, has a way of coming at you slowly, if at all. And when it does, it emerges from within the machine, a Bauhaus ethic that is evident even in the very first BMW, the R32. With this new design, Robb had an opportunity to make a serious mark on motorcycle design; he was not content simply to let the styling of his new motorcycle happen by accident.

As an American, Robb had very clear ideas about how to make a machine look, well, *American*. His own design impulses are deeply rooted in the American automotive tradition. Raymond Loewy, a giant of postwar American product design, spotted Robb's talent when he was still a student at the Art Center College of Design in Pasadena, California. Robb has worked with Larry Shinoda, the designer of the Corvette Sting Ray, the seminal car of the 1960s, and he did stints at Chrysler and Audi before joining BMW. His road to motorcycles is replete with powerful and positive influences, all of which show clearly in the R1200 C.

The BMW Cruiser is a brilliant achievement. Technically, it is all BMW: a 1,170-cc, four-valve, flat-twin Boxer, with the Telelever suspension technology of the newer Boxer generation. Electronic engine management and a three-way catalytic converter are standard. The bike is high-tech, environmentally friendly, and safe.

Stylistically, the R1200 C is the only important statement to have been made in the otherwise moribund cruiser niche since the introduction of the Indian Chief some 50 years ago. That the bike is not a Harley is quite clear. Its use of chrome and the motorcycle's soft, flowing lines set it far apart from the rest of the pack. A truly American design, borne out of a quintessentially German automotive tradition, the R1200 C is a perfect marriage of Old World and New Age. On Robb's quiet, efficient motorcycle, you can cruise at 55 mph while smelling the flowers. That is not the Harley-Davidson way; it is David Robb's way. His is the vision of one of the most important motorcycle designers of the moment. —*UG*

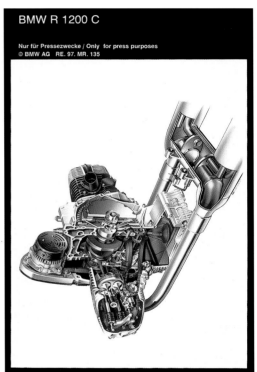

BMW R 1200 C

Nur für Pressezwecke / Only for press purposes
© BMW AG   RE. 97. MR. 135

Engine drawing of the BMW R1200 C, 1997.
Courtesy of BMW AG, Munich.

Morbidelli V8

847 cc • 1997 • Italy

Bore x stroke: 55 x 44.6 mm • Power output: 120 hp @ 11,000 rpm •
Top speed: 149 mph (240 km/h) • Courtesy of SCM Group, Rimini

Giancarlo Morbidelli grew up with a deep passion for racing motorcycles. He was born in 1938 and spent his teens during the 1950s, the so-called Golden Age of Italian participation in the sport. During the 1960s the young Morbidelli built up a thriving woodworking machinery factory in his home town of Pesaro, on the Adriatic Coast, a short distance from the old Benelli works.

After a short apprenticeship in karting, in 1968 Morbidelli entered his first motorcycle, a Benelli 60, as a team owner. This was soon followed by the Motobi that Luciano Mele had used to win the Italian junior title.

From these relatively humble beginnings was to come a stream of lightweight two-stroke racing machines, culminating in a pair of bikes that took the 125-cc world championships in 1975 and 1976, followed in 1977 by the ultimate accolade, the 250-cc crown, with Mario Lega at the helm. Morbidelli then went into the 500-cc category with a four-cylinder model (still a two-stroke), but the combination of great expense and poor results led Morbidelli to quit racing at the beginning of the 1980s.

But Morbidelli's enthusiasm for motorcycling was not dimmed, and when, in 1992, the news first leaked that he was working on a V-8, 847-cc (55 x 44.6 mm) luxury street bike, no one who knew the man was surprised. The design, however, was a different story. Nobody expected him to produce a leisure bike. But Morbidelli obviously saw the the burgeoning leisure sector of the motorcycle market, and the success of companies such as Ducati and Bimota, as promising a wealth of commercial opportunities. In the Morbidelli V8, he envisioned a machine that was far more glamorous than those produced by his Italian rivals.

Unfortunately, breaking into this market proved to be more difficult than he had bargained for. First, one would think that any motorcycle propelled by a V-8 engine would be dominated by its power unit. But in truth it was to be the bodywork that everyone would talk about—and for all the wrong reasons! Pininfarina, the world-famous automotive designer engaged by Morbidelli for the V8, might well be a legendary name in the four-wheel world. But the fact is, with its cross between a CX500 Turbo and a Pacific Coast (both made by Honda!), the Morbidelli V8, Pininfarina's first motorcycle, garnered the wrong type of headlines when it was finally launched in summer 1994.

Its styling was criticized—a great pity, since the oversquare, longitudinally mounted 90-degree V engine offered instant, free-revving response and liquid-smooth power delivery. With its $60,000 price tag, the Morbidelli V8 was one man's dream that no one else wanted. — *MW*

Italjet Formula 50 LC

49 cc • 1998 • Italy
Bore x stroke: 41 x 37.4 mm • Power output: 7 hp @ 7,200 rpm •
Top speed: 50 mph (80 km/h) • Courtesy of Italjet, USA, Huntington,
New York

Designer Leopoldo Tartarini has been deeply involved in Italian motorcycle design since the 1950s when, as one of the star riders of his generation, he was courted by Count Agusta to join the legendary MV team. Tartarini's mother, however, feared for the safety of her beloved only son and intervened, preventing him from joining the MV team. Instead he became a development rider and designer for Ducati, under their renowned designer Fabio Taglioni.

As a designer, Tartarini has had a hand in some of motor-cycling's most interesting projects. These include several Ducatis, notably a range of midsized Desmodromic singles from the '60s and '70s, as well as the wonderful 900-cc Darmah, a seminal Ducati design of the '70s, which Tartarini refined after initial efforts by prod-uct designer Giorgetto Giugiaro. Tartarini was also responsible for some of the more notable eccentrics of motorcycle design, including the abortive Indian Velo project launched by maverick American producer Floyd Clymer in the '70s. The Indian Velo was a last-gasp attempt to keep the aesthetic of the British motorcycle alive in a world market dominated by Japanese bikes of exceptional quality and reliability. That it failed was not the fault of Tartarini's lovely designs; in fact, the Indian Velo is much prized today.

Meanwhile, Tartarini's own company, Italjet, founded in the early '60s, achieved some success producing smaller motorcy-cles and scooters aimed at young, beginner motorcyclists. For a time, Italjet was the leading manufacturer of off-road miniature bikes for children.

Tartarini now concentrates on designing top-of-the-line scooters best known for technical innovations not seen on far bigger and more expensive motorcycles. The Formula 50 LC scooter has a liquid-cooled engine; independent, hydraulically operated disc brakes; and a unique independent steering system intended to neutralize some of the more heart-stopping handling quirks of the traditional small-wheeled scooter. His designs are not only functional but also extremely pretty, drawing on a design lineage going back to the Vespa and the Lambretta, but without any concessions to "retro" styling. The designs are also successful: Italjet produces some 90,000 scooters a year. The Formula 50's earlier, air-cooled version was twice voted scooter of the year in Italy. —*UG*

MV Agusta F4

750 cc • 1998 • Italy

Bore x stroke: 73.8 x 43.8 mm • Power output: 126 hp @ 12,200 rpm •

Top speed: 171 mph (275 km/h) • Collection of King Juan Carlos of Spain, Courtesy of Cagiva Motor SpA, Varese

During the mid-to-late 1980s, Claudio and Gianfranco Castiglioni, acquired the manufacturing rights for the names of several of Europe's leading motorcycle marques, notably: Ducati, Husqvarna, Moto Morini, and MV Agusta. The latter is probably the most glamorous in the two-wheel world, with its record-breaking score-card of racing world championship titles and the glorious memories of legendary riders such as Surtees, Hailwood, Agostini, and Read.

What was to emerge as the F4 project began some years ago at the beginning of the 1990s, when Massimo Tamburini, the founder of Bimota, and Claudio Castiglioni were discussing future tactics for the Cagiva Group. (Tamburini had joined Cagiva in 1985 and already had several design credits to his name, including the Ducati Paso and Cagiva Freccia.)

The Ferrari car company also played a leading role in the F4's development—the engine was a joint Ferrari-Cagiva venture. The remainder of the machine was developed solely by CRC (Cagiva Research Center) in Varese, with Tamburini heading the group of engineers that was responsible for Cagiva's 500-cc world championship racing effort, which spanned the 1980s and early 1990s.

At the center of the F4 is a liquid-cooled double-overhead-cam 750-cc (73.8 x 43.8 mm) engine with a Weber-Marelli electronic fuel and ignition system. Items of particular technical interest include a radial cylinder head with four valves per cylinder and a six-speed cassette gearbox. The latter allows the owner of the four-cylinder motorcycle to optimize the exact ratios required for road or track use, for the first time on a mass-produced level.

The F4's frame is constructed out of a combination of steel and aluminum, enabling the division of the bike into two distinct sections. Another feature is the adjustable steering head. The method on the F4 is one of several features of the design on which special patents have been taken out.

For all its superb technical merit, the F4's styling really sets it apart—together with its famous brand name. The visual appeal of the new MV Agusta is stunning. The work of Massimo Tamburini and his CRC staff makes all other sports bikes seem dull by comparison.

Eventually MV plans to produce the F4 in 600 and 900 engine sizes, in addition to the original 750. The latter will also be used if the machine enters World Superbike racing. —*MW*

Charles M. Falco

Motorcycle Books

The following bibliography attempts to document comprehensively significant English-language books published on motorcycles over the past one hundred years. Important books in other languages also are included, as are multiple editions of titles containing additional valuable information. Excluding works of fiction, children's literature, repair-related books, and factory manuals, this bibliography is estimated to contain approximately ninety percent of all relevant titles.

GENERAL AND HISTORICAL

Abel, Friedhelm. *The Kettenkrad*. Atglen, Pa.: Schiffer, 1991.

Allen, C. E. *The First Vintage Road Test Journal*. Leatherhead, England: Bruce Main-Smith, 1973.

———. *The Second Vintage Road Test Journal*. Leatherhead, England: Bruce Main-Smith, 1974.

———. *The Third Vintage Road Test Journal*. Leatherhead, England: Bruce Main-Smith, 1975.

———. *The First Post-Vintage Scene*. Leatherhead, England: Bruce Main-Smith, 1976.

———. *The Fourth Vintage Road Test Journal*. Leatherhead, England: Bruce Main-Smith, 1976.

———. *The Fifth Vintage Road Test Journal*. Leatherhead, England: Bruce Main-Smith, 1977.

———. *The First Military Machine Scene*. Leatherhead, England: Bruce Main-Smith, 1978.

———. *The Sixth Vintage Road Test Journal*. Leatherhead, England: Bruce Main-Smith, 1986.

Ansell, David. *British Racing Motor Cycles*. London: B. T. Batsford, n.d.

———. *Military Motor Cycles*. London: B. T. Batsford, 1985.

———. *The Illustrated History of Military Motorcycles*. London: Osprey Publishing, 1996.

Les Archives du Collectionneur. *Monocylindres et vertical twins anglais 1948–1960*. Boulogne: Editions Techniques pour l'Automobile, 1990.

Arctander, Erik. *The Book of Motorcycles, Trail Bikes and Scooters*. New York: Fawcett, 1965.

———. *The New Book of Motorcycles*. New York: Arco Publishing, 1968.

Armstrong, Douglas. *ABC of British Motor Cycles*. London: Ian Allan, 1954.

Ashby, J. B., and D. J. Angier. *Catalog of British Motor Cycles*. Los Angeles: Floyd Clymer, 1951.

Avery, Derek. *Motorcycles, A Select Colour Handbook*. Ware, England: Wordsworth, 1994.

Axon, Jo. *Our Sidecars*. Tiverton, England: Maslands, 1990.

———. *Sidecars*. Princes Risborough, England: Shire Publications, 1997.

Ayton, Cyril J. *The Great Japanese Motorcycles: Honda, Kawasaki, Suzuki, Yamaha*. Abbotsham, England: Herridge, 1981.

———. *Guide to Postwar British Motor Cycles*. Feltham, England: Temple Press, 1982.

———. *World Motorcycles*. Sparkford, England: Haynes, 1983.

———. *Guide to Italian Motorcycles*. Feltham, England: Temple Press, 1985.

———. *Guide to Pre-War British Motor Cycles*. Feltham, England: Temple Press, 1985.

———. *A-Z Guide to British Motorcycles*. Bideford, England: Bay View, 1991.

Ayton, Cyril J., Bob Holliday, Cyril Posthumus, and Mike Winfield. *The History of Motor Cycling*. London: Orbis, 1979.

Bacon, Roy. *The Motorcycle Manual*. London: Butterworths, 1976.

———. *Foreign Racing Motorcycles*. Sparkford, England: Haynes, 1979.

———. *Military Motorcycles of World War Two*. London: Osprey Publishing, 1985.

———. *British Motorcycles of the 1930s*. London: Osprey Publishing, 1986.

———. *British Motorcycles of the 1960s*. London: Osprey Publishing, 1988.

———. *Motorcycles of the 1940s and 1950s*. London: Osprey Publishing, 1989.

———. *An Illustrated History of Motorcycles*. London: Sunburst Books, 1995.

Ball, Kenneth. *Motor Cycle Index 1925–1936*. Brighton, England: Autopress, ca. 1960.

———. *Motor Cycle Index 1928–1939*. Brighton, England: Autopress, ca. 1960.

Ball, Kenneth, ed. *Motor Cycle Index 1913–1924*. Brighton, England: Autopress, 1964.

Ball, K. Randall. *Easyriders: Ultimate Custom Bikes*. New York: Thunder's, 1997.

Beaumont, W. Worby. *Motor Vehicles and Motors*. 2nd ed. Westminster, England: A. Constable, 1902.

———. *Motor Vehicles and Motors*. Vol. 2. London: A. Constable, 1906.

Betts, R. G., and G. H. Perry. *Helping Hand Book*. N.p., ca. 1905.

Big Chief I-Spy [pseud.]. *I-Spy Motorcycles and Cycles*. London: Dickens, 1963.

Bishop, George. *The Encyclopedia of Motorcycling*. New York: Putnam's, 1980.

Bishop, George and Shaun Barrington. *Encyclopedia of Motorcycling*. New York: Southmark, 1995.

Boulton, Jim. *Men and Machines in the Banbury Run*. Leeds: Turntable, 1973.

———. *Powered Vehicles Made in the Black Country (1900–1930s)*. Tipton, England: Black Country, 1976.

Bourne, Arthur B., ed. *Motor Cycle Engines*. London: Iliffe & Sons, 1951.

Bourdache. *La motocyclette en France 1894–1914*. N.p.: Edifree, 1989.

Bowman, Peter, ed. *The Motorcycle Book*. New York: Fawcett, 1951.

Bridges, John F. *Early Country Motoring: Cars and Motorcycles in Suffolk, 1896–1940*. Ipswitch, England: J. F. Bridges, 1995.

British Motor Cycles of the Year 1951. London: Stone and Cox, 1951.

British Motor Cycles of the Year 1952. London: Stone and Cox, 1952.

British Motor Cycles of the Year 1953. London: Stone and Cox, 1953.

British Motor Cycles of the Year 1954. London: Stone and Cox, 1954.

Brown, Roland. *Superbikes: Road Machines of the '60s, '70s, '80s and '90s*. Secaucus, N.J.: Chartwell, 1993.

———. *The Encyclopedia of Motorcycles*. New York: Smithmark, 1996.

———. *The World of Motorcycling*. New York: Smithmark, 1997.

Bull, Maureen A. *New Zealand's Motorcycle Heritage*. N.p.: Masterton, 1981.

Burns, Max and Ken Messenger. *The Winged Wheel Patch*. St. Catharines, Canada: Vanwell, 1993.

A Buyer's Guide to the British Bicycle and Motor Cycle Industries. Coventry, England: British Cycle and Motorcycle Industries, 1958.

Bygrave, Mike, and Jim Dowdall. *Motor Bike*. London: Hamilton, 1976.

Caddell, Laurie. *Powerbikes.* Dorset, England: Blandford, 1981.

———, ed. *Purnell's New Book of Bikes*. Bristol, England: Purnell, 1982.

Caddell, Laurie, and J. Smith. *Modern Motorbikes in Colour*. Dorset, England: Blandford, 1979.

Caddell, Laurie, and M. Winfield. *The Book of Superbikes*. Tucson: HP Books, 1981.

Carroll, John. *The Motorcycle: A Definitive History*. New York: Smithmark, 1997.

Carter, Ernest F. *The Burke Book of Cycles and Motor Cycles*. London: Burke, 1962.

Cathcart, Alan. *Classic Motorcycle Racer Tests*. London: Osprey Publishing, 1984.

———. *Road Racers Revealed*. London: Osprey Publishing, 1987.

———. *Dream Bikes*. London: Crescent, 1989.

———. *The Ultimate Racers*. Osceola, Wis.: Motorbooks International, 1990.

Caunter, C. F. *Cycles: History and Development*. Part 1. London: Her Majesty's Stationery Office, 1955.

———. *Motor Cycles: Handbook of the Collection*. Part 2. London: Her Majesty's Stationery Office, 1958.

———. *Motorcycles: A Technical History*. London: Her Majesty's Stationery Office, 1970.

———. *Motorcycles: A Technical History*. 3rd ed. London: Her Majesty's Stationery Office, 1982.

Chamberlain, Peter. *Motor Cycling Year Book 1951*. London: Temple Press, 1951.

———. *Motor Cycling Year Book 1953*. London: Temple Press, 1953.

Chirinian, Alain. *Motor-Cycles*. Englewood Cliffs, N.J.: M. Messner, 1989.

Clarke, Massimo. *La moto classica*. Vol. 1, no. 1. Milan: International Publishing Group, 1987.

———. *One Hundred Years of Motorcycles*. New York: Portland House, 1988.

399

Clew, Jeff. *British Racing Motorcycles*. Sparkford, England: Haynes, 1976.

———. *Lucky All My Life*. Sparkford, England: Haynes, 1979.

———. *Veteran Motorcycles*. Buckinghamshire, England: Shire, 1995.

Clymer, Floyd. *Floyd Clymer's Historical Motor Scrapbook*. Nos. 1–8. Los Angeles: Floyd Clymer, 1944–55.

———. *Motorcycle Road Tests (1949–1952)*. Los Angeles: Floyd Clymer, 1952.

———. *Motorcycle Road Tests (1950–1953)*. Los Angeles: Floyd Clymer, 1954.

———. *A Treasury of Motorcycles of the World*. Los Angeles: Floyd Clymer, 1965.

Concise Color Guides: Motorcycles. London: Longmeadow, 1993.

Connolly, Harold. *Motorcycle Story: 1875–1905*. Peterborough, England: E. M. Art & Publishing, 1962.

———. *Pioneer Motorcycles*. Leatherhead, England: Bruce Main-Smith, ca. 1975.

Cook, R.A.B., ed. *Motor Cycling Year Book 1957*. London: Temple Press, 1957.

———, ed. *Motor Cycling Year Book 1961*. London: Temple Press, 1961.

Corbishley, H. *Motor Cycles and Side-Cars*. London: Cassell, 1925.

Croucher, Robert. *The Observer's Book of Motorcycles*. 1st ed. London: Fredrick Warne, 1976.

———. *Observer's Motorcycles*. 7th ed. London: Bloomsbury, 1991.

Crowley, T. E. *Discovering Old Motor Cycles*. 2nd ed. Buckinghamshire, England: Shire, 1977.

Currie, Bob. *The Second Post-Vintage Scene (1931–1953)*. Leatherhead, England: Bruce Main-Smith, 1978.

———. *Great British Motor Cycles of the Fifties*. London: Ivy Leaf, 1980.

———. *Great British Motor Cycles of the Sixties*. London: Hamlyn Publishing, 1981.

———. *Classic British Motor Cycles: The Final Years*. Feltham, England: Temple Press, 1984.

———. *Classic Competition Motorcycles*. Cambridge, England: Patrick Stephens, 1987.

———. *Classic British Motorcycles of Over 500cc*. Cambridge, England: Patrick Stephens, 1988.

———. *Great British Motor Cycles of the Thirties*. London: Ivy Leaf, 1991.

Cutts, John and Michael Scott. *The World's Fastest Motor Cycles*. London: Apple, 1990.

Czechoslovak Motor Vehicles. N.p., ca. 1960.

Davies, B. H. *The Modern Motor Cycle*. London: C. Arthur Pearson, 1915.

Davies, Roland. *Daily Mail Motorcycling Book*. Birmingham, England: Daily Mail, 1950.

Davison, G. S. *The Motor Cyclist's Annual and Buyer's Guide 1939–40*. London: H.E.W. Publications, 1939.

The Dealer and Repairman, April 1902. Reprint. Los Angeles: Floyd Clymer, ca. 1955.

Deane, Charles. *Motorcycles*. London: Sundial, 1978.

Deane, Charles E., and B. Crichton. *The Pictorial History of Motorcycling*. London: Chancellor, 1993.

Dumble, David B. *Veteran Motorcycles in Australia*. Noble Park, Australia: Vintage Motorcycle Club of Victoria, 1974.

———. *Classic Motorcycles in Australia*. Noble Park, Australia: Dumble, 1977.

Du Pont, S. *The German Motorcycle Industry since 1938*. London: Her Majesty's Stationery Office, 1946.

Ellacott, S. E. *Wheels on the Road*. London: Methuen, 1953.

Ford, Taylor. *Best Motorcycle Investments*. Dallas: Keyway, 1996.

Forsdyke, Graham. *Motorcycles*. Secaucus, N.J.: Chartwell, 1977.

Garside, George I., ed. *The Image of Motorcycling in the Sixties*. West Yorkshire, England: Garside, 1986.

Gaspard, Gilbert. *Les demoiselles de Herstal*. Liège: Vaillant, 1975.

———. *Les dames de la Basse-Meuse*. Liège: Vaillant, 1978.

Georgano, G. N. *The World's Commercial Vehicles 1830–1964*. London: Temple Press, 1965.

Galbiati, Fermo, and Nino Ciravegna. *Bicycles: Le Biciclette*. San Francisco, Calif.: Chronicle, 1994.

Gardiner, Mark. *Classic Motorcycles*. New York: MetroBooks, 1997.

Girdler, Allan. *The Harley-Davidson and Indian Wars*. Osceola, Wis.: Motorbooks International, 1997.

Goyard, Jean. *Le temps des mobs*. Paris: E.P.A., 1995.

Goyard, Jean, and Dom Pascal. *Tous les scooters du monde*. Paris: Ch. Massin, 1993.

Griffin, Al. *Motorcycles: A Rider's and Buyer's Guide*. Chicago: Henry Regnery, 1972.

———. *Motorcycles: A Buyer's and Rider's Guide*. 2nd ed. Chicago: Henry Regnery, 1974.

Griffith, John. *Famous Racing Motorcycles*. London: Temple Press, 1961.

———. *Built for Speed*. London: Temple Press, 1962.

———. *Historic Racing Motorcycles*. London: Temple Press, 1963.

Griffin, Michael. *Motorcycles from the Inside Out*. Englewood Cliffs, N.J.: Prentice-Hall, 1978.

Hasluck, Paul N., ed. *Motor Bicycle Building*. London: Cassell, 1906.

Hatfield, Jerry. *American Racing Motorcycles*. Sparkford, England: Haynes, 1982.

———. *Antique American Motorcycle Buyer's Guide*. Osceola, Wis.: Motorbooks International, 1996.

Hawks, Ellison. *Buying a Motorcycle*. Harrogate, England: E. Hawks, ca. 1925.

Henshaw, Peter. *Classic Bikes*. London: Regency House, 1995.

Herrmann, Siegfried. *The Motor Cycle*. N.p.: Technical Fundamentals, 1967.

Hicks, Roger W. *V-Twins: The Classic Motorcycle*. Dorset, England: Blandford, 1985.

———. *Classic Motorbikes*. London: Tiger, 1992.

———. *Classic Motorbikes*. Secaucus, N.J.: Chartwell, 1993.

———. *The Complete Book of Motorcycles*. London: Tiger, 1993.

Higgins, L. R. *Britain's Racing Motor Cycles*. London: Foulis, 1952.

Hingston, I. R. *Scooters and Mopeds*. London: Iliffe & Sons, 1958.

Hinrichsen, Horst. *Motorcycles of the Wehrmacht*. Atglen, Pa.: Schiffer, 1994.

Hiscox, Gardner D. *Gas, Gasoline, and Oil Vapor Engines*. N.p.: Henley, 1897.

———. *Horseless Vehicles, Automobiles, Motor Cycles Operated by Steam, Hydro-carbon, Electric and Pneumatic Motors*. N.p.: Munn & Co., 1900.

Hodgdon, T. A. *Motorcycling's Golden Age of the Fours*. Lake Arrowhead, Calif.: Bagnall, 1974.

Holliday, Bob. *Motor Cycle Parade*. New York: David and Charles, 1974.

———. *Motorcycle Panorama*. New York: Arco Publishing, 1975.

Homans, James E. *Self-Propelled Vehicles*. New York: Theo. Audel, 1910.

———. *Self-Propelled Vehicles*. 1909. Reprint, New York: Theo. Audel, 1917.

Hough, Richard, and L.J.K. Setright. *A History of the World's Motorcycles*. New York: Harper and Row, 1966.

———. *A History of the World's Motorcycles*. Rev. ed. New York: Harper and Row, 1973.

Howard, Dennis, ed. *Vintage Motor Cycle Album*. London: F. Warne, 1982.

Howdle, Peter. *Best of British: Classic Bikes of Yesteryear*. Cambridge, England: Patrick Stephens, 1979.

Hudson-Evans, Richard. *The Lightweight Bike Book*. London: B. T. Batsford, 1981.

Hume, William Elliot. *The Register of Machines of the VMCC*. 3rd ed. Thornton Heath, England: VMCC, 1991.

Jennings, Gordon. *Motorcycles*. Englewood Cliffs, N.J.: Prentice-Hall, 1981.

Johnstone, Gary. *Classic Motorcycles*. Osceola, Wis.: Motorbooks International, 1993.

Johnson, Jessamy, ed. *Miller's Classic Motorcycles Price Guide: 1994*. London: Reed Books, 1993.

Jones, Peter. *Historic Motor Cycling*. Rushcutters Bay, Australia: Modern Magazines, 1978.

Joyce, Daryl, ed. *The Biker's Bible*. London: Windrow & Greene, 1994.

Judge, Arthur W., ed. *Modern Motor Cars*. 2nd ed. 3 vols. London: Caxton, ca. 1930.

Karolevitz, Bob. *Yesterday's Motorcycles*. Mission Hill, S.D.: Homestead, 1986.

Keig, S. R., and Bob Holliday. *The Keig Collection*. Vols. 1–3. Leatherhead, England: Bruce Main-Smith, 1975.

———. *The Keig Collection*. Vol. 4. Leatherhead, England: Bruce Main-Smith, 1984.

Keig, S. R., and Bill Snelling. *The Keig Collection*. Vol. 5. Laxey, Isle of Man: Amulree, 1996.

Kemp, Andrew, and Mirco De Cet. *Classic British Bikes*. Leicester, England: Abbeydale, 1997.

Kennedy, Rankin. *The Book of the Motor Car*. 4 vols. London: Caxton, 1913–1920.

Knittel, Stefan. *German Motorcycles in World War Two*. West Chester, Pa.: Schiffer, 1990.

Koch, Don. *Chilton's Complete Guide to Motorcycles and Motorcycling*. Radnor, Pa.: Chilton, 1974.

Koerdt, Volker, ed. *Custom Bikes: From Factory to Fantasy*. Oxfordshire, England: Transedition, 1994.

Kosbab, William H. *Motorcycle Dictionary of Terminology*. Orange, Calif.: Career, 1984.

Lacombe, Christian. *The Guinness Guide to Motorcycling*. Enfield, England: Guinness, 1974.

———. *The Motorcycle*. New York: Grossett Dunlap, 1974.

Leek, S., and S. *The Bicycle, That Curious Invention*. N.p.: Nelson, 1973.

Leonard, Grant. *Motorcycle Classics*. N.p.: Arlington, 1992.

Lewis, Valerie. *Miller's Classic Motorcycles Price Guide: 1995*. London: Reed Books, 1994.

———. *Miller's Classic Motorcycles Price Guide: 1996/1997*. London: Reed Books, 1995.

Louis, Harry, and Bob Currie. *The Classic Motorcycles 1896–1950*. New York: E. P. Dutton, 1976.

Luraschi, Abramo Giovanni. *Storia della motocicletta*. Vol. 1. Milan: La Moto, 1962.

———. *Storia della motocicletta (1915–1925)*. Vols. 2–5. Milan: Edisport, ca. 1975.

Macauley, Ted, and Paul Butler, eds. *The International Motor Cycle File*. London: Pictorial, 1972.

MacDonald, B. C. *Motor Cyclist's Handbook*. London: Sir I. Pitman & Sons, 1951.

Main-Smith, Bruce. *Road Tests Republished*. Vols. 1–3. Leatherhead, England: Bruce Main-Smith, 1974, 1975.

———. *The Veteran Scene*. Leatherhead, England: Bruce Main-Smith, 1976.

———. *The First Vintage Racing Scene (pre-1931)*. Leatherhead, England: Bruce Main-Smith, 1977.

———. *The First Post-Vintage Racing Scene (1931–1951)*. Leatherhead, England: Bruce Main-Smith, 1977.

———. *The Second Post-Vintage Racing Scene (1931–1953)*. Leatherhead, England: Bruce Main-Smith, 1978.

———. *The Book of Super Bike Road Tests*. Leatherhead, England: Bruce Main-Smith, 1984.

———, ed. *The Motorcyclist's Encyclopedia*. Leatherhead, England: Bruce Main-Smith, 1972.

Mazza, Franco. *Concise Guide to Motorcycles*. London: Grange, 1994.

McDiarmid, Mac. *Classic Super Bikes from Around the World*. New York: Smithmark, 1996.

The MC Staff. *British Motorcycle Engines*. Los Angeles: Floyd Clymer, 1951.

———. *Autocycles and Cyclemotors*. 3rd ed. London: Iliffe & Sons, 1953.

———. *The Motor Cycle Buyers' Guide for 1958*. London: Iliffe & Sons, 1957.

Melling, Frank. *Track Tests of the World's Greatest Enduro Motorcycles*. London: Osprey Publishing, 1981.

Middlehurst, Tony. *The Pictorial History of Motorcycling*. New York: Mallard, 1989.

Miller, Denis N. *A Source Book of Motor Cycles*. London: Ward Lock, 1977.

———. *A Source Book of Motorcycles and Sidecars*. London: Ward Lock, 1983.

Minton, Dave. *Motorcycles of the World*. London: Phoebus, 1980.

Minton, Dave, and Frank Melling. *Superbikes*. London: Hamlyn Publishing, 1975.

Mitchel, Doug. *American Motorcycle Classics*. Lincolnwood, Ill.: Publications International, 1994.

———. *Motorcycle Classics*. Lincolnwood, Ill.: Publications Internatioinal, 1995.

———. *Memorable Japanese Motorcycles, 1959–1996*. Atglen, Pa.: Schiffer, 1997.

Miyato, Kimiaki, ed. *Japanese Motorcycle History, 1945–1997*. Tokyo: Yaesu-shuppan, 1997. In Japanese.

The Modern Motor Cycle. N.p.: Aeroshell, ca. 1935.

Montague, Lord, and M. Bourdon, eds. *Cars and Motorcycles*. 3 vols. London: Sir I. Pitman & Sons, 1928.

Morley, Don. *Everyone's Book of Motor Cycling*. London: Hamlyn Publishing, 1983.

———. *Classic British Trials Bikes*. London: Osprey Publishing, 1984.

———. *Classic British Scramblers*. London: Osprey Publishing, 1986.

———. *Classic British Two-Stroke Trials Bikes*. London: Osprey Publishing, 1987.

———. *Spanish Trials Bikes*. London: Osprey Publishing, 1988.

———. *The Story of the Motorcycle*. London: Tiger, 1991.

The Motor Cycle Index. Norwich, England: Fletcher & Son, 1923.

'Motor Cycling' Sports Model Road Tests. London: Temple Press, 1959.

'Motor Cycling' Sports Road Tests. London: Temple Press, 1959.

Nabinger, Manfred. *Deutsche Fahrrad Motoren, 1898 bis 1988*. Brilon, Germany: Podszun, 1988.

Nakaoki, Mitsuru. *Autobiography: Japanese Bike History*. N.p.: Sony Magazine, ca. 1990.

Nicks, Mike, ed. *Golden Oldies: Classic Bike Roadtests*. Cambridge, England: Patrick Stephens, 1981.

1994 Vintage Cycle Price Guide. West Chester, Pa.: Vintage Cycle, 1994.

Noakes, Keith. *Post War Independent Motorcycle Frame Makers*. London: Osprey Publishing, 1995.

Nutting, John. *Superbikes of the Seventies*. London: Hamlyn Publishing, 1978.

Olyslager, Piet. *Motorcycles to 1945*. London: Frederick Warne & Company, 1974.

———. *Motorcycles and Scooters from 1945*. London: Frederick Warne & Company, 1975.

Orchard, C. J., and S. J. Madden. *British Forces Motorcycles*. Gloucestershire, England: Alan Sutton, 1995.

Osborne, Bernal. *Modern Motor Cycles*. London: Temple Press, 1951.

Pagé, Victor W. *Motorcycles, Sidecars and Cyclecars*. N.p.: N. W. Henley, ca. 1915.

———. *Early Motorcycles*. Reprint. Arcadia, Calif.: Post, 1916.

Parker, Tim. *Italian Motorcycles: Classic Sport Bikes*. London: Osprey Publishing, 1984.

———. *Japanese Motorcycles*. London: Osprey Publishing, 1985.

Partridge, Michael. *Motorcycle Pioneers: The Men, The Machines, The Events, 1860–1930*. New York: Arco Publishing, 1977.

———. *An Introduction to Classic British Motorcycles*. London, Canada: Partridge, 1991.

Pascal, Dominique. *50 Ans de Motocyclettes Françaises*. Paris: E.P.A., 1979.

———. *Le Grand Dictionnaire des motos françaises*. Paris: Ch. Massin, ca. 1980.

Patrignani, Roberto, and Brizio Pignacca. *Le moto da corsa italiane*. Novara, Italy: Agostini, 1985.

Patrignani, Roberto, and M. Colombo. *Motorcycles: Classics and Thoroughbreds*. London: Orbis, 1971.

Paulson, Tim, and Fredric Winkowski. *Harleys, Popes, and Indian Chiefs*. Edison, N.J.: Wellfleet, 1995.

Perriam, Gerard. *Flyweight Motor Cycles*. Peterborough, England: E. M. Art & Publishing, 1964.

Pfeiffer, Michael, and Jurgen Gassebner. *Custom Motorcycles*. Oxford, England: MetroBooks, 1997.

Phoenix [Charles S. Lake]. *Motor Cyclist's Handbook*. London: Percival Marshall, 1911.

Pickard, Derek. *British 250 Racer*. Burwood, Australia: Pickard, 1984.

Porazik, Juraj. *Motorcycles 1885–1940*. Leicester, England: Galley Press, 1983.

Posthumus, Cyril. *First Motorcycles*. London: Phoebus, 1977.

Posthumus, Cyril, and Dave Richmond. *Fifty Years of Motorcycles*. London: Phoebus, 1978.

———. *Motor Cycle Story*. London: Phoebus, 1979.

Prior, Rupert. *Motorcycling: The Golden Years*. London: Tiger Books International, 1994.

Pucket, Alan, and Warren Penney. *Classic Motorbikes*. London: Hamlyn Publishing, 1979.

Rae, Ronald L. *The Goulding Album*. Southfield, Mich.: Rae, 1990.

Rance, George. *Vintage Motor Cycles Illustrated*. London: Vintage Motorcycle Club, 1968.

———. *Vintage Motorcycles Illustrated*. Rev. ed. London: Vintage Motorcycle Club, 1970.

Redman, Martin. *Superbike: Modern High Performance Motorcycles*. New York: Harper and Row, 1975.

Renstrom, Richard. *Motorsport on Two Wheels*. Long Beach, Calif.: Parkhurst, ca. 1970.

———. *Great Motorcycle Legends*. Newfoundland, N.J.: Haessner, 1977.

———. *Motorcycle Milestones*. Vol. 1. Caldwell, Idaho: Classics, 1980.

Reynaud, Claude. *Le mythe des 4 cylindres en ligne 1904–1954*. Domazan, France: C. Reynaud, 1991.

———. *Guide Reynaud International de la Moto de Collection*. Franconville, France: Reynaud, 1995.

Reynolds, Jim. *Best of British Bikes*. Cambridge, England: Patrick Stephens, 1990.

Richmond, Dave. *The Superbook of Bikes*. N.p.: Willowisp, 1987.

Rivers, K. *History of the Traffic Department of the Metropolitan Police*. N.p.: Styletype, ca. 1970.

Rivola, Luigi. *Racing Motorcycles*. Chicago: Rand McNally, 1978.

Roberts, Derek. *The Invention of Bicycles and Motorcycles*. London: Usborne, 1975.

Ryder, Julian. *Motorcycles*. Los Angeles: Aladdin, 1987.

Salvat, Bernard. *Motos de course 1902–1958*. Charnay-les Macon, France: A.H.M.A., 1988.

———. *Les motos francaises: Cent ans d'histoire*. Paris: E.P.A., 1994.

Sanderson, G. *Superbike Road Tests*. London: Hamlyn Publishing, 1982.

Saward, Robert. *A-Z of Australian-Made Motorcycles, 1893–1942*. Sydney: Turton & Armstrong, 1996.

Scalzo, Joe. *The Motorcycle Book*. Englewood Cliffs, N.J.: Prentice-Hall, 1974.

Schiller, Colin. *Fast Bikes: The New Generation*. London: Osprey Publishing, 1987.

Schilling, Phil. *The Motorcycle World*. New York: Ridge, 1974.

———. *Motorcycles*. New York: Ridge, 1975.

Schmidt, Oscar C., ed. *Practical Treatise on Automobiles*. Vol. 2. Philadelphia: American Text Book Company, 1909.

Schultz, Jean-Paul. *Histoire de la Moto Militaire*. Brussels: Sagato, ca. 1980.

Scott, Michael, and John Cutts. *The World's Fastest Motor Cycles*. London: Apple, 1986.

Setright, L.J.K. *Some Unusual Engines*. London: Mechanical Engineering Publications, 1975.

———. *Motorcycles*. London: Arthur Barker, 1976.

Sheldon, James. *Veteran and Vintage Motor Cycles*. London: B. T. Batsford, 1961.

———. *Veteran and Vintage Motor Cycles*. Brentford, England: Transport Bookman, 1971.

Shelley, Les. *The First Vintage Scene*. Leatherhead, England: Bruce Main-Smith, 1977.

Statnekov, Daniel K. *Pioneers of American Motorcycle Racing*. Http://www.roadrunner.com/~maraz/motorcycles.html. World Wide Web: D. Statnekov, 1996.

Sumner, Philip. *Motorcycles*. London: Her Majesty's Stationery Office, 1972.

Taylor, Rich. *Street Bikes: Superbikes/Tourers/Café Racers*. New York: Golden Press, 1974.

———. *Café Racers: Customs/Production Bikes/Road Racers*. New York: Golden Press, 1976.

Tessera, Vittorio. *Scooters: Made in Italy*. Milan: Giorgio Nada, 1993. In Italian.

Thompson, Eric E. *Motor Cycles in Colour*. London: Blandford, 1974.

Thompson, Eric E., and Laurie Caddell. *From Motorcycle to Superbike: The History of the Motorbike*. Dorset, England: New Orchard, 1986.

Thoms, Dave, and Tom Donnelly. *The Motor Car Industry in Coventry Since the 1890's*. New York: St. Martin's, 1985.

Tragatsch, Erwin. *The World's Motorcycles 1894–1963*. London: Temple Press, 1964.

———. *The Complete Illustrated Encyclopedia of the World's Motorcycles*. New York: Holt, Rinehart and Winston, 1977.

———. *Motorcycles: An Illustrated History*. Leicester, England: Galley Press, 1980.

———. *The Complete Illustrated Encyclopedia of the World's Motorcycles: New Edition*. New York: Holt, Rinehart and Winston, 1985.

———. ed. *The Illustrated History of Motorcycles*. London: New Burlington, 1979.

Tragatsch, Erwin, and Brian Wooley. *The New Illustrated Encyclopedia of Motorcycles*. Edison, N.J.: Wellfleet, 1992.

Turner, Dave. *Scooters*. Leeds: Malvern House, 1996.

Vanderheuvel, Cornelis. *Pictorial History of Japanese Motorcycles*. Rijswijk, The Netherlands: Uitgeverij Elmar B.V., 1997.

V.M.C.C. *Vintage and Veteran: An Illustrated Brochure*. Thornton Heath, England: Vintage Motorcycle Club, ca. 1954.

Walford, Eric W. *Early Days in the British Motor Cycle Industry*. Coventry, England: British Cycle, 1932.

———. *Floyd Clymer's Historical Scrapbook: Foreign Motorcycle Edition*. Vol. 1. Los Angeles: Floyd Clymer, 1955.

Walker, Mick. *Spanish Post-War Road and Racing Motorcycles*. London: Osprey Publishing, 1986.

———. *German Motorcycles: Road and Racing Bikes*. London: Osprey Publishing, 1989.

———. *Classic British Racing Motorcycles*. London: Osprey Publishing, 1990.

———. *Classic Italian Racing Motorcycles*. London: Osprey Publishing, 1991.

———. *Classic German Racing Motorcycles*. London: Osprey Publishing, 1991.

———. *Classic Japanese Racing Motorcycles*. London: Osprey Publishing, 1991.

———. *Classic Motorcycles*. Secaucus, N.J.: Chartwell, 1991.

———. *Italian Motorcycles*. Buckinghamshire, England: Aston, 1991.

———. *Mick Walker's Italian Classic Gallery: The Road Bikes*. Sparkford, England: Haynes, 1991.

———. *Classic American Racing Motorcycles*. London: Osprey Publishing, 1992.

———. *Classic European Racing Motorcycles*. London: Osprey Publishing, 1992.

———. *Café Racers of the 1960s*. London: Windrow & Greene, 1994.

———. *Superbike Specials of the 1970s*. London: Windrow & Greene, 1994.

———. *Hamlyn History of Motorcycles*. London: Hamlyn Publishing, 1997.

———. ed. *Miller's Classic Motorcycles Price Guide: 1997/1998*. London: Reed Books, 1996.

———. ed. *Miller's Classic Motorcycles Price Guide: 1998/1999*. London: Reed Books, 1997.

Ward, Ian, ed. *The Illustrated Encyclopedia of Motorcycling*. N.p.: Cavendish, 1979.

Ward, Ian, and Laurie Caddell, eds. *Great British Bikes*. London: Black Cat, 1994.

Webster, Michael. *Motor Scooters*. Buckinghamshire: Shire, ca. 1986.

Willoughby, Vic. *Classic Motorcycles*. N.p.: Dial, 1975.

———. *The Racing Motorcycle*. London: Hamlyn Publishing, 1980.

———. *Exotic Motorcycles*. London: Osprey Publishing, 1982.

———. *Classic Motorcycles*. 2nd ed. Feltham, England: Temple Press, 1983.

———. *Classic Motorcycle Engines*. Croydon, England: Motor Racing Publications, 1986.

———. *Winning Motorcycles Engines*. London: Osprey Publishing, 1989.

Wilson, Hugo. *The Ultimate Motorcycle Book*. London: Dorling Kindersley, 1993.

———. *The Encyclopedia of the Motorcycle*. London: Dorling Kindersley, 1995.

Wilson, M. J. *ABC Motor Cycles*. London: Ian Allan, ca. 1962.

Wilson, Steve. *British Motorcycles since 1950*. 6 vols. Cambridge, England: Patrick Stephens, 1982–1992.

———. *Practical British Lightweight Two-Stroke Motorcycles*. Sparkford, England: Haynes, 1990.

———. *Practical British Lightweight Four-Stroke Motorcycles*. Sparkford, England: Haynes, 1994.

Wise, David Bugess. *Historic Motor Cycles*. London: Hamlyn Publishing, 1973.

Wood, Geoffrey, and Richard C. Renstrom. *The Great Motorcycles: Histories of Twenty-two Famous Makes*. Newport Beach, Calif.: Bond/Parkhurst, 1972.

Woollett, Mick. *Racing Motorcycles*. London: Hamlyn Publishing, 1973.

———. *Bike and Superbike*. London: B. T. Batsford, 1977.

———. *Lightweight Bikes*. London: B. T. Batsford, 1981.

———. *Speedbikes*. New York: Arco Publishing, 1984.

Woolley, Brian. *Directory of Classic Racing Motorcycles*. Osceola, Wis.: Aston, 1988.

World Motorcycle Guide. London: Phoebus, 1979.

Worthington-Williams, Michael. *Cycles and Motorcycles*. Glasgow: Collins, 1976.

Wright, Stephen. *American Racer 1900–1940*. Huntington Beach, Calif.: Megden, 1979.

———. *American Racer 1940–1980*. Huntington Beach, Calif.: Megden, 1986.

Wrobel, Peter, ed. *World Motorcycle Catalogue: 1977–78*. London: Phoebus, 1977.

Zimmerman, Mark. *Street Bikes*. London: Bison, 1995.

RIDING AND MOTORCYCLING

America's Fifty Best Touring Roads, by Harley-Davidson. Chicago: Rand McNally, 1987.

Annuario ANCMA (Associazione Nazionale Ciclo Motociclo Accessori). Milan: ANCMA, 1972.

Archbold, G. *Not So Innocent Abroad*. N.p.: Jarrold, 1957.

Ashley, F. J. *With a Motor Bike in the Bush*. N.p.: Blackie, ca. 1938.

Auburn, Robert B. *The Endless Ride*. Newport Beach, Calif.: Endless Ride, 1994.

Barnes, Richard. *Mods!* London: Plexus, 1979.

Battson, Roy K. *The Land Beyond the Ridge: A Motor Cycle Memoir*. Cambridge, England: Goose, 1974.

Beagle, Peter S. *I See by My Outfit*. New York: Penguin, 1985.

Behme, B., and M. Jaderquist. *The Motorcycle and Trail Bike Handbook*. New York: Pyramid, 1971.

Bennett, Jim. *The Complete Motorcycle Book: A Consumer's Guide*. New York: Facts On File, 1995.

Bjornstad, Harvey. *Mandatory Motorcycle Helmets*. Glendale, Calif.: Bridgeport, 1996.

Blessing, Arthur R. *List of Books on Automobiles and Motorcycles*. New York: New York State Library Board, 1918.

Blom, Dick. *Rider's Complete Guide to Motorcycle Touring*. Agoura, Calif.: T. L. Enterprises, 1981.

Brobst, Bill. *Pulling Your Tail*. Kitty Hawk, N.C.: The Transport Environment, 1982.

Brooks, Sammy Kent. "The Motorcycle in American Culture: From Conception to 1935." Ph.D. diss.,
    George Washington University, 1975.

Brown, E. T. *Everything about a Motor Cycle*. N.p.: Morgan Hoadly, ca. 1920.

———. *The Complete Motor-Cyclist*. London: Hodder and Stoughton, 1925.

———. *The Practical Motor-Cyclist*. London: Cassell, 1926.

Brownell, Bob. *Dr. Bob's Southern California Motorcycle Guide*. N.p.: Dr. Bob, 1992.

Bull, M. A. *Vintage Motor Cycling*. N.p.: Hedley's Book, 1970.

Capitalist Toys: A Selection of Toy Boats and Motorcycles. New York: Sotheby's, 1994.

Caddell, Laurie, ed. *Purnell's New Book of Bikes*. Bristol, England: Purnell, 1982.

Caiati, Carl. *Collecting Harley-Davidson*. Brooklyn, N.Y.: Alliance, 1997.

Camm, F. J., ed. *The Motor Cyclist Reference Book 1929–30*. 2nd ed. N.p.: T.G. Simpson, 1930.

Carrick, Peter. *Motorcycling: A Guinness Superlatives Guide*. New York: Sterling, 1980.

———. *Superbikes: Road-Burners to Record-Breakers*. London: Octopus, 1982.

Chidgey, David. *Motorcycle Discussion Paper*. London: Liberal Democrats, 1996.

Christensen, Richard D. *Motorcycles in Magazines, 1895–1983*. Metuchen, N.J.: Scarecrow, 1985.

Christenson, Ron, ed. *Motorcycle Price Guide, 1905–1985*. St. Paul, Minn.: Mid-America Publications, 1996.

Clampett, Bob. *The Motorcycle Handbook*. New York: Fawcett, 1975.

Clay, Mike. *Café Racers*. London: Osprey Publishing, 1990.

Clew, Jeff. *Motorcycling in the 50s*. Godmanstone, England: Veloce, 1995.

Clymer, Floyd. *Floyd Clymer's Popular Motor Books, Catalog 118*. Los Angeles: Floyd Clymer, ca. 1960.

Cole, Lee S. *Motorcycle Identification*. Novato, Calif.: Lee Books, ca. 1990.

Congdon, Kirby. *Motorcycle Books: A Critical Survey and Checklist*. Metuchen, N.J.: Scarecrow, 1987.

Craven, Ken. *Ride It! The Complete Book of Motor Cycle Touring*. Sparkford, England: Haynes, 1977.

Crichton, Brian. *You and Your Bike*. London: Treasure Press, 1985.

Culberson, Ed. *Obsessions Die Hard*. N.p.: Teak Wood, 1990.

Currie, Bob. *Motor Cycling in the 1930's*. London: Hamlyn Publishing, 1981.

Cutter, Robert A. *The New Guide to Motorcycling*. New York: Arco Publishing, 1974.

Dandy, R. *Motor-Cyclist's Handbook*. London: Cassell, 1977.

Del Monte, Frank. *Motorcycle Arizona!* Phoenix: Western States MC Tours, 1993.

Demaus, A. B. *Victorian and Edwardian Cycling and Motoring*. London: B. T. Batsford, 1977.

Dempsey, Paul. *The Complete Mini-Bike Handbook*. Blue Ridge Summit, Pa.: TAB, 1973.

de Ville, Susie, ed. *Motorcycle Touring, An International Directory: 1991–92*. Boston: Whitehorse, 1991.

———, ed. *1993–94 Supplement to Motorcycle Touring, An International Directory*. Boston: Whitehorse, 1993.

Ditchburn, Blackett. *Superbiking: A Manual for Fast Street Riding*. London: Osprey Publishing, 1983.

Domokos, D., and Len Weed. *Wheelyin' With the King*. Tarzana, Calif.: Cleansheet, 1980.

Donaldson, Sandra, ed. *Car and Cycle Stories from Sports Illustrated*. Middletown, Conn.: Xerox, 1972.

Drake, Albert. *Riding Bike in the Fifties*. N.p.: Stone, 1973.

Dunbar, Leila. *Motorcycle Collectibles*. Atglen, Pa.: Schiffer, 1996.

Dyson, John. *The Motorcycling Book*. New York: Penguin, 1977.

Edmonds, I. G. *Motorcycling for Beginners, A Manual for Safe Riding*. Hollywood, Calif.: Wilshire, 1972.

———. *Minibikes and Minicycles*. N.p.: Archway, 1975.

Edwards, C., ed. *Daily Mail Motorcycling Guide, 1952*. London: Associated Newspaper, 1952.

———, ed. *Daily Mail Motorcycling Guide, 1955*. London: Associated Newspaper, 1955.

Engel, Lyle Kenyon. *The Complete Motorcycle Book*. New York: Four Winds, 1974.

———. *The Complete Book of Minibikes and Minicycles*. New York: Arco Publishing, 1975.

English, Richard, and Mopsa. *Full Circle*. Sparkford, England: Haynes, 1989.

Falco, Charles. *Motorcycling at the Turn of the Century*. Tucson: Star Press, 1995.

Farren, Mick. *The Black Leather Jacket*. New York: Abbeville, 1985.

Felsen, Henry Gregor. *Living With Your First Motorcycle*. New York: Berkley, 1976.

Ferrar, Ann. *Hear Me Roar: Women, Motorcycles, and the Rapture of the Road*. New York: Crown, 1996.

Forsdyke, Graham. *The Love of Motorcycling*. London: Octopus, 1977.

Frazier, Gregory W. *Motorcycle Sex, or Freud Would Never Understand the Relationship Between Me and My Motorcycle*. Denver: Arrowstar, 1994.

Fulton, Robert E., Jr. *One Man Caravan*. New York: Harcourt Brace, 1937.

Garfinkel, Martin. *Sturgis, South Dakota: Motorcycle Mecca*. Carbondale, Colo.: ZG Publishing Company, 1990.

Garnier, Peter. *The Motor Cycling Club*. London: David and Charles, 1989.

Gawne, Jack. *Motor Cycle Moonshine*. Birmingham, England: The T.T. Special, ca. 1950.

———. *Gawne Crazy*. Birmingham, England: The T.T. Special, ca. 1952.

Gibson-Downs, S., and C. Gentry. *Motorcycle Toys: Identification and Values*. Paducah, Ky.: Collector Books, 1995.

Gordon, J., and C. *Three Lands on Three Wheels*. N.p.: Harrap, 1932.

Grant, Malcolm, and Harold H. Paynting, eds. *The James Flood Book of Motorcycling in Australia 1899–1980*. Footscray, Australia: James Flood Charity Trust, 1982.

Gray, Jack. *Motorcycling Through the Thirties*. Romford, England: Gannet Books, 1995.

Guevara, Ernesto Che. *The Motorcycle Diaries*. Trans. Ann Wright. London: Verso, 1995.

Gutkind, Lee. *Bike Fever*. Chicago: Follett, 1973.

Hampton, William. *Expert Motorcycling*. Chicago: Contemporary, 1979.

Hanrahan, Byran. *Bikes and Bikies*. N.p.: Lansdowne, 1974.

Harris, Maz. *Bikers: Birth of a Modern Day Outlaw*. London: Faber & Faber, 1985.

Harrison, J. *How to Ride a Motor Cycle*. London: Percival Marshall, ca. 1927.

Hauser, Marc, and Judy Robb. *Road Pirates*. Chicago: Chicago Review, 1991.

Heath, F. P. *Buyer's Guide to Used Motor-Cycles and Scooters*. London: Cassell, 1967.

Hicks, Roger W. *Motorcycle Touring in Europe*. Glasgow: William Collins Sons and Company, 1985.

Hollern, Susie. *Women and Motorcycling*. Freeville, N.Y.: Hollern, 1992.

Holmes, Tim, and Rebekka Smith. *Collecting, Restoring and Riding Classic Motor Cycles*. Cambridge, England: Patrick Stephens, 1986.

———. *Collecting, Restoring and Riding Classic Motorcycles*. N.p.: Bookmart, 1995.

Hopwood, Bert. *Whatever Happened to the British Motorcycle Industry?* Sparkford, England: Haynes, 1981.

Howard, Dennis. *An Old Motor Kaleidoscope of Motor Cycling*. N.p.: Old Motor Mag, 1977.

Hudgeons, T. E., ed. *Official Collector's Price Report*. Orlando, Fla.: House of Collectibles, 1983.

Hung, Christopher. *Sparring With Charlie: Motorbiking down the Ho Chi Minh Trail*. New York: Anchor-Doubleday, 1996.

Hurdle, David. *Motorcycling: Time to Apply the Brakes?* London: Center for Independent Transportation, 1997.

Hylands, George J. *Fifty Years on British Bikes*. London: Minerva, 1997.

Irving, Phil. *Rich Mixture*. Surrey Hills, Australia: Vincent Publications, 1976.

———. *Black Smoke*. Surrey Hills, Australia: Research Publications, 1978.

Ixion [B. H. Davies]. *Motor Cycle Reminiscences*. London: Iliffe & Sons, ca. 1920.

———. *Further Motor Cycle Reminiscences*. London: Iliffe & Sons, ca. 1928.

———. *Motor Cycle Cavalcade*. London: Iliffe & Sons, 1950.

Jackson, Bob. *How To Ride to Save Your Hide Street Biking*. Tucson: HP Books, 1980.

Jones, Bernard E., ed. *Motor Cycles: A Practical Handbook*. London: Cassell, 1915.

Kaysing, William. *Intelligent Motorcycling*. Long Beach, Calif.: Parkhurst, 1966.

Koerner, Steve. "Trade Unionism and Collective Bargaining at Two British Motorcycle Factories." Master's thesis, University of Warwick, ca. 1993.

Ladd, James. *The White Helmets*. Sparkford, England: Haynes, 1977.

The Lady Drives. N.p.: Royal Enfield, 1917.

Lange, Eitel and Rolf. *Around the World with Motorcycle and Camera*. Los Angeles: Floyd Clymer, 1957.

Lavigne, Yves. *Hell's Angels: Three Can Keep a Secret If Two Are Dead*. Secaucus, N.J.: Lyle Stuart, 1996.

Lovin, Roger. *The Complete Motorcycle Nomad*. Boston: Little, Brown, 1974.

Lucas, Frederick. *English-French and French-English Dictionary of the Motor Car, Cycle, and Boat*. N.p.: Spon, 1905.

Lyon, Danny. *The Bikeriders*. New York: Macmillan, 1968.

Malins, Geoffrey. *Going Further*. London: Elkin Mathews Marrot, 1931.

Manly, H. P. *The Motor Cycle Handbook*. N.p.: Drake, 1920.

Mann, D., and R. Main. *Races, Chases and Crashes*. Osceola, Wis.: Motorbooks International, 1994.

Manners for Motorcyclists. Los Angeles: Floyd Clymer, ca. 1965.

Marriott, Andrew, ed. *Barry Sheene's Book of Motor Cycling*. Knutsford, England: Stafford Pemberton, 1978.

Marriott, Michael. *Two-Up by Scooter to Australia*. London: Travel Book Club, 1960.

———. *The Handbook for Motorcyclists and Scooter Owners*. London: Hamlyn Publishing, 1964.

Masters, A. St. J. *Motor Cycling Holidays Abroad*. London: C. Arthur Pearson, 1957.

McClure, M. *Freewheelin Frank: Secretary of the Angels*. N.p.: Grove, 1967.

McIntyre. *Motorcycling Today*. N.p.: Barker, 1963.

McLintock, J.D. *Come Motor-Cycling With Me*. 2nd ed. London: Fred Muller, 1960.

The MC Staff. *How and Where to Tour by Motorcycle and Cyclecar*. London: Temple Press, ca. 1914.

———. *Art of Driving a Motorcycle*. 1st ed. London: Temple Press, 1915.

———. *Art of Driving a Motorcycle*. 3rd ed. London: Temple Press, 1920.

Melling, Frank. *Ride It! The Complete Book of Trail Bike Riding*. Sparkford, England: Haynes, 1978.

———. *All About Motorcycles*. Sparkford, England: Haynes, 1992.

Mercer, Ian. *Europe on Wheels*. London: Power and Pedal, 1957.

The Methods of the Experts. London: Iliffe & Sons, 1956.

Miles, J., and N. Tennant, eds. *Talking Bikes*. London: Macdonald, 1979.

Miller-Bohman, Cyndi, Patricia Doerman, and Alan L. Doerman, eds. *A. D. Farrow Uncrated, Pages of History*. Columbus, Ohio: A. D. Farrow, 1997.

Minton, David, ed. *The Complete Motorcyclist's Handbook*. New York: Simon and Schuster, 1981.

———, ed. *The Complete Motorcyclist's Handbook*. N.p.: Marshall Editions, 1981.

Mo-Peds and Scooters. N.p., ca. 1960.

Morley, Don. *Crescent Color Guide to Motorcycling*. London: Crescent, 1982.

Mortimer, Charles. *The Constant Search: Collecting Motoring and Motorcycling Books*. Sparkford, England: Haynes, 1982.

The Motor Cycle Diary, 1949. London: Iliffe & Sons, 1949.

Motorcycle Industry Council. *Motorcycle Statistical Annual 1993*. Irvine, Calif.: Motorcycle Industry Council, 1993.

Motor Cycle Roadcraft. 2nd ed. London: Her Majesty's Stationery Office, 1973.

Motor Cycle Route Book for the British Isles. London: Iliffe & Sons, ca. 1920s.

Motor Cycling Diary, 1951. London: Temple Press, 1951.

Newell, Malcolm. *Streetwise: The Alternative Motorcycle Survival Manual*. London: Osprey Publishing, 1989.

Nicholson, J. Bernie. *How to Ride a Motorcycle, Including Trouble Tracing*. Los Angeles: Floyd Clymer, ca. 1965.

———. *Motorcycling with Safety*. 2nd ed. Calgary: Nicholson Foundation, ca. 1990.

Noble, Dudley. *Teach Yourself Motor Cycling*. London: England University Press, 1956.

———. *Teach Yourself Motorcycling and Scootering for Beginners*. London: England University Press, 1961.

Norman, Mick. *Angels from Hell: The Angel Chronicles*. N.p.: Creation, 1994.

Osborne, Bernal. *Motorcycling Abroad*. London: Temple Press, 1956.

———. *Your Scooter: How to Choose, Manage and Maintain It*. London: Temple Press, 1960.

Periam, Gerard. *How to Start Motorcycling*. London: MC News, 1964.

Perry, Robin. *The Woods Rider*. New York: Crown, 1973.

———. *The Road Rider*. New York: Crown, 1974.

Phoenix [Charles S. Lake]. *How to Drive a Motor Cycle*. London: Percival Marshall, ca. 1915.

Pierson, Melissa Holbrook. *The Perfect Vehicle: What It Is About Motorcycles*. New York: W. W. Norton, 1997.

Poteet, Lewis and Jim. *Car and Motorcycle Slang*. Quebec: Pigwidgeon, 1992.

Quinn, Paul. *The Yellow Motorbike*. Polegate, England: Paul Quinn, 1982.

Rafferty, Tod. *Harley Memorabilia*. Edison, N.J.: Chartwell, 1997.

Reid, Peter C., and Don Lehrbaum. *The Motorcycle Book*. Garden City, N.Y.: Doubleday, 1967.

Richmond, Dave. *The Book of the Motorcycle*. London: Ward Lock, 1979.

Richmond, Doug. *How to Select, Ride and Maintain Your Trail Bike*. Tucson: HP Books, 1972.

Robinson, Ed. *Old Timer's Motorcycle Tall Tales*. Delaware, Ohio: Knightwood, 1996.

Rogers, Jim. *Investment Biker*. New York: Random House, 1994.

Rothe, Jon P., and Peter J. Cooper, eds. *Motorcyclists: Image and Reality*. Vancouver: Insurance Corp., 1987.

Rowland, Elijah. *Economical Motor Cycling*. London: J. M. Ouseley, ca. 1914.

Sagnier, Thierry. *Bike! Motorcycles and the People Who Ride Them*. New York: Harper and Row, 1974.

Salinger, Peter H. *Motorcycling and the New Enthusiast*. New York: Grosset & Dunlap, 1973.

Sanford, Bob. *Riding the Dirt*. Newport Beach, Calif.: Bond-Parkhurst, 1972.

Sands, Jack M. *The Motorcycle Marines: An Illustrated History*. Bloomfield, N.J.: Portrayal Press, 1984.

Sato, Ikuya. *Kamikaze Biker: Parody and Anomy in Affluent Japan*. London: University of Chicago, 1991.

Sauer, J. L., and D. R. Hobart, eds. *Motorcycle Manual*. N.p.: Motorcycle Illustrated, ca. 1912.

Schleicher, Robert. *Model Car, Truck, and Motorcycle Handbook*. Philadelphia: Chilton, 1978.

Scott, Chris. *Desert Biking*. 2nd ed. London: Travellers' Bookshop, 1995.

———. *Desert Travels: Motorcycle Journeys in the Sahara and West Africa*. London: Travellers' Bookshop, 1996.

———. *The Adventure Motorbiking Handbook*. N.p., ca. 1997.

Setright, L.J.K. *Motorcycling Facts and Feats: A Guinness Superlatives Book*. Enfield, England: Guinness
        Superlatives, 1979.

————, ed. *Twistgrip*. London: Allen and Unwin, 1969.

Shannon, Alyn. *Women of the Road*. Minneapolis: Shannon, 1995.

Shedenhelm, W.R.C. *Motorcycle and Trailbike Handbook*. New York: Pyramid, 1973.

————. *Motorcycle and Trailbike Handbook*. New York: Pyramid, 1976.

————. *Motorcycle and Trailbike Handbook*. New York: Pyramid, 1977.

Shepherd, C. K. *Across America by Motor Cycle*. N.p.: Arnold, 1922.

Sheppard, Tom. *Motor Cycle as an Expedition Tool*. N.p.: Expedition Advisor, 1988.

Sheridan, Clare. *Across Europe with Satanella*. N.p.: Duckworth, 1925.

Shilton, Neale. *A Million Miles Ago*. Sparkford, England: Haynes, 1982.

Shipman, Carl. *The Boonie Book*. 2nd ed. Tucson: HP Books, 1974.

Shreve, Herbie. *Riding the Crossroads*. Hatfield, Ark.: Christian Motorcyclists Association, 1995.

Sieman, Rick. *Monkey Butt!* Baja, Calif.: Sieman, 1995.

Simon, Ted. *Jupiter's Travels*. Garden City, N.Y.: Doubleday, 1980.

————. *Riding Home*. Harmondsworth, England: Viking, 1984.

Smith, Anthony. *High Street Africa*. London: Allen & Unwin, 1961.

————. *Smith and Son*. London: Hodder and Stoughton, 1984.

Soboleff [Sobolev], I.S.K. *Cossack at Large*. N.p.: Davies, 1960.

Sobolev, I.S.K. *Nansen Passport: Round the World on a Motor-Cycle*. N.p.: Bell, 1936.

Stermer, Bill. *Motorcycle Touring*. Tucson: HP Books, 1982.

Stewart, Dorothy G., ed. *"Going Some" 1913: A True Adventure*. Bridgeport, Calif.: D and D Enterprises, 1992.

Stratil-Sauer, G. *From Leipzig to Cabul*. N.p.: Hutchinson, ca. 1928.

Streano, Vince. *Touching America with Two Wheels*. New York: Random House, 1974.

Stuart, Johnny. *Rockers!* London: Plexus, 1987.

Sucher, Harry V. *Inside American Motorcycling*. Laguna Niguel, Calif.: Infosport, 1995.

Swallow, Tom. *Flywheel: Memories of the Open Road*. N.p.: Webb and Bower, 1987.

Thacker, Bill. *Rocker Box: A Collection of The Cartoons of Bill Thacker*. N.p., ca. 1985.

Thompson, Hunter S. *Hell's Angels*. New York: Ballantine, 1967.

Thiffault, Mark, ed. *Motorcycle Digest*. Chicago: Follett, 1972.

Thoeming, Peter, and Peter Rae. *Motorcycle Touring*. London: Osprey Publishing, 1982.

Thorpe, John. *Motor Cycling Guide to the Driving Test*. London: Temple Press, 1958.

————. *Motorcycling Manual*. London: Hamlyn Publishing, 1979.

Tobey, Peter W., ed. *Two Wheel Travel: Motorcycle Camping and Touring*. New Canaan, Conn.: Tobey, 1972.

The Trader Handbook 1949. 43rd ed. London: Iliffe & Sons, 1949.

Vermps, Philippe. *Straightening Out the Corners*. Boca Raton, Fla.: Iris, 1989.

Wagner, Wiltz, and Bill Brokaw. *How to Ride a Trail Bike*. Colorado Springs: Wagner/Brokaw, ca. 1970.

Wallace, Carlton. *Motor Cyclist's Pocket Book*. London: Evans Brothers, 1954.

Wallach, Theresa. *Easy Motorcycle Riding*. New York: Sterling, 1970.

Ward, Patrick. *Bike Riders*. London: W. H. Smith, 1981.

Warren, Lady. *Through Algeria and Tunisia*. N.p.: Cape, 1922.

Warth, Thomas E. *The Car Book Value Guide*. 1996 ed. Marine on St. Croix, Minn.: T. E. Warth, 1996.

Watson, W.H.L. *Adventures of a Despatch Rider*. N.p.: Blackwood, 1915.

Wilde, Sam. *Barbarians on Wheels*. Secaucus, N.J.: Chartwell, 1977.

Williamson, Mitch. *Safe Riding*. New York: Everest, 1980.

Wilson, James C. *Three-Wheeling through Africa*. 1st ed. New York: Bobbs Merrill, 1936.

Wineland, Lynn, ed. *The Complete Book of Motorcycling*. Hollywood, Calif.: Hot Rod, 1964.

Wyatt, Horace M., ed. *Motor Cyclists' ABC*. London: Newnes, 1916.

Wyatt, John H. *Motorcycling*. N.p.: C. G. Harrap, 1925.

Yeager, Trisha. *How to be Sexy with Bugs in Your Teeth*. Chicago: Contemporary, 1978.

Zonker, Patricia. *Murdercycles: The Facts about America's Number One Blood Sport*. Chicago: Nelson-Hall, 1978.

INDIVIDUAL MARQUES

Aermacchi

Walker, Mick. *Aermacchi*. Great Britain: Transport, 1995.

AJS

Bacon, Roy. *AJS and Matchless: The Postwar Models*. London: Osprey Publishing, 1983.

———. *AJS and Matchless Postwar Twins, 1948–1969*. Ventor, England: Niton Publishing, 1989.

———. *AJS and Matchless Postwar Singles, 1945–1969*. Ventor, England: Niton Publishing, 1990.

Clarke, R. M., ed. *AJS and Matchless Gold Portfolio, 1945–1966*. Cobham, England: Brooklands, 1997.

Grant, Gregor. *AJS: The History of a Great Motorcycle*. Cambridge, England: Patrick Stephens, 1974.

Main-Smith, Bruce. *The First AMC Racing Scene*. Leatherhead, England: Bruce Main-Smith, 1980.

Mills, S. J. *AJS of Wolverhampton*. Sutton, England: S. J. Mills, 1994.

Redman, Martin. *Illustrated AJS and Matchless Buyer's Guide*. Bourne End, England: Aston, 1993.

Manuals

Emmott, Jack. *A Jack Emmott Book of Engines: AJS 7R and Matchless G45–G50*. London: Emmott, 1964.

Haycraft, W. C. *The Book of the AJS*. 1st ed., with supplement. London: Sir I. Pitman & Sons, 1928.

———. *The Book of the AJS*. 4th ed. London: Sir I. Pitman & Sons, 1935.

———. *The Book of the AMC Singles*. London: Sir I. Pitman & Sons, 1973.

Neil, F. *AJS and Matchless Single Motorcycles (1948–1966)*. Chislehurst, England: Lodgemark, ca. 1970.

Neil, F. *AJS and Matchless Twin Motorcycles (1955–1965)*. Chislehurst, England: Lodgemark, ca. 1970.

Neil, F. *Service and Overhaul Manual for the AJS and Matchless Single Motorcycles (1957–1966)*. Chislehurst, England: Lodgemark, ca. 1970.

Neill, F. W. *AJS Motor Cycles*. London: C. Arthur Pearson, 1948.

Ariel

Bacon, Roy. *Ariel: The Postwar Models*. London: Osprey Publishing, 1983.

———. *Ariel Leader and Arrow*. Ventor, England: Niton Publishing, 1990.

Harper, Roy. *Ariel Square Four Super Profile*. Sparkford, England: Haynes, 1984.

Hartley, Peter. *The Ariel Story*. Watford, England: Argus, 1980.

Main-Smith, Bruce. *The First Classic Ariel Scene*. Leatherhead, England: Bruce Main-Smith, 1981.

Manuals

Davison, G. S. *The Book of the Ariel*. 4th ed. London: Sir I. Pitman & Sons, 1932.

Haycraft, W. C. *The Book of the Ariel*. 7th ed. Los Angeles: Floyd Clymer, 1947.

———. *The Book of the Ariel Leader and Arrow*. London: Sir I. Pitman & Sons, 1964.

Waller, C. W. *Ariel Motor Cycles: A Practical Guide Covering All Models from 1933*. Los Angeles: Floyd Clymer, ca. 1952.

Benelli

Ainscoe, Raymond. *Benelli Grand Prix Motorcycles*. Osceola, Wis.: Motorbooks International, 1993.

Ainscoe, Raymond, and G. Perrone. *Benelli Road Racers*. Ilkley, England: Ilkley Racing, 1995.

Walker, Mick. *Benelli*. Ipswitch, England: Transport, 1995.

Bianchi

Gentile, Antonio. *Edoardo Bianchi*. Milan: Giorgio Nada, 1992.

Blackburne

Collin, Eddie. *The History of Blackburne Engines and Some of the Motorcycle Manufacturers Who Used Their Engines*. Grantham, England: Collin, ca. 1987.

BMW

Bacon, Roy. *BMW Twins and Singles*. London: Osprey Publishing, 1986.

———. *BMW Postwar Models Twins and Singles*. Ventor, England: Niton Publishing, 1991.

———. *The Illustrated Motorcycle Legends*. Secaucus, N.J.: Chartwell, 1994.

Croucher, Robert. *The Story of BMW Motor Cycles*. Cambridge, England: Patrick Stephens, 1982.

Dymock, Eric. *BMW*. New York: Orion, 1990.

Frostick, Michael. *BMW: The Bavarian Motor Works*. London: Dalton Watson, 1976.

Härtel, Heinz. *BMW-Motorräder: Typen und Technik*. Munich: Ariel Verlag, 1976.

Harper, Roy. *BMW R69 and R69S Super Profile*. Sparkford, England: Haynes, 1983.

Knittel, S., and R. Slabon. *Illustrated BMW Motorcycle Buyer's Guide*. Osceola, Wis.: Motorbooks International, 1990.

Minton, David, ed. *The BMW Story*. London: Phoebus, 1979.

Morley, D., and M. Woollett. *Classic Motorcycles: BMW*. London: Osprey Publishing, 1992.

Setright, L.J.K. *Bahnstormer: The Story of BMW Motorcycles*. Brentford, England: Transport Bookman, 1977.

Piekalkiewicz, J. *BMW Motorcycles in World War Two*. Atglen, Pa.: Schiffer, 1991.

Preston, Bruce. *BMW: The Complete Story*. Ramsbury, England: Crowood Press, 1990.

Slabon, Roland. *How To Restore Your BMW Motorcycle Twins 1950–1969*. Osceola, Wis.: Motorbooks International, 1994.

Walker, M. *BMW Twins Restoration*. London: Osprey Publishing, 1992.

Walker, M., and P. Dobson. *BMW K-Series Motorcycles*. Sparkford, England: Haynes, 1989.

Brough-Superior

Allen, C. E., ed. *Brough-Superior from 1923*. Bideford, England: Bay View, 1990.

Clark, Ronald H. *Brough-Superior: The Rolls-Royce of Motorcycles*. Norwich, England: Goose, 1964.

———. *Brough-Superior: The Rolls-Royce of Motorcycles*. Sparkford, England: Haynes, 1984.

Gibbard, Bill. *Maintaining Your Brough Superior*. N.p.: Brough Superior Club, ca. 1960.

Simms, Colin. *Brough-Superior SS100 Super Profile*. Sparkford, England: Haynes, 1984.

BSA

Bacon, Roy. *BSA Twins and Triples: The Postwar A7/A10, A50/A65, and Rocket III*. London: Osprey Publishing, 1980.

———. *BSA Gold Star and Other Singles*. London: Osprey Publishing, 1982.

———. *BSA A7/A10 Twins: All Models, 1946–1963*. Ventor, England: Niton Publishing, 1989.

———. *BSA Bantam: All Models*. Ventor, England: Niton Publishing, 1989.

———. *BSA A50/A65 Twins: All Models, 1962–1972*. Ventor, England: Niton Publishing, 1990.

———. *BSA Unit Singles: C15 to B50, 1958–1973*. Ventor, England: Niton Publishing, 1990.

———. *Illustrated BSA Buyer's Guide*. Ventor, England: Niton Publishing, 1990.

———. *BSA Pre-Unit Singles: B, C, and M Ranges*. Ventor, England: Niton Publishing, 1991.

———. *BSA Rocket 3 and Triumph Trident, 1968–1976*. Ventor, England: Niton Publishing, 1991.

Bacon, Roy. *The Illustrated Motorcycle Legends: BSA*. London: Sunburst Books, 1995.

Clark, R. M., ed. *BSA Twins A7 and A10 Gold Portfolio, 1946–1962*. Cobham, England: Brooklands, ca. 1996.

———, ed. *BSA Twins, A50 and A65 Gold Portfolio, 1962–1973*. Cobham, England: Brooklands, ca. 1996.

Clew, Jeff. *BSA Bantam Super Profile*. Sparkford, England: Haynes, 1983.

Cycle World. *Cycle World on BSA 1962–1971*. Cobham, England: Brooklands, 1987.

Falco, Charles. *The Gold Star Buyer's Companion*. Ventura, Calif.: Pacific Motorbooks Press, 1996.

Gardner, John. *BSA Goldstar Super Profile*. Sparkford, England: Haynes, 1985.

Golland, A. *Goldie: The Development History of the Gold Star BSA*. Sparkford, England: Haynes, 1978.

Holliday, Bob. *Story of BSA Motorcycles*. Cambridge, England: Patrick Stephens, 1978.

Main-Smith, Bruce. *The Gold Star Book*. Leatherhead, England: Bruce Main-Smith, 1974.

———. *The First Classic BSA Scene*. Leatherhead, England: Bruce Main-Smith, 1982.

Morley, Don. *Classic Motorcycles: BSA*. London: Osprey Publishing, 1991.

Parkhurst, Joe. *A Hurricane Named Vetter: The Story of the Last BSA Motorcycle*. N.p.: Vetter, 1978.

Report on Strip Examination of Motor Cycle G.S. Mk. I (BSA B40). Ref. no. VS 819. Farnborough, England: Government Inspection, 1969.

Ryerson, Barry. *The Giants of Small Heath: The History of BSA*. Sparkford, England: Haynes, 1980.

Vanhouse, Norman. *BSA Competition History*. Sparkford, England: Haynes, 1986.

Ward, Donovan M. *The Other Battle*. N.p.: BSA, 1946.

Wright, Owen. *BSA M20 and M21 Super Profile*. Sparkford, England: Haynes, 1985.

———. *BSA A7 and A10 Twins Super Profile*. Sparkford, England: Haynes, 1984.

———. *BSA: The Complete Story*. Ramsbury, England: Crowood Press, 1992.

Manuals

Bacon, Roy. *BSA Twin Restoration*. London: Osprey Publishing, 1986.

———. *BSA Singles Restoration*. London: Osprey Publishing, 1988.

B.S.A. Motorcycles 1935–1940. London: Temple Press, 1958.

BSA Motorcycles 1935–1940. 1959. Reprint, Leatherhead, England: Bruce Main-Smith, 1974.

Waysider [F. J. Camm]. *The Book of the BSA*. 1st ed., with author's notes. London: Sir I. Pitman & Sons, 1924.

Chilton's BSA 250, 500, 650, and 750 Unit Construction. Philadelphia: Chilton, 1972.

Daniels, Marcus. *BSA Singles Owners Workshop Manual*. Sparkford, England: Haynes, 1986.

Darlington, Mansur. *BSA Pre-Unit Singles*. Sparkford, England: Haynes, 1977.

Haycraft, W. C. *The Book of the BSA*. 9th ed. London: Sir I. Pitman & Sons, 1939.

———. *The Book of the BSA*. Los Angeles: Floyd Clymer, 1947.

———. *The Book of the BSA Bantam*. London: Sir I. Pitman & Sons, 1956.

———. *The Book of the BSA*. 15th ed. London: Sir I. Pitman & Sons, 1961.

———. *The Book of the BSA Twins (1948–62)*. 2nd ed. London: Sir I. Pitman & Sons, 1963.

———. *The Book of the BSA (B and M)*. 17th ed. London: Sir I. Pitman & Sons, 1971.

———. *The Book of the BSA Bantam*. London: Sir I. Pitman & Sons, 1972.

Lupton, A. G. *The Second Book of the BSA Twins (1962–69)*. London: Sir I. Pitman & Sons, ca. 1970.

———. *The Book of the 250cc BSA*. London: Sir I. Pitman & Sons, 1973.

Munro, D. W. *BSA Motor Cycles*. 2nd ed. London: C. Arthur Pearson, 1950.

———. *BSA Motor Cycles*. 3rd ed. London: C. Arthur Pearson, 1951.

———. *BSA Twin Motor Cycles*. 2nd ed. London: C. Arthur Pearson, 1960.

Reynolds, Mark. *Owner's Workshop Manual: BSA A50 and A65 Series, 1962–1973*. Sparkford, England: Haynes, 1974.

Ritch, OCee. *Chilton's BSA Repair and Tune-Up Guide: A, B, C and M Group Models*. Philadelphia: Chilton, 1968.

Thorpe, John. *The Book of the BSA Sunbeam and Triumph Tigress Motor Scooters*. London: Sir I. Pitman & Sons, 1967.

Bultaco

Fullgraf, ed. *Two Wheel Horse: The Enjoyment of Dynamic Balance*. Barcelona: Fullgraf, 1971.

Herros, Francisco. *Bultaco: La pasion por el deporte*. Barcelona: Moto Retro, 1992.

Manuals

Jorgensen, E., ed. *Bultaco 125–370cc Singles through 1977*. Los Angeles: Floyd Clymer, ca. 1980.

CCM

Lawless, Bill. *Rolling Thunder: The History of the BSA-Based CCM Four-Strokes*. Newport, Wales: Willow, 1990.

Chater-Lea

Collin, Eddie. *The History of Chater-Lea*. Grantham, England: Collin, ca. 1987.

Cotton

Collin, Eddie. *The Chronicle of the Cotton*. Grantham, England: Collin, 1987.

Coventry-Eagle

Collin, Eddie. *The History of Coventry-Eagle*. Grantham, England: Collin, ca. 1987.

Cushman

Dregni, Michael, and Eric. *Illustrated Motorscooter Buyer's Guide: Cushman, Vespa, Lambretta and More*. Osceola, Wis.: Motorbooks International, 1993.

Somerville, Bill. *The Complete Guide to Cushman Motor Scooters*. Springfield, Mo.: Cantrell-Barnes, 1988.

———. *A History of the Cushman Eagle*. Springfield, Mo.: Cantrell-Barnes, ca. 1990.

———. *Cushman Photo Album and Scooter Memories*. Springfield, Mo.: Cantrell-Barnes, ca. 1990.

DKW

Knittel, Stefan. *DKW Motorräder, 1949–1958*. Munich: Schrader, 1988.

———. *DKW Motorräder, 1922–1939*. Munich: Schrader, 1993.

Douglas

Briercliffe, H., and E. Brockway. *The Illustrated History of Douglas Motorcycles*. Sparkford, England: Haynes, 1991.

Carrick, Peter. *Douglas*. Cambridge, England: Patrick Stephens, 1982.

Clew, Jeff. *Douglas: The Best Twin*. Norwich, England: Goose, 1974.

———. *The Douglas Motorcycle*. Rev. ed. Sparkford, England: Haynes, 1981.

Frost, Doug. *Douglas Motor Cycle Range, 1907–1926*. N.p.: Frost, ca. 1979.

———. *Douglas Motor Cycle Range, 1927–1939*. N.p.: Frost, ca. 1979.

———, ed. *Douglas Motor Cycle Range, Mark Series 1945 to 1957*. N.p.: Frost, ca. 1979.

Manuals

Heathcote, Leslie K. *The Book of the Douglas*. 6th ed. London: Sir I. Pitman & Sons, 1948.

Knott, E. W. *The Book of the Douglas*. 1st ed. London: Sir I. Pitman & Sons, 1925.

Ducati

Bacon, Roy. *Ducati V-Twins, Bevel-Drive Models*. Ventor, England: Niton Publishing, 1991.

Cathcart, Alan. *Ducati Motorcycles*. London: Osprey Publishing, 1983.

———. *Ducati: The Untold Story*. London: Osprey Publishing, 1987.

Clarke, R. M., ed. *Ducati Gold Portfolio, 1960–1973*. Cobham, England: Brooklands, ca. 1996.

———, ed. *Ducati Gold Portfolio, 1974–1978*. Cobham, England: Brooklands, ca. 1996.

Conti, Paolo. *Ducati Super Bikes: 851, 888, 916*. Osceola, Wis.: Motorbooks International, 1995.

Cycle World. *Cycle World On Ducati: 1962–1980*. Cobham, England: Brooklands, 1987.

Cycle World. *Cycle World On Ducati: 1982–1991*. Cobham, England: Brooklands, 1993.

Ducati, Bruno Cavalieri. *Storia della Ducati*. Bologna: Editografica, 1991.

Ducati, Style-Sophistication-Performance, A Retrospective. N.p.: CNA Press, 1994.

Falloon, Ian. *The Ducati Story*. Cambridge, England: Patrick Stephens, 1996.

Walker, Mick. *Ducati Singles*. London: Osprey Publishing, 1985.

———. *Ducati Twins*. London: Osprey Publishing, 1985.

———. *Ducati Desmo: The Making of a Masterpiece*. London: Osprey Publishing, 1989.

———. *Illustrated Ducati and Cagiva Buyer's Guide*. Bourne End, England: Aston, 1989.

———. *Ducati Singles Restoration*. London: Osprey Publishing, 1991.

———. *Ducati Twins Restoration*. London: Osprey Publishing, 1993.

———. *Ducati*. London: Osprey Publishing, 1993.

———. *Illustrated Ducati Buyer's Guide*. 2nd ed. Osceola, Wis.: Motorbooks International, 1994.

Manuals

Cox, Penny, and Matthew Coombs. *Ducati 600, 750 and 900 2-Valve V-Twins*. Sparkford, England: Haynes, 1996.

Cycleserv. *Servicing Ducati Motorcycles: 750 GT/Sport, 860*. Sydney, Australia: Cycleserv, 1975.

Eke, Stephen. *Ducati Tuning: V-Twins with Bevel Drive Camshafts*. Chislehurst, England: Lodgemark, 1986.

Excelsior

Collin, Eddie. *The History of Excelsior*. Grantham, England: Grantley, 1987.

Francis-Barnett

Manuals

Goddard, J. H. *Francis-Barnett Motor Cycles*. London: C. Arthur Pearson, 1961.

Gilera

Ainscoe, Raymond. *Gilera Road Racers*. London: Osprey Publishing, 1987.

Colombo, Sandro. *Gilera Quattro: Technica e storia*. Milan: Automototecnica, 1992.

Greeves

Carrick, B., and M. Walker. *Greeves*. London: Osprey Publishing, 1988.

Conley, Frank F. *Greeves Motorcycles*. Carmel Valley, Calif.: Conley, 1990.

Harley-Davidson

Bacon, Roy. *Illustrated Motorcycle Legends: Harley-Davidson*. London: Sunburst Books, 1995.

Birkitt, Malcolm. *Harley-Davidson*. London: Osprey Publishing, 1992.

———. *Harley-Davidson: A Pictorial Celebration*. Osceola, Wis.: Motorbooks International, 1993.

———. *Harley-Davidson Electra Glide*. London: Osprey Publishing, 1994.

Bolfert, Thomas C. *The Big Book of Harley-Davidson*. Osceola, Wis.: Motorbooks International, 1989.

Bolfert, Thomas C., Buzz Buzzelli, M. B. Chubbuck, and Martin Jack Rosenblum. *Harley Davidson, 1903–1993 Historical Overview*. Milwaukee: Harley-Davidson, 1994.

Briel, Dorthea. *Harley-Davidson*. London: Tiger, 1994.

Buzzelli, Buzz. *Harley-Davidson Sportster Performance Handbook*. Osceola, Wis.: Motorbooks International, 1992.

Caiati, Carl. *Customizing Your Harley*. Blue Ridge Summit, Pa.: TAB, 1993.

Carmona, R. F. *The Iron Stallion: An American Love Story*. Los Angeles: Hirshberg, 1990.

Carroll, John, and G. Stuart. *Harley-Davidson 45s: Workhorse and Warhorse*. London: Osprey Publishing, 1994.

Caroll, John. *The Gatefold Book of Harley-Davidson*. New York: Barnes and Noble, 1997.

Conner, Rick. *Harley-Davidson Data Book*. Osceola, Wis.: Motorbooks International, 1996.

Field, Greg. *Harley-Davidson Panheads*. Osceola, Wis.: Motorbooks International, 1995.

———. *Harley-Davidson Knuckleheads*. Osceola, Wis.: Motorbooks International, 1997.

Foster, Gerald. *Cult of the Harley-Davidson*. London: Osprey Publishing, 1982.

———. *Harley-Davidson: The Cult Lives On*. London: Osprey Publishing, 1984.

———. *Harley-Davidson: The Motorcycle that Built a Legend*. Osceola, Wis.: Motorbooks International, 1986.

Genat, Robert, and Robin. *Harley-Davidson Police Motorcycles*. Osceola, Wis.: Motorbooks International, 1995.

Girdler, Allan. *Illustrated Harley-Davidson Buyer's Guide*. Osceola, Wis.: Motorbooks International, 1986.

———. *Harley Racers*. Osceola, Wis.: Motorbooks International, 1987.

———. *Harley-Davidson XR750: The Complete History*. Osceola, Wis.: Motorbooks International, 1991.

———. *Harley-Davidson: The American Motorcycle*. Osceola, Wis.: Motorbooks International, 1992.

———. *Illustrated Harley-Davidson Buyer's Guide*. 2nd ed. Osceola, Wis.: Motorbooks International, 1992.

Green, William. *Harley-Davidson: The Living Legend*. New York: Crescent, 1993.

Harvard Business School. "AMF-Harley Davidson Motor Company, Inc." Case Study 9-579-153, Rev. 3/79. Cambridge, Mass.: Harvard University, 1979.

Hatfield, Jerry. *Inside Harley-Davidson*. Osceola, Wis.: Motorbooks International, 1990.

———. *Illustrated Buyer's Guide, Harley-Davidson Classics, 1903–1965*. Osceola, Wis.: Motorbooks International, 1997.

Hendry, Maurice D. *Harley-Davidson*. New York: Ballantine, 1972.

Jaspersohn, William. *Motorcycle: The Making of Harley-Davidson*. Boston: Little, Brown and Co., 1984.

Kayama, Tomoko, ed. *Harley-Davidson*. N.p.: Green Arrow, 1992. In Japanese.

Leffingwell, Randy. *Harley-Davidson: Myth and Mystique*. Osceola, Wis.: Motorbooks International, 1995.

Leonard, Grant. *Harley-Davidson: The Legend*. Secaucus, N.J.: Chartwell, 1993.

Ludel, Moses. *Harley-Davidson Evolution V-Twin Owner's Bible*. Cambridge, Mass.: Robert Bentley, 1997.

Mann, Dave. *Harley-Davidson Performance Parts Directory*. Osceola, Wis.: Motorbooks International, 1993.

Marselli, Mark. *Classic Harley-Davidson Big Twins*. Osceola, Wis.: Motorbooks International, 1994.

Middlehurst, Tony. *Harley-Davidson*. New York: Mallard Press, 1990.

Mitchel, Doug. *Harley-Davidson Chronicle*. Lincolnwood, Ill.: Publications International, 1996.

Murphy, Tom. *Harley-Davidson Shovelhead*. Osceola, Wis.: Motorbooks International, 1996.

———. *How to Build Harley-Davidson Horsepower*. Osceola, Wis.: Motorbooks International, 1997.

Norris, Martin. *Rolling Thunder: The Harley-Davidson Legend*. Philadelphia: Courage, 1992.

Palmer, Bruce, III. *How To Restore Your Harley-Davidson*. Osceola, Wis.: Motorbooks International, 1994.

Rafferty, Tod. *Harley-Davidson: The Ultimate Machine*. Philadelphia: Courage, 1994.

———. *The Complete Harley-Davidson: A Model-by-Model History of the American Motorcycle*. Osceola, Wis.: Motorbooks International, 1997.

Reid, Peter C. *Well Made in America: Lessons from Harley-Davidson on Being the Best*. New York: McGraw-Hill, 1990.

Remus, Timothy. *Arlen Ness: Master Harley Customizer*. Osceola, Wis.: Motorbooks International, 1990.

———. *How To Customize Your Harley-Davidson*. Osceola, Wis.: Motorbooks International, 1992.

———. *How to Custom Paint Your Harley-Davidson*. Osceola, Wis.: Motorbooks International, 1994.

———. *Harley-Davidson Customs*. Osceola, Wis.: Motorbooks International, 1995.

Saladini, Albert, and Pascal Szymezak. *Harley-Davidson: History, Meetings, New Models, Custom Bikes*. New York: Barnes and Noble, 1997.

Sarafan, David. *The Liberators: Military Harley-Davidson Motorcycles*. Spring Valley, N.Y.: David Sarafan, 1986.

Schrader, Halwart, and Klaus Vollmar. *Harley-Davidson Motorcycles: Singles and Twins, 1918–78*. West Chester, Pa.: Schiffer, 1990.

Scott, Graham. *Harley-Davidson: A Celebration of the Dream Machine*. Stamford, Conn.: Longmeadow, 1990.

Sucher, Harry V. *Harley-Davidson: The Milwaukee Marvel*. Sparkford, England: Haynes, 1981.

———. *Harley-Davidson: The Milwaukee Marvel*. 4th ed. Sparkford, England: Haynes, 1990.

Vermps, Philippe. *A Pictorial Essay of Harley Owners*. Boca Raton, Fla.: Iris, 1990.

Wagner, Herbert. *Harley-Davidson: 1930–1941*. Atglen, Pa.: Schiffer, 1996.

Wright, David K. *The Harley-Davidson Motor Company: An Official Eighty Year History*. Osceola, Wis.: Motorbooks International, 1987.

———. *The Harley-Davidson Motor Company: An Official Eighty Year History*. 3rd ed. Osceola, Wis.: Motorbooks International, 1993.

Wiesner, Wolfgang. *Harley-Davidson Photographic History*. Osceola, Wis.: Motorbooks International, 1989.

Williams, Mark. *The Classic Harley*. London: Salamander, 1993.

Manuals

Arman, Mike, and Kurt Heinrichs. *Special Tools for Harley-Davidson*. N.p.: M. Arman, 1982.

———. *What Fits What on Harley-Davidson Motorcycles*. N.p.: M. Arman, 1983.

Denish, D. William. *The V-Twin Tuner's Handbook*. Gates Mills, Ohio: Crystal, 1993.

———. *The Big Twin High-Performance Guide*. Gates Mills, Ohio: Crystal, 1994.

Fox, Randy G. *Half-Priced Harley*. Agoura Hills, Calif.: Paisano, 1987.

McClanahan, Carl. *V-Twin Thunder!* N.p.: Arman, 1984.

Murphy, Tom. *Harley-Davidson Big Twin Performance Handbook*. Osceola, Wis.: Motorbooks International, 1995.

Questions and Answers Covering All Harley-Davidson Models. N.p., 1930.

Henderson

Schultz, Richard Henry. *Hendersons: Those Elegant Machines*. Freeman, S.D.: Pine Hill Press, 1994.

Honda

Bacon, Roy. *Honda: The Early Classic Motorcycles*. London: Osprey Publishing, 1985.

———. *The Illustrated Motorcycle Legends: Honda*. London: Sunburst Books, 1995.

Birkitt, Malcolm. *Honda Gold Wing*. London: Osprey Publishing, 1995.

Brown, Roland. *Honda: The Complete Story*. Ramsbury, England: Crowood Press, 1991.

Carrick, Peter. *The Story of Honda Motor Cycles*. Cambridge, England: Patrick Stephens, 1976.

Hilton, Christopher. *Honda: Conquerors of the Track*. Cambridge, England: Patrick Stephens, 1990.

Morley, Don. *Honda Motorcycles—Osprey Color Library*. London: Osprey Publishing, 1993.

Sakiya, Tetsuo. *Honda Motor: The Men, The Management, The Machines*. N.p.: Kodansha, 1982.

Seigo-Ishikura, ed. *Honda Collection*. 4 vols. Tokyo: Neko, 1994–97. In Japanese.

Myers, Chris. *Honda*. New York: Arco Publishing, 1984.

Rae, Peter. *Honda Golden Wing*. London: Osprey Publishing, 1984.

Sanders, Sol. *Honda: The Man and His Machines*. Boston: Little, Brown and Co., 1975.

Sandham, Tony, and John Dickinson. *Four-Stroke Finale? The Honda Trials Story*. Glossop, England: Willow, 1989.

Scott, Michael. *Kimberley's Grand Prix Bike Team Guide No. 2: Honda*. London: Kimberley's, ca. 1986.

Shoemark, Peter. *Honda CB750 SOHC Super Profile*. Sparkford, England: Haynes, 1983.

Shook, Robert L. *Honda: An American Success Story*. Englewood Cliffs, N.J.: Prentice-Hall, 1988.

Vreeke, Ken, ed. *Gold Wing: The First 20 Years*. Westlake Village, Calif.: Honda, 1994.

Walker, Mick. *Honda*. London: Osprey Publishing, 1993.

Woollett, Mick. *Honda*. London: Newness, 1983.

———. *Honda Racers in the Golden Age*. Tokyo: Neko, 1990.

Manuals

Clymer, Floyd. *Honda 50 (C100 and C110) Shop Manual and Handbook*. Los Angeles: Floyd Clymer, ca. 1963.

———. *Honda 750cc Models, 1969–74*. Los Angeles: Floyd Clymer, 1974.

Honda Motorcycle Identification Guide: 1959–1988. N.p.: Honda, 1988.

Robinson, Steve. *Tuning the Honda Four*. N.p.: Robinson, ca. 1995.

Thorpe, John. *The Book of the Honda*. Los Angeles: Floyd Clymer, 1967.

———. *The Book of the Honda Twins*. London: Sir I. Pitman & Sons, 1969.

H.R.D. (see Vincent/H.R.D.)

Humber

Demaus, A. B., and J. C. Tarring. *The Humber Story 1868–1932*. Gloucester, England: Alan Sutton, 1989.

Freeman, Tony. *Humber: An Illustrated History, 1868–1976*. London: Academy, 1991.

Indian

Hatfield, Jerry. *Illustrated Indian Motorcycle Buyer's Guide*. Osceola, Wis.: Motorbooks International, 1989.

———. *Indian Motorcycle Photographic History*. Osceola, Wis.: Motorbooks International, 1993.

———. *Indian Motorcycles Restoration Guide 1932–53*. Osceola, Wis.: Motorbooks International, 1995.

Hatfield, Jerry, and Hans Halberstadt. *Indian Motorcycles*. Osceola, Wis.: Motorbooks International, 1996.

Hamacher and Nicholsen. *Indian Motocycle Patents from Beginning to End*. Springfield, Ohio: M. Hamacher, 1993.

Kanter, Buzz. *Indian Motorcycles*. Osceola, Wis.: Motorbooks International, 1993.

Stuart, Garry, and John Carroll. *Indian*. London: Osprey Publishing, 1994.

Sucher, Harry V. *The Iron Redskin*. Sparkford, England: Haynes, 1977.

J.A.P.

Buchanan, D. J. *The J.A.P. Story 1895–1951*. Tottenham, England: J.A.P., ca. 1951.

Clew, Jeff. *JAP: The Vintage Years*. Sparkford, England: Haynes, 1985.

———. *JAP: The End of an Era*. Sparkford, England: Haynes, 1988.

May, Cyril. *The Story of the Racing J.A.P.* N.p.: Cyril May, n.d.

Manuals

Fenner, A. C., and W. H. Phillips. *The J.A.P. Engine*. London: C. Arthur Pearson, 1952.

Haycraft, W. C. *The Book of the J.A.P.* 3rd ed. London: Sir I. Pitman & Sons, 1951.

Kawasaki

Bacon, Roy. *Kawasaki: Sunrise to Z1*. Ventor, England: Niton Publishing, 1993.

———. *The Illustrated Motorcycle Legends: Kawasaki*. Secaucus, N.J.: Chartwell, 1994.

Carrick, Peter. *The Story of Kawasaki Motor Cycles*. Cambridge, England: Patrick Stephens, 1978.

Walker, Mick. *Kawasaki*. London: Osprey Publishing, 1993.

Manuals

Kawasaki Model Recognition Manual. N.p.: Kawasaki, 1982.

Laverda

Ainscoe, Raymond. *Laverda*. London: Osprey Publishing, 1991.

Borghesi, Massimo. *Registro Laverda 750 SFC Italia*. Milan: Borg Edizioni, 1994.

Clarke, R. M., ed. *Laverda Gold Profile, 1967–1977*. Cobham, England: Brooklands, 1997.

Manuals

Parker, Tim. *Laverda Twins and Triples Repair and Tune-Up Guide*. Stillwater, Minn.: Olive Street, 1993.

Lambretta (see also Cushman)

Cox, Nigel. *Lambretta Innocenti, An Illustrated History*. Sparkford, England: Haynes, 1996.

Sparrow, Andrea and David. *Innocenti Lambretta, Colour Family Album*. Godmanstone, England: Veloce, 1997.

Manuals

Broad, Raymond. *Lambretta*. 2nd ed. London: C. Arthur Pearson, 1967.

Page, Sydney F. *The Cassell Book of the Lambretta (1953–59)*. London: Cassell, 1961.

Warring, R. H. *The Book of the Lambretta Motor-Scooter*. Los Angeles: Floyd Clymer, ca. 1958.

Lea-Francis

Price, Barrie. *The Lea-Francis Story*. London: B. T. Batsford, 1978.

Levis

Collin, Eddie. *The Story of Levis*. Grantham, England: Grantley, 1989.

Matchless

Hartley, Peter. *Matchless*. London: Osprey Publishing, 1981.

Jackson, Keith, and Deryk Wylde. *Matchless G3L and G80 Super Profile*. Sparkford, England: Haynes, 1984.

Manuals

Bacon, Roy. *Matchless and AJS Restoration*. London: Osprey Publishing, 1989.

Matchless Motor Cycles, 1939–1955. London: Temple Press, 1958.

Osborne, Bernal, ed. *Matchless 350 and 500cc Heavyweight Singles 1939–1955*. Leatherhead, England: Bruce Main-Smith, 1976.

Morgan

Alderson, J. D., and D. M. Rushton. *Morgan Sweeps the Board: The Three-Wheeler Story*. London: Gentry, 1978.

Boddy, William. *The Vintage Years of the Morgan Three Wheeler*. London: Grenville, 1970.

Bowden, G. H. *More Morgan: A Pictorial History of the Morgan Sports Car*. New York: Dodd, Mead & Co., 1977.

Clarke, R. M. *Morgan Three-Wheeler Gold Portfolio, 1910–1952*. Cobham, England: Brooklands, ca. 1990.

Manuals

Coombes, Clarrie. *The Best of Clarrie*. Newbury, England: Morgan, ca. 1994.

Douglass, F. H. *Morgan-3-Wheelers: The Matchless Engine*. Ealing, England: Douglas, ca. 1940.

Morgan Restoration and Buying. Beckenham, England: Kelsey, 1992.

Moto G.D.

Ruffini, Enrico. *Moto G.D.* Milan: Giorgio Nada, 1990. In Italian.

Moto Guzzi

Clarke, R. M., ed. *Moto Guzzi Gold Portfolio, 1949–1973*. Cobham, England: Brooklands Books, ca. 1997.

Colombo, Mario. *Moto Guzzi: Genius and Sport*. Milan: Automobilia, 1983.

———. *Moto Guzzi*. Milan: Giorgio Nada, 1990.

Walker, Mick. *Moto Guzzi Twins*. London: Osprey Publishing, 1986.

———. *Moto Guzzi Singles*. London: Osprey Publishing, 1987.

———. *Illustrated Moto Guzzi Buyer's Guide*. Bourne End, England: Aston, 1992.

———. *Moto Guzzi*. London: Osprey Publishing, 1994.

———. *Illustrated Moto Guzzi Buyer's Guide*. 2nd ed. Osceola, Wis.: Motorbooks International, 1995.

Moto MM

Ruffini, Enrico, and Giampaolo Tozzi. *Moto MM*. Milan: Giorgio Nada, 1988. In Italian.

Münch

Scheibe, Winni. *Münch: The Legend Friedel Münch and His Motorcycles*. Rosrath, Germany: Art Motor Verlag, 1995.

MV Agusta

Carrick, Peter. *The Story of MV Agusta Motor Cycles*. Cambridge, England: Patrick Stephens, 1979.

Clew, Jeff. *MV Agusta 750S America Super Profile*. Sparkford, England: Foulis, 1983.

Columbo, Mario, and Roberto Patrignani. *MV Agusta*. Milan: Giorgio Nada, 1991.

———. *Moto MV Agusta*. 2nd ed. Milan: Giorgio Nada, 1997.

Ferdinandsson, Erik. *MV Agusta Italy, 4 DOHC History, 1945–1979*. Smaland, Sweden: Ferdinandsson, 1984.

Spahn, Christian. *MV Agusta: Technik un Geschichte der Rennmotorräder*. Pfäffikon, Switzerland: Serag AG, 1986.

Walker, Mick. *MV Agusta*. London: Osprey Publishing, 1987.

MZ

Leek, Jan. *MZ: The Racers*. Altrincham, England: 650 Publications, 1991.

Walker, Mick. *MZ*. Ipswitch, England: Transport Source Books, 1996.

New Imperial

Collin, Eddie. *The History of New Imperial*. Grantham, England: Collin, ca. 1987.

Manuals

Haycraft, W. C. *The Book of the New Imperial*. 6th ed. London: Sir I. Pitman & Sons, 1952.

Norton

Ayton, Cyril. J. *International Norton Super Profile*. Sparkford, England: Haynes, 1985.

———. *Norton from 1946*. Bideford, England: Bay View, 1988.

Bacon, Roy. *Norton Twins*. London: Osprey Publishing, 1981.

———. *Norton Singles*. London: Osprey Publishing, 1983.

———. *Norton Commando: All Models*. Ventor, England: Niton Publishing, 1989.

———. *Norton Dominator Twins, 1949–1970*. Ventor, England: Niton Publishing, 1990.

———. *Norton Singles OHV and SV*. Ventor, England: Niton Publishing, 1991.

———. *Illustrated Norton Buyer's Guide*. Ventor, England: Niton Publishing, 1991.

———. *The Illustrated Motorcycle Legends: Norton*. London: Sunburst Books, 1996.

Clarke, R. M., ed. *Norton Commando Gold Portfolio, 1968–1977*. Cobham, England: Brooklands, 1996.

Clew, Jeff. *Norton Commando Super Profile*. Sparkford, England: Haynes, 1983.

Cycle World. *Cycle World on Norton 1962–1971*. Cobham, England: Brooklands, 1987.

Holliday, Bob. *The Norton Story*. Rev. ed. Cambridge, England: Patrick Stephens, 1976.

———. *The Unapproachable Norton*. London: Dalton Watson, 1979.

———. *The Norton Story*. 3rd ed. Cambridge, England: Patrick Stephens, 1986.

Howard, Dennis. *Norton*. New York: Ballantine, 1972.

Magrath, D. *Norton, The Complete Story*. Ramsbury, England: Crowood Press, 1991.

Main-Smith, Bruce. *The First Knocker Norton Scene*. Leatherhead, England: Bruce Main-Smith, 1979.

Morley, Don. *Classic Motorcycles: Norton*. London: Osprey Publishing, 1991.

Perkins, Kris. *Norton Rotaries*. London: Osprey Publishing, 1991.

Reynolds, J. *Pictorial History of Norton Motorcycles*. Feltham, England: Temple Press, 1985.

Reynolds, Jim. *Norton: A Racing Legend*. London: Apple, 1995.

Walker, Mick. *Manx Norton*. Bourne End, England: Aston, 1990.

Woolett, Mick. *Norton*. London: Osprey Publishing, 1992.

Manuals

Bacon, Roy. *Norton Twin Restoration*. London: Osprey Publishing, 1987.

Dunstall, Paul. *Norton Tuning*. N.p.: Dunstall, ca. 1970.

Franks, E. M. *Norton*. London: C. Arthur Pearson, 1948.

———. *Norton*. 2nd ed. London: C. Arthur Pearson, 1949.

Garratt, P. L. *Norton*. 5th ed. London: C. Arthur Pearson, 1962.

Haycraft, W. C. *The Book of the Norton*. 4th ed. Los Angeles: Floyd Clymer, 1947.

———. *The Book of the Norton Dominator Twins 1955–65*. London: Sir I. Pitman & Sons, 1966.

Neill, F. *Norton Service and Overhaul Manual, Singles and Twins*. Chislehurst, England: Lodgemark, ca. 1970.

Norton Motorcycles 1928 to 1955. Reprint. London: BMS, ca. 1975.

Robinson, Steve. *Tuning the Norton Twin*. Forncett St. Mary, England: Robinson, 1993.

NSU

Manuals

Waring, R. H. *The Book of the NSU Quickly*. London: Sir I. Pitman & Sons, 1964.

———. *The Book of the NSU Prima*. London: Sir I. Pitman & Sons, 1964.

OEC

Collin, Eddie. *The History of OEC*. Grantham, England: Grantley, 1987.

OK Supreme

Collin, Eddie. *The History of OK Supreme*. Grantham, England: Collin, ca. 1987.

Panther (and P and M)

Jones, Barry M. *The Story of Panther Motorcycles*. Cambridge, England: Patrick Stephens, 1983.

Manuals

Haycraft, W. C. *The Book of the P and M*. 1st ed. London: Sir I. Pitman & Sons, 1927.

———. *The Book of the Red Panther*. 2nd ed. London: Sir I. Pitman & Sons, 1942.

———. *The Book of the Panther (Lightweight Models)*. 4th ed. London: Sir I. Pitman & Sons, 1951.

———. *The Book of the Panther (Heavyweight Models)*. 2nd ed. London: Sir I. Pitman & Sons, 1958.

Raleigh

Mentor [pseud.]. *The Raleigh Handbook*. 3rd ed. London: Sir I. Pitman & Sons, 1930.

Collin, Eddie. *The History of Raleigh*. Grantham, England: Grantley, 1991.

Manuals

Warring, R. H. *The Book of Raleigh Mopeds*. London: Sir I. Pitman & Sons, 1971.

Rex-Acme

Collin, Eddie. *The History of Rex-Acme*. Grantham, England: Grantley, 1988.

Rickman

[Rickman, Don]. "Our Lessons from the USA." Mimeograph. New Milton, England: Rickman, 1967.

Royal Enfield

Bacon, Roy. *Royal Enfield: The Postwar Models*. London: Osprey Publishing, 1982.

Bradford, Anne. *Royal Enfield, From the Bicycle to the Bullet*. Laxey, Isle of Man: Amulree, 1996.

Hartley, Peter. *The Story of Royal Enfield*. Cambridge, England: Patrick Stephens, 1981.

Manuals

Booker, C.A.E. *Royal Enfield Motor Cycles: A Practical Guide Covering All Models from 1937 to 1960*. 6th ed. London: C. Arthur Pearson, 1960.

Haycraft, W. C. *The Book of the Royal Enfield*. 5th ed. London: Sir I. Pitman & Sons, 1953.

———. *The Book of the Royal Enfield*. 6th ed. London: Sir I. Pitman & Sons, 1958.

———. *The Book of the Royal Enfield Crusader*. London: Sir I. Pitman & Sons, 1966.

———. *The Second Book of the Royal Enfield*. London: Sir I. Pitman & Sons, 1972.

Ryder, R. E. [pseud.]. *The Book of the Royal Enfield*. With 1928 supplement. London: Sir I. Pitman & Sons, 1926.

Rudge

Hartley, Peter. *The Story of Rudge Motorcycles*. Cambridge, England: Patrick Stephens, 1985.

Reynolds, Bryan. *Don't Trudge It, Rudge It*. Sparkford, England: Haynes, 1977.

The Rudge Book of the Road. Coventry, England: Rudge Whitworth, ca. 1928.

Manuals

Cade, L. H. *The Book of the Rudge*. 1st ed. London: Sir I. Pitman & Sons, 1929.

Cade, L. H., and F. Anstey. *The Book of the Rudge*. 5th ed. London: Sir I. Pitman & Sons, 1953.

Cushing, Douglas. *Introduction to Rudge Wrinkles 1922*. Easingwold, England: G. H. Smith, 1974.

Ransom, R. P. *Rudge Motor Cycles*. 2nd ed. London: C. Arthur Pearson, 1952.

Scott

Clew, Jeff. *The Scott Motorcycle: The Yowling Two-Stroke*. Sparkford, England: Haynes, 1974.

Shelley, Les. *The First Scott Scene*. Leatherhead, England: Bruce Main-Smith, 1977.

Stevens, George. *Made to Limit Gauge, Pictorial Supplements "A–D."* 4 vols. Coed-y-Park, Wales: G. Stevens, ca. 1965.

Solex

Salvat, Bernard. *Le VeloSolex: La bicyclette qui roule toute seule*. Paris: Massin Editeur, ca. 1985.

Sunbeam

Champ, Robert Cordon. *The Sunbeam Motorcycle*. Sparkford, England: Haynes, 1980.

———. *Sunbeam S7 and S8 Super Profile*. Sparkford, England: Haynes, 1983.

———. *The Illustrated History of Sunbeam Bicycles and Motorcycles*. Sparkford, England: Haynes, 1989.

———. *Sunbeam Bicycles and Motorcycles*. Sparkford, England: Haynes, 1989.

Hide, Reg, ed. *Sunbeam Four-Stroke Singles 1928–1939*. Leatherhead, England: Bruce Main-Smith, 1977.

Manuals

Heathcote, Leslie K. *The Book of the Sunbeam*. London: Sir I. Pitman & Sons, 1932.

———. *The Book of the Sunbeam*. London: Sir I. Pitman & Sons, 1958.

Munro, D. W. *Sunbeam Motor Cycles*. London: C. Arthur Pearson, 1954.

Suzuki

Aspel, Geoff. *Suzuki*. New York: Arco Publishing, 1984.

Bacon, Roy. *Suzuki Two-Strokes*. London: Osprey Publishing, 1984.

———. *Illustrated Motorcycle Legends: Suzuki*. London: Sunburst Books, 1996.

Battersby, Ray. *Team Suzuki*. London: Osprey Publishing, 1982.

Bennett, Chris, and Michael Scott. *Grand Prix Suzuki*. London: Osprey Publishing, 1995.

Clew, Jeff. *Suzuki*. Sparkford, England: Haynes, 1980.

Pinchin, Gary. *Suzuki GSX-R750*. Ramsbury, England: Crowood Press, 1997.

Walker, Mick. *Suzuki*. London: Osprey Publishing, 1993.

Manuals

Thorpe, John. *The Book of the Suzuki*. London: Sir I. Pitman & Sons, 1967.

Triumph

Ayton, Cyril J., ed. *Triumph Twins from 1937*. Bideford, England: Bay View, 1990.

Bacon, Roy. *Triumph Twins and Triples*. London: Osprey Publishing, 1981.

———. *Triumph Singles*. London: Osprey Publishing, 1984.

———. *Illustrated Triumph Motorcycle Buyer's Guide*. Ventor, England: Niton Publishing, 1989.

———. *Triumph Bonneville T120, 1959–1974*. Ventor, England: Niton Publishing, 1989.

————. *Triumph Tiger 100 and 110, 1939–1961*. Ventor, England: Niton Publishing, 1989.

————. *Triumph T90 and T100 Unit Twins: 1960–1974*. Ventor, England: Niton Publishing, 1990.

————. *Triumph T140 Bonneville and Derivatives*. Ventor, England: Niton Publishing, 1990.

————. *Triumph Touring Twins: 3T-5T-6T-5TA, 1938–1966*. Ventor, England: Niton Publishing, 1990.

————. *Illustrated Triumph Motorcycle Buyer's Guide*. 2nd ed. Ventor, England: Niton Publishing, 1993.

————. *The Illustrated Motorcycle Legends: Triumph*. Secaucus, N.J.: Chartwell, 1994.

Bird, Richard. *Triumph Bonneville*. London: Osprey Publishing, 1994.

Brooke, Lindsay. *Triumph Racing Motorcycles in America*. Osceola, Wis.: Motorbooks International, 1996.

Brooke, Lindsay, and David Gaylin. *Triumph in America*. Osceola, Wis.: Motorbooks International, 1993.

Clark, R. M., ed. *Triumph Bonneville Gold Portfolio, 1959–1983*. Cobham, England: Brooklands, 1996.

Cycle World. *Cycle World on Triumph 1967–1972*. Cobham, England: Brooklands, 1987.

Davies, Ivor. *It's a Triumph*. Sparkford, England: Haynes, 1980.

————. *Triumph Thunderbird Super Profile*. Sparkford, England: Haynes, 1984.

————. *Triumph Trident Super Profile*. Sparkford, England: Haynes, 1984.

————. *Pictorial History of Triumph Motorcycles*. Feltham, England: Temple Press, 1985.

————. *It's Easy on a Triumph*. Sparkford, England: Haynes, 1990.

————. *Triumph: The Complete Story*. Ramsbury, England: Crowood Press, 1991.

Duckworth, Mick. *Triumph and BSA Triples*. Ramsbury, England: Crowood Press, 1997.

Guislain, Christian. *Les trois cylindres Triumph et BSA Trident/Rocket 3*. Arques, France: Gallet, 1993.

Hancox, Hughie. *Triumph Motorcycles and the Meriden Factory*. Godmanstone, England: Veloce, 1996.

Louis, H., and Bob Currie. *The Story of Triumph Motorcycles*. Cambridge, England: Patrick Stephens, 1975.

————. *The Story of Triumph Motorcycles*. 2nd ed. Cambridge, England: Patrick Stephens, 1978.

Main-Smith, Bruce. *The First Classic Triumph Scene*. Leatherhead, England: Bruce Main-Smith, 1984.

Meriden: Historical Summary 1972–1974. N.p.: Norton Villiers Triumph, ca. 1975.

Minton, David. *The Return of the Legend: Triumph*. London: Apple, 1995.

Morland, Andrew, and Peter Henshaw. *Triumph Triples*. London: Osprey Publishing, 1995.

Morley, Don. *Classic Motorcycles: Triumph*. London: Osprey Publishing, 1991.

Nelson, J. R. *Bonnie: The Development History of the Triumph Bonneville*. Sparkford, England: Haynes, 1979.

————. *The Triumph Tiger 100/Daytona: The Development History of the Pre-Unit and Unit Construction 500cc Twins*. Sparkford, England: Haynes, 1988.

————. *Bonnie: The Development History of the Triumph Bonneville*. 2nd ed. Sparkford, England: Haynes, 1994.

Nelson, John. *Triumph Bonneville Super Profile*. Sparkford, England: Haynes, 1985.

Remus, Tim. *Triumph Motorcycles, Twins and Triples*. Osceola, Wis.: Motorbooks International, 1997.

Tipler, John. *Triumph Motorcycles: Their Renaissance and the Hinckley Factory*. Ramsbury, England: Crowood Press, 1997.

Woolridge, H. *Triumph Speed Twin: The Development History of the Pre-Unit and Unit Construction 500cc Twins*. Sparkford, England: Haynes, 1989.

Manuals

Bacon, Roy. *Triumph Twin Restoration*. London: Osprey Publishing, 1985.

Brotherwood, Clive. *Triumph 350/500 Unit Twins Owners Workshop Manual*. Sparkford, England: Haynes, 1974.

Brown, E. T. *The Book of the Triumph*. 1st ed. London: Sir I. Pitman & Sons, 1925.

————. *The Book of the Triumph*. London: Sir I. Pitman & Sons, 1940.

Glenn, H. T. *Glenn's Triumph 500, 650 and 750 (Twins)*. New York: Crown, 1973.

Gaylin, David. *Triumph Motorcycle Restoration Guide*. Osceola, Wis.: Motorbooks International, 1997.

Haycraft, W. C. *The Book of the Triumph Twins*. 13th ed. London: Sir I. Pitman & Sons, 1969.

Masters, A. St. J. *Triumph Motor Cycles*. 2nd ed. London: C. Arthur Pearson, 1949.

————. *Triumph Motorcycle Owner's Handbook*. Los Angeles: Floyd Clymer, 1951.

————. *Triumph Motor Cycles*. 4th ed. London: C. Arthur Pearson, 1956.

————. *Triumph Twin Motor Cycles*. 2nd ed. London: C. Arthur Pearson, 1963.

Meek, Frank. *Triumph Trident and BSA Rocket 3 Owners Workshop Manual, 741cc, 1969–1975*. Sparkford, England: Haynes, 1988.

Shenton, Stan. *Triumph Speed Tuning*. N.p.: Arman, 1982.

————. *Triumph Tuning*. Bromley, England: Boyer Bromley, 1982.

Triumph (German)

Knittel, Stefan. *Triumph Motorräder*. Rosrath, Germany: Schrader Verlag, 1991.

Velocette

Allen, C. E. "Titch." *The Velocette Saga*. Laxey, Isle of Man: Amulree, 1994.

Bacon, Roy. *Velocette Flat Twins*. London: Osprey Publishing, 1983.

———. *Velocette Viper, Venom and Thruxton*. Ventor, England: Niton Publishing, 1990.

Beresford, George. *The Story of the Velocette*. Birmingham, England: The T.T. Special, 1950.

Burgess, R. W. *Velocette*. London: C. Arthur Pearson, 1952.

Burgess, R. W., and Jeff Clew. *Always in the Picture: A History of the Velocette Motorcycle*. Sparkford, England: Haynes, 1980.

Burris, Rod. *Velocette: A Development History of the MSS, Venom, Viper, Thruxton and Scrambler Models*. Sparkford, England: Haynes, 1982.

Clew, Jeff. *KSS Velocette Super Profile*. Sparkford, England: Haynes, 1984.

Main-Smith, Bruce. *The First Velocette Scene*. Leatherhead, England: Bruce Main-Smith, 1977.

Masters, Dave. *Velocette: A List of Models*. N.p.: D. J. Masters, 1974.

———. *Velocette 1905–1971: An Illustrated Reference*. Brentford, England: Transport Bookman, 1976.

Moseley, Leonard J. *My Velocette Days*. Brentford, England: Transport Bookman, 1974.

Rhodes, Ivan. *Velocette: Technical Excellence Exemplified*. London: Osprey Publishing, 1990.

Manuals

Clew, Jeff. *Owner's Workshop Manual: Velocette Singles 349 and 499cc, 1953–71*. Sparkford, England: Haynes, 1975.

Heathcote, Leslie K. *The Book of the Velocette*. London: Sir I. Pitman & Sons, 1937.

Leigh, Ferrers. *The Book of the Velocette*. London: Sir I. Pitman & Sons, 1956.

———. *The Book of the Velocette*. London: Sir I. Pitman & Sons, 1970.

Main-Smith, Bruce. *Velocette Viper/Venom/Thruxton 350 and 500 Singles, All Years*. Leatherhead, England: Bruce Main-Smith, 1978.

Velocette Motorcycles 1925 to 1952. London: Temple Press, 1960.

Velocette Motorcycles 1925 to 1952. Reprint. Leatherhead, England: Bruce Main-Smith, 1974.

Vespa (see also Cushman)

Brockway, Eric. *Vespa: An Illustrated History*. Sparkford, England: Foulis, 1993.

Calabrese, Omar, ed. *The Cult of the Vespa*. Pisa: Lupetti, 1996.

Sparrow, Andrea and David. *The Colour Vespa Family Album*. Godmanstone, England: Veloce, 1995.

Manuals

Cornish, H. G. *Vespa*. London: C. Arthur Pearson, 1957.

Emmott, J. *The Book of the Douglas Vespa*. London: Sir I. Pitman & Sons, 1958.

Thorpe, J. *Second Book of the Vespa, All Models, 1959–63*. London: Sir I. Pitman & Sons, 1964.

———. *The Third Book of the Vespa*. London: Sir I. Pitman & Sons, 1972.

Villiers

Bacon, Roy. *Villiers Singles and Twins*. London: Osprey Publishing, 1983.

The Story of Villiers: 1898–1948. Wolverhampton, England: Villiers, ca. 1948.

Manuals

Browning, B. E. *The Villiers Engine*. London: C. Arthur Pearson, 1949.

———. *The Villiers Engine for Industrial, Agricultural, and Horticultural Use*. London: C. Arthur Pearson, 1954.

Burgess, A. T. *Villiers Engines*. Chislehurst, Kent, England: Lodgemark, ca. 1965.

Carrick, Rob, and John Wood. *Villiers Singles Improvements Handbook*. Birmingham, England: Carwood, 1995.

Grange, Cyril. *The Book of the Villiers Engine*. London: Sir I. Pitman & Sons, 1929.

———. *The Book of the Villiers Engine*. 7th ed. London: Sir I. Pitman & Sons, 1947.

———. *The Book of the Villiers Engine*. London: Sir I. Pitman & Sons, 1972.

Osborne, Bernal, ed. *Villiers Engines, 1935–55, All Models*. London: Temple Press, 1959.

Vincent/H.R.D.

Ayton, Cyril J. *Vincent from 1938*. Bideford, England: Bay View, 1988.

Bickerstaff, J. P. *Vincent Twins Super Profile*. Sparkford, England: Haynes, 1984.

———. *Original Vincent Motorcycle*. Bideford, England: Bay View, 1997.

Carrick, Peter. *Vincent-HRD*. Cambridge, England: Patrick Stephens, 1982.

Clarke, R. M., ed. *Vincent Gold Portfolio, 1945–1980*. Cobham, England: Brooklands Books, ca. 1997.

Guirao, Antoine. *La 1000 Vincent*. Nimes: Guirao, 1992.

Harper, Roy. *Vincent H.R.D. Gallery*. Great Britain: Vincent Publications, 1974.

———. *The Vincent H.R.D. Story*. Great Britain: Vincent Publications, 1979.

———. *Vincent Vee Twins*. London: Osprey Publishing, 1982.

Main-Smith, Bruce. *The First HRD-Vincent Scene*. Leatherhead, England: Bruce Main-Smith, 1977.

Miller, Zachary. *Illustrated Vincent Motorcycle Buyer's Guide*. Osceola, Wis.: Motorbooks International, 1994.

Minett, Denis. *The Denis Minett Notebook*. N.p.: Victoria Section, Vincent Owners Club, 1983.

Preece, Geoff. *H.R.D. Motor Cycles*. Daventry, Northants, England: J. Bickerstaff, 1992.

Vincent, P. C. *Fifty Years of the Marque*. Great Britain: Vincent Publications, 1977.

Wherrett, Duncan. *Vincent*. London: Osprey Publishing, 1994.

Wilkins, Paul. *The Vincent HRD Story in South Australia*. South Australia: P. Wilkins, 1994.

Manuals

Bowen, Jeff, ed. *Forty Years On*. N.p.: Jeff Bowen, 1991.

Richardson, Paul. *Vincent Owner's Handbook*. Los Angeles: Floyd Clymer, 1955.

———. *Vincent: Motor Cycle Maintenance and Repair Series*. 2nd ed. Great Britain: C. A. Pearson, 1960.

———. *Vincent: Motor Cycle Maintenance and Repair Series*. 2nd ed. Reprint, Great Britain: C. A. Pearson, 1960.

———. *Vincent: Motor Cycle Maintenance and Repair Series*. 3rd ed. Great Britain: Vincent Owners Club, 1996.

Stevens, E.M.G. *Know Thy Beast*. 2nd ed. Great Britain: Vincent Publications, 1977.

———. *Know Thy Beast*. 3rd ed. Great Britain: Vincent Owners Club, 1989.

Vincent-H.R.D. Motorcycles, 1947–55. London: Temple Press, 1960.

Vincent-HRD Motorcycles 1947 to 1955. Reprint. Leatherhead, England: BMS, 1973.

Yamaha

Argus editors. *Wild World of Yamaha*. Los Angeles: Argus, 1973.

Bacon, Roy. *Illustrated Motorcycle Legends: Yamaha*. London: Sunburst Books, 1996.

Macauley, Ted. *The Yamaha Legend*. New York: St. Martin's, 1979.

———. *Yamaha*. London: Cadogan, 1983.

Mackellar, Colin. *Yamaha Two-Stroke Twins*. London: Osprey Publishing, 1985.

———. *Yamaha Dirtbikes*. London: Osprey Publishing, 1986.

———. *Yamaha*. Ramsbury, England: Crowood Press, 1995.

Scott, Michael. *Yamaha (Kimberly Team Guide One)*. London: Kimberley, ca. 1986.

Takahashi, Norihiko, ed. *Yamaha SR File*. Vol. 3. Tokyo, Japan: Studio Tac, 1996.

Walker, Mick. *Yamaha*. London: Osprey Publishing, 1993.

Woolett, Mick. *Yamaha*. London: B. T. Batsford, 1984.

Manuals

Genibrel, Jean Louis. *Racing the Yamaha KT100-S*. Santa Ana, Calif.: Steve Smith, 1986.

Zenith

Collin, Eddie. *The History of Zenith*. Grantham, England: Grantley, 1988.

RACES, RACING, AND COMPETITION

Road Racing

AMA ProRacing '95 Superbike Series Racing Guide. Westerville, Ohio: AMA, 1995.

Bacon, Roy. *Taking Up Motor Cycle Racing*. Chislehurst, England: Lodgemark, 1964.

Bargy, Ed. *Introduction to Motorcycle Roadracing*. N.p.: Ed Bargy, 1994.

Bayley, Joseph. *The Vintage Years at Brooklands*. Norwich, England: Goose, 1968.

The Book of Motorcycle Road Racing Champions. Ipswitch, England: Studio Publications, 1977.

Boyer, David B. *The Racer's Image: A Look Inside the World of Canyon Racing*. Columbia, Ga.: Brentwood Christian Press. 1994.

Brown, Norman. *History of the Manx Grand Prix*. N.p.: Shell, ca. 1960.

Bula, Maurice. *Grand Prix Motorcycle Championships of the World, 1949–1975*. Sparkford, England: Foulis, 1975.

Cade, L. H. *T.T. Thrills*. N.p.: Muller, 1957.

Carrick, Peter. *The Book of Motor Cycle Racing*. London: Stanley Paul, 1967.

———. *Great Moments in Sport: Motor Cycle Racing*. London: Pelham Books, 1977.

————. *Hell Raisers*. London: Pelham Books, 1973.

Carter, C., F. Clarke, and E. Fitch. *Who's Who of Motor-Cycle Road Racing*. Ipswitch, England: Studio Publications, ca. 1975.

Carter, Chris, ed. *Motocourse 1976–77*. New York: Arco Publishing, 1977.

Cathcart, Alan. *Track Secrets of Champion Road Racers*. London: Osprey Publishing, 1987.

Clifford, Peter, ed. *Motocourse, 1987/88*. Richmond, England: Hazleton, 1987.

Clifford, Peter. *The Art and Science of Motor Cycle Road Racing*. Richmond, England: Hazleton, 1982.

Code, Keith. *A Twist of the Wrist*. Los Angeles: Acrobat, 1983.

————. *A Twist of the Wrist*. Vol. 2. Los Angeles: Acrobat, 1993.

————. *The Soft Science of Road Racing Motorcycles*. Los Angeles: Acrobat, 1986.

Colquhoun, Gordon D. *Brands Hatch and Beyond*. Seaton, England: Motoprint, 1995.

Crellin, Ralph. *Japanese Riders in the Isle of Man*. Laxey, Isle of Man: Amulree, 1995.

Davison, G. S. *The Story of the T.T.* 1st ed. Birmingham, England: The T.T. Special, 1947.

————. *The Story of the Manx*. Birmingham, England: The T.T. Special, 1948.

————. *The Story of the T.T.* 2nd ed. Birmingham, England: The T.T. Special, 1948.

————. *The Story of the Ulster*. Birmingham, England: The T.T. Special, 1949.

————. *The Story of the T.T.* 4th ed. Birmingham, England: The T.T. Special, ca. 1950.

————. *Motorcycle Road Racing*. Los Angeles: Floyd Clymer, 1950.

————. *T.T. Tales*. Birmingham, England: The T.T. Special, 1950.

————. *The Racing Year*. Birmingham, England: The T.T. Special, 1950.

————. *Racing Through the Century*. Birmingham, England: The T.T. Special, 1951.

————. *The 1951 T.T. Who's Who*. Birmingham, England: The T.T. Special, 1951.

————. *Geoff Davison's T.T. Anecdotes*. N.p.: M. Davison, 1956.

————, ed. *Racing Reminiscences*. Birmingham, England: The T.T. Special, 1948.

————, ed. *The T.T. Races: Behind the Scenes*. Birmingham, England: The T.T. Special, 1949.

————, ed. *The Racing Game*. Birmingham, England: The T.T. Special, ca. 1956.

————, ed. *The Racing Game*. Los Angeles: Floyd Clymer, 1956.

Davison, G. S., and Phil Heath. *Short Circuits!* Birmingham, England: The T.T. Special, 1951.

Davison, G. S., Phil Heath, and W. J. McGowan. *A Million Miles of Racing*. Birmingham, England: T.T. Special, 1950.

Deane, Charles. *Isle of Man T.T.* Cambridge, England: Patrick Stephens, 1975.

The Diamond Jubilee Manx Grand Prix. Birmingham, England: The T.T. Special, 1983.

Dixon, Alan. *The T.T. Riders*. London: Stanley Paul, 1967.

Duke, Geoff. *The T.T.: as Geoff. Duke Sees It*. N.p.: Castrol, 1950.

EMAP. *T.T. '78*. Bretton, England. EMAP, 1978.

Emde, Don. *The Daytona 200*. Laguna Niguel, Calif.: Motorcycle Heritage, 1991.

Emde, Don. *Legends: The BMW Battle of the Legends, 1992–1996*. Laguna Niguel, Calif.: Don Emde, 1997.

Freudenberg, M. *The Isle of Man T.T.: An Illustrated History 1907–80*. Bourne End, England: Aston, 1990.

Georgano, G. N. *Brooklands, A Pictorial History*. London: Daton Watson, 1978.

Grant, Mick. *Road Racing*. London: Hamlyn Publishing, 1979.

Guichard, A., ed. *Motorcycle Year No. One, 1975/1976*. N.p.: Edita, 1975.

————, ed. *Motorcycle Year 1976–77*. Lausanne, Switzerland: Haessner, 1977.

Hailwood, Mike and Peter. Carrick. *Bikes: Thirty Years of Motor Cycle Championships*. N.p.: Trafalgar, 1984.

Hailwood, Mike, and Murray Walker. *The Art of Motorcycle Racing*. 4th ed. London: Cassell, 1966.

Harris, Nick. *Motocourse History of the Isle of Man Tourist Trophy Races, TT 1907–1989*. Richmond, England: Hazleton, 1990.

Hartley, Peter. *Bikes at Brooklands in the Pioneer Years*. Norwich, England: Goose, 1973.

————. *Brooklands Bikes in the Twenties*. Los Angeles: Argus, 1980.

Hendricks, J. *Superbike Preparation*. Osceola, Wis.: Motorbooks International, 1988.

Hetzler, Dave, ed. *Popular Cycling's How to Ride Motorcycles*. N.p.: Coronado, 1971.

Higgins, L. R. *Private Owner*. Sparkford, England: Foulis, 1948.

Higgins, L. R., and C. Quantrill. *Fifty Years of T.T. History*. London: Shell/BP, 1956.

————. *History of the T.T. Races, 1907–1960*. London: BP, ca. 1960.

Hilton, Christopher. *Two Wheel Showdown!* Cambridge, England: Patrick Stephens, 1994.

Hislop, S., P. Beighton, and A. Douglas. *Steve Hislop's You Couldn't Do It Now!* N.p.: Mannin, 1993.

Holliday, Bob. *Racing Round the Island*. Newton Abbot.: David and Charles, 1976.

Holmes, Ron. *Motorcycle Science*. N.p., 1977.

Jenkinson, Denis. *Motorcycle Road Racing: The 1950s in Photographs*. Bourne End, England: Aston, 1989.

Kelly, Robert. *How the T.T. Started*. Laxey, Isle of Man: Island Development, ca. 1970.

Kneale, P. E., and G. E. Kniveton. *The T.T. Experience*. Laxey, Isle of Man: The Manx Experience, 1984.

Knight. *TT Racing*. N.p.: Speed Sports, 1974.

Knight, Ray. *Racing and Tuning Production Motorcycles*. London: SpeedSport, 1970.

———. *How to Start Production Motorcycle Racing*. London: SpeedSport, 1973.

———. *Road Bike Racing and Preparation*. London: Osprey Publishing, 1989.

———. *Isle of Man TT Rider's Guide*. London: Osprey Publishing, 1991.

Knight, Ray, and Nick Jefferies. *Ride the TT Mountain Course With Ray Knight*. Laxey, Isle of Man: Amulree, 1997.

Macauley, Ted, ed. *International Motor Cycle Racing Book*. London: Souvenir, 1971.

Main-Smith, Bruce. *The Second Post-Vintage Racing Scene (1931–1953)*. Leatherhead, England: Bruce Main-Smith, 1978.

Mallet, David D., and John V. Imre. *The Canyon Racer's Pocket Guide to Advanced Motorcycle Riding Techniques*. Seattle: Canyon Racer, 1983.

The Manx Grand Prix. N.p.: Shell, 1963.

The Manx Motor Racing Bulletin. Liverpool: Fullerton Lloyds, 1949.

McKinnon, Andrew. *Motorcycle Road Racing in the Fifties*. London: Osprey Publishing, 1982.

Miller, Robin, and C. Rous. *T.T. Golden Greats*. Bretton, England: Motor Cycle News, 1973.

Morrison, Ian. *Guinness Motorcycle Sport Fact Book*. Enfield, England: Guinness, 1991.

Mortimer, Charles. *Brooklands and Beyond*. Norwich, England: Goose & Son, 1974.

———. *Brooklands: Behind the Scenes*. Sparkford, England: Haynes, 1980.

Mutch, Ronnie. *The Last of the Great Road Races*. Brentford, England: Transport Bookman, 1975.

———. *The Last of the Great Road Races: Isle of Man T.T.* Brentford, England: Transport Bookman, 1975.

Nicks, Mick. *Motorcycle Racing Manual*. Cambridge, England: Patrick Stephens, 1973.

1963 T.T. Races. London: BP, 1963.

1965 T.T. Races. London: BP, 1965.

O'Dell, G., and I. Beacham. *Sidecar Championships*. London: Hamlyn Publishing, 1978.

Pinchin, Gary, ed. *Tourist Trophy*. Stamford, England: Key Publishing, 1997.

Rae, Rusty. *The World's Biggest Motorcycle Race: The Daytona 200*. Minneapolis: Lerner Publications, 1978.

Roberts, Kenny. *Techniques of Motor Cycle Road Racing*. Richmond, England: Hazleton, 1988.

Robinson, John. *Ride It! The Complete Book of Endurance Racing*. Sparkford, England: Haynes, 1979.

Ryder, Julian. *World Superbikes, The First Ten Years*. Sparkford, England: Haynes, 1997.

Sakkis, Tony. *Anatomy and Development of the Grand Prix Motorcycle*. Osceola, Wis.: Motorbooks International, 1995.

Scott, Michael. *Motocourse, 1993–94*. Richmond, England: Hazleton, 1993.

———. *Motorcycle Grand Prix Year 1989/1990*. London: Scott, 1989.

Smyth, John. *Bike Sport Ireland*. South Humberside, England: McKinnon Farmer, 1989.

Snelling, Bill. *The Tourist Trophy in Old Photographs*. Gloucester, England: Alan Sutton, 1994.

Surtees, John. *John Surtees on Racing*. London: Iliffe & Sons, 1960.

Swift, Jim. *Ride It! The Complete Book of Big Bike Racing*. Sparkford, England: Haynes, 1976.

Wallace, P. J. *Brooklands*. New York: Ballantine, 1971.

Wernham, M., and M. Walker. *World Motorcycle Endurance Racing*. London: Osprey Publishing, 1994.

Windrum, Norman. *The Ulster Grand Prix*. Belfast, Ireland: Blackstaff, 1979.

Woollett, Mick. *World Championship Motor Cycle Racing*. London: Hamlyn Publishing, 1980.

Motocross, Enduro, and Cross-Country

Archer, Les. *Scrambles and Moto-Cross*. London: Temple Press, 1962.

Bailey, Gary, and C. Shipman. *How to Win Motocross*. Tucson: HP Books, 1974.

Bailey, Gary, and Tom Mueller. *Gary Bailey Teaches Rider Technique*. Axton, Va.: G. Bailey, ca. 1985.

Bales, Donnie with Gary Semics. *Pro Motocross and Off-Road Motorcycle Riding Techniques*. Osceola, Wis.: Motorbooks International, 1996.

Bonnello, Joe. *Supercross*. Osceola, Wis.: Motorbooks International, 1977.

Booth, S., and B. Palormo. *Championship Enduro*. N.p., n.d.

Bradley, Harry. *The Scott Trial*. St. Harmon, Powys: Ariel, 1994.

Brown, Don J., and Evan Aiken, eds. *How to Ride and Win!* Los Angeles: National Sports, 1956.

Coonfield, Ed. *Enduro Secrets Revealed*. N.p.: Hourglass, 1985.

Engel, Lyle K. *Off-Road Racing*. New York: Dodd Mead & Co., 1974.

Johns, Smokey. *Enduro Riding!* Mauldin, S.C.: N-DuroSpec., 1970.

Jones, Thomas Firth. *Enduro*. Philadelphia: Chilton, 1970.

Eighth Annual Catalina Grand Prix, Souvenir Program. Westerville, Ohio: AMA Dist.37, 1958.

Forsdyke, Graham. *Off Road Motor Cycle Sport*. London: Hamlyn Publishing, 1976.

Gorr, Eric. *Motocross and Off-Road Motorcycle Performance Handbook*. Osceola, Wis.:
Motorbooks International, 1996.

Hertfelder, Ed. *Duct Tapes Eighty*. Haddonfield, N.J.: Hertfelder, 1980.

Jonsson, Ake, and Vin Gilligan. *The Technique of Motocross*. Santa Ana, Calif.: Oxman, 1974.

Kelley, John D., ed. *ISDT '73: The Olympics of Motorcycling*. Philadelphia: Chilton, 1973.

Lackey, Brad, and Len Weed. *Motocross: Techniques, Training and Tactics*. Tarzana, Calif.: Cleansheet, 1982.

Melling, Frank. *Ride It! The Complete Book of Motocross*. Sparkford, England: Haynes, 1975.

———. *Ride It! The Complete Book of Motocross*. Sparkford, England: Haynes, 1977.

———. *Motocross, the Big Leap*. London: Hamlyn Publishing, 1979.

———. *The Complete Book of Motocross*. Sparkford, England: Foulis, 1986.

Patrignani, R., and C. Perelli. *Motorcycle Competition: Off-Road Riding and Racing*. London: Orbis, 1974.

Sandham, Tommy. *The Castrol Book of the Scottish Six Days Trial.* Sparkford, England: Haynes, 1982.

———. *The "Scottish" 1900–1962*. Newport, England: Willow, 1988.

———. *The "Scottish" 1963–1989*. Newport, England: Willow, 1989.

Semics, Gary. *The Moto-Cross Racing Manual*. N.p.: Semics, 1989.

Seventh Annual Catalina Grand Prix, Souvenir Program. Westerville, Ohio: AMA Dist. 37, 1957.

Sixth Annual Catalina Grand Prix, Souvenir Program. Westerville, Ohio: AMA Dist. 37, 1956.

Smith, Jeff. *Jeff Smith on Scrambling*. London: Iliffe & Sons, 1960.

Smith, Jeff, and Bob Currie. *The Art of Moto-Cross*. London: Cassell, 1966.

Smith, Philip H. *The Greatest of All Trials*. Melksham, Wiltshire, England: Scott, 1963.

Venables, Ralph. *Schoolboy Scrambling and Other Motorcycle Sports*. 2nd ed. Oxford, England:
Oxford Illust., 1978.

———. *British Scrambles Motorcycles*. Leatherhead, England: Bruce Main-Smith, 1986.

Walker, Mick, and Rob Carrick. *International Six Days Trial*. London: Osprey Publishing, 1992.

Observed Trials

Beesley, Tom. *The Mick Andrews Book of Trials*. Irvine, Calif.: Trippe, Cox Specialist Publications, 1976.

Beesley, Tom, and M. Andrews. *Mick Andrews Book of Trials*. Cambridge, England: Patrick Stephens, 1976.

Bourne, A. B. *Trials and Trials Riding*. London: Iliffe & Sons, ca. 1940.

Candellone, Mario. *PhotoTrial, 1994*. Torre Pelice, Italy: FunTrials, 1994. In English and Italian.

———. *PhotoTrial, 1995*. Torre Pelice, Italy: FunTrials, 1995. In English and Italian.

Cattone. *Get Back to Nature: Get Into Trials*. N.p.: Fantic Motors, ca. 1970.

King, Max. *Trials Riding*. 1st ed. London: Sir I. Pitman & Sons, 1955.

———. *Trials Riding*. 2nd ed. London: Sir I. Pitman & Sons, 1960.

———. *Motor Cycle Trials Riding*. 4th ed. London: Pelham Books, 1972.

———. *Motor Cycle Trials Riding*. 5th ed. London: Pelham Books, 1975.

Leavitt, Lane, and Len Weed. *Motor Cycle Trials: Techniques and Training*. Tarzana, Calif.: MC Trials, 1978.

Miller, Samuel H. *The Way to Win Motor Cycle Trials*. N.p.: Miller, 1980.

Mathieson, Peter, ed. *Observed Trials Coaching Manual*. Http://www.trials.net/trialsman/trialman.html.
World Wide Web: Mathieson, 1994.

Miller, Sammy. *Sammy Miller on Trials*. Newport Beach, Calif.: Parkhurst, 1969.

———. *Sammy Miller on Trials*. 2nd ed. Newport Beach, Calif.: Parkhurst, 1971.

———. *Clean to the Finish*. Leatherhead, England: Bruce Main-Smith, 1974.

Morley, Don. *Trials: A Rider's Guide*. London: Osprey Publishing, 1990.

Perry, Robin. *The Trials Motorcyclist*. New York: Crown, 1975.

Schreiber, Bernie, and Len Weed. *Observed Trials*. Tarzana, Calif.: Cleensheet, 1983.

Shipman, C. *How to Ride Observed Trials Just for Fun*. N.p., 1973.

Smith, Don. *Ride It! The Complete Book of Motor Cycle Trials*. Sparkford, England: Haynes, 1975.

———. *Ride It! The Complete Book of Motor Cycle Trials*. Sparkford, England: Haynes, 1977.

———. *Trials Bike Riding*. Tucson: HP Publishing, 1980.

Smith, Philip H. *Scott Motorcycle Trials*. N.p., 1969.

Venables, Ralph. *British Trials Motorcycles*. Leatherhead, England: Bruce Main-Smith, 1985.

Wylde, Deryk. *The Pre-65 Yearbook: 1990–91*. Newport, Gwent, England: Willow, 1991.

Speedway

Abraham, I., and C. Irwin. *Speedway Spectacular*. N.p.: Lodestar Press, 1983.

Bott, Richard. *The Champion's Book of Speedway*. London: Stanley Paul, 1970.

———. *The Champion's Book of Speedway*. No. 4. London: Stanley Paul, 1973.

———, ed. *The Peter Collins Speedway Book*. London: Stanley Paul, 1977.

Briggs, Barry. *Briggo's World of Speedway*. London: Souvenir, 1973.

———. *Trackin' with Briggo*. London: Souvenir, 1975.

Crossley, Lionel. *Crystal Palace Speedway*. London: Crystal Palace, 1986.

Domhnullach, Alasdair. *Speedway*. N.p.: Empire, 1992.

Dracket, Phil. *Speedway*. London: W.G. Foyle, 1951.

Elder, Sprouts. *The Romance of the Speedway*. London: Frederick Warne, 1930.

Festival of Speedway. Ipswitch, England: Studio Publications, ca. 1980.

Jones, Maurice. *World Speedway Final: A History from 1929*. London: MacDonald and Janes, 1979.

Higgins, L., ed. *The Book of British Speedway*. N.p.: Bonar, 1950.

Hoare, Ron. *Speedway Panorama*. Sparkford, England: Haynes, 1979.

Hoskins, J. *Roarin' Round the Speedways*. N.p.: McCorquodale, 1930.

———. *Johnnie Hoskins' Speedway Walkabout*. London: Studio, 1977.

Lanning, Dave. *Speedway and Short Track Racing*. London: Hamlyn Publishing, 1974.

Louis, John. *A Second Look Inside Speedway*. London: Studio, 1976.

Mauger, Ivan. *Triple Crown Plus*. London: Pelham Books, 1971.

Mauger, Ivan, and Peter Oakes. *Ivan Mauger's Speedway Book*. London: Pelham Books, 1972.

———. *Ivan Mauger's World Speedway Book*. London: Pelham Books, 1973.

———. *Ivan Mauger's Speedway Spectacular*. London: Pelham Books, 1975.

———. *Ivan Mauger's Speedway Extravaganza No. Two*. London: Studio, 1976.

———. *Ivan Mauger's Speedway Extravaganza*. No. 1. Ipswitch, England: Studio Publications, 1977.

May, Cyril. *Ride It! The Complete Book of Speedway*. Sparkford, England: Haynes, 1976.

Morgan, T. *Speedway Guide*. N.p.: Odhams, 1947.

Oakes, Peter, and Ivan Mauger. *Speedway Quiz Book No. One*. N.p., 1977.

Olsen, Ole. *Ole Olsen's Speedway Scrapbook*. London: Souvenier, 1980.

Patrick, Mike. *Focus on Speedway*. London: Studio, 1975.

Penhall, Bruce. *Stars and Bikes*. London: Studio, 1980.

Racing at Crystal Palace. Croydon, England: Motor Racing Publications, 1991.

Ridding, F., ed. *Speedway Pictorial Album*. N.p., 1954.

Roberts, Gary. *California Speedway 97*. San Jose, Calif.: Sherbourne, 1997.

Rogers, Martin. *The Illustrated History of Speedway*. London: Studio, 1978.

Stallworthy, Dave. *Sidecar Speedway Racing*. Bristol, England: Stallworthy, 1991.

Stallworthy, Dave, and Lethhbridge. *The Story of Grass Track and Speedway in Cornwall*. N.p., ca. 1997.

Stenner, Tom. *Thrilling the Million: The Lure of the Speedway*. London: John Miles, 1934.

Wingrove and Wilson, eds. *Yarns of the Speedway*. N.p.: Aldine, ca. 1930.

Miscellaneous Competition and Racing

AMA ProRacing '95 Grand National Series Media Guide. Westerville, Ohio: AMA, 1995.

Bentley, Pat. *Stalking the Motorsports Sponsor*. Santa Ana, Calif.: Steve Smith, 1979.

Bowman, Hank W. *Motorcycles in Competition*. New York: Fawcett, 1952.

Carrick, Peter. *Motor Cycle Racing*. London: Hamlyn Publishing, 1969.

———. *Great Moments in Sport: Motor Cycle Racing*. London: Pelham Books, 1977.

———. *Encyclopedia of Motor Cycle Sport*. New York: St. Martin's, 1977.

Davis, Anthony. *Tackle Motorcycle Sport This Way*. London: Stanley Paul, 1963.

Drag Racing Rules and Procedure. Los Angeles: Floyd Clymer, ca. 1965.

Dubler, Jürg, ed. *Motor Cycle Racing Guide 1974*. Zürich: Sil Sports Book, 1973.

Edwards, Guy. *Sponsorship and the World of Motor Racing*. Richmond, England: Hazleton, 1992.

Foster, Gerald. *Ride It! The Complete Book of Flat Track Racing*. Sparkford, England: Haynes, 1978.

Gardner, Col. Goldie, ed. *Motor Cycle and Motor Racing 1951*. London: Country & Sporting Publications, 1951.

Goodwin, Carl. *How to Get a Racing Sponsorship*. Grosse Ile, Michigan: Goodwin, 1985.

Griffin, Mike. *Motorcycle Drag Racing*. Osceola, Wis.: Motorbooks International, 1982.

Hodder, M., and B. McLouglin, eds. *Sixty Years of Speed*. Peterborough, England: M.C.N., 1967.

Holden [Holder], Bill. *Motorcycle Racing*. Secaucus, N.J.: Chartwell, 1994.

Holder, Bill. *Motorcycle Racing*. Leicester, England: Magna, 1994.

Hudson-Evans, Richard. *Handbook of Motorcycle Sport*. New York: Arco Publishing, 1978.

Jackson, Jeremy. *Champions: A Profile of the Westcountry Motorcycle Champions*. Cornwall, England: J and S Publishers, 1996.

Kenyon, James W. *Racing Wheels*. London: Nelson, 1944.

Loughborough, T. W., ed. *World's Motor Cycle Records as at First January, 1949*. Hawkhurst, England: Federation International des Clubs Motocyclistes, 1949.

Macauley, Ted, ed. *International Motor Cycle Racing Book, No. 1*. London: Souvenier, 1971.

Masters, A. St. J. *Motor-Cycle Sport*. London: C. Arthur Pearson, 1958.

Motor Cycle Sport in Pictures. London: Iliffe & Sons, 1951.

Nelson, Mike. *A Guide to Motorcycle Drag Racing*. Englewood, Ohio: Atlantic Digital, 1992.

Patrignani, Roberto, and Carlo Perelli. *Color Treasury of Motorcycle Competition*. London: Orbis, 1974.

Reynolds, J. C., ed. *Speed: The Book of Racing and Records*. London: Temple Press, 1950.

Shell Successes, 1960. N.p.: Shell, 1960.

'64 Successes. N.p.: Shell, 1964.

Spence, James, and G. Brown. *Motorcycle Racing In America*. Chicago: J. P. O'Hara, 1974.

Walker, Murray, ed. *The BP Book of Motor Cycle Racing*. London: Stanley Paul, 1960.

Woods, Stanley, ed. *Your Motorcycle on Road and Track*. London: Vacuum Oil, ca. 1938.

BIOGRAPHIES AND AUTOBIOGRAPHIES

Briggs, Barry. *Briggo*. London: Souvenir, 1972.

Brown, Cliff. *George Brown, Sprint Superstar*. Sparkford, England: Haynes, 1981.

Carrick, Peter. *Great Motor-Cycle Riders*. London: Robert Hale, 1985.

Clew, Jeff. *Sammy Miller: The Will to Win*. Sparkford, England: Haynes, 1977.

———. *Francis Beart, A Single Purpose*. Sparkford, England: Haynes, 1978.

———. *Sammy Miller Story*. New Milton, England: Chard, 1993.

Clifford, Peter. *Kevin Schwantz, the World's Champion*. Wanganui, New Zealand: Schwantz/Clifford, 1997.

Cox, Don, and Will Hagon. *Australian Motorcycle Heroes: 1949–1989*. North Ryde, Australia: Angus, 1989.

Duke, Geoff. *Geoff Duke: In Pursuit of Perfection*. London: Osprey Publishing, 1988.

Gundersen, Erik. *My Two Lives*. N.p.: Pinegen, 1990.

Hailwood, Mick, and Ted Macauley. *Hailwood*. London: Cassell, 1968.

Hailwood, Stan. *The Hailwood Story: My Son Mike*. Peterborough, England: M.C.N., 1966.

Harris, Nick, and Peters Clifford. *Fast Freddie*. Croydon, England: Motor Racing Publications, 1986.

Hartgerink, Nick. *The Wayne Gardner Story*. Waterloo, Australia: Fairfax, 1987.

———. *Gardner: A Dream Come True*. Milsons Point, Australia: Hutchinson, 1989.

Harvard, Jan. *A Bit on the Side*. Croydon, England: Motor Racing Publications, 1992.

Henry, Alan. *John Surtees: World Champion*. Richmond, England: Hazelton, 1991.

Hilliard, Frank. *Deeley: Motorcycle Millionaire*. N.p.: Orca, 1994.

Hilton, Christopher. *A Man Called Mike*. Croydon, England: Motor Racing Publications, 1992.

Irving, P. E. *Phil Irving: An Autobiography*. Sydney, Australia: Turton and Armstrong, 1992.

Jackson, Jeremy. *Champions: A Profile of the Westcountry Motorcycle Champions*. Cornwall, England: J & S Publications, n.d.

Jonas, George. *A Passion Observed*. New York: Macmillan, 1989.

Macauley, Ted. *Mike the Bike Again*. London: Cassell, 1980.

———. *Mike, The Life and Times of Mike Hailwood*. London: Buchan Enright, 1984.

Mann, Dick with Joe Scalzo. *Motorcycle Ace, The Dick Mann Story*. Chicago: Henry Regnery, 1972.

Marriott, Andrew, ed. *Sheene Machine*. London: Pelham Books, 1979.

Marshall, Roger. *Roger and Out*. N.p.: Mckinn. Farm, 1989.

McCleery, W. F. *Stanley Woods*. Ulster, Northern Ireland: Ulster Museum, 1987.

May, Dennis. *Pastmasters of Speed*. London: Temple Press, 1958.

Mellors, Ted. *Continental Circus*. Birmingham, England: The T.T. Special, 1949.

Minter, Derek. *Racing All My Life*. London: Arthur Barker, 1965.

Mortimer, Charles. *We Went Racing: The Griff Jenkins Story*. London: M.C. News, 1966.

Moss, Stirling, and Mike Hailwood. *Racing and All That*. London: Pelham Books, 1980.

Nolan, William. *Steve McQueen: Star on Wheels*. N.p.: Berkley, 1972.

Peck, Alan. *No Time to Lose: The Fast Moving World of Bill Ivy*. Croydon, England: Motor Racing Publications, 1972.

Perryman, A. C. *A Clubman at Brooklands*. Sparkford, England: Haynes, 1979.

Peters, Victor. *Frank Varey, Red Devil of the Speedway*. Timperley, England: Sherratt Hughes, 1937.

Pope, Noel B. *Full Chat*. Croydon, England: Motor Racing Publications, 1952.

———. *Full Chat*. 2nd ed. Croydon, England: Motor Racing Publications, 1972.

Read, Phil. *Prince of Speed*. London: Arthur Barker, 1970.

Read, Phil, and Graeme Wright. *Phil Read: The Real Story*. N.p.: Futura, 1979.

Redman, Jim. *Wheels of Fortune*. London: Stanley Paul, 1966.

Robb, Tommy. *From T.T. to Tokyo*. Laxey, Isle of Man: Courier Herald, 1974.

Ryder, Julian. *Carl Fogarty, the Complete Racer*. Cambridge, England: Patrick Stephens, 1996.

Sallon. *Motor-Cycling Personalities Past and Present*. N.p.: Shell-Mex, 1957.

Savage, Mike. *TT Heroes*. Laxey, Isle of Man: Amulree, 1997.

Scalzo, Joe. *Racer: The Story of Gary Nixon*. Newport Beach, Calif.: Parkhurst, 1970.

———. *The Bart Markel Story*. Newport Beach, Calif.: Bond-Parkhurst, 1972.

Scott, Michael. *Barry Sheene: A Will To Win!* London: Comet, 1983.

———. *Freddie Spencer*. London: Kimberley, 1987.

———. *Wayne Rainey, His Own Story*. Sparkford, England: Haynes, 1997.

Sheene, Barry. *Barry Sheene: The Story So Far. . . .* Ipswitch, England: Studio Publications, 1976.

Sheene, Barry with Ian Beacham. *Leader of the Pack*. London: Queen Anne, 1983.

Small, Gordon. *The Life and Work of Rex McCandless*. Ulster, Northern Ireland: Ulster Museum, 1989.

———. *Jimmie Guthrie, Hawick's Racing Legend*. Hawick, England: Hawick Archaeological Society, 1997.

Snelling, Bill. *Aurora to Ariel: The Motorcycling Exploits of J. Graham Oates*. Laxey, Isle of Man: Amulree, 1993.

Surtees, John. *John Surtees' Motorcycling Book*. London: F. Muller, 1961.

———. *Speed: John Surtees' Own Story*. London: Arthur Barker, 1963.

A Tribute to Bob McIntyre. Lesmahagow, Scotland: M & R Promotions, 1997.

Vincent, Philip. *P.C.V.: The Autobiography of Philip Vincent*. Great Britain: Vincent Publications, 1976.

Whyte, Norrie, ed. *Motor Cycle Racing Champions*. Cambridge, England: Patrick Stephens, 1975.

Wiggin, Maurice. *My Life on Wheels*. London: John Baker, 1963.

Woollett, Mick, and Peter Clifford. *The Grand Prix Riders*. Richmond, England: Hazleton, 1990.

Acknowledgments

The Art of the Motorcycle could never have been made possible without the remarkable generosity of our lenders, who have given up these superb examples of the best of motorcycle design from their collections. We are most grateful to those private collectors and public institutions who are listed separately for parting with their motorcycles. In particular, our thanks go to Otis Chandler and George Barber, who have been invaluable in their support of this exhibition, and who have made available large and important parts of their collections.

Obtaining these loans has required the assistance of many people. In particular we would like to express our gratitude to those who have contributed their time to advise and assist us in the details of fine-tuning the exhibition: Glenn Bator; Tim Buche and Beverly St. Clair Baird (Discover Today's Motorcycling); Gary Christopher; Nobby Clark; Josh Cohen; David Edwards; David Gross; Federico Minoli; Jeff Ray; Phil Schilling; Brian Slark; Pete terHorst; Philip Tooth; and Ed Youngblood, president of the American Motorcyclist Association.

The realization of this project was truly a team effort. Curatorial Advisors Ultan Guilfoyle and Charles Falco were essential in the selection process for the bikes in the show and played key roles in securing loans. Matthew Drutt, Associate Curator for Research, was responsible for overseeing the scope, content, and design of the catalogue, and also provided the early drafts that formed the foundation of the exhibition. Sarah Botts, Executive Assistant to the Director, not only coordinated the myriad aspects of the exhibition, but also participated in the debates surrounding the selection of bikes and helped secure specific loans. Furthermore, she was responsible for coordinating the catalogue photography and exhibition design, and for locating the historical support material. Project Curatorial Assistant Vanessa Rocco became the main support center for all of this activity, managing the exhibition database, tracking loans, and providing editorial assistance with the catalogue. Finally, Judith Cox, Lisa Dennison, Nicolas Iljine, Ben Hartley, Max Hollein, Greg Jordan, and Min Jung Kim were invaluable for their sustained effort and initiative in working with the executive aspects of this project. To all of the members of this tightly knit team, I am most grateful for the dedication and hard work that has resulted in the successful staging of this exhibition.

Without the conceptual support and working contributions of Richard Gaul and Erbo Hermanns representing BMW, this project could not have gone forward. Their insight, advice, and flexibility helped create a truly dramatic cultural event.

Our ambitions for this catalogue were fully realized by the Guggenheim Museum Publications Department. We have benefited greatly from the expertise of Anthony Calnek, Director of Publications; Elizabeth Levy, Managing Editor/Editor of Foreign Editions;

Elizabeth Franzen, Manager of Editorial Services; Esther Yun, Assistant Production Manager; Domenick Ammirati, Editorial Assistant; Melissa Secondino, Production Assistant; and Stephanie Fleischmann. For the dynamic design of the catalogue we are indebted to Pandiscio design studio.

Guggenheim Museum Chief Photographer David Heald, Randy Leffingwell, Marc Bondarenko, Jean-Pierre Praderes, and the rest of the photographic team deserve special thanks for the magnificent photographs of every motorcycle in the exhibition. Also, a special note of thanks must be extended to Frank O. Gehry and Associates for their striking exhibition design.

Finally, we would like to thank and acknowledge the contributions of the following organizations and individuals: American Historical Racing Motorcycle Association; American Motorcyclist Association; The Antique Motorcycle Club of America Inc.; Motorcycle Heritage Museum; National Motor Museum, Beaulieu, England; Frank R. Arnold; Terry Beale (Yamaha Motor Corp.); Martino Bianchi, Claudio Castiglioni, and Miguel Galluzzi (Cagiva); John Bishop; Erik Buell (Buell Motorcycle Company); Kevin Cameron; Court Canfield (Buell Motorcycle Company); Brian Catterson; Peter Cocks; Cosmopolitan Motors Corp.; Bob Cox; Sue Davis (Roper Archive); Creighton Demerest; Peter Egan; Bill Eggers; Jeff Elghanayan; Bruce Fairey (Ducati); Aaron Fitch (Motorcycle Heritage Museum); Mike FitzSimons; Chris Garville; David Gaylin (Motorcycle Days); Sandy Gilbert; Pauline Hailwood; Kirk House (Curtiss Museum); Tom Hayes; Dennis Hopper; Don Huey; Julie Hernandez; Bill Jackson (Harley-Davidson Archives); David Koh; Alan Lindsay; Jim Miller; Federico Minoli; Jerry Mortimore; David Robb (BMW); Richard Rosenthal (*Classic Bikes* Archives); Clement Salvadori; David Sarafin; Eleanora Scali (Moto Guzzi); Steve Seid (Pacific Film Archive); Jeffrey Slobodian; Daniel Statnekov; Stewart Engineering; Doug Strange; Mick Walker; Buzz Walneck; Brad Wilmarth; and George Yarocki.

In conclusion, I want to acknowledge the contribution of Peter Noever, Director of the Museum of Applied Arts in Vienna. His encouragement in the early stages of this project helped frame its importance both as a historical exhibition and as a design exhibition. Frank Gehry, of course, worked his special magic once again with the design for the installation. As with the Guggenheim Museum Bilbao, his team of Edwin Chan and Randy Jefferson helped carry the project through its critical phases to realize a truly unique and startling transformation of the Frank Lloyd Wright building.

—*Thomas Krens, Curator,* The Art of the Motorcycle, *and Director, The Solomon R. Guggenheim Foundation*

Photo Credits

By catalogue number

i © Jean-Pierre Pradères • ii David Heald • iii © Chester Goosen, F22 Photography • iv David Heald •
v David Heald • vi David Heald • 1 David Heald • 2 © Randy Leffingwell • 3 © National Air and Space Museum,
Smithsonian Institution, photo by Erik Long, Mark Avino • 4 David Heald • 5 © Randy Leffingwell •
6 © Randy Leffingwell • 7 © Randy Leffingwell • 8 © Randy Leffingwell • 9 © Jean-Pierre Pradères •
10 © Randy Leffingwell • 11 © Randy Leffingwell • 12 © Randy Leffingwell • 13 David Heald •
14 © Jean-Pierre Pradères • 15 David Heald • 16 David Heald • 17 © Randy Leffingwell • 18 © Alessandro
Bersani • 19 © John Colley • 20 David Heald • 21 © Marc Bondarenko • 22 © Jean-Pierre Pradères •
23 © Ralph Bradatsch, In-Pro • 24 © Jean-Pierre Pradères • 25 © Jean-Pierre Pradères •
26 © Marc Bondarenko • 27 David Heald • 28 © Marc Bondarenko • 29 © Randy Leffingwell •
30 © David Edwards • 31 David Heald • 32 David Heald • 33 © Randy Leffingwell • 34 © Marc Bondarenko •
35 David Heald • 36 © Jean-Pierre Pradères • 37 David Heald • 38 © Marc Bondarenko • 39 David Heald •
40 © Marc Bondarenko • 41 © Randy Leffingwell • 42 © Marc Bondarenko • 43 © Jean-Pierre Pradères •
44 © Marc Bondarenko • 45 © Randy Leffingwell • 46 © Marc Bondarenko • 47 © Marc Bondarenko •
48 © George C. Anderson • 49 David Heald • 50 © Randy Leffingwell • 51 © Marc Bondarenko •
52 © Marc Bondarenko • 53 © Marc Bondarenko • 54 © Randy Leffingwell • 55 © J. Asquni/Asquini Inc. •
56 © George C. Anderson • 57 © Tony Higgins • 58 © Jean-Pierre Pradères • 59 David Heald •
60 © Marc Bondarenko • 61 © Randy Leffingwell • 62 © Richard Bell • 63 © Randy Leffingwell •
64 David Heald • 65 © Studio Pascucci-Barcelona • 66 © David Edwards • 67 © Randy Leffingwell •
68 © Randy Leffingwell • 69 © Randy Leffingwell • 70 © Marc Bondarenko • 71 David Heald •
72 © Randy Leffingwell • 73 © Randy Leffingwell • 74 David Heald • 75 © Randy Leffingwell •
76 © Marc Bondarenko • 77 © Randy Leffingwell • 78 © Randy Leffingwell • 79 © Marc Bondarenko •
80 Jim Boyle • 81 David Heald • 82 David Heald • 83 © Marc Bondarenko • 84 © Marc Bondarenko •
85 © Ducati Motor SpA, photo by Antonio Vigarani, Sinergia • 86 David Heald • 87 David Heald •
88 © Ducati Motor SpA, photo by Antonio Vigarani, Sinergia • 89 © Marc Bondarenko •
90 © American Honda Motor Company, Inc. • 91 David Heald • 92 David Heald • 93 © Morbidelli •
94 David Heald • 95 © Cagiva Motor SpA.

Original materials accompanying catalogue images photographed by Ellen Labenski, with the following
exceptions: Cat. no. 22: Géo Ham (© Bernard Salvat) • Cat. no. 48: Thomas Reed • Cat. no. 64: Alan Davidson at
Stills. Other ephemera reproductions: Cat. no. 4, Cat. no. 6 (p. 113), Cat. no. 62: National Motor Museum, Beaulieu,
England • Cat. no. 9, Cat. no. 24, Cat. no. 43: © Bernard Salvat • Cat. no. 74, Cat. no. 92: © BMW AG. Additional
photos accompanying plates: Cat. no. 55, Cat. no. 61: Photofest • Cat. no. 88: © Gold & Goose Photography.

Additional copyrights

Cat. no. 12, Cat. no. 32, Cat. no. 44, Cat. no. 45, Cat. no. 67, Cat. no. 75: © Harley-Davidson Motor Company •
Cat. no. 16, Cat. no. 27, Cat. no. 82: © BMW AG • Cat. no. 34: © David Holyoake, Stewart Engineering •
Cat. no. 39: © Archiv Auto Union • Cat. no. 42: © Classic Bike • Cat. no. 48, Cat. no. 56, Cat. no. 66, Cat. no. 78,
Cat. no. 90: © American Honda Motor Company, Inc. • Cat. no. 86: © Yamaha Motor Corporation, USA •
Cat. no. 87: © Britten Motorcycle Company Ltd. (from material provided by *Riders Club* magazine) •
Cat. no. 91: © Betamotor SpA.

Note on Catalogue Entries

In documenting the history of the motorcycle from an art and design perspective, the Guggenheim has attempted to strike a balance between industry standards and the interests of a diverse audience. Specifications for pre-World War II American motorcycles are listed in imperial measurements; subsequent measurements are given in metric. Displacement and top speed have been rounded to the nearest whole number, while bore and stroke and power output have been rounded to the nearest tenth. Finally, our lenders have emphasized that top speeds are subjective figures that depend on varying conditions and should thus be considered approximate.

Guggenheim Museum Publications

1071 Fifth Avenue

New York, New York 10128

Hardcover edition distributed by

Harry N. Abrams, Inc.

100 Fifth Avenue

New York, New York 10011

ISBN 0-8109-6912-2 (hardcover)

ISBN 0-89207-207-5 (softcover))

Design by Richard Pandiscio

Printed in Germany by Cantz

Front cover: Megola Sport, 640 cc, Germany, 1922 (detail). Deutsches Museum, Munich.

Back cover: Triumph X75 Hurricane, 750 cc, United Kingdom, 1973 (detail). The Barber Vintage Motorsports Museum, Birmingham, Ala.